Adventure Travel

Adventure Travel

by *Pat Dickerman*

Thomas Y. Crowell Company

Established 1834 New York

Photo on pages 2 and 3: Grizzly Ranch, Wy.

ADVENTURE TRAVEL. Copyright © 1972, 1974, 1976, 1978 by Adventure Guides, Inc.
All rights reserved. Printed in the United States of America. No part of this book may
be used or reproduced in any manner whatsoever without written permission except
in the case of brief quotations embodied in critical articles and reviews. For information address Thomas Y. Crowell, 10 East 53d Street, New York, N.Y. 10022. Published simultaneously in Canada by Fitzhenry & Whiteside Limited, Toronto.

ISBN: 0-690-01750-2 (cloth)
    0-690-01751-0 (pbk)

LIBRARY OF CONGRESS CATALOG CARD NUMBER: 77-25745

Contents

A Note of Appreciation. . .

Thousands of communications have passed through our office in the last twelve months of updating, rewriting and expanding the fourth edition of this book. For cheerfully keeping the maelstrom of details organized, and for their meticulous work in analyzing, drafting and proofreading, Connie Smith and Linnea Leedham have my grateful thanks. Credit goes also to Carol Eannarino and Christina Madaio for their research and design contributions. And I am most grateful to Paul Fargis and Joe Montebello at T.Y. Crowell whose concept of the book has so enriched this 1978 edition.

The book would be far less informative were it not for the quantities of information provided by the outfitters and services about whom it is written, and for the valuable insight which hundreds of vacationers have generously shared. Thanks are due, also, for the important contributions of many tourism centers in the states and Canadian provinces.

Lastly, my thanks in advance to everyone who reads these pages and catches the spirit we have attempted to convey. We have thought about you constantly for months, wondering who will decide to go where. We trust that each one who uses this book will reap joy along with the jouncing!

Gratefully,
Pat Dickerman

Introduction

The trend toward adventurous travel has burst upon the vacation scene with amazing effect. Suddenly thousands of vacationers are discovering that even the neophyte outdoorsperson can learn to scale a sheer rock wall, backpack or ride horseback into a wilderness a million miles (or so it seems) from civilization, or hang on for dear life to a roller-coasting raft as it twists, turns, flies and plunges through roaring rapids.

If you know nothing of navigating, orienteering, topographical map reading, campcraft skills, how to steer a boat, how to read a river or how to mount a horse . . . if you have not spent a night in a sleeping bag camped under the stars, or in the rain . . . if you have never journeyed on treks powered by horse, mule, burro, paddle, pole, wind, water current or your own two feet . . . still you can safely venture on these expeditions into the wilds. Outfitters and other services make it possible.

And that is what this book is all about. It tells of the experts who can guide you and teach you what you need to know to become a genuine trekker. It tells what their trips are like, the areas they explore, their rates and what is required of participants. It contains all the details you will need to contact each service for brochures, answers to your questions and reservations. The information in these pages can open up a whole new world of travel for you.

Adventure travel, it should be remembered, is for anyone with an adventurous and inquisitive spirit. It bears little resemblance to the deluxe tour. Depending upon the ruggedness of the expedition, you may have to put up with blistering sun or chilling cold, with drought or drenching rain, with bouncing, jostling, dunking, bruising and predictable as well as unpredictable hazards. It's not that adventurers yearn for the discomforts of roughing it. It's more a question of their being sporty enough to endure whatever difficulties come along in the process of reaping the rewards of their treks.

What they yearn for is the beauty of an isolated canyon or remote valley, seeing the world from the top of a high peak, camping beside an alpine lake or an uninhabited coastal island. Or the closeness to nature . . . watching a black bear eat berries, spotting deer at the water's edge, waking to the bugling of an elk or the honking of geese. Or the exhilaration of mastering a difficult climb, navigating turbulent water, achieving a goal that did not seem within reach. Or the thrill of exploration and discovery, the joy of being surrounded with unbelievable beauty, the camaraderie of sharing a rugged experience with others and the special reward when it's shared between parent and child, the immense satisfaction of learning new skills and insights and successfully meeting a challenge. The hazards and discomforts are insignificant in comparison with the rewards.

This is the fourth edition of *Adventure Travel,* the first having been published in 1972. A year earlier its parent publication about farm and ranch vacations carried an adventure supplement. As the first draft came out of the typewriter, it was obvious that *Adventure Travel* would become a book in its own right.

Our focus is on adventurous travel throughout North America. Not only are we directly in touch with the experts who have developed the excursions we describe, but we have received the viewpoints and advice of hundreds of people who have taken their trips. We write also from our own participation on a variety of expeditions. To be covered, outfitters or services must answer our many questions and provide references or other recommendations that attest to their reliability. Most belong to regional associations seeking to establish standards of service and safety. We hope that our care in double-checking and interpreting the vast number of facts that our research produced has resulted in accurate reporting on every page. To the best of our ability we have tried to achieve this goal.

The chapters cover categories of adventurous travel on land, water, snow and in the air, with introductions to give an overview of each activity and italicized paragraphs with reminders of things to check when booking trips. A special chapter, "Wilderness Living," outlines excursions that include adventure travel combinations, and one titled "Youth Adventures" tells of programs especially for teens. A final chapter notes several organizations that specialize in developing and booking adventure travel, including our own. And we have added a bibliography of recent books related to the activities covered—books which can enrich the treks you undertake.

Under each adventure category we list services alphabetically by state and province, with cross-referencing from one category to another for those that offer more than one type of trip. *Though their trips may be scheduled in widely separated regions, each service (with few exceptions) appears under the area of its headquarters location.* In many cases we have named the *arrival city* which can be reached by public transportation prior to a trip departure. When outdoor camping is involved we have indicated whether sleeping gear is provided or whether you should bring your own. Each service's brochure spells out further details.

The rates given are somewhat generalized, and are for one person in a group unless otherwise noted. It is inevitable, however, that rates will change, some excursions will be canceled and new ones will be offered—all of which should be checked when planning trips. Policies concerning deposits, full payment and cancellations vary and should be clearly understood when making reservations. One way of protecting vacation funds where prepayment is required is through low-cost cancellation insurance.

Safety measures—like wearing life jackets on rivers—are not to be taken lightly. Once a trip is launched the outfitter's word is law, and potential dangers will be reduced if it is obeyed. Some services require participants to sign waivers releasing the outfitter from liability in case of accident or loss of personal possessions. Vacation trip insurance can be arranged if desired.

What are the age requirements for these trips? That is a question frequently asked. We find that a rugged little six-year-old can do as well on a not-too-difficult pack trip, riding a gentle horse, as any neophyte adult. And we hear of youngsters aged nine who have outhiked their parents on the exhausting climb up the Bright Angel Trail at the Grand Canyon. Though twelve years is considered minimum by most outfitters for a river run like the one down the Colorado, some even younger have made the trip happily. It's more a matter of being a good sport and adventurous in spirit.

That holds true at the other end of the age scale as well. A California vacationer wrote us recently: "In June I will journey to the Arctic, flying to Yellowknife, then down the MacKenzie in a cruiser for 1,200 miles to where it empties into the Arctic Ocean. I'll visit Eskimo villages, then fly into Dawson City. Once again I will be floating down the Yukon River for several days with my outfitter friends for my annual dip into the Fountain of Youth!" This trekker's age? You figure it. She is a Sourdough, having crossed the White Pass in the Klondike Gold Rush with her parents when she was a very small child. The year was 1898!

So . . . whatever your age, and whatever your wilderness expertise, these pages will lead you to great adventure if you want it, and if you'll let them. We hope you'll write us about your journeys and share your ideas of what should be added to our next edition.

Pat Dickerman, *President*
ADVENTURE GUIDES, INC.
36 E. 57TH ST.
NEW YORK, NY 10022

Northern Lights Alpine Recreation, B.C.—Arnör Larson.

I ON FOOT

Backpacking/Hiking

The prime difference between the backpacker and the hiker is that the packer can trek deep into the wilderness with everything needed for housekeeping right on his (or her) back. The hiker, carrying at most a light daybag, covers more ground in a day but must reach shelter and food by nightfall.

"Ten years ago," sighs a backpacker, "people had climbed no higher than their attic. Now they've climbed every mountain within 300 miles."

With a week or ten days of provisions crammed into an aluminum-frame nylon pack, the backpacker, looking like an earthly version of an Apollo moon walk, carries 30 to 40 pounds of air mattress, wool socks, flashlight, a down or polyester sleeping bag that rolls into a small bundle, a plastic ground cloth and sleeping pad, dehydrated or freeze-dried foods, toilet articles, clothing, cooking equipment, raingear, a first-aid kit and maybe a tent. A kerosene or gas stove obviates the possibility of leaving a fire scar behind and eliminates having to find dry firewood each night.

Backpackers have a fetish for reducing weight. They rip labels off tea bags, cut towels in half and chop handles off toothbrushes. At the end of a long day, those few ounces could feel like pounds. The tyro backpacker should seriously underestimate the weight he can carry comfortably, and practice carrying a pack on short trips before starting off on an extended hike.

As for clothing, most neophytes can find T-shirts, long-sleeved cotton and wool shirts, lightweight and heavy wool sweaters, a windbreaker jacket, shorts and some sturdy but comfortable pants if they look thoroughly through their closets. But when it comes to boots, choose with special care. For day hiking, tennis sneakers will do unless the terrain is rough. For more extensive backpacking, your choice is between lightweight, mediumweight or heavy boots, roomy enough for a light wool liner sock and heavy wool oversock to fit inside. (Wool socks provide cushioning and absorb perspiration better than cotton or synthetics.) Lightweight boots are easier to break in, cost less and will serve the average backpacker well. They will not stay as dry as the medium or heavy boot, which should be chosen for extremely wet or rugged use, but wet-boot discomfort generally can be alleviated by changing to dry socks.

Boots have an intense plus or minus effect on the joy of backpacking. If they're new, wear them around for a few days to get them well broken in before you head for the trail. It used to be said that the way to break in boots was to soak them in water, then wear them. Today's experts nix this old theory as not only outmoded but damaging for boots as they are constructed today. Give them a dry run to get them in shape, is their advice. Though most backpackers are a self-sufficient lot, learning from one another how to cope with wilderness trails and camping, there are out-fitters whose guide services are a great boon for first-timers who are unacquainted with the techniques of map and compass reading, orienteering, foraging and campcraft in unfamiliar territory, and with the skills of minimum-impact camping. And the guides are sources of vast information on the plant and animal life, geology, archaeology and ecology of their various regions. With such background, any expedition becomes more meaningful.

On a guided trip you may learn about Alaska's tundra world and gold rush towns, its ice caves and fjords, for example, or trek into remote areas of the Canadian Arctic. You can search for Bigfoot in Oregon, combine hiking with nontechnical climbing in Colorado, catch rainbow trout in Idaho's Big Horn Crags, or hike into the back country of Glacier National Park in Montana, the Grand Canyon in Arizona, or a subtropical swamp in Georgia. There are outfitters who trek across stretches of the East's Appalachian Trail and the West's Pacific Crest Trail, the initial components of the National Trails System Act of 1968. And outfitters who treat backpackers to a combination of hiking and rafting in the Grand Canyon. And one outfitter (in Wyoming) who circumvents the backpacker's fetish for reducing weight by packing steaks and fresh produce on the back of a mule who trudges to each night's campsite by a different route, while the hikers, carrying half their usual load, follow the more rugged and scenic trail!

Check with your outfitter on what equipment he supplies and what you should bring. How heavy a pack can you carry? How many miles can you cover? Are you good for rugged terrain or should you try easier trails? Will there be some layover days? Other details to double-check: departure dates, what rates include, state tax, rendezvous point and how to get there. Also find out about elevations, weather, fishing license, and who will make reservations for before and after the trip. Is this trip just for your own party, or do you expect to join others?

ALASKA

Camp Denali, Box 67CA, McKinley Park, AK 99755. Att.: Wally & Jerry Cole. Summer: (907) 683-2290. Winter: (907) 683-2302. Mt. McKinley Natl. Park. 1–24 backpackers. 3 or more days $72–$80/day, incl. camp lodgings, food, backpacking gear & transport in Mt. McKinley Natl. Park; group rates. Arrival: Fairbanks, AK.

"This is a personal 'bush' country living experience," say the Coles. Camp Denali, with a magnificent view of Mt. McKinley, is your base for day or overnight hikes across rolling tundra, rocky ridges, braided glacial streams. You follow the trail of bear, sheep or caribou. The program (individualized, not regimented) acquaints you with plant, bird and animal life and interprets the phenomena of the tundra world. "An exceedingly fine outdoor experience, excellent food, and one of the prime locations in Alaska," writes a guest.

Kenai Guide Service, Box 40-A, Kasilof, AK 99610. Att.: George R. Pollard. (907) 262-5496. Kenai Natl. Moose Range. Jun.–Aug. 5–10 backpackers. 3–10 days. 10 days, $400, all-incl. Arrival: Kenai, AK. (See also *Kayaking*.)

"From blackspruce muskeg near sea level to the Harding Ice Field at 5,000 feet, this is a land of constant surprises," writes George Pollard. "Photograph a golden eagle eyrie or bog orchids. Smell the fragrance of budding cottonwood and Labrador tea. Hear the marmot's warning whistle, the lonely cry of a loon. Watch a cow moose and calf crossing a braided glacial stream and butterflies flitting over one of the largest landbound ice masses in North America. It's all here in this magnificent setting of mountains and glaciers."

Klondike Safaris, PO Box 1898-A, Skagway, AK 99840. Att.: Skip Burns. (907) 983-2496. [Oct.–May: 823 6th St., Juneau, AK 99801. (907)586-3924.] Chilkoot Trail. Jun.–Sept. 4–20 backpackers. 5 days, $225, everything incl. Group rates. Arrival: Skagway, AK. (See also *Float Trips, Youth Adventures*.)

The '98 gold rush comes alive as you follow the famous Chilkoot Trail to Klondike. You stop at an old gold rush town and other historic points, then return by way of Lake Lindeman in British Columbia and a ride on the White Pass and Yukon Railway. "It's a strenuous trip," Skip Burns warns. "The trail is not the place to get in shape."

Mountains North Guide Service, 851 University Ave., Fairbanks, AK 99701. Att.: Ev Wenrick. (907) 479-2984. Brooks & Alaska Ranges; White, Kenia & Chugach mts. Jun.–Aug. 3–10 backpackers. 3 or more days. $35/day; fly-in trips, $45/day. Bring or rent sleeping gear. Group, family & youth rates. Arrival: Fairbanks, AK. (See also *Mountaineering, Canoeing, Ski Touring*.)

Ev Wenrick describes his trips as "learning and doing adventures for active people, novice or experienced." Climbing, fishing and photography are part of the action. "We provide wilderness experiences at as low a cost as possible," he says, "consistent with safety, quality gear, small groups and responsible leadership. And we eat well!"

Sourdough Outfitters, Bettles, AK 99726. Att.: David Ketscher. (907) 692-5252. Brooks Range. Jul.–Aug. Up to 8 backpackers. 5–30 days. $45/day. Bring pack & sleeping gear. Arrival: Bettles, AK, via Fairbanks. (See also *Canoeing, Float Trips, Ski Touring, Dog Sledding*.)

"True wilderness as we never saw it before," says one backpacker. These trips take you to spectacular Arrigetch Peaks, Gates of the Arctic area. You follow game trails, creeks and ridges where there are no established hiking trails. Terrain can be rugged—be prepared to carry enough food for the duration of the trip or between airdrops.

Wilderness Alaska, PO Box 81266, College, AK 99701. Att.: Bob Waldrop & Deborah Vogt. (907) 479-2592. [Oct.–May: Box 1042, Auke Bay, AK 99821. (907) 789-2218.] Brooks Range & Lake Clark areas. Apr.–Sept. 4–12 backpackers. 10–30 days. 2-wk. trip, $450–$750, according to remoteness & length of bush flight. Bring or rent sleeping gear & packs. Group rates. Arrival: Fairbanks or Anchorage, AK.

The vast Brooks Range, which stretches across Alaska above the Arctic Circle, is approximately the size of the state of California—a great untouched wilderness of rugged beauty with valleys carved by past glaciers, with peaks and crags, and tundra and lichen at the higher elevations. "We go into different areas each year," Bob Waldrop explains, "especially those being proposed for inclusion in the National Parks System, such as the Gates of the Arctic (Brooks Range) or the Lake Clark area (200 miles west of Anchorage)." Backpacking and mountaineering trips are WA specialties, but its program also includes river trips, ski trips and a few dog sled excursions.

Wildernorth, Inc., Mile 102 Glenn Hwy., SRC Box 92E, via Palmer, AK 99645. Att.: Joe & Suzi LaBelle & Stu Ashley. No tel. Chugach & Talkeetna mts; Prince William Sound. All yr. 3–10 backpackers. 1–8 days. About $30/day (Blackstone Bay, $48/day; 1-day trips, $20); group rates. Bring pack & sleeping gear. Arrival: Anchorage, AK. (See also *Mountaineering, Snowshoeing*.)

Sailing up Blackstone Bay, "the most spectacular fjord in Prince William Sound," you pass hanging waterfalls, harbor seals resting on floating icebergs, and kittiwakes and glaucous-winged gulls nesting on Blackstone Glacier. Other trips explore glaciers, ice caves and petrified wood in the Chugach Mountains or tundra, gemstones and lowbush cranberries in the Talkeetnas. Guides are well versed in local geology.

ARIZONA

Canyoneers, Inc., PO Box 2997, East Flagstaff, AZ 86003. Att.: Gaylord Staveley. (602) 526-0924 (all yr.). [Apr.–Oct.: PO Box 735, Grand Canyon, AZ 86023. (602) 638-2391.] Grand Canyon, Havasupai Canyon. Up to 14 people. 1–6 days. Guided trips, $26–$38/day. Rentals. Arrival: Flagstaff, AZ. (See also *Jeeping, Float Trips.*)

"Our guides will design a backpacking hike to your specifications—for length, difficulty, terrain and locality," Gaylord Staveley promises, "if you'll let us know what kind of self-propelled experience you want." He combines some hiking trips with rafting the Colorado, and has a hikers' rental shop at the Grand Canyon for equipment for unguided trips.

Grand Canyon Youth Expeditions, Inc., RR 4, Box 755, Flagstaff, AZ 86001. Att.: Dick & Susan McCallum. (602) 774-8176. Colorado Plateau. All yr. 10–20 backpackers. Sample rates: Grand Canyon, 2 days, $15; Thunder River–Havasu, 7 days, $250. Bring pack & sleeping gear. Arrival: Flagstaff, AZ. (See also *Float Trips, Ski Touring, Youth Adventures.*)

Some of the McCallums' family trips are run with the Museum of Northern Arizona, with interpreters on the geology, biology and archaeology of the region. Their hikes range from easy to strenuous, and each provides an opportunity to explore, have fun and learn at the same time. The 7-day Havasu hike includes a day of running the Colorado's rapids.

CALIFORNIA

Beamer Expeditions, PO Box 285, Dept. AT8, Canoga Park, CA 91305. Att.: Billy Beamer. (Tel. starting May '78). S.W. OR, N.W. CA. Dec.–Feb., May–Aug. 4–16 people. Inquire re rates. Family discounts. Bring pack & sleeping gear. Arrival: Medford, OR.

It had to happen—expeditions in search of Bigfoot! Scientists, naturalists or trackers lead groups into wilderness areas near the Oregon–California border that are rich in unique landforms, rare plants, invertebrates, fish, amphibians, reptiles, birds "and 93 mammal species including Bigfoot." You must be a hiker, backpacker or snowshoer to join these groups—18 years or older, or 12 to 17 if mature. You'll learn the basics of tracking, will collect data, and will see an abundance of plant and animal life as you help solve a scientific mystery and keep safe an endangered species.

Sierra Guides, 1720 Santa Cruz Ave., Menlo Park, CA 94025. Att.: Ed Murphy. (415) 326-1636. Sierra Nevada & Cascade mts. (CA, OR, WA). June.–Sept. 5–12 backpackers. 3–15 days. $11.50/day, everything incl.; group rates. Also custom trips. Arrival: San Francisco, CA.

Big Sur, Bench Canyon, Valentine Lake, Emigrant Basin, Kings-Kern and Great Western Divides, Silver Divide—backpackers enjoy these and other beauteous areas on hikes designed for everyone from 11 years up. With an ecological nonimpact approach, guides teach basic mountaineering skills, survival techniques, campcraft, compass navigation and rock climbing. Hiking days with packs are short, side trips challenging. "We do a lot of fishing, swimming, peak climbing and relaxing," Ed Murphy explains.

Squaw Valley Mountaineering Center, Box 2288-B, Olympic Valley, CA 95730. Att.: Skip Reedy. (916) 583-4316. Sierra Nevadas. Jun.–Sept. 3–25 backpackers. 1–7 days. 5 days, $64. Group rates. Bring or rent pack & sleeping gear. Arrival: Reno, NV, or Truckee, CA. (See also *Ski Touring, Youth Adventures.*)

Northern Lights Alpine Recreation, B.C.—Arnör Larson.

Skip Reedy's 5-day trips for families and individuals who are new to backpacking follow the Pacific Crest Trail overlooking Squaw Valley. Wildflowers, deep blue-green lakes and spectacular vertical granite walls provide the backdrop for informal lessons in trip planning, camp cooking, wilderness travel ethics and equipment.

COLORADO

Colorado Wilderness Experience Trips, 2912 Aspen Dr., Box K, Durango, CO 81301. Att.: Adolph Kuss, Jr. (303) 247-1159. Weminuche Wilderness. Jul.–Aug. 6–14 backpackers. 7-day trips, $200, everything incl.; group & family rates. Arrival: Durango, CO.

Your trip into the Colorado high country begins with a narrow-gauge train ride from Durango to the edge of the wilderness. There you put on a backpack, and Mike Elliott (cross-country ski racer) and Dolph Kuss (U.S. ski coach for the 1972 Winter Olympics) guide you on what they call "true wilderness experiences, not canned outings." Groups are coed, both novice and experienced backpackers. Along with camping, cooking, map reading, mountain hiking, safety and outdoor skills, you can also learn basic rock climbing.

Mountain Guides and Outfitters, Inc., PO Box 2001, Aspen, CO 81611. Att.: Kenneth R. Wyrick. (303) 925-6680. White Riv. Natl. Forest & adj. wilderness. May–Oct. 2–40 backpackers. 1–30 days $35/day; bring or rent pack & sleeping gear. Family rates. Arrival: Aspen, CO. (See also *Mountaineering, Float Trips, Dog Sledding, Ski Touring*—Aspen Ski Touring School.)

From Aspen you ascend high valleys of the White River National Forest, mostly over easy terrain, but there are more ambitious routes, too. Guides know the local history, geology and wildlife, point out fishing spots and teach camp skills. They also guide special youth trips in these scenic mountains.

Rocky Mountain Backpack Tours, PO Box 2781, Evergreen, CO 80439. Att.: Michael R. Carter. (303) 674-0519. Roosevelt & Arapahoe natl. forests. May–Sept. 2–16 backpackers. 3 or more days. Guided 3-day wkend, $118; 6 days, $262. Experienced backpackers $82 for guide service in & pickup out, plus $7/day for food, all-incl. 15% discount w./own equipment; group & family rates. Arrival: Denver, CO.

"Our emphasis is on having fun while learning the skills required to plan and enjoy mountain backpacking excursions," says Michael Carter. All trips begin and end at the Sundance Lodge in Nederland, and on most trips the first and last nights are spent there. Groups can be picked up in Denver and delivered to the lodge or the mountains with all equipment and food packed and ready to go. Guides spend the first day reviewing equipment and area topo maps and accompany novice backpackers. Experienced groups may take off on their own for as long as they like, with pickup at a designated point and time.

Rocky Mountain Expeditions, Inc., PO Box CC-AG, Buena Vista, CO 81211. Att.: Dick Scar. (303) 395-8466. Rocky Mts. incl. Yellowstone (CO, MT, WY), Canyon de Chelly & Grand Canyon (AZ), Guadalupe Mts. (TX). Apr.–Nov. 1–12 backpackers. 1–10 days. Sample rates: 4 days, $125; 10 days, $210; everything incl. Group rates. (See also *Float Trips, Ski Touring, Wilderness Living.*)

Dick Scar stresses an understanding of the environment as a whole on all trips into majestic wild areas of the West. Supplying "top-quality equipment," he takes beginners on progressive or base camp trips, and seasoned trekkers on more strenuous trips involving nontechnical climbing. Outdoor study camps, most for 5 days (about $175), focus on orienteering, water quality, wilderness philosophy and angling. There are many scheduled dates for outings, and RME also arranges custom trips tailored to the needs of individuals and groups.

Rocky Mountain Ski Tours and Backpack Adventures, 130 E. Riverside Dr., Box 413P, Estes Park, CO 80517. Att.: Bill Evans, Peter or Rick Marsh. (303) 586-3553. [Nov.–Apr.: 156 Elkhorn Ave., Box 413P, Estes Park, CO 80517. (303) 586-2114.] Rocky Mt. Natl. Park, Rawah Wilderness, Roosevelt Natl. Forest. Jun.–Sept. 4–10 backpackers. 1–10 days. $20-$30/day. 5 days w./8-10 backpackers, $100. Rates all-incl. (See also *Ski Touring.*)

"Our trips are primarily instructional," explains Peter Marsh. "We travel through open meadows, conifer forests and high mountain peaks of the Rockies, while our instructors teach orienteering, first aid, fishing, and trail, camp and wilderness skills. In 10 days individuals can learn skills that would normally take years to acquire."

Wilderness Adventures, Moon Valley Resort, Box 265-CA, South Fork, CO 81154. Att.: Larry Ehardt. (303) 873-5331. Weminuche Wilderness. May–Oct. 3–30 backpackers. 3–7 days. 6 days, $132. Equipment rental, $11/day. Group rates. Arrival: South Fork, CO. (See also *Hiking with Packstock, Pack Trips, Snowmobiling.*)

With short distances between camping sites, we're told, there's time for study, observing, fishing, hiking or just relaxing. Larry's trips emphasize wilderness education. On some you climb 14,000-foot peaks.

GEORGIA

Wilderness Southeast, Rt. 3, Box 619-L, Savannah, GA 31406. Att.: Dick Murlless. (912) 355-8008. Joyce Kilmer-Slickrock Wilderness, Great Smoky Mts., Big Cypress Swamp, Cumberland Is. All yr. 10–20 backpackers. 3–7 days. $20/day all-incl. Group & youth rates. (See also *Canoeing, Scuba Diving*—FL, *Youth Adventures.*)

One veteran of a WS expedition writes, "The working together—sharing difficulties as well as joys—is a great experience for families, including single-parent families like mine. Our trip was beautifully planned. Even the cooking and cleanup were fun.'' Participants can hike in the footsteps of Indians and pioneers in the Joyce Kilmer Wilderness; climb to the top of a rock summit in the soft green Smokies; discover alligators, egrets and dwarf cypress trunks in subtropical Big Cypress Swamp; or explore slave cabin ruins, high dunes and miles of unspoiled beach on Cumberland Island.

IDAHO

Fog Mountain, Salmon and Selway Expeditions, Box 585-D, Salmon, ID 83467. Att.: Stanton C. Miller. (208) 756-2319. Selway Wilderness, Big Horn Crags & Chamberlain Basin. Jul.–Sept. 4–12 backpackers. 3–10 days. $40/day. Custom & sched. Arrival: Salmon, ID. (See also *Hiking with Packstock, Pack Trips.*)

''We traverse varied topography up to 10,000 feet,'' says Stan Miller. His trips foster personal involvement for enjoying this country of alpine glaciers and remote lakes (some with rainbow trout over 4 pounds) nestled among the high peaks.

M&M Outfitter, RR 1, c/o M. B., Cambridge, ID 83610. Att.: Mike Bishop. (208) 257-3472. Clearwater Natl. Forest, Kelly Creek Ranger District. Jun.–Aug. 6–15 backpackers. 7–10 days. $30/day. Bring pack & sleeping gear. Arrival: Lewiston, ID. (See also *Pack Trips.*)

''Unspoiled landscape, clear mountain streams, forests and high meadows make this an ideal setting for a family vacation,'' Mike Bishop writes. ''We point out safety precautions and how to get along in the wilderness. There's fishing and picture-taking that can't be beat.''

The Wilderness Institute, PO Box 338, Bonners Ferry, ID 83805. Att.: Larry E. Fidler. (208) 267-3013. Wilderness areas of CO, WY, AK, MT, WA & BC. Jun.–Aug. 5–12 backpackers. 6–20 days. 9 days, $215; 10 days, $235; 11 days, $250. Sleeping gear incl. Group & youth rates. (See also *Mountaineering, Canoeing, Ski Touring.*)

The Wilderness Institute, a nonprofit educational organization dedicated to preservation of wild lands, leads journeys into many of North America's spectacular wilderness areas. They supply instructors, guides, equipment, food and itineraries for a series of scheduled as well as custom trips. Some are easy backpacking treks covering 6 to 8 miles every other day, others difficult trips involving longer distances and fewer layover days. Age limit is 15 to 55 years—with some exceptions.

Wilderness River Outfitters & Trail Expeditions, PO Box 871-AG, Salmon, ID 83467. Att.: the Tonsmeires. (208) 756-3959. White Clouds of Boulder Mts. Jul.–Sept. 2–8 backpackers. 2–10 days. 8 days, $375; 5 days, $275; group rates & charters. Everything incl. Arrival: Sun Valley, ID. (See also *Float Trips, Ski Touring.*)

On these trips you climb high peaks for breathtaking vistas extending 100 miles in every direction. Group participation is featured in menu planning, route selection, map and compass reading, first aid and ecology.

IOWA

Iowa Mountaineers, 30 Prospect Pl., Iowa City, IA 52240. Att.: John & Jim Ebert. (319) 337-7163. 25–35 backpackers. Mar.: 5 days in Grand Canyon, $90. Aug.: 12-day camp, $220–$250. Bring pack & sleeping gear. (See also *Mountaineering, Ski Touring.*)

On the Grand Canyon Trip you hike down the Kaibab Trail, 6,000 feet in 7 miles, to the bottom. Explore, camp, hike to Ribbon Falls and finally up the Bright Angel

Canatrek Mountain Expeditions, Ltd., Alta.

Trail. At the Eberts' camp in the Beartooth Mountain Wilderness of Montana, activities include mountaineering, fishing and photography as well as backpacking. "It's a hiker's and climber's paradise," says Jim Ebert, "with high alpine hiking and dozens of attractive peaks, including Montana's highest."

LOUISIANA

Pack & Paddle, 601 Pinhook Rd. E., Lafayette, LA 70501. Att.: Joan & Dick Williams. (318) 232-5854. Kisatchie Natl. Forest. All yr. 10–15 backpackers. 2–10 days. $26.50/overnight ($10 less w./own equipment) incl. all but food. Arrival: Lafayette, LA. (See also *Canoeing*.)

The Kisatchie National Forest near Natchitoches is an area of hilly terrain and clear running streams with rock outcroppings. This is the setting for Pack & Paddle's overnight backpacking trips. The outfitter provides guides, equipment, transportation and an instructional session for each trip. You bring the food.

MINNESOTA

Bear Track Outfitting Co., Box 51, Grand Marais, MN 55604. Att.: David & Cathi Williams. (218) 387-1162. Boundary Waters Canoe Area & Isle Royale Natl. Park (MI). May–Oct. 2–10 backpackers. 1–10 days. Guided trips about $12/day, all-incl. Group & family rates, complete or partial outfitting. Arrival: Duluth, MN. (See also *Canoeing, Ski Touring, Youth Adventures*.)

"Personalized service and instruction are the strong points of our trips," remarks Dave Williams. "I am a teacher by profession, and explain the area's fascinating history—the Indians, fur traders and loggers. The Isle Royale trip begins with a ferry ride. From there we hike, study the predator-prey relationship of wolf and moose, identify wildflowers and learn about local geology. BWCA trips start along the Gunflint Trail or Grand Portage."

MONTANA

Backpacking with Barrow, Box 183-A, Whitefish, MT 59937. Att.: Shirley M. Barrow. (406) 862-3100. Flathead Natl. Forest in the Bob Marshall Wilderness. Jul.–Sept. 4–24 backpackers. 5–12 days. $100/5-day trip, $220/12-day trip, everything incl.; discount w./own equipment; group & family rates. Arrival: Whitefish or Glacier Natl. Park, MT.

From Whitefish, near Glacier National Park, Barrow's 5-day trip is ideal for families or novice backpackers. You follow a trail along Gorge Creek to a picturesque Indian tipi base camp. From here you make day trips in this very scenic area of lofty peaks, glacial cirques and green meadows, and one overnight trek to Sunburst Lake. Or take the more strenuous 12-day trip, criss-crossing the Continental Divide at 8,000 feet. "The equipment, food, everything was well done—just great!" exclaims one guest. "Taking people into this area is a rewarding experience," Shirley Barrow comments. "I love them all—the slow walkers and the fast ones, the young and old."

Montana Mountain Trips, 3401 14th Ave. So., Great Falls, MT 59405. Att.: John H. & T. Brice Addison. No tel. Mission Mts., Beartooth Primitive Area, Bob Marshall Wilderness, Cabinet Mts., Madison Range. Jul.–Sept. 3–8 backpackers. 3–6 days. Approx. $30/day, all-incl. Arrival: Kalispell or Great Falls, MT. (See also *Mountaineering.*)

Brothers John and Brice Addison have been backpacking and mountaineering in Montana's Rockies since childhood. They offer custom and regularly scheduled 5-day backpacking trips into these glorious mountains, pointing out local history, geology, botany and meteorology and giving tips on safe and comfortable travel along the way. The third day is the only day without packs—hikers cross alpine meadows and snowfields seen by very few. Open to anyone, families especially.

Walk in the Wilderness, PO Box 4041, Missoula, MT 59801. Att.: Daniel Mullan. (406) 543-6157. Glacier Natl. Park, Bob Marshall, Mission Mts., Scapegoat, Selway-Bitterroot & Anaconda-Pintlar wilderness areas. Jul.–Aug. 2–6 backpackers. 5–14 days. About $20–$25/day, everything incl.; family & group rates. Less w./own equipment. Arrival: Missoula, MT.

Daniel Mullan plans trips of 5, 7, 10, 12 and 14 days for backpackers "to experience nature in its purest state with a minimum of intrusion by man." Each hiker carries approximately one-fifth his weight over distances that vary with the terrain and hiking ability of the group. Trout fishing, flower and plant identification, birdwatching, orienteering, geology, wildlife identification and just plain relaxing are among the activities.

Wildlife Outfitters, Rt. 1, Box 99B-AG, Victor, Mt 59875. Att.: Jack & Shirley Wemple. (406) 642-3262. Selway-Bitterroot Wilderness, Bitterroot Natl. Forest. Apr.–Aug. 6–10 backpackers. 7–10 days. 7-day trips, $250. Group & family rates. Bring pack & sleeping gear. Arrival: Missoula, MT. (See also *Hiking with Packstock, Pack Trips.*)

"Our backpacking expeditions are the ideal way to travel in harmony with this grand wilderness," writes Jack Wemple. "With parties limited to 10, impact on the environment is minimized." The Wemples recommend these trips for families as long as everyone is in good physical condition and can carry a pack.

NEW JERSEY

Odyssey, Ltd., 26 Hilltop Ave., Berkeley Heights, NJ 07922. Att.: Art Fitch. (201) 322-8414. Grand Canyon, Canadian Rockies, Adirondack Mts., North Cascades & AK. Apr.–Oct. 6–12 backpackers. 2–15 days. 15 days, $450; shorter trips, $30/day; all-incl. Group & youth rates. (See also *Ski Touring, Mountaineering*—Northeast School of.)

A combination backpack/float trip in the Grand Canyon in April (7 days), October weekends in the ancient Adirondacks, and 2-week summer trips in the spectacular Canadian Rockies—Yoho, Banff, Kootenay and Jasper parks—are among Odyssey's wilderness treks. The friendly and responsible leadership features "pleasure packing" with moderate loads, small parties and imaginative cuisine. Nature photography, plant and animal identification, orienteering and basic wilderness survival are some of the skills hikers acquire.

NEW YORK

Glen Durham, Sunside, Cairo, NY 12413. Att.: David Nascimbeni. (518) 622-9878. Catskill Mts. All yr.

Hikes over mountain trails overlooking the Hudson and Mohawk valleys cover from 4 to 32 miles, and in winter you do it on snowshoes. There are lean-to shelters or tents for overnights—or lodging at Glen Durham.

Timberlock, Adirondacks, Sabael, NY 12864. Att.: C. R. Catlin. (518) 648-5494. [Sept.–May: Sugar Hill Farm, RD 2, Woodstock, VT 05091. (802) 457-1621.] High Peaks & Adirondack wilderness. Jun.–Aug. 5–10 backpackers. 2–7 days. $24/day. Group & family rates. Bring pack & sleeping gear. Arrival: Indian Lake, NY. (See also *Canoeing*.)

These relaxed trips are geared to the pace of the slowest member. They're guided by college students who know wilderness routes where there are few hikers, excellent fishing, sparkling mountain lakes and 4,000-foot peaks. Catlin recommends a stay at Timberlock before or after.

NORTH CAROLINA

Folkestone Lodge Guide and Outfitting Service, Rt. 1, Box 310, West Deep Creek Rd., Bryson City, NC 28713. Att.: Bob Kranich. (704) 488-2730. Smoky Mt. Natl. Park. Jun.–Oct. 2–7 backpackers. 2–7 days. $45/day, everything incl.; family rates. Arrival: Asheville or Bryson City, NC.

"Our trips allow families to share and appreciate a unique wilderness experience," promises Bob Kranich. "Backpackers need not have experience. We provide a dependable guide service and share backpacking skills, wilderness conservation techniques and mountain lore." Bob has hiked more than 2,500 miles, with one 850-mile stretch from Georgia to Key West, and has been editor of *American Hiker* magazine.

Nantahala Outdoor Center, Star Rt., Box 68-B, Bryson City, NC 28713. Att.: Payson Kennedy. (704) 488-6407. So. Appalachians. All yr. 1–10 backpackers. Any no. of days. Guided 2-day wkend trips, $50; longer, $50/day; all-incl. Group rates. Arrival: Asheville, NC, or Chattanooga, TN. (See also *Mountaineering, Canoeing, Float Trips*.)

The Appalachian Trail crosses the Nantahala River just outside NOC's door. Weekend clinics for beginners emphasize the basics of backpacking. Private instruction or guide service can be arranged to meet the needs of most any group. NOC will also help plan trips for those who want to go out on their own.

OHIO

Wilderness Trails, 728 Prospect Ave., Cleveland, OH 44115. Att.: Gary Newman. (216) 696-5222 or 543-8639. PA, WV, NY, CO, WY. All yr. 6–12 backpackers. 2–30 days. PA, 2 days, $7; WV, 5 days, $40. (See also *Ski Touring, Wilderness Living*.)

Gary sums up his view simply: "I like the woods, people, teaching and laughing."

He arranges both custom and scheduled trips, such as 2-day Pennsylvania hikes in Allegheny National Forest, a 2-day "tyke hyke" in the same locale for hikers with babies riding the backpacks, and 5-day hikes in West Virginia's Monongahela National Forest. The outfit also offers basic climbing and compass classes and a 5-day New Year's mountaineering trip in the Adirondacks. It's a nonprofit organization with all surplus funds donated to "groups working to create and/or enhance the quality of worthy outdoor areas."

OREGON

Johann Mountain Guides, Inc., PO Box 19171, Portland, OR 97219. Att.: Ed Johann. (503) 244-7672. Pacific Northwest. All yr. 3–12 backpackers. 2–10 days. About $20/day; bring or rent sleeping gear. Group & youth rates. Arrival: Portland, OR. (See also *Mountaineering.*)

Backpacking among the major peaks of the Cascade Mountains, a watercolor course in the Mt. Hood Wilderness, beach trekking along the headlands and reefs of the Oregon coast—these are a few of the specialties of Johann Mountain Guides. Remarks one hiker: "Ed Johann fosters enjoyment of nature and shows excellent judgment and teaching ability." Minimum age for trips is 10 years.

PENNSYLVANIA

Mountain Streams & Trails Outfitters, Trails Division, Ohiopyle, PA 15470. Att.: Ralph McCarty. (412) 329-8810. PA, WV, MD. All yr. Up to 32 backpackers. 2 or more days. Rates on request. Arrival: Uniontown, PA, or Morgantown, WV. (See also *Float Trips.*)

"We'll 'gear you up' for most any trail in this beautiful tristate area," says Ralph McCarty, "and provide a topo map or, if you want one, a guide. We don't organize tours. We meet people at the trailheads."

UTAH

Tu-Kay Renegades' Frontier Escapades, 49 No. Main, Clawson, UT 84516. Att.: Keith Wright. (801) 384-2608. San Rafael Riv., Wasatch Mts., Book Cliffs, Desolation/Gray canyons. May–Oct. 10–20 backpackers. 10 days, $495. Bring sleeping gear. Group rates. Also custom trips. Arrival: Green River, UT.

The Wrights describe their trips: "We generally spend 7 days backpacking and 3 days river-running, but we have no set routine. Whether the backpacking takes place in desert canyons or mountains will depend on such things as weather and water supplies. We stay off beaten paths and do not follow the same trails every trip. You can count on a real frontier escapade." They encourage charter trips for 10 to 20

Rocky Mountain Expeditions, Inc., CO.

people designed around the group's special interests—photography, writing, sketching, meditating—"You name it."

VERMONT

Killington Adventure, Killington, VT 05751. Att.: Dave Langlois. (802) 422-3333 (or 422-3139, evenings). Jun.–Aug. Adirondacks (NY), White Mts. (NH), Green Mts. (VT). 1 wk., $170 + $30 for equipment pkg. if needed. Arrival: Killington, VT. (See also *Youth Adventures*.)

"All trips are rugged, but within reach of any person in reasonably good physical condition," Dave Langlois says. It's a great way for a novice to start backpacking. Trips begin with 2 days of training at Killington, followed by a 5-day mountain expedition.

WASHINGTON

Northwest Alpine Guide Service, Inc., 1628 Ninth Ave. #2, Seattle, WA 98101. Att.: Linda Bradley Miller. (206) 622-6074. Brooks Range (AK), Queen Charlotte Is. (BC), Olympics & Cascades (WA). Sched. Apr.–Sept., custom all yr. 1–20 backpackers. 1–21 days. Rates average $35/day. Bring or rent sleeping gear. Youth rates. (See also *Mountaineering, Canoeing, Float Trips, Ski Touring, Wilderness Living, Youth Adventures.*)

Backpackers hike "from the ruggedly beautiful Pacific Coast beaches through the world-famous rain forest to the alpine meadows and glacier-clad rock summits" in the Olympics, with other spectacular scenery in the Cascades. On Alaska's Brooks Range you pass through the calving ground of the Porcupine caribou herd, and in the Carcajou Mountains explore from a base camp at Porter Lake. In the Yukon you hike the Chilkoot Trail of gold rush fame, and on the Queen Charlotte Islands it's wilderness beaches, tundralike peat bogs, bald eagles, wild cranes and other scenes of the "Misty Islands." Many departures offered year-round.

Pacific Northwest Float Trips, 829 Waldron St., Sedro Woolley, WA 98284. Att.: David E. Button. (206) 855-0535. Cascade Mts. Aug.–Nov. 5–12 backpackers or hikers. 1–3 days. Bring sleeping gear. Group rates. Arrival: Seattle, WA. (See also *Float Trips.*)

Sauk Mountain, Suaittle and the Glacier Peak area around Darrington are some of the majestic regions covered on these strenuous hikes. Guide Dave Button provides food and transportation to and from the trailhead. Fishermen: Bring a rod for high mountain lakes.

WYOMING

Game Hill Ranch, Box A, Bondurant, WY 82922. Att.: Pete & Holly Cameron. (307) 733-2015. [Nov.–May: (307) 733-3281.] Gros Ventre Mts.: Wyoming Range. Jun.–Oct. 2–6 backpackers. Sample rates: 5 days, $253; 7 days, $338; 10 days, $462. Bring or rent sleeping gear. Arrival: Jackson, WY. (See also *Hiking with Packstock, Pack Trips, Ski Touring.*)

What an area for backpackers—sage-covered ridges, acres of wildflowers, stands of fir and expansive views of mountain ranges. Pete Cameron provides small groups with "well-planned campsites, simple but good food, dependable equipment and enthusiastic, well-qualified guides." You can stay at Pete's ranch before and after trips.

L. D. Frome, Outfitter, Box G, Afton, WY 83110. (307) 886-5240. Teton, Washakie, Bridger & Yellowstone wilderness (WY), redrock canyons (UT), Grand Canyon (AZ). Apr.–Oct. Up to 20 backpackers. 5–10 days. $35/day incl. sleeping gear, pack frame & all equip. exc. boots & clothing. Arrival: Jackson, WY; Salt Lake City, UT; Las Vegas, NV. (See also *Hiking with Packstock, Horse Trekking, Pack Trips, Covered Wagons*.)

L. D. Frome, a hearty eater, believes that backpackers should not have to subsist on dehydrated rations. So he packs in steaks and fresh vegetables on the backs of sturdy mules who leave camp each morning and take the quickest route to the evening's destination. Backpackers, carrying only their personal clothing and sleeping gear, are able to follow the more scenic and rugged trails with only half of the usual load on their backs. In summer they hike trails in the Wyoming Rockies, and in spring and fall trek into the canyons of Utah and Arizona.

Richard Brothers, Inc., 2215 Rangeview Lane, Laramie, WY 82070. Att.: Paul & Jim Richard. (307) 742-4872. Mt. Zirkel Wilderness. Jul.–Aug. 10–15 backpackers. 4–7 days. $35/day. Bring pack & sleeping gear. Custom trips. Arrival: Laramie, WY. (See also *Float Trips*.)

These are specially arranged trips in the Colorado Rockies where hikers cross the Continental Divide twice. They climb from aspen groves at 8,500 feet through montane, subalpine and alpine life zones to over 12,000-foot elevations. Both Paul and Jim are biology teachers in other months, so they're well versed in mountain flora and fauna and readily share their expertise.

Yellowstone Wilderness Guides, Crossed Sabres Ranch, Box Z, Wapiti, WY 82450. Att.: Lee Hanchett. (307) 587-3750. Yellowstone Natl. Park & surrounding wilderness areas. Jun–Oct. 2–10 backpackers. 2–22 days. Average: $40/day, all-incl. Arrival: Cody, WY, or Billings, MT. (See also *Youth Adventures*.)

"Witness the awesome splendor of such untouched areas as the Absaroka Wilderness, Yellowstone's Mirror Plateau, the amazing Sunlight Basin or the Beartooth Mountain Range," encourages Lee Hanchett. "With small custom groups we can give you individual attention. Our college-educated guides will help sharpen your skills—orienteering, first aid, nontechnical climbing, environmental awareness, routing techniques, fishing and high country exploration."

ALBERTA

Canatrek Mountain Expeditions Ltd., PO Box 1138, Dept. AG, Banff, Alta. TOL OCO. Att.: John Amatt. (403) 762-2528. Baffin & Ellesmere is., St. Elias Mts. Jul.–Aug. 4–12 backpackers. 14–22 days. $35–$55/day; bring pack & sleeping gear.

In 1974 Canatrek initiated its program of small-group expeditions to remote and little-visited mountain corners of the world, especially the Canadian Arctic. They are basically backpacking explorations, with some climbing. In the Northwest Territories and the Yukon you travel in a magnificent Arctic land with brilliant wildflowers or bare icecap, where in summer the sun shines 24 hours a day. Whales, seals, polar bears, caribou, and other wildlife inhabit this region of fjords, glaciers and high peaks. Travel in some areas is by snowmobile and sledge, in others by Eskimo canoe, and there is opportunity to become familiar with the Inuit culture.

BRITISH COLUMBIA

Whitewater Adventures Ltd., PO Box 46536, Vancouver, B.C. V6R 4G8. Att.: Dan Culver. (604) 736-2135. Coastal Range (BC). Jun.–Sept. 5 days, $185, incl. transport. Bring sleeping gear & backpacks. Group, family & early-payment discounts. Arrival: Vancouver, BC. (See also *Float Trips, Windjammers*.)

No previous camping experience needed for these relaxed hikes. After the train ride to D'Arcy, it's an easy trail to base camp. From there you follow trails each day in alpine meadows below towering mountain peaks.

Clifton R. Merritt for Wilderness Society.

Hiking with Packstock

"Packstock" means a friendly, maybe amusing, sometimes ornery four-legged pack animal, be it horse, mule or burro. The wild burros at home on the terraces of the Grand Canyon are reminders that in an earlier era settlers and prospectors trekked with pack animals out of necessity. There was no other transport for packing in supplies. "A burro," says one expert, "can be managed by any camper who is more intelligent than he." Are you?

Essentially, you hike while the horse (or whatever) does all the toting of grub and gear. With less urgency to keep weight at a bare minimum, more comforts can be taken along than in a backpack, and the hiker is usually free from carrying anything at all. This makes it a great excursion for families with young children if it is planned for not-too-difficult terrain and distances that youngsters can manage.

As with pack trips, outfitters for these hiking expeditions offer *moving* or *progressive trips* (on to a new camp each day) as well as *base camp trips* (staying put at one camp and circling the area on daily hikes). The latter is the more relaxed approach to wilderness living, since it's your choice whether you join the hikers each day, or spend hours fishing, or just goof off and read a book in the shade of the rustling pines. *Custom trips*—planned for you—are offered by all the outfitters, and some also schedule group departure dates for trips you can join.

The outfitters listed here offer a splendid choice to hikers. Does the scenic trail system in Alaska's Mt. McKinley National Park appeal to you? Or the fragrant forests and trout-laden streams of the High Sierras in California? Perhaps you would like exploring the high country of the Colorado Rockies, Idaho's Salmon River Breaks, the Bob Marshall Wilderness or Mission Mountains of Montana, Utah's canyonlands, Washington's North Cascades, Glacier and Olympic national parks or the mountains in Wyoming.

You can walk in and camp in the most beautiful wilderness imaginable. For an average rate of $35 or so per day (less for children), your outfitter will plan an itinerary especially for you, provide the guides, camping know-how and food, and handle all the logistics. It's a tremendous way to see and experience the wilderness. Only the foot power is up to you.

Will the animals carry all the gear, or is some to be on your back? Is this a flexible trip where you plan length of hikes and layovers as you go along? Will you stay at a base camp, or will you camp out? Check what the rates cover, whether there is a transportation charge, how many miles a day you'll walk, over what terrain, and the weight limits (if any) for personal gear. For fishing, will you need a license? Where will you meet—ranch, road's end or canyon head? What should you bring? Are you joining a scheduled departure or is this a custom trip for your own group? And if it matters, find out who your other walking companions will be—horses, mules or burros.

ALASKA

Alaskan Adventure, Hope, AK 99605. Att.: Keith Specking. No tel. [Jan.–Jun.: Juneau, AK. (907) 465-3500.] Brushkana Creek, Mt. McKinley Natl. Park area. Jul.–Aug. Moving & base camp trips. 4–10 hikers. 7 days, $495. Bring sleeping gear. Arrival: Cantwell, AK. (See also *Pack Trips.*)

The Speckings pick you up in Cantwell for the drive to their Brushkana Creek headquarters camp below Nenana Glacier. Next morning you hike to a remote cabin in a land of Dall mountain sheep, moose, grizzlies, grayling, glaciers, mountains and an exceptionally scenic trail system. The congenial Speckings orient their trips for truly enjoying the Alaskan environment.

CALIFORNIA

McGee Creek Pack Station, Box 1054, Bishop, CA 93514. Att.: David MacRoberts. (714) 935-4324. [Sept.–May: (714) 873-4350.] John Muir Wilderness. Jun.–Sept. Moving & base camp trips. 2–25 hikers. 3–14 days. Packer & mule, $60/day; ea. addl. mule, $15/day. Bring sleeping gear. Arrival: Bishop, CA. (See also *Pack Trips.*)

The High Sierras make spectacular hiking country, with their mighty peaks, fragrant forests and trout-laden lakes and streams. Dave MacRoberts will carry your gear on mules to a predesignated spot while you hike in. Ideal for large groups.

Red's Meadow, Agnew Meadows and Mt. Whitney Pack Outfits, Box 395-G, Mammoth Lakes, CA 93546. Att.: Bob Tanner. (714) 934-2345. [Oct.–Jun.: (714) 873-3928.] Yosemite & Sequoia natl. parks, John Muir & Minaret wilderness areas. Jun.–Oct. Moving & base camp trips. 1–25 hikers. 1–21 days. $24–$29/day. Group rates. Bring sleeping gear. Arrival: Mammoth Lakes or Bishop, CA. (See also *Pack Trips.*)

Red's Meadow Pack Outfits prides itself on being the High Sierra's largest outfitter. Hiking trips with packstock cover the same fabulous country as pack trips—high mountain trails, dense forests and fish-laden lakes and streams.

Rock Creek Pack Station, Box 248, Bishop, CA 93514. Att.: Herbert & Craig London. (714) 935-4493. [Oct.–Jun.: (714) 872-8331.] John Muir Wilderness, Sequoia & Yosemite natl. parks. Jun.–Oct. Moving & base camp trips. 1–25 hikers. 2–21 days. $45/day for packer, $12/day per mule. Group rates. Bring sleeping gear. Arrival: Bishop, CA. (See also *Horse Drives, Pack Trips.*)

Countless lakes, streams and meadows, major Sierra passes and peaks up to 13,000 feet welcome the Rock Creek hiker. Herb London's experience includes outfitting several college and university groups for hiking trips with packstock. Free parking and overnight camping at the pack station for guests.

COLORADO

Cottonwood Cove Lodge, Box 2, Wagon Wheel Gap, CO 81154. Att.: W. W. (Bibs) Wyley. (303) 658-2242. La Garita & Weminuche wilderness. Jun.–Sept. Moving & base camp trips. 4–18 hikers. 3–8 days. $30/day. Bring sleeping gear. Arrival: Alamosa or South Fork, CO. (See also *Pack Trips.*)

"Each day's hike is long enough to offer a variety of beautiful alpine scenery and views," writes Bibs Wyley, "yet short enough to give guests time to climb a peak or have added leisure in camp. We cater to our guests. Very little is left out of their vacations."

Wilderness Adventures, Moon Valley Resort, Box 265-CA, South Fork, CO 81154. Att.: Larry Ehardt. (303) 873-5331. May–Oct. Weminuche Wilderness. 3–15 hikers. 3–7 days. 6-day trips, $210. Bring or rent sleeping gear. Group rates. Arrival: South Fork, CO. (See also *Backpacking, Pack Trips, Snowmobiling*.)

"We are natives of this area," say the Ehardts, "and have spent a big part of our lives in these mountains—working, learning and teaching. You can expect an educational as well as an enjoyable recreational experience." On these scenic, conservation-oriented trips you'll walk the Continental Divide and learn about plant and animal life.

IDAHO

Fog Mountain, Salmon and Selway Expeditions, Box 585-D, Salmon, ID 83467. Att.: Stanton C. Miller. (208) 756-2319. Selway & Salmon wilderness, Big Horn Crags, Chamberlain Basin-Continental Divide. Jul.–Sept. Moving & base camp trips. 3–12 hikers. 4–10 days. $50/day incl. sleeping gear. Arrival: Salmon, ID. (See also *Backpacking, Pack Trips*.)

"We work out of several comfortable tent camps," Stan Miller says, "sometimes spending a day around camp to fish and explore before moving on to the next." There are well-maintained trails, good fishing in the alpine lakes and "the most breathtaking high country to be found anywhere."

Nez Perce Outfitters & Guides, PO Box 1454-S, Salmon, ID 83467. Att.: Val B. Johnson. (208) 756-3912. Salmon River Breaks Primitive Area. Jul.–Sept. Moving & base camp trips. 3–10 hikers. 3 or more days. $35/day; bring or rent sleeping gear. Group & youth rates. Arrival: Salmon, ID. (See also *Pack Trips, Float Trips*.)

Writes Val Johnson: "The terrain we hike is varied—steep and rocky in some areas, in others level and grassy—and the distance we cover depends on your abilities. Our basic but protective camps allow for mobility. Once we're in the high country, we do whatever you want—fish the well-stocked lakes, pan for gold, hike scenic trails and stalk game with cameras."

MONTANA

Black Tail Ranch, Box 77, Wolf Creek, MT 59648. Att.: Tag & Lyla Rittel. (406) 235-4330. Bob Marshall Wilderness, Scapegoat Wilderness. Jul.–Sept. Moving & base camp trips. 4–12 hikers. 7–14 days. $35–$40/day for 12 people, 10 days. Bring sleeping gear. Arrival: Helena, MT. (See also *Pack Trips*.)

Tag Rittel organizes adventure trips for the whole family, traveling about 10 miles between points with layover days for side trips or just resting. Equipment and guests' gear are packed on mules. "In this beautiful country, cameras and fishing rods are musts!"

Cheff Guest Ranch, RFD 1, Box 124-B, Charlo, MT 59824. Att.: Vern (Bud) Cheff. (406) 644-2557. Mission Mts., Bob Marhsall Wilderness. Jul.–Aug. Moving & base camp trips. 4–20 hikers. Any no. of days. $30/day. Bring sleeping gear. Arrival: Missoula, MT. (See also *Pack Trips*.)

From the ranch, you pass under the towering peaks of the "Little Alps of America." Abundant wildlife, flower-carpeted meadows, waterfalls, glaciers, cedars, spruce and piñon pines surround you on the trail, and the lakes are full of trout. "Expect to hike about 5 miles a day," Bud Cheff advises, "and limit your dunnage to 40 pounds. Too many packhorses will damage this fragile wilderness."

Double Arrow Outfitters (AG), PO Box 505, Seeley Lake, MT 59868. Att.: C. B. Rich. (406) 677-2411 or 2467. Bob Marshall Wilderness. Jul.–Sept. Moving & base camp trips. 4–15 hikers. 3–14 days. $35/day incl. food & cook, less w./own supplies. Bring sleeping gear. Arrival: Missoula, MT. (See also *Pack Trips.*)

C. B. Rich provides pyramid tents that accommodate 2 to 3 people and a 20-foot-by-20-foot kitchen fly. He also takes an extra saddle horse or two to be prepared for any emergency—and for sore feet. If hikers bring their own gear, C.B. charges only for each day his pack service is required. And if they have their own floating equipment, he'll drop them off on the South Fork of the Flathead River for a rafting trip, and pick them up where they come out.

Montana Sports Ranch, Box 501, Hwy. 209, Condon, MT 59826. Att.: Ron Hummel. (406) 754-2351. Mission Mts. Wilderness. Jul.–Sept. Base camp trips. 4–8 hikers. 6 days, $248. Bring sleeping gear. Arrival: Missoula or Kalispell, MT. (See also *Snowmobiling.*)

Ron Hummel's packstock transports your gear to a base camp on a wilderness lake with tents, a cook and a guide. Hike a challenging but not too strenuous 5-mile mountain trail. Try your luck at hooking a trout for supper. Practice your photography till you run out of film. Take a trip to a glacier. Predicts Ron: "Your week will end all too soon."

Seven Lazy P Guest Ranch, Box 193A, Choteau, MT 59422. Att.: Chuck Blixrud. (406) 466-2044. Bob Marshall Wilderness Area. Jul.–Sept. Moving & base camp trips. 4–15 hikers. 6–14 days. $40/day. Bring sleeping gear. Arrival: Choteau or Great Falls, MT. (See also *Pack Trips.*)

You start from the ranch at 5,200 feet and reach high alpine basins at 7,000 feet, with about 10 miles of hiking each day. Much of it is fragile high country where horses are not allowed—"some of God's greatest work," as Chuck describes this scenic wilderness. He schedules two trips in July, which anyone may join. For a day or more at the ranch before the trip starts, the rate is $35/day.

Wild Country Outfitters (A), 713 W. Poplar, Helena, MT 59601. Att.: Don & Meg Merritt. (406) 442-7127. Bob Marshall & Scapegoat wilderness. Jun.–Sept. Moving & base camp trips. 8–16 hikers. 7–12 days. $32/day. Bring sleeping gear. Arrival: Helena, MT. (See also *Pack Trips.*)

Reports a Wild Country hiker: "This trip will rejuvenate your spirits. Sturdy pack animals do the real work while you soak up the grandeur of the vast Big Sky country and relax in the leisurely pace of the hike. With only a collapsible wood-burning stove, Meg Merritt fixes outstanding meals—thick, juicy steaks, wild huckleberry pancakes. On layover days, the fishing and wildlife sighting are fun and rewarding."

Wildlife Outfitters, Rt. 1, Box 99B-AG, Victor, MT 59875. Att.: Jack & Shirley Wemple. (406) 642-3262. Selway-Bitterroot Wilderness, Bitterroot Natl. Forest. Jun.–Aug. Moving & base camp trips. 5–12 hikers. 7–9 days. About $50/day. Group & family rates. Bring sleeping gear. Arrival: Missoula, MT. (See also *Backpacking, Pack Trips.*)

"Explore wild lands the way the early prospectors did on one of our leisurely hiking trips," urges Jack Wemple. "We'll show you the wilderness as it was meant to be seen."

OREGON

Cal Henry, Box 26-A, Joseph, OR 97846. (503) 432-3872. Snake Riv. & Eagle Cap Wilderness. Mar.–Sept. Moving & base camp trips. 4–10 hikers. 1–10 days. Custom trip rates on request. Bring sleeping gear. Arrival: Enterprise, OR. (See also *Pack Trips.*)

On Cal Henry's trips you visit Hells Canyon, the deepest gorge in North America, or the alpine peaks of the Eagle Cap Wilderness. On travel days hikes cover 6 to 10 miles, and on layover days there's time for fishing and "learning firsthand nature's secrets."

UTAH

Horsehead Pack Trips, Box 68B, Monticello, UT 84535. Att.: Pete Steele. (801) 587-2929. Canyonlands Natl. Park, Grand Gulch, Blue Mt. & Dark Canyon. Apr.–Nov. Moving camp trips. 4–20 hikers. 2–7 days. $40/day incl. sleeping gear. (See also *Pack Trips.*)

Pete Steele has been packing through these areas for several years. "We move camp each day," he explains. "There's variety for all, and a qualified hiker can hike twice as far as the one who prefers to take it slow on the shortest route between each camping point."

WASHINGTON

Cascade Corrals, Box A, Stehekin, WA 98852. Att.: Ray Courtney. (509) 663-1521. North Cascades Natl. Park, Glacier Peak Wilderness, Wenatchee Natl. Forest. Jul.–Oct. 5–10 hikers. 7 days, $225. Sched. & custom trips. (See also *Pack Trips, Ski Touring.*)

"Hike-and-Like-It" treks take you to alpine meadows, high peaks, jewel-like lakes, glaciers, valleys—the very heart of the wilderness and the scenic Cascade Crest Trail. There are layover days for exciting side trips or for lazy relaxing up where the goats live. Right from the start it's an adventure, as the scenic approach to the Courtneys' headquarters is by charter plane or by excursion boat up beautiful Lake Chelan.

Indian Creek Corral, Star Rt., Box 218-A, Naches, WA 98937. Att.: Edward H. Cristler. No tel. Cascade Crest. Spring & fall. Moving & base camp trips. 2–20 hikers. 3 or more days. $30/day & up. Bring sleeping gear. Arrival: Yakima, WA. (See also *Pack Trips.*)

"We take our hikers into an area familiar to us and make it a learning as well as a fun experience," explains Ed Cristler. "We hope they have as good a time on these trips as we do! This almost inaccessible country is a perfect haven of alpine meadows and flowery parks for those who want peace and solitude." He picks up his guests in Yakima.

Lost Mountain Packing & Guide Service, Rt. 6, Box 920, Sequim, WA 98382. Att.: Mike Jeldness. (206) 683-4331. Olympic Natl. Park. Apr.–Oct. Moving & base camp trips. 2–10 hikers. 2–10 days. $35/day; under 12, $30/day. Bring sleeping gear. Arrival: Sequim or Port Angeles, WA. (See also *Pack Trips.*)

Mike Jeldness custom-tailors each trip to the wishes of his clients, and gourmet trail cooking is his specialty. On some trips you have a spectacular view of the Olympic Range on one side and the Strait of Juan de Fuca on the other. It's a 2½-hour bus or car ride from Seattle to Sequim.

WYOMING

Box Y Ranch, Box 1172-A, Jackson, WY 83001. Att.: Bud Callahan. (307) 733-4329. Wyoming & Salt Riv. ranges of Bridger-Teton Natl. Forest. Jul.–Aug. Moving & base camp trips. 4–12 hikers. 3–10 days. Rates vary. Arrival: Jackson, WY, or Idaho Falls, ID. (See also *Pack Trips.*)

Bud Callahan's custom trips match the desires and abilities of each group. On the trail along the top of the Wyoming Range you're in spectacular mountain scenery with lots of wildlife. The Salt River route follows a series of high mountain lakes—

beautiful country and excellent fishing. "Trips are well equipped and the food is the best," a vacationer writes.

Game Hill Ranch, Box A, Bondurant, WY 82922. Att.: Pete & Holly Cameron. (307) 733-2015. [Nov.-May: (307) 733-3281.] Gros Ventre Mts., Wyoming Range. Jun.-Oct. Moving & base camp trips. 2-6 hikers. Sample rates: 5 days, $319; 7 days, $431; 10 days, $594. Bring or rent sleeping gear. Arrival: Jackson, WY. (See also *Backpacking, Pack Trips, Ski Touring.*)

Pete Cameron teaches hikers about the flora, fauna, geography and history of this beautiful country. Each trip is planned for weather and hiker, abilities, so the number of layover days varies. They usually cover 5 to 10 miles when traveling, and stay in comforgable but simple camps.

Greys River Outfitting, Box 2453, Jackson, WY 83001. Att.: Derrell Roden. (307) 733-6218. N.W. Wyoming. Jun.-Sept. Moving & base camp trips. 2-20 hikers. 2-14 days. Custom trips. Rates vary for size of group; children half price. Bring sleeping gear. Arrival: Jackson or Afton, WY; Idaho Falls, ID. (See also *Pack Trips.*)

With pack horses lugging the gear, you can hike 10 to 15 miles each day, if you wish, through "very beautiful scenery, a multitude of wild flowers and the home of deer, elk, moose, eagles, coyotes, beaver and trout." For large groups Derrell provides tents, cooking gear, food, cook and wrangler. Small groups usually bring their own equipment.

L. D. Frome, Outfitter, Box G, Afton, WY 83110. (307) 886-5240. Teton, Washakie, Yellowstone Park & Gros Ventre wilderness areas. Jun.-Sept. Moving & base camp trips. 1-20 hikers. 4 or more days. $40/day for 5 days & min. 4 hikers. Bring sleeping gear. Arrival: Jackson, WY. (See also *Backpacking, Horse Trekking, Pack Trips, Covered Wagons.*)

One ecstatic hiker remarks: "The mountains were spectacular—a moose at the edge of a clearing, waterfalls and snowball fights in the middle of July! L.D.'s services were terrific, the crew was great and the food excellent!" On these trips you usually move camp every other day, use layover days for exploring and fishing, and sleep-in in a tent or under the stars.

Low Gardner, PO Box 107, Smoot, WY 83126. (307) 886-5665. Salt Riv. Range, Wyoming Range in Bridger Natl. Forest. Jul.-Aug. Moving & base camp trips. 8-20 hikers. Rates on request. Bring sleeping gear. Arrival: Jackson, WY. (See also *Pack Trips.*)

On Low Gardner's trips, hikers travel 8 to 10 miles a day and stay at a teepee base camp. You'll fish, climb peaks and find magnificent scenery wherever you go in this area. Low shares his wilderness knowledge based on years of guiding experience with each group. "He's one of the most competent woodsmen I've ever had the pleasure of spending time with," writes one participant.

Mountaineering/Rock Climbing

The early mountaineers climbed for a logical reason. They had to get over a mountain in the course of their trapping, exploring or pioneer migrating.

Now, with access by road or by air to the mountain areas that people need to reach, climbing is no longer the only way to get there. Yet vastly more climbers are in high altitudes today than in years past. They are there simply for the sport of it.

The facetious answer to "Why climb a mountain?" was given by Mallory of Everest fame: "Because it is there." But the real incentives are far deeper. Perhaps the basic one is the desire to meet a challenge that involves great physical endurance and the mastering of important skills—skills that minimize the risks and dangers of the sport.

"The mind's desire to explore and the body's desire to find its limits are all part of climbing," explains an instructor. According to one participant of a basic rock climbing seminar on Mt. Hood, "You go beyond what you think you're capable of and you have one hell of a lot of fun in the process.

"Mountaineering is as physically demanding as any activity I've tried," he continues, "and I've been into a lot of things, including white-water canoeing and semipro hockey. But there are infinite, subtle satisfactions that you can derive from the sport, even if you never get to Everest . . . the companions, the mental and physical challenge, the incredible scenery. It's not everyone's bag, but some will turn on."

If you get that "elevator" feeling looking down from the roof of a tall building—or perhaps out of your second-floor window—mountaineering is definitely not for you. A serious climber, you must recall, is as adept on a perpendicular incline as a fly on a Sunday picnic. Clinging to footholds and handholds on sheer rock faces, or wielding an ice ax to kick out steps for cramponed feet on snowy ice walls, is ultimate joy to a climber.

Yet there are degrees of climbs—some rugged and ambitious, others easy and safe—choices that range from a major expedition up a high peak to a day's lope in the foothills. And there are courses for those who want to spend the night suspended in a hammock on an overhang. . . and courses for those who don't ever want to be more than ten feet off the ground.

The term "mountaineering" covers the entire scope of mountain climbing, and courses include campcraft, map reading, orienteering, survival techniques and mountain medicine. They also include the specific techniques of rock climbing—such as basic rope handling, rappeling, glissading, belaying and the use of pitons,

Mt. Adams Wilderness Institute, WA.

nuts and slings. And they cover the skills of alpine climbing—steep climbs that involve snow and ice as well as rock and require proficiency with an ice ax, rope and crampons.

There are mountaineering services to provision and guide climbers into practically any part of North America's mountain ranges. If you're expert enough, you can join a climb up the 22,834-foot summit of Mt. Aconcagua in Alaska, America's highest mountain. With only basic experience you are eligible for ascents of volcanic peaks in Mexico. Or spend five days in Montana's Mission Mountains, a trek designed for families and anyone who'd like to learn the fundamentals of route finding and mountaineering. There are courses, seminars and guided climbs for every level of expertise.

It's a sport that is strenuous and can demand all the strength you possess. It presents difficulty and danger, unpredictable hazards, enormous discomfort, freezing sleet, drenching rains, precarious footholds and falls. The rewards? A surge of self-confidence, the exaltation of achievement, the discovery of what you can do if you have to, and indescribable exhilaration at the summit. Climbers will agree— it's a fantastic sport!

Equipment is important, and so are instructors. Get to know your instructor before you start the climb. His abilities and judgment are invaluable. Also let him know your capabilities or limitations. What should you bring? What do rates cover? Are you arranging for a beginner, intermediate or advanced excursion? How much weight will you carry? What preconditioning should you have? What are the health requirements or age limits? Be clear on whether you are signing up for a course, an expedition, a trip from a base camp, rock climbing, glacier climbing, peak climbing or whatever. Is the terrain rugged? Is the excursion for enjoyment, for survival training, or for both? Are you joining a group or is this a custom trip? Find out whether transportation to and from your meeting point is supplied, what other activities are included, and who arranges pre- and posttrip lodging. Check dates. And for excursions especially for teens, see the chapter, "Youth Adventures."

ALASKA

Genet Expeditions, Talkeetna, AK 99676. Att.: Ray Genet. (907) 733-2306. Alaska Range (Mts. McKinley, Foraker, Hunter & Aconcagua). Apr.–Jul. 12 people. 14–30 days, $880–$1,800. Bring sleeping & personal climbing gear. Arrival: Air to Anchorage, train to Talkeetna, AK. (See also *Ski Touring.*)

In one of the world's coldest but most spectacular mountain ranges, Ray Genet and his guides lead expeditions on various routes. Some are not technically difficult but require excellent physical and mental condition and proficiency in use of ice ax and crampons. Others are for very experienced climbers with good snow and ice background. On the Mt. Aconcagua climb, America's highest summit at 22,834 feet, high-altitude experience is a prerequisite. Genet offers ascents up Mt. McKinley's West Buttress, Kahiltna-Muldrow Traverse, or South Buttress; also up Mt. Hunter's West Ridge and Mt. Foraker's east approach. Genet provides access to this challenging terrain by bush plane from his Talkeetna headquarters. They return by plane, bus, train or river raft. "Climbers must be prepared to work very hard," he warns, "and convinced that they are going 'to the summit.'"

Mountain Trip, PO Box 10078, South Station, Anchorage, AK 99502. Att.: Gary Bocarde & Jim Hale. (907) 349-1161. Alaska Range & Chugach Mts. All yr. 5–10 people. 2-day courses, $45; 2-wk. seminars, $650; guided climbs, 2–3 wks., $895–$1,180. Arrival: Anchorage, AK.

This comprehensive mountaineering school offers small expeditions and classes in rock and ice climbing and glacier travel. A special expedition training program is taught over a 2-summer period in the magnificent Ruth Amphitheater, where Mt. Huntington, Moose's Tooth and Mt. McKinley rise spectacularly from the glacial floor. Also in its program: demanding guided climbs of McKinley, Foraker, Hunter and other peaks, and expeditions in such areas as the Ruth Gorge, Kichatna Spires and Talkeetna Mountains. Gary Bocarde's advice: "Train hard!"

Mountains North Guide Service, 851 University Ave., Fairbanks, AK 99701. Att.: Ev Wenrick. (907) 479-2984. Alaska Range, Brooks Range, Chugach Mts.

May–Aug. 3–8 participants. 1- & 2-day seminars, $30–$80; guided climbs, $45/day; group & family rates. Arrival: Fairbanks, AK. (See also *Backpacking, Canoeing, Ski Touring*.)

With easy access to McKinley, the Brooks Range and the Alaska Range, Wenrick offers seminars on rock climbing that include holds and balance techniques, roping, knots, belaying and rappeling. Also snow and glacier travel with rope, ice ax and crampon work, belaying, route finding and crevasse rescue. He also plans guided climbs.

Wildernorth, Inc., Mile 102 Glenn Hwy., SRC Box 92E, via Palmer, AK 99645. Att.: Joe & Suzi LaBelle & Stu Ashley. No tel. Chugach & Talkeetna Mts., Prince William Sound fjords. All yr. 4–8 people. 1–25 days. 1 day, $20; 2 days, $90; 5 days, $275; incl. food & flight. Arrival: Anchorage, AK. (See also *Backpacking, Snowshoeing*.)

Travel by foot and airplane onto, over and around several of the most spectacular mountain glacier systems in Alaska. Study huge tumbling icefalls, complex moraine systems, nunataks, sharp aretes, ogives—and if you're not sure what these are, you'll know by the end of your trip. Instruction in roped glacier travel is given on Matanuska Glacier and climbs made of Mt. Sgt. Robinson (10,650 feet) and Mt. Marcus Baker (13,176 feet) in the Chugach Mountains and high peaks in the Talkeetnas.

CALIFORNIA

Mountain People School, 157 Oak Spring Dr., San Anselmo, CA 94960. Att.: Terry Halbert. (415) 457-3664. Sierra Nevada Mts. & San Francisco Bay area. All yr. 4–7 people. 2–14 days. 2-day course, $25; 7-day trip, $125; 14-day trip, $225. Group & family rates. Arrival: San Rafael or San Francisco, CA. (See also *Ski Touring*.)

Mountain People operates in Tahoe National Forest, part of the Sierra Nevada Range. Their 7-day adventure offers exposure to "tough hiking and problem-solving." We're told groups will try to stay off trails whenever possible so they will learn to negotiate fallen timber, boulder fields or snow. There's a 14-day expedition to "climb high mountain peaks, eat wild natural foods, enjoy some of the best trout fishing in the state and find your own routes." Also beginning and intermediate classes in rock climbing.

Mountain Travel, Inc., 1398-G Solano Ave., Albany, CA 94706. Att.: Leo LeBon. (415) 527-8100. Aug.–Nov. 6–15 people. Mexico, 19 days $1,085. Arrival: Mexico City.

Mountain Travel organizes over 80 climbing expeditions world-wide. For hikers who want to expand their basic mountaineering experience, the Mexico trip introduces snow climbing techniques during ascents of four volcanic peaks: Pico de Orizaba (18,851 feet), Popocatepetl (17,887 feet), Ixtacihuatl (17,343 feet) and Nevado de Toluca (15,016 feet).

Palisade School of Mountaineering, PO Box 694, Bishop, CA 93514. Att.: John Fischer. Sierra Nevada. Mar., Jun.–Sept. 6–9 people. 3–18 days. 6-day courses, $390. Arrival: Bishop, CA.

Unique to PSOM training is the opportunity for students and guides to work closely together for a week, with curriculum tailored to fit personal goals. Small groups led by top climbers take intensive courses in ski mountaineering, mountain medicine rescue (a special 2-day course), basic and advanced rock climbing, mountaineering, and ice and snow climbing. The school's base camp is in the Palisades Range, one of the best climbing areas of the Sierras. It's the oldest climbing school in California.

Rainier Mountaineering, Inc., WA.

COLORADO

The Bob Culp Climbing School, 1335 Broadway, Boulder, CO 80302. (303) 442-8355. Rock climbing all yr.; ice climbing & ski touring Dec.-Mar. Boulder area & Rocky Mts. 1-3 people, ½ day or more days. Semipvt. lesson or climb, $25; pvt. lesson or guided climb, $35-$65. Arrival: Boulder, CO.

"Climbing is an intense experience that can open up new worlds for you," Bob Culp believes. His school offers comprehensive instruction in the craft of climbing. "It is thorough, presents the most up-to-date techniques, and is entirely practical—that is, the student learns while actually climbing with an instructor," Culp explains. He also provides a guide service for climbs in the Southwest, Wyoming and abroad as well as in the Colorado Rockies.

Colorado Mountain Club, 2530 W. Alameda Ave., Denver, CO 80219. (303) 922-8315.

Founded in 1912, CMC has nearly 5,000 members and conducts backpacking trips, climbs, snowshoe and ski tours, walks and outings—most for members only. There are 13 groups in Colorado. Dues vary. For outing details send CMC $3 for its *Summer Schedule* or $2.50 for the *Winter Schedule*.

Fantasy Ridge Alpinism, Mountain Guides of Colorado, Box 2106, Estes Park, CO 80517. Att.: Michael Covington. (303) 586-5758. Rocky Mt. Natl. Park all yr., Mt. McKinley May–Aug. 1–5 people. 1 or more days. 1-day guided climbs, $40 w./3, grade V or VI, $80 w./2. 1-day courses, $10–$60. Rates incl. all equip. Group rates. Arrival: Denver, CO.

High in the Rockies of north-central Colorado are many steep-walled cirques and permanent snowfields. This is where FRA does much of its mountaineering and technical rock-climbing. Across the valley are summits of 11,000 feet to 14,255 feet—some easy mountaineering routes, some involving multiday rock climbs. FRA's year-round instruction includes basic through advanced mountaineering, guided climbs, and rock, snow and ice techniques. Their instructor/guide qualifications are high, Covington tells us, and low student/instructor ratios encourage maximum comprehension. They also arrange guided climbs world-wide.

International Alpine School, Dept. CCA, Eldorado Springs, CO 80025. Att.: Michael R. Lowe. (303) 494-1015. Sangre de Cristo Mts. All yr. 3–12 people. 1–10 days. Courses: 3 & 5 days rock climbing, 5 & 7 days mountaineering, about $30/day; 5 days ice climbing, 7 days outdoor adventure, $200. Arrival: Denver or Boulder, CO.

Highly skilled teachers, a 3-to-1 student-teacher ratio and a superb teaching area in the Sangre de Cristo Mountains are IAS's major ingredients. Their goal: to impart knowledge of classical and contemporary mountaineering through instruction and actual climbing experience. Safety techniques, mental and physical conditioning, and exposure to ecology are emphasized in courses on rock climbing, mountaineering, winter ice climbing (new techniques) and outdoor adventure (an introduction to technical rock climbing, white-water rafting and high-alpine mountaineering).

Mountain Guides and Outfitters, Inc., PO Box 2001, Aspen, CO 81611. Att.: Kenneth R. Wyrick. (303) 925-6680. White Riv. Natl. Forest, Utah desert, Wind River & Teton Mts. (WY). Apr.–Oct. 2–20 people. ½–30 days. Rock-climbing classes, ½ day $15, full day $25; private lessons, ½ day $40, full day $75; guided climbs, $50/day. Arrival: Aspen, CO. (See also *Backpacking, Float Trips, Ski Touring*—Aspen Ski Touring School, *Dog Sledding.*)

Writes Ken Wyrick: "We teach small classes the latest and safest techniques, beginning with belaying and basic movements and progressing to vertical rock and more advanced rope handling. Our climbs take place on 13,000-foot and 14,000-foot peaks, with steep snow gullies." There are spectacular but not difficult ridge routes—"perfect for the novice."

The Mountaineering School at Vail, Inc., PO Box 3034, Vail, CO 81657. Att.: Ted Billings. (303) 476-4123. Gore Range, White Riv. Natl. Forest. Jun.–Aug. 4–8 people. 1-wk. ski mountaineering & basic courses, $205. 3½-wk. mountaineering trips, $545. Arrival: Vail, CO.

From a base camp at 11,000 feet, the basic course covers all phases of mountaineering and is taught at progressive levels, suitable to each student's ability. Those enrolling in early June can combine ski touring with basic rock climbing. The 3½-week mountaineering trip extends the basic course teaching into a 25-day wilderness trek through the magnificent Gore Range. "Excellent, thorough instruction," is a former student's endorsement.

IDAHO

The Wilderness Institute, PO Box 338, Bonners Ferry, ID 83805. Att.: Larry E. Fidler. (208) 267-3013. Uncompahgre Primitive Area (CO), Gros Ventre & Absaroka wilderness (WY), Beartooth Primitive Area & Cabinet Mts. (MT). Jun.–Aug. 5–12 people. 12 days, $260; 14 days, $295. (See also *Backpacking, Canoeing, Ski Touring.*)

Intended for people between 15 and 45 seeking in-depth wilderness training, these trips cover the fundamentals of wilderness living (orientation, finding shelter, preparing food) and mountaineering techniques (using a climbing rope, knots, belaying, rappeling). Participants climb 14,000-foot peaks in spectacular country. Near the end there's a survival solo.

IOWA

Iowa Mountaineers, 30 Prospect Pl., Iowa City, IA 52240. Att.: John & Jim Ebert. (319) 337-7163. Devil's Lake State Park (WI). May–Jun. 7 days, $100. (See also *Backpacking, Ski Touring.*)

The Eberts say their 7-day intensive course is "one of the finest and safest courses in the country." In the outstanding rock climbing area of Devil's Lake State Park, they give thorough instruction on rope management, static and dynamic belaying, rappeling, use of pitons, nuts and slings, and other skills. Evening lectures and slides amplify daytime instruction, which begins each Saturday.

MONTANA

Hondo Rast and Company, PO Box 231-A, Hamilton, MT 59840. Att.: Haven Holsapple. (406) 363-1382 or 3440. AK, MT, Mexico. Jun. Aug. Dec.–Jan. 3–10 people. 14–30 days, $330-$995.

"Expeditioning is an art—born of dreams and turned into the reality of experiencing nature's beauty and challenge," writes Haven Holsapple, professional outdoorsman, mountaineer and caver. He turns his dreams into adventurous ascents of Mexico's Citlaltepetl, Popocatepetl and Ixtacihuatl (all over 17,000 feet); 30-day Alaskan mountaineering expeditions in Glaciér Bay and the Brooks, Chugach and Talkeeetna Ranges; and 15-day winter expeditions in Montana's Rockies. They are for anyone 16 years or over. "An outstanding feature is that we offer full-scale expeditions in glacial mountaineering," Holsapple adds.

Montana Mountain Trips, 3401 14th Ave. So., Great Falls, MT 59405. Att.: John H. & T. Brice Addison. No tel. Mission Mts., Beartooth Primitive Area, Bob Marshall Wilderness, Cabinet Mts. & Madison Range. Jul.–Aug. 3–8 people, 3–14 days. Approx. $30/day all-incl. Arrival: Kalispell or Great Falls, MT. (See also *Backpacking.*)

The Addisons recommend their 5-day mountaineering trips for "families and anyone who'd like to learn the fundamentals of route finding and mountaineering." Participants ford streams, climb a mountain, travel over snow and through woods—and fish in four beautiful lakes. A more intensive 8-day mountaineering trip equips teenagers with basic wilderness and mountaineering skills—and gives them an opportunity for self-discovery through challenging physical and mental limits.

NEW HAMPSHIRE

International Mountain Equipment, Box 494, North Conway, NH 03860. Att.: Paul Ross. (603) 356-5287. Presidential Range & White Mts. 1–5 people. 2–5 days recommended. Instruction $20–$30/day; pvt. $40. Arrival: Portland, ME. (See also *Ski Touring.*)

"All you need is a pair of boots; we supply everything else," says Director Paul Ross. He has been rock climbing for over 20 years and has made many first ascents in Britain, the U.S. and Canada, and early ascents in the Alps. IME's instruction includes all aspects of mountaineering, and Ross describes his instructors as

Mt. Adams Wilderness Institute, WA.

"responsible, experienced and very competent—the most experienced in the East." Never more than 5 students per instructor in beginners' classes, or 3 in intermediate and advanced.

NEW JERSEY

Northeast School of Mountaineering, 26 Hilltop Ave., Berkeley Heights, NJ 07922. Att.: Art Fitch. (201) 322-8414. All yr. $30–$35/day, incl. instruction, food, most climbing equip., local transport. 15 days mountaineering in Bugaboos (BC), $500; 15 days in Mexico, $700. (See also *Backpacking, Ski Touring*—Odyssey.)

NSM students scramble up the New Paltz cliffs (NY) on weekends spring through fall, learning the fine points of rock climbing. Winter weekends include ice climbing instruction at Chapel Pond in the Adirondacks. For prospective mountaineers all phases of high climbing are taught during 2-week summer camps in the Bugaboos (British Columbia), while on other expeditions sturdy hikers can venture up the Mexican volcanos Orizaba and Popocatepetl. Included in the price of any trip are instruction, food and lodging.

NORTH CAROLINA

Nantahala Outdoor Center, Star Rt., Box 68-B, Bryson City, NC 28713. Att.: Payson Kennedy. (704) 488-6407. Western NC. All yr. 1–3 students on 2-day weekend clinics, $75. Pvt. lessons. Arrival: Asheville, NC, or Chattanooga, TN. (See also *Backpacking, Canoeing, Float Trips*.)

NOC assures rock climbers a safe indoctrination into the sport. The novice spends his weekend learning knots, signals, rope handling and basic techniques. He learns to use small holds and almost undetectable variations—how to move in balance with the rock. Fee includes meals Friday through Sunday night and instruction from "some of the best climbers in the South."

OREGON

Johann Mountain Guides, Inc., PO Box 1917l, Portland, OR 97219. Att.: Ed Johann. (503) 244-7672. Pacific Northwest & Mexico. All yr. 3–12 people, 1–10 days. Instruction, $10/day; climbs & expeditions, $25/day; 4-day ascent of Popocatepetl, $125. Arrival: Portland, OR, or Mexico City. (See also *Backpacking.*)

Explains Ed Johann: "Our rock and snow practices, and ascents of Mt. Hood, Mt. St. Helens and Mt. Adams are designed for the beginner. But they'll also help the experienced climber since we demonstrate the use of all the latest equipment. We help you enjoy the out-of-doors and live safely in a sometimes hostile environment." A 4-day summit ascent of Mexico's Popocatepetl includes transportation from Mexico City and meals and lodging on the mountain.

Lute Jerstad Adventures, Inc., PO Box 19527, Portland, OR 97219. (503) 244-4364. Pacific Northwest. Jun.–Sept. 8–20 people. 5-day seminars, $210–$300. Arrival: Portland, OR. (See also *Pack Trips, Float Trips.*)

Lute Jerstad's 5-day ice and rock climbing seminars give every climber, beginner or advanced, a chance to improve and perfect his climbing techniques with recognized authorities. To assure an optimum level of safety and attention, no more than six climbers are taken by any one instructor. Also a mountain medicine and rescue seminar for outdoor leaders. One climber's comment is typical: "The instruction is thorough . . . Lute's program is fantastic. He gets you to go beyond what you think you're capable of and you have one hell of a lot of fun in the process."

VERMONT

Dakin's Vermont Mountain Shop, 227 Main St., Burlington, VT 05401. Att.: Helmut Lenes. (802) 864-4122. Green Mts. (VT), White Mts. (NH), Adirondack Mts. (NY). May–Sept. 3–5 people. 1–2 days. $20/day for beginners; more for difficult climbs.

"Our goal is to teach you to enjoy safely the beauty of nature," Helmut Lenes writes. He became a registered Austrian guide at 17 and has scaled all the major peaks in the Alps. He takes beginners to the Green Mountains and Adirondacks, and advanced climbers to Franconia Notch in the White Mountains.

VIRGINIA

Geneva Spur Limited, Inc., 1109 Lakewood Dr., Vienna, VA 22180. Att.: Barry Allen Nelson. (703) 281-3316. Mts. of VA, WV, MD, NH, & NY. All yr. 1–6 people, or more. 1-day classes, $15–$20; pvt. instruc., $25/day; also guided climbs. Arrival: Washington, DC.

"Mountaineering builds confidence in a person's own abilities," Barry Nelson believes. "Climbing is not so much taught as it is discovered. From basic rock climbing, through alpinism, we provide the know-how and the experience for any adventurer to safely enjoy the mountains and receive their wisdom." Their classes deal with basic through advanced rock climbing, ice climbing and mountaineering. And they offer private instruction on a 1-to-1 basis, and guided climbs that enable students to improve their technique.

WASHINGTON

Mt. Adams Wilderness Institute, Rt. 2, Flying L Ranch, Glenwood, WA 98619. Att.: Darryl Lloyd. (509) 364-3511. Mt. Adams in Cascade Range. Jun.–Aug. 6–10 people. 8 days, $300; 12 days, $400. Arrival: Portland, OR.

Darryl Lloyd characterizes his course as "a total mountain experience," which includes intensive instruction in snow and ice climbing, glacier travel, backpacking in remote alpine wilderness and a strenuous climb to the 12,276-foot summit of Mt. Adams. No previous experience is necessary; however, participants should be over the age of 18 and in excellent physical condition. Students rate this course in their comments to us as: "Tremendous! Far exceeding our expectations . . . not only enjoyable but an extraordinary learning experience as well."

Northwest Alpine Guide Service, Inc., 1628 Ninth Ave. #2, Seattle, WA 98101. Att.: Linda Bradley Miller. (206) 622-6074. WA, May–Dec.; Mexico, Dec.–Jan. 2–18 people. 1 or more days. About $40–$45/day. (See also *Backpacking, Canoeing, Float Trips, Ski Touring, Wilderness Living, Youth Adventures.*)

Director Brad Bradley is convinced his basic snow, glacier and rock climbing school is outstanding for beginners. Each student receives personal attention from people-oriented instructors who feel climbing safely is more important than making a summit. Three-day climbs tackle every major mountain peak in Washington. In winter Bradley offers 12-day ascents of Mexico's Popocatepetl, Ixtacihuatl and Citlaltepetl.

Northwest Wilderness Traverse, PO Box 1732, Bellevue, WA 98009. Att.: Frank King. (206) 885-7469. North Cascade, Olympic & Sawtooth mts. Jun.–Sept. 4–12 people. 6 days, $215–$335. Arrival: Seattle, WA.

"Our specialty is navigating off-trail wilderness areas," says Frank King, "choosing a route and negotiating whatever lies in the way." His expeditions involve on- and off-trail (mountain and cross-country) backpacking and hiking, and, on some routes, climbs and snow, rock and glacier travel. On these King and his leaders, graduates of the Seattle Mountaineers Climbing Course, teach rope technique, ice ax and crampon use en route. The spectacular area has the greatest concentration of glaciers in the contiguous U.S. As once climber writes, "These are excellent, very rugged and incredibly beautiful trips."

Rainier Mountaineering, Inc., Paradise, WA 98397. Att.: Lou Whittaker & W. Gerald Lynch. (206) 569-2227. [Sept.–May: 201 St. Helens, Tacoma, WA 98402. (206) 627-6242.] Mt. Rainier Natl. Park (WA), Mt. McKinley Natl. Park (AK), Mexico. Feb.–Oct. 4–24 people. 1–30 days. 1-day rock, snow, ice school, $25; 5-day seminars, $225; 20–30 day Mt. McKinley Expeditions, $1,100; pvt. climbs, $75/day.

RMI has the largest professional staffs of trained snow, ice and rock climbing instructors in the U.S. according to Lou Whittaker. "We pride ourselves in our safety record and the comments made by thousands of novice climbers whose experience with us was a highlight of their lives." His wide-ranging offerings—from Mexico's 17,887-foot Popocatepetl to Alaska's 20,230-foot McKinley—suit mountaineers of all levels of experience.

WYOMING

Exum Mountain Guide Service & School of American Mountaineering, Moose, WY 83012. Att.: Glenn Exum. (307) 733-2297. [Sept.–Jun.: (307) 733-2276.] Grand Teton Natl. Park. Jun.–Sept. 1–10 people. Daily classes, $15–$25; snow and ice, $30. Guided climbs: 1 day, $25–$65; 2 days, $50–$60/day. Arrival: Jackson, WY.

Glenn Exum, a pioneer in American mountaineering, and his guides have climbed world-wide. Among his first ascents was his solo on the Exum Ridge of the Grand Teton in 1931. He operates basic, intermediate and advanced schools, a snow and ice school and special seminars. You must qualify through climbing schools before taking guided climbs. If in good condition, you can qualify for climbing the Grand Teton with a day of basic and one of intermediate instruction. "The mind's desire to explore and the body's desire to find its limits are all a part of climbing,'' Exum says.

Jackson Hole Mountain Guides, Box 124-A, Teton Village, WY 83025. Att.: Dr. William E. Thompson. (307) 733-4979. Grand Teton Natl. Park, Wind Riv. Range. Jun.-Sept. 1-4 people, 1-8 or more for special trips. 1-day schools, $22-$75; 4-day seminars, $175; 8-day camps, $46-$100/day; guide service, $48-$100/day. Arrival: Jackson Hole, WY; Idaho Falls, ID.

Jackson Hole Mountain Guides is committed to providing personalized, quality instruction. Students can enroll in 1-day schools covering everything from basic to advanced and snow climbing. Four-day ice and snow seminars and 8-day high-altitude living and climbing camps sharpen skills. JHMG "graduates," and climbers with previous experience, can participate in guided alpine and ice climbs. "We climb only aesthetic routes," asserts Dr. Thompson, "those that are less used, sometimes more difficult, but always more exciting."

National Outdoor Leadership School, PO Box AA, Dept. K, Lander, WY 82520. (307) 332-4381. Absaroka, Beartooth, North Cascades, Teton, Uinta & Wind Riv. ranges, Mt. McKinley. All yr. 15-40 days. Sample rates: 15 days, Absaroka Range, $600; 35 days, Wind Riv. Range, $765. (See also *Ski Touring, Wilderness Living, Youth Adventures.*)

Year-round expeditions are scheduled, involving every type of mountaineering skill and technique, from beginning to advanced, on rock, snow, glaciers, ice, trails and mountain peaks. Most are 35 days, with minimum ages 16 to 18 and no top limit. NOLS provides full details.

REGIONAL CLUBS—U.S.

Adirondack Mountain Club, 172 Ridge St., Dept. 51, Glens Falls, NY 12801. Att.: Mrs. Doris M. Herwig. (518) 793-7737. All yr. Membership, $15. (See also *Ski Touring.*)

Mt. Adams Wilderness Institute, WA.

The Adirondack Mountain Club was formed in 1922 to promote forest conservation, camping, hiking and canoeing. The club maintains 2 lodges, miles of trails, and sponsors winter mountaineering and rock climbing schools and summer seminars. Local chapters (25 in New York and New Jersey) offer hiking and backpacking trips all year.

Appalachian Mountain Club, 5 Joy St., Boston, MA 02108. (617) 523-0636.
Organized in 1876 to advance mountain exploration in New England, AMC maintains hiking trails, a hut system, camps and shelters. Its 10 chapters sponsor rock climbing, hiking, canoeing, skiing, snowshoeing and bicycling trips. Membership is $20; initiation fee, $5; spouse, $15; and under 23 years, $5—or $10 with club publications.

Appalachian Trail Conference, Box 236, Harpers Ferry, WV 25425. (304) 535-6331.
Established in 1925, ATC has built and maintains the 2,000 miles of the Appalachian Trail from Maine to Georgia. For a list of more than 100 affiliate clubs with year-round hiking, camping and mountaineering programs, write ATC.

BRITISH COLUMBIA

Adventure Unlimited, Box 1881, Golden, B.C. VOA 1HO. Att.: Pete Austen. (604) 344-2380. Bugaboos, Selkirks & Rockies (BC). Jun.–Sept. 3–15 people. 6-day climbing courses, $199–$209. Bring sleeping gear & pack. Group rates. (See also *Canoeing, Ski Touring*.)
These "noninstitutional, happy and relaxed trips" teach wilderness skills in fabulous mountain settings. The introductory course covers orienteering, bush survival and rock climbing; the more advanced course covers rock, ice and glacier climbing with mountain ascents. For the less ambitious, there are day and weekend trips at all levels. Accommodations on these excursions are in climbing huts, tents or lean-tos deep in the mountains.

Northern Lights Alpine Recreation, Box 399, Invermere, B.C. VOA 1KO. Att.: Arnör Larson. (604) 342-6042. Southern Canadian Rockies & Purcell Range (BC & Alta), other areas by arr. May–Oct. 2–4 people. Alpine hiking, $85–$90/wk.; climbing, $160/wk.; exploratory climbing, $350/2 wks. Arrival: Calgary, Alta., or Invermere, B.C. (See also *Ski Touring*.)
"Our specialty is personally arranged trips," says Arnör Larson, whose activities run the gamut from basic to advanced mountaineering. Whatever your interests—photography, mountain rescue, rock climbing, snow and ice, bivouac techniques, new routes—he'll tailor the expedition for you. With no more than four in each party, you receive individual attention. "You supply the food, Arnör supplies the technical knowledge," explains a confirmed climber. "He stresses exploring places few people have seen."

YUKON TERRITORY

Yukon Expeditions, 2 Kluhini Crescent, Whitehorse, Y.T. Y1A 3P3. Att.: Monty Alford. (403) 667-7960. Kluane & Auriol Ranges, St. Elias & Selwyn mts. 1–4 people. 4–30 days. $65/day w./1 person, $55/day w./2, $50/day w./3 or 4. Charters. Arrival: Whitehorse, Y.T. (See also *Kayaking*.)
Monty Alford has had over 20 years of mountaineering and exploration experience world-wide, with climbs and expeditions from Switzerland to the Antarctic. He runs what he states is the first guide service of its kind in the starkly beautiful Yukon terrain. He leads upland treks, high alpine climbs and, by special arrangement, expeditions in the St. Elias Mountains involving high snow and ice climbs with air support.

Rockhounding

It's the best of all possible treasure hunts, combining exercise and the outdoors with the excitement of discovery. No wonder rockhounding has such a captive following!

The term "rockhounding" is a broad one, including everyone from serious hobbyists in search of rare specimens to those out just for the fun of it. They may hunt everything from ancient fossils and petrified wood to sparkling—and often valuable—gemstones and minerals.

Hunting expeditions take place almost anywhere. Indeed, it's actually hard *not* to see rocks and minerals. Outcrops—places where bedrock is naturally exposed, such as ridges and cliffs—are obvious starting points, and are common in parts of the Southwest and New England. In the Middle States, the soil is thicker, and outcrops may occur along river valleys and on steep hilly slopes.

While rockhounding is possible almost anywhere (including downtown Los Angeles, where the La Brea tar pits yield fantastic fossils!), some areas sparkle with certain treasures. New Mexico is one of the top collecting states, since there are many old mines and mineralized sections. Rockhound State Park is one, the first state park so designated, where the rockhounder can snoop until he finds his special something—maybe a beautiful banded agate, or other quartz family gems. The state also has the fabled turquoise mines at Los Cerrillos, the blue-green smithsonite of Kelly (now a quiet ghost town where the famous old dumps are open for a fee), quartz along the Pecos River and many other spots productive for rockhounders.

You can hunt for jade around Yreka, California, or pan for gold near the historic gold rush towns of Auburn, Nevada City and Placerville. Indeed, nuggets are picked up (though not by the handful) on streams throughout the West.

Or find emerald mines near Hiddenite, Spruce, Pine and Shelby in North Carolina. How about looking for sparkling treasures in the nation's only diamond mine—located in the crater of an ancient volcano south of Murfreesboro, Arkansas? Or hunting along the beaches of northern Michigan for exotic pastel agates?

The possibilities are endless; the treasures, bountiful. You'll need some simple equipment, of course, particularly a geologist's hammer and coal chisel. You'll also need some good advice: Best to read a bit on basic geology before venturing out.

Be sure to ask permission to collect on private property. And follow this tip from the U. S. Department of the Interior: "While it's illegal to collect rocks in National Parks and Monuments—and in many State Parks—similar rocks commonly crop out on land nearby, and can be collected there."

In all states, you can get the best information on rockhounding from local gem shops, generally through local Chambers of Commerce and particularly through local mineral and lapidary clubs. The annual issue of *Lapidary Journal* provides an extensive list of gem and mineral clubs and bulletins; the *Journal* also has a variety of books on the subject for sale. For further information write them at: P.O. Box 2369, San Diego, CA 92112.

Irene Bulterman, Eastern Federation of Mineral and Lapidary Societies, Inc.

Spelunking

Slowly they descend into the earth's inner realms, through secret passages and narrow crevices to crystal caverns where the only sounds are stone icicles dripping in the dark. . . .

The term "spelunking" is deprived from "speleology," the science of studying caves. The sport demands the same spirit of adventure and physical challenge as mountaineering, with one big difference: The cave explorer has a stalactite-studded ceiling over his head, and can spelunk to his heart's content in any weather.

The number of cave *aficionados* has jumped to an estimated 100,000—and that's not counting curious-but-careful tourists who take guided tours through the country's 175 commercial caves. The more rugged explorers brave the mud and moisture of the country's 10,000-odd below-ground caverns, predominant in the country's limestone areas—particularly in Missouri and Virginia, where new ones are being discovered all the time.

Yet, while the subterranean depths offer unparalleled thrills, they can also spell danger—both for the cave's environment and for the neophyte explorer. The National Speleological Society (NSS) is trying to combat these dangers by encouraging would-be explorers to learn safety and environmentalism from experts.

Since the cave ecology is a delicate one, the NSS seeks to prevent insensitive explorers from turning caves into litter-strewn subways. The NSS motto—"Take nothing but a picture; leave nothing but footprints; kill nothing but time"—stresses the urgency of conserving the rare and delicate creatures who dwell in the depths, as well as the eons-in-the-making crystalline formations.

To prevent human mishaps, the NSS encourages safety with their cardinal rules for spelunkers. Chief among the rules: "Never cave alone!" They urge four cavers in each group to provide a safety margin in case of emergency. More tips: Dress properly for chilly and damp caves, wear heavy-duty shoes and a protective hard hat, and carry three separate sources of light. And, since special techniques and equipment are needed to negotiate vertical drops, the NSS says to learn the proper skills from experts before attempting such caving.

Particularly important for the preservation of the sport is the NSS advice: "Caves have owners: courtesy pays." In the East, South and Midwest, most caves are privately owned, generally by farmers; in the Far West, more are managed by government agencies. But everywhere more and more caves are being closed because of the thoughtlessness of cavers. The NSS urges spelunkers to seek out the cave's owners to enter, and to treat the property with care.

The NSS, with 130 local chapters, or "grottos," nationwide, welcomes those interested in caves to their meetings and field trips. Additional information may be obtained by writing: National Speleological Society, Inc., Cave Avenue, Huntsville, AL 35810.

Kenneth Goddard for National Speleological Society.

II BY HORSE

Cattle/Horse Drives

If anyone has told you that the long cattle drive is as obsolete as the Texas longhorn, they're almost, but not quite, right. What's even more astonishing is that, for a fee, the city dude can hitch along as a part-time cow puncher.

Although the object is no longer to drive cattle north to the railroads, cattle are shifted to greener pastures in spring, summer or fall. It can be a modest 30 miles in the saddle, or 100 miles. It's up at 7 A.M., sorting stock, chasing after drifting cattle all day, and riding behind them in the cloud of dust their slow-moving hooves kick up. Before dusk you set up camp, and after a chuckwagon dinner and some fireside talk, crawl into tents and sleeping bags.

You are expected to help out, and you should be able to ride without clutching the saddle horn. If you don't think you can fend for yourself very well, you can always ride the range in the chuckwagon, which tends to be a station wagon these days. Oh well.

Can you ride well enough? Are you to supply your sleeping gear? Where do you meet? Will you be on roads or rugged trails? Will you need reservations before and after the trip? A fishing license? Cattle drives are as unstandardized as anything you'll ever book. Double-check rates, dates, tax and other details.

CALIFORNIA

Rock Creek Pack Station, Box 248, Bishop, CA 93514. Att.: Herbert London. (714) 872-8331. Owens Valley & High Sierra Mts. (CA). Jun. For 25 riders. 4 days, $145, incl. dinner & lodging night before. Bring sleeping gear. Arrival: Bishop, CA. (See also *Hiking with Packstock, Pack Trips.*)

Herb London believes that this is your only chance to help herd horses and mules from the winter range, an Old West activity. "We like to get an early start, ride in the cool of day, and make camp early in the afternoon. The cook and camp crew set up a comfortable camp in advance with tents, but many prefer to sleep under the stars." There's chuckwagon-style food, swimming at every camp, beautiful country and plenty of wrangling.

COLORADO

Canyon Ranch, Rt. 1, Box 61-A, Olathe, CO 81425. Att.: Bob & Bea Frisch. (303) 323-5288. Black Canyon of the Gunnison. Summer & fall. ½-day mini cattle drive,

$15, or combined with ½-day jeep trip w./lunch & supper, $35. Arrival: Montrose, CO. (See also *Jeeping*.)

"We rotate our cattle from different pastures about every 10 days during summer and fall," explains Bob. "If someone wants a half-day mini cattle drive, he would ride down the canyon with us, across the creek, and help us round up the cattle and get them into greener pastures." It's a full morning's work. Might as well stay on for an afternoon mini jeep ride through Indian country up the canyon.

711 Ranch, Parlin A, CO 81231. Att.: Rudy & Virginia Rudibaugh. (303) 641-0666. Missouri Riv. Breaks (MT). Jun. 10 & Sept. 10. 15–25 people. 7 days, $400; bring sleeping gear. Arrival: Billings, MT. (See also *Pack Trips.*)

"Every spring we round up and move 1,000 head of cattle to summer pasture; every fall we round them up again for market." And the Rudibaughs invite you to take part in their old-time cow camp with chuckwagon, camp cook and tents. You cover about 10 miles each day (knowing how to ride helps) through grasslands and the Missouri River Breaks area, made famous by Butch and the Kid and their Hole-in-the-Wall Gang. The first drive, 7 days, begins at the Two Crow Ranch near Malta, Montana. You spend a day getting fitted to your horse and saddle. Then it's 5 days of driving the herd with the Two Crow cowboys. The Rudibaughs also take people on 5-day cattle drives in the Colorado Rockies near Gunnison—"some of the most scenic areas in the state." On some roundups there are as many as 800 head of cattle.

WYOMING

Tillett Ranch, Box 453, Lovell, WY 82431. Att.: Lloyd & Royce Tillett. (406) 484-2583. MT/WY border & Crow Indian Res. Apr.–Oct. 1–20 people. 6 or more days. $200/wk. or $35/day. Bring sleeping bag. Arrival: Billings, MT; Cody or Lovell, WY.

The day after guests arrive at this family-operated cow ranch they're helping brand calves in the old-time way—roping them out of the herd. Next they're cutting herd. "Guests aren't always proficient," Abbie Tillett lets on, "but it's lots of fun." The rest of the time is spent trailing herd various places, traveling 10 to 15 miles a day. "At night we fill up on great campfire cooking and sleep in tents. Sleeping bags never felt so good!" The Tilletts work their 1,000 head of cattle on open range at all times, so there's always something going on. Guests are housed in campers and the ranch house.

S Bar S Ranch, CO.

Horse Trekking

"Get a horse!" That's not a bad idea these days, and it's also not a bad way to have a really different and fun vacation. For years the British have been enjoying their pony trekking over the hills and dales of northern and southwestern England. They find it a good show, indeed.

We, in turn, passed the idea on to L. D. Frome, one of our outfitter friends in Wyoming, and he now has saddled up an honest-to-goodness horse trek.

What is horse trekking? It's pretty simple, and we can't understand why it hasn't been done in this country. Instead of going out on the trail and back again, riders continue on to a destination that they must reach before nightfall—a dude ranch or a mountain lodge, for example, where a hot shower, family-style dinner and comfortable bed are awaiting them. Next morning, after breakfast, they trek on to the next destination.

Although L.D. is the only one offering our concept of a real ranch-to-ranch or ranch-to-lodge horse trek, we tell here of three other rides that bear at least some similarity to the horse trek idea. And before long we expect a group of Vermont inns to develop a horse trekking program, as they have done with inn-to-inn hiking, biking and ski touring.

If you are someone who enjoys riding but can do without sleeping under the stars (or in the rain), horse trekking should be right down your trail.

ARIZONA

Grand Canyon National Park Lodges, Grand Canyon, AZ 86023. (602) 638-2401. (Group bookings: 638-2525.) All yr. 4–8 riders. 1 day, $22; 2 days, $82 incl. meals & accom. Arrival: Flagstaff or Williams, AZ, with bus or plane connection.

Mule trains leave the South Rim every day for a spectacular zig-zagging ride down the canyon trail to the banks of the Colorado River, nearly a mile below—a 5- to 6-hour trek. You spend the night at Phantom Ranch, deep in a side canyon along Bright Angel Creek, where the shade of olive trees and tall cottonwoods and a swimming pool are a boon to trekkers when summer temperatures hit 120 degrees Fahrenheit. The ride back up the trail begins after breakfast the next day. This trek is recommended for anyone with moderate horseback riding experience who is physically fit, 12 years or older but not too advanced in age, and (with the patient mules in mind) for those weighing not more than 200 pounds fully clothed.

Wyoming Travel Commission.

MISSOURI

Cross Country Trail Rides, Box A, Bland, MO 65014. Att.: Ralph A. Branson. (314) 226-3492. Ozark Natl. Scenic Riverways. Jun.–Oct. 5–7 days. $80/wk. incl. elec. hookups, showers, food, entertainment. Youth & nonrider rates. Rental horses, $14/day. Bring sleeping gear. Arrival: Willow Springs, MO.

For families who love to vacation with their horses, Ralph Branson offers campsites on the banks of the beautiful spring-fed Jacks Fork River, from which riders follow old logging roads through the scenic Missouri Ozarks. You can ride every day for a week without taking the same trail twice. A 24-hour dining tent and 345 horse-tie stalls are provided. And there's also canoeing, swimming and dancing.

WYOMING

Jackson Hole Trail Ride, Box 110, Moran, WY 83013. Att.: Walt Korn. (307) 543-2407. Teton Natl. Forest. 5-day trek, 1st wk. of Aug. Up to 75 riders. $250 incl. meals, tents, horse & riding gear, or $198 w./own horse & gear. Bring sleeping bag. Arrival: Jackson, WY. (See also *Pack Trips*—Box K Ranch.)

"Hike up your britches and tighten your cinch," instructs Walt Korn at the start of his 5-day trek in the scenic Teton National Forest. From a tent base camp, you take spectacular daily rides skirting sparkling alpine lakes and crossing lush green meadows, returning to camp at night for "the best cowboy chow" and rousing hoedowns. The ride ends with an awards banquet—a sterling silver trail pin for each rider and a hand-tooled saddle for one. "One of the most satisfying experiences of our lives," writes a trekking couple. "Walt is a terrific guide and his crew is great. Most fabulous was riding a high open ridge to the Continental Divide, where the Grand Tetons, Yellowstone Park and the Dubois area surrounded us—we were on top of the world, spellbound."

L. D. Frome, Outfitter, Box G, Afton, WY 83110. (307) 886-5240. Teton Wilderness. Jun.–Sept. 1 or more people. 5 days, $250 incl. lodging, meals, horses, guide & transport to/from Jackson. Arrival: Jackson, WY. (See also *Backpacking, Hiking with Packstock, Pack Trips, Covered Wagons.*)

L. D. Frome, an old hand at pack trips, adds a new twist with his horse trek. You ride each day through the back country of the Teton foothills just north of Jackson Hole from one ranch to another, or to a mountain lodge. Arrangements include lodging, dinner and breakfast at each night's destination, and a guide and trailside lunch for the day's ride. Stopovers for an extra day or so at the same ranch can be arranged. L.D. plans each trip to fit your requirements. Daily trail rides cover about 8 miles up and over the mountains, or 15 miles at the most, and luggage is transported from one ranch to the next by car.

Pack Trips by Horse

There are many kinds of pack trips you can take, depending on your riding ability, stamina and yen for roughing it. But first, to understand what you are booking, you need some outfitter lingo.

A *pack trip* or *horse pack trip* are the same thing. In their brochures, outfitters differentiate a vacationer's pack trip from a hunting trip (which this book does not cover) by calling it a *summer trip,* or a *sightseeing, scenic, custom, deluxe or private trip.*

A key idea to remember in choosing your trip is the *layover day.* "It's hard on inexperienced riders to be on the trail every day," one outfitter explains. "They get very sore on the rear." The problem is greatly eased by a layover day in camp, with side-trip riding or just relaxing, whichever you wish.

Sometimes outfitters schedule dates for rides into specific areas, and you can reserve a place on these trips, generally limited to 15 riders or less. Other trips are tailored especially for your own group of family or friends. This tailored arrangement is called a *custom trip,* a service that almost every outfitter gives for the same rate as his scheduled-date excursions.

The ultimate trip is one on which you ride to a new location each day (or sometimes take a layover day) and set up camp for the night. In the morning you break camp, pack all the gear, and your pack train moves on to another un-believably beautiful camping spot. This is called a *moving* or *progressive pack trip,* with an extensive route that covers the most scenic features of the region. Such trips are frequently offered for scheduled-date departures. They also can be arranged on a custom basis, with the route, the length of each day's ride, and the number of layover days planned according to the group's requirements.

An outfitter may have a wilderness camp in some picturesque spot already equipped with tents, cots and cooking gear. Here he arranges what is known as a *base camp trip.* By horseback he packs you, your personal gear and the food into this camp, where you and the camp crew will stay, making loop trips into the wilderness each day. Or if he has several such camps, you can stay at one, then ride on to the next. Base camp trips are less expensive than progressive trips, since pack animals are not needed to haul in the camping equipment, nor do the guide and wranglers have to unpack and set up camp each time you arrive at your base.

If you are experienced in wilderness camping, you'll enjoy a *drop* or *spot pack trip.* This service includes the riding and pack horses to take you and the camping gear—your own gear, or equipment rented from the outfitter—into the wilderness, where the outfitter sets up your camp and leaves you there. On an appointed day he comes back to pack you out again. This is the least expensive trip, as you pay only for the days he is packing you in and out, and for any gear or horses that he leaves with you.

The pack trip rates quoted in these pages generally refer to moving or base camp trips, on either scheduled or custom excursions. They are somewhat generalized, and the outfitter will supply details—such as the rate for group bookings, for children (12 years or under), for drop pack service, and for specific itineraries.

Factors that determine rates are the size of camp crew required, the amount of equipment, the number of riding horses and pack animals, the length of the trip, and special features (such as a fresh-food airdrop along the way). An average rate of $50 to $60 per day for each rider represents one of the best travel buys of our day. It covers experienced guides and wranglers who attend to your needs and safety and are well versed on the region's history, geology, animals and plants; a camp cook who turns out Dutch oven cooking described by riders as "fabulous"; sure-footed

Montana Fish and Game Department, by Bob Cooney.

horses and pack animals; an array of equipment; plus scenery, adventure and fun.

You'll want only durable and practical essentials on a pack trip, stuffed into a duffel bag that a pack horse or mule will carry. You'll have a saddlebag for things you may need on the day's ride, such as a sweater, raingear and camera. On most trips you'll want soft jeans, longjohns to prevent chafing if you haven't ridden for a while, a long-sleeved shirt and gloves for protection from sunburn and brush scratches, a sweater and windbreaker, and belt pouch for personal effects (comb, lip gloss, sunglasses and suntan lotion). For sun protection you'll need a wide-brimmed hat (preferably a western hat if you're in the West). Some outfitters provide sleeping gear. All provide a specific checklist of what to bring.

The requirements and rewards of a pack trip have poured into our office from vacationers in all areas. "Expect to get tired and to ride through temperatures that can range from the 90s at midday to freezing at night," writes one. "You can experience everything from drought to downpours and blizzards and arrive in camp with ice-sheathed Levi's. If you don't ride frequently, resign yourself to a sore backside. But the temporary discomforts are well worth the feeling of accomplishment and the memories of being in the high pines, listening to a stream flowing down the mountain and catching trout in an alpine lake."

One rider told us of Prince, a horse who loved to gaze at the scenery. The only problem was that he preferred to walk out on the jutting overlooks to get a better view of the distant forests and especially a creek some one-and-a-half miles straight down. "Thank God he was a loving horse," his rider recalls, "because I had my arms around his neck during his sightseeing excursions and he didn't seem to mind."

A veteran packtripper in Montana's Bob Marshall Wilderness Area expresses her reasons for coming back each year. "It's because when I stand on a 9,000-foot pass and can see nearly 100 miles in four directions, I become the size I am supposed to be. Because one early morning we looked up at a ridge and saw a 'pack train' of 40 elk moving along the crest. Because a curious trout nudged my wading boot with his nose in a glass-clear stream—more exciting than catching him would have been. Because once we threw our bedrolls down and slept in a field of blue gentian. Because for five minutes on a very narrow, very sheer trail I was as scared as I've ever been—and made it across. Because the early-morning sun shining on a dew-spangled spider web is one of the loveliest sights in the world. Because I'm hooked."

Reasonable health and an open mind are the basic requirements for packtrippers. If you're coming from near sea level to trails at high elevations, you might spend several days at a ranch to get accustomed to the altitude—and riding. Most outfitters can recommend a place to stay in the area.

Double-check on who provides sleeping gear, the services and equipment included in rates, and what items you should bring. Your outfitter will want to know your ages, weight and riding ability so he can assign horses accordingly. Ask his advice on which trip you should take. He knows the areas that best fit your requirements. Also ask about state tax, fishing licenses, where the trip starts, accomodations for before and after, and the outfitter's policy on deposits, payments and cancellation refunds.

ALASKA

Alaskan Adventure, Hope, AK 99605. Att.: Keith Specking. No tel. [Jan.–Jun.: Juneau, AK. (907) 465-3500.]. Mt. McKinley Natl. Park area. Jul.–Aug. Moving & base camp trips. 2-8 riders. 7 days, $595. Bring sleeping gear. Arrival: Cantwell, AK. (See also *Hiking with Packstock*.)

For 20 years Keith Specking has been developing a trail system in this beautiful region at the headwaters of the Jack and Nenana rivers. "My wife and I are experts on the flora and fauna," Keith writes. "We see game and vast stretches of wildflowers on these trips, ride to Nenana Glacier, and have some exciting river crossings." You pan for gold, pack through precarious mountain passes to beautiful valleys, and feast on Alaskan delicacies such as wild blueberry pie, caribou sausage and moose roast.

Lee Spears Outfitter, SR Box 20237, Fairbanks, AK 99701. (907) 479-3351. Central Alaska Range. Jun.–Sept. Moving & base camp trips. 1–6 riders. 7 or more days. $150/day, sleeping gear incl.; group & family rates. Arrival: Fairbanks, AK.

Lee Spears plans unstructured trips with the individual in mind. His small groups ride through a vast, remote wilderness of glacier-fed streams, tundra, and aspen, birch and spruce woods, with a day or more at each camp to fish and explore. "A tough but very satisfying experience," remarks a vacationer. "Lee runs a good traditional camp in Robert Service country." He provides transportation from Fairbanks to base camp by car or air charter.

ARIZONA

Granite Mountain Outfitters, 2194 Dineh Dr., Prescott, AZ 86301. Att.: M.J. Doyle. (602) 455-0142. Northern AZ. Apr.–Oct. Base camp custom trips for 2–6 riders. 2 days, $100; 4 days, $175. Bring sleeping bag. Arrival: Prescott, AZ.

This vast canyon country is a land of red rock spires and Ponderosa pines—and prehistoric Indian ruins, most of which are reached only by horse or foot. "You needn't be an experienced trail hand to enjoy these trips," Doyle says. "We ride to a tent camp the first day and circle out from there through Zane Grey country—the rugged Granite Mountain area, forests of the Mogollon Rim, scenic Sycamore Canyon Wilderness Area, and the upper Verde River Canyon." You won't go hungry. Doyle promises first-class chuckwagon-style meals "prepared by a cantankerous cowboy cook or mule packer." Ample time for swimming, climbing, swapping tales, photographing and poking around the ancient ruins.

Price Canyon Ranch, PO Box 1065, Douglas, AZ 85607. Att.: Scotty & Alice Anderson. (602) 558-2383. Chiricahau Mts. Moving, base camp & drop pack trips for 4–20 riders. 1–12 days (or longer). $35/day, sleeping gear incl. Arrival: Douglas or Tucson, AZ.

Experienced rancher-cowboy Scotty Anderson takes you into the breathtakingly beautiful Chiricahua Mountains, passing through five life zones from 5,000 feet to 9,000 feet. He is a specialist on the differing forms of wildlife and vegetation along the way. "You'll see hidden canyons, Indian caves, scenic grandeur—a fascinating area for hikers, rockhounds, naturalists and birders," Scotty promises. The trail starts on the 18,000-acre ranch, where he also can give riding lessons before you hit the trail, and can put you up overnight or longer. It has been described as "the most beautiful ranchland in Arizona."

CALIFORNIA

McGee Creek Pack Station, Box 1054, Bishop, CA 93514. Att.: David MacRoberts. (714) 935-4324. [Sept.–May: (714) 873-4350.] John Muir Wilderness. Jun.–Sept. Moving, base camp & drop pack trips. 2–25 riders. Guided trips, $40–$55/day, 5 or more days. Drop pack trip about $200 for 7–10 days, family of 4. Group & youth rates. Bring sleeping gear. Arrival: Bishop, CA. (See also *Hiking with Packstock*.)

The Sierra peaks of McGee Canyon are noted as the most colorful in California. David MacRoberts packs you into the canyon to camp, or over McGee Pass into Upper Fish Creek for great fishing. It's the home of golden, rainbow and brook trout. In either case, it's an exciting experience for adults and children alike, with safe trails and gentle stock.

Rainbow Pack Outfit, RR 1, Box 26A, Bishop, CA 93514. Att.: James W. Howell. (714) 873-4485. [Sept. 15–Jun. 15: 719A Springfield Ave., Ventura, CA 93003. (805)

647-5351.] Inyo Natl. Forest and King's Canyon Natl. Park. Jun.-Oct. Moving, base camp & drop pack trips for 5-20 riders. 2 or more days. $30-$45/day, less with your own food & camping gear; bring sleeping gear. Arrival: Bishop, CA.

This pack station is "the natural starting point for trips over Bishop Pass (elev., 11,988 feet) to the Middle Fork of the King's River, the most secluded wilderness area of King's Canyon National Park," James Howell remarks. Trips take you either north over Muir Pass and out over Piute Pass or south over Mather Pass, an area "unsurpassed for beauty—and for golden trout fishing."

Red's Meadow, Agnew Meadows & Mt. Whitney Pack Outfits, Box 395-G, Mammoth Lakes, CA 93546. Att.: Bob Tanner. (714) 934-2345. [Oct.-Jun.: (714) 873-3928.] Yosemite & Sequoia natl. parks, John Muir & Minaret wilderness areas. Jun. Oct. Moving, base camp & drop pack trips. 1-25 riders, 1-21 days. $33-$40/day. Group rates. Bring sleeping gear. Arrival: Mammoth Lakes or Bishop, CA. (See also *Hiking with Packstock*.)

From Agnew Meadows take spectacular trips into the Minaret Wilderness or to Shadow, Ediza, Garnet and Thousand Island lakes—excellent areas for the novice. Red's Meadow is near Devil's Post Pile National Monument on the Middle Fork of the San Joaquin River, with over 100 lakes. Moving trips are a specialty, packing into Sequoia and the Upper Kern areas, with rides between camps from 3 to 4 hours.

Rock Creek Pack Station, Box 248, Bishop, CA 93514. Att.: Herbert & Craig London. (714) 935-4493. [Oct.-Jun.: (714) 872-8331.] Yosemite & Sequoia natl. parks, John Muir Wilderness. Jun.-Oct. Moving, base camp & drop pack trips. Max. 25 riders. 1-30 days. Guided trips avg. $40/day, sleeping gear incl. Arrival: Bishop or Lone Pine, CA. (See also *Hiking with Packstock, Horse Drives*.)

"We've made a specialty of wilderness trail rides and are pleased to share our experience with you," states Herb London. If you bring your own horse, it will receive "expert care and good feed." Mules carry your packs as you travel through varied terrain with wildlife, glaciers and 13,000-foot peaks that made it John Muir's favorite back country. Herb's "rambling tales" keep riders in high spirits, we're told.

COLORADO

All Season's Guest Ranch, Box 412-G, Hayden, CO 81639. Att.: William & Donna Hellyer. (303) 276-3463. Flat Top Wilderness. Jun.-Sept. Base camp & drop pack trips. 3-12 riders. 3 or more days. 3 riders, $60/day; 4-6 riders, $55/day; 7-12 riders, $50/day; sleeping & fishing gear incl. Arrival: Hayden, CO.

"Ten minutes into the mountains I was having the time of my life," raves one enthusiastic vacationer. "Anyone who can stay on a horse for no more than two hours at a time can enjoy this delightful trip. Bill and Donna Hellyer did everything for us—from lending us spare clothes when it got cold and baking fresh sourdough rolls for dinner, to teaching us how to fish and answering our questions about wildflowers." The Hellyers recommend their trips for families. "Our horses are gentle, and the mountains are unbelievably beautiful." Everyone pitches in with the camp chores.

Bar X Bar Ranch, PO Box 27-P, Crawford, CO 81415. Att.: Dellis Ferrier. (303) 921-6321. West Elk Wilderness & Gunnison Natl. Forest. Jul. & Aug. Moving, base camp & drop pack trips. 8-25 riders. 2-14 days. 6 days, $170; $40/day for shorter trips; bring sleeping gear. Arrival: Delta or Montrose, CO.

"Our trips are for the average family. If you haven't ridden, we'll teach you how," is Dellis Ferrier's reassuring comment. "We ride each day but not so much that you get too tired. We fish mountain streams and ride to 13,000 feet, where you can see for 100 miles." Adds a vacationer, "There was time to think, scenery beyond compare and the cleanest air imaginable. The skilled, experienced trail hands make even the greenest dude feel like the most confident trail rider."

Budge's South Fork Resort, Box 71, Glenwood Springs, CO 81601. Att.: Ross Utt & Dennis Bergstad. (303) 328-6544. [Nov.–May: 1759 South Ironton, Aurora, CO 80012. (303) 751-9274.] Flat Tops Wilderness Area, White Riv. Natl. Forest. Jun.–Sept. Moving, base camp & drop pack trips. 4–16 riders. 3–14 days. 3 days, $195; 5 days, $275; addl. days, $45. Rates incl. first & last nights at Budge's Resort with meals. Bring sleeping gear. Arrival: Eagle, CO.

"Ours are true wilderness trips," says Dennis Bergstad, "with no vehicles, no roads and very few people in a 235,000-acre wilderness area." He writes of unmatched scenery, good food and beds, the best in fishing, horsemanship lessons—and the largest elk herd in Colorado. "This country gives the soul a lift."

Colorado Back Country Pack Trips, PO Box 110-E, La Jara, CO 81140. Att.: Jake Neal. (303) 274-5655. Cumbres Pass & Wolf Creek Pass on Continental Divide in the Rockies. Jun.–Sept. Moving, base camp & drop pack trips. 2–5 riders. 2 or more days. $60/day. Bring or rent sleeping gear. Custom & sched. Arrival: Alamosa, CO.

Features of the trip? "Good, well-balanced meals, well-prepared horses, and clear, cold headwater streams and high-altitude lakes." One packtripper calls the Neals "modern-day mountain men who know their business, don't drink, and run a good camp." On a 7-day trip you'll ride about 70 miles from one beautiful scene to another.

Cottonwood Cove Lodge, Box 2, Wagon Wheel Gap, CO 81154. Att.: W.W. (Bibs) Wyley. (303) 658-2242. Rio Grande, San Juan & Gunnison Natl. Forest. Jun.–Sept. Moving, base camp & drop pack trips. 4–12 riders. 2–8 days. $37.50/day. Bring sleeping gear. Arrival: Alamosa or South Fork, CO. (See also *Hiking with Packstock*.)

"A pack trip into La Garita, Weminuche or San Juan wilderness areas will unite you with the beauties of nature in a never-to-be-forgotten way," writes Bibs Wyley. "You follow the Continental Divide at 9,000 feet to 12,500 feet. It's a vacation that enriches your life. We offer the very best of Colorado's scenery."

Delby's Triangle 3 Ranch, Box 14, Steamboat Springs, CO 80477. Att.: Delbert Heid. (303) 879-1257. Mt. Zirkel Wilderness. Jul.–Nov. Moving & base camp trips. 5–10 riders, 1–10 days. $50/day; 3-day trip, $125. Arrival: Steamboat Springs, CO. (See also *Youth Adventures*.)

Del Heid likes to take families into this 114-square-mile wilderness with over 40 lakes, streams and miles of beautiful trails. His trips feature "very good mountain horses, good equipment, good food and helpful, knowledgeable hands to assist you with everything."

Dick Pennington Guide Service, 2371 H Road NW, Grand Junction, CO 81501. (303) 242-6318. White Riv. Natl. Forest near Aspen. Jun.–Aug. Moving, base camp & drop trips. 2–10 riders. 3–5 days. 3 days, $175; 5 days, $250. Bring sleeping gear. Family rates. Arrival: Grand Junction, CO.

"Come see and enjoy the West like people did years ago," invites Dick Pennington. "We use gentle, well-trained, sure-footed horses. Our magnificent mountains are over 13,000 feet. There are wildflowers, deer, elk, eagles, cold, clear mountain streams and lakes with wild native trout. We start from a remote tent camp or a roving campsite, and plan specifically for each group's needs."

K. E. Schultz Guide & Outfitting Service, 0010 Ponderosa Rd., Glenwood Springs, CO 81601. (303) 945-7120. Flat Tops Wilderness, Holy Cross-Sawatch Range.

Joe E. Clark, Fort Collins, CO.

Jul.–Sept. Moving & base camp trips. 2–10 riders. 3–14 days. $40–$60/day, sleeping gear incl.; group rates. Arrival: Glenwood Springs or Grand Junction, CO.

"A great get-away-from-it-all," is one rider's reaction. "I found everything interesting. The most fun was wondering 'what's up there'—and then riding up to see, with no time limits or other restrictions." Kurt Schultz emphasizes custom trips—"personalized service, with each trip designed around the group's needs." Trips are planned for a layover day at each base camp. Or you can pack in and stay at one camp, usually on a lake, and make day trips from there.

711 Ranch, Parlin R, CO 81239. Att.: Rudy & Virginia Rudibaugh. (303) 641-0666. West Elk & La Garita wilderness. Jun.–Sept. Moving, base camp & drop pack trips. 4–20 riders. 5–7 days. $50/day. Group & family rates. Bring sleeping gear. Arrival: Gunnison, CO. (See also *Cattle Drives.*)

"We have a permanent camp, or can plan roving campsites, for photographic and scenic pack trips," explains expert horseman Rudy Rudibaugh, "and quiet, well-mannered horses, good equipment, good food and plenty of it." Each year some of Rudy's trips are for Boy Scouts or college students majoring in outdoor education. Usually accompanied by a professor, they receive college credits for instruction on how to handle a wilderness pack trip.

Seven-W Ranch, Gypsum, CO 81637. Att.: Burt & Claudia George. (303) 524-9328. Flat Tops Primitive Area, White Riv. Natl. Forest. Jun.–Sept. Moving, base camp & drop pack trips. 4–10 riders. Min. 2 days. $50/day ($25 for ranch guests), incl. sleeping gear. Arrival: Eagle or Gypsum, CO. (See also *Snowmobiling.*)

Trails in the 9,000-foot-high Flat Tops Primitive Area lead you through stately spruce and aspen trees, along stretches of grass dotted with colorful mountain flowers, and bring you to spectacular views of mountain ranges, valleys and canyons. "The rides are well supervised and informal," comments a guest. "Burt George is a capable and entertaining guide."

Sid Simpson Guide Service, RR 1, Box 161, Paonia, CO 81428. (303) 527-3486. West Elk Wilderness, Gunnison Natl. Forest. Jun.–Sept. Moving, base camp & drop pack trips. 2–30 riders. 2–6 days. 6 days, $180/adult, $160/youth; sleeping gear incl. Arrival: Gunnison or Montrose, CO.

"Re-explore with us high mountain meadows, dense forests and deep canyons once traveled by Indians, trappers and miners," invites Sid Simpson. "With our fine horses, top-notch equipment and mountain savvy, we welcome all who like the out-of-doors: youngsters, old-timers, the experienced horseman and the beginner. The typical 6-day trip is divided between two camps a day's ride apart, which are accessible only by horse." One packtripper writes, "Sid gave us the most memorable family vacation we ever had. We'll go again before the kids get out of high school."

Stewart Brothers Outfitters and Guides, Rt. 4, Box 246, Montrose, CO 81401. Att.: Larry Stewart. (303) 249-8375. Uncompahgre Wilderness Area. Jul.–Sept. Moving, base camp & drop pack trips. 5–15 riders. 5–8 days. $35/day; bring sleeping gear. Arrival: Montrose, CO.

"From the lofty summit of Uncompahgre Peak (14,309 feet) there's a breathtaking view across a sea of peaks into three adjoining states—Utah, New Mexico and Arizona," declare the Stewarts. The area is rich in elk, deer, bighorn sheep, blue grouse, ptarmigan, songbirds and wildflowers (particularly outstanding in the higher elevations), and the streams abound in cutthroat, rainbow and brook trout. "A fascinating trip and excellent outfitters," riders report.

Sun Valley Guest Ranch, Box 470, Grand Lake, CO 80447. Att.: Ken Bruton. (303) 627-3670. Rocky Mt. Natl. Park, Arapaho Natl. Forest. Jun.–Oct. Moving pack trips for 6–12 riders, 2–5 days. 2 days, $66; 3 days, $100; 1 wk., $300, w./ 2 nights at ranch; sleeping gear incl. Arrival: Denver or Granby, CO.

Trail boss Ken Bruton promises "an exciting new trail each day" on Sun Valley's 5-day pack trips which cover approximately 75 miles and reach altitudes of more than 12,000 feet. "You'll camp beside snow-fed lakes and trout-filled streams and enjoy the fantastic food and trailwise horses. We care about you and for you." And to prove it, Ken asks that you arrive at the ranch on Sunday to get acquainted with your horse and receive trail instruction before setting out on Tuesday.

Sunset Ranch, PO Box 876, Steamboat Springs, CO 80477. Att.: Patsy M. Wilhelm. (303) 879-0954. Routt Natl. Forest. Jun.-Sept. Moving, base camp & drop pack trips. 3-12 riders. 3 or more days. $50/day; bring sleeping gear. Arrival: Steamboat Springs or Hayden, CO.

Patsy's family has outfitted trips for 30 years, so it's a way of life for her. She likes introducing families to "the excitement and beauty of a wilderness pack trip," and structures each trip to the group's specifications. You ride into breathtaking scenery of Mt. Zirkel Wilderness, up to 11,000 feet, on gentle, trailwise horses. "Our horses are people," Patsy says.

Wilderness Adventures, Moon Valley Resort, Box 265-CA, South Fork, CO 81154. Att.: Larry Ehardt. (303) 873-5331. Weminuche Wilderness. May-Oct. 3-15 riders. 3-7 days. 6 days, $270. Bring or rent sleeping gear. Group rates. Arrival: South Fork, CO. (See also *Backpacking, Hiking with Packstock, Snowmobiling*.)

"With a gentle, mountain-acclimated horse, you ride into remote back country—scenic and breathtaking, with rugged peaks knit together in long, flowing canyons and massive valleys," Larry explains. You learn much about animal and plant life on his trips. He also provides cabins and a unique rustic restaurant in a garden setting for before and after these treks.

HAWAII

Molokai Guided Mule Tours, PO Box 1067, Kaunakakai, Molokai, HI 96748. (808) 537-3050. Island of Molokai. 25 riders max. 1-day tour, $35, incl airport or hotel (Molokai or Pau Hana Inn) pickup. Arrival: Molokai Airport.

While not truly a pack trip, this mule tour's rugged ride into Molokai's isolated and majestically beautiful Kalaupapa Peninsula qualifies it for inclusion here. Your mounts are sure-footed animals who confidently carry you 2,000 feet down a steep cliff (26 hairpin trail turns). Tour includes a 3-hour tour of the peninsula and the quaint village which began as Father Damien's leprosy colony. (It's really quite pleasant today.) Tour cost includes lunch at Kalawao Park.

IDAHO

Bar BQ Ranch, Box 173, Harrison, ID 83833. Att.: Lloyd & Rowena Jones. (208) 689-3528. St. Joe & Clearwater riv. Jun.-Aug. Moving pack trips for 6-15 riders. 5-22 days. $40/day; bring sleeping gear. Arrival: Coeur d'Alene, ID, or Spokane, WA.

"Real wilderness experience, good equipment, good saddle horses, excellent pack mules and guides who know the country, the plants, wildflowers and wildlife," is how the Joneses bill their treks in this scenic region in the Bitterroot Mountains of the northern Idaho Panhandle. "Great food prepared mountain style" is another specialty offered by this family, whose pioneer forebears trekked West in covered wagons.

Coolwater Ranch, 1376 Walenta Dr., Moscow, ID 83843. Att.: Harry Vaughn. (208) 882-5367. Selway-Bitterroot Wilderness. Jun.-Sept. Moving, base camp & drop pack trips. 4-20 riders. 3-10 days. $45/day; bring sleeping gear. Group & family rates. Arrival: Lowell, ID.

"Because of its rugged solitude this land has been bypassed and retains the charm

Outlaw Trails, Inc., UT.

and romance of wild mountain country," reports Harry Vaughn. You ride on sparsely maintained old forest service and game trails. "Come and see, appreciate, and understand this national wilderness of yours," he urges. "We visit 26 high mountain lakes and backpack into beautiful pristine areas."

Fog Mountain, Salmon and Selway Expeditions, Box 585-D, Salmon, ID 83467. Att.: Stanton C. Miller. (208) 756-2319. Selway & Salmon riv. wilderness, Big Horn Crags, Chamberlain Basin-Continental Divide. Jun.–Sept. Moving, base camp & drop pack trips. 4–12 riders. 4–10 days. $50/day, incl. sleeping gear. Group & youth rates. Arrival: Salmon, ID. (See also *Backpacking, Hiking with Packstock*.)

"We ride through remote meadows and basins in the vast wilderness," Stan says, "to our tent camps, some of them next to alpine glacier lakes." If at night you wake to a shrill, eerie sound, don't be alarmed—it's just a bull elk bugling.

Happy Hollow Camps, Box 694-A, Salmon, ID 83467. Att.: Martin R. Capps. (208) 756-3954. Idaho Primitive Area. May–Sept. Moving, base camp & drop pack trips. Max.: 20 riders, 10 days. Base camp trips, about $35/day. Bring sleeping gear. Group & children's rates. Arrival: Salmon, ID. (See also *Float Trips*.)

Martin Capps leads you over the skyline of the Salmon River Mountain Range to his comfortable base camp. Here you ride remote trails or just relax. "Martin lets you pick your own level of roughing it on these trips," comments a guest. "There's more food than you can eat, more breathtaking scenery than you can absorb and more fun than you can keep track of."

M & M Outfitter, RR 1, c/o M.B., Cambridge, ID 83610. Att.: Mike Bishop. (208) 257-3472. Clearwater Natl. Forest, Kelly Creek Ranger District. Jun.–Aug. Base camp trips. 6–10 riders. 7–10 days. $35/day. Bring sleeping bag. Arrival: Lewiston, ID. (See also *Backpacking*.)

"See elk, deer, bear, moose, birds, flowers and clear mountain streams," tempts Mike Bishop. "We offer a real wilderness experience, ideal as a family vacation. Our camp is in a big, flat meadow where the younger members of the group can run and play. No poisonous plants in our area," he adds.

Muleshoe Pack Camp, PO Box 34-B, Harrison, ID 83833. Att.: Stan Gootrad. (208) 689-3422 or 3315. Jun.–Sept. Moving, base camp & drop pack trips. 2–14 riders. 7 days, $385–$400. Bring sleeping gear. Arrival: Missoula, MT; Spokane, WA; or Coeur D'Alene, ID.

Stan Gootrad describes Muleshoe Pack Camp as "your gateway into the Selway-

Bitterroot Wilderness with cedar forests, pure rushing rivers and perpetually snow-clad mountain peaks more than 10,000 feet high.'' And he speaks of great food, top-flight guides, excellent equipment and gentle horses to take you into country little changed since Sacajawea led Lewis and Clark through it in 1805. A special trip for painters and photographers is hosted by an accomplished artist/instructor.

Mystic Saddle Ranch, Box AG, Stanley, ID 83340. Att.: Jeff & Max J. Bitton. (208) 774-3591. [Nov.–May: Box 461, Mt. Home, ID 83647. (208) 587-5091.] Sawtooth Wilderness. Jun.–Oct. Moving, base camp & drop pack trips. 4–20 riders. 2–15 days. $42.50/day; $30.50/day with own food. Bring sleeping gear. Arrival: Boise or Hailey, ID.

Mystic Saddle's trips take you into America's Alps where glaciers carved a country of rugged peaks and gem-blue lakes. At one point you can see five lakes in a row, with the Sawtooth Valley and the White Cloud mountains in the background. Families love this country—it has something for everyone. Comments one rider: ''The Bittons are ecology-conscious outfitters with excellent stock. A very well done trip.''

Nez Perce Outfitters & Guides, PO Box 1454-S, Salmon, ID 83467. Att.: Val B. Johnson. (208) 756-3912. Salmon River Breaks Primitive Area. Jun.–Sept. Moving, base camp & drop trips. 3–10 riders. 3 or more days. $45/day; bring or rent sleeping gear. Group & youth rates. Arrival: Salmon, ID. (See also *Hiking with Packstock, Float Trips.*)

Val Johnson speaks of personalized service—''Working with each group, gauging mileage to ability, and exposing guests to the wonderful variety of terrain, views and activities in the high country.'' Each day is a new adventure—fishing, hiking, riding, even a summer snowball fight in the north slopes. When he's not in the mountains, Val teaches courses in government at the Salmon high school.

Palisades Creek Ranch, PO Box 594-H, Palisades, ID 83437. Att.: Elvin Hincks. (208) 483-2545. ID & WY high country. May–Oct. Moving, base camp & drop pack trips. 5–10 riders. 6-day trips. Bring sleeping gear. Arrival: Idaho Falls, ID.

Elvin Hincks has guided hunters for years and taken out trail riders, and now invites riders on pack trips in this wilderness he knows so well. ''There's outstanding fishing, photographing, hiking, mountain climbing and wildflowers. Sometimes see a herd of 300 elk. The best part is no worries, no cares. Just the great outdoors.''

Peck's Ponderosa, PO Box 57-I, Challis, ID 83226. Att.: Joseph M. Peck. (208) 879-2303. Idaho Primitive Area. Jun.–Aug. Moving & base camp trips. 5–20 riders. 5–14 days. $50/day; bring sleeping gear. Arrival: Boise or Challis, ID.

In this fabulous wilderness there are neither roads nor vehicles. You reach the base camp on the Middle Fork of the Salmon River by charter flight from Challis or Boise. From there you ride into ''1,250,000 acres of rugged mountains and majestic beauty,'' as Joe Peck describes it, ''where cameras are a necessity. We camp in tents whenever night overtakes us.''

Salmon River Lodge, PO Box 58A, Salmon, ID 83467. Att.: Dave & Phyllis Giles. (208) 756-2646. Idaho Primitive Area, Salmon River Breaks Primitive Area. Jul.–Sept. Moving & base camp trips. 5–15 riders. 3 or more days. 7 days, $325, incl. first & last nights at lodge. Arrival: Salmon, ID. (See also *Float Trips, Jet Boating.*)

Dave and Phyllis Giles especially like families on their trips. In this lightly traveled area, snow-capped mountains tower above timbered valleys and flower-carpeted meadows. Lake fishermen usually return to camp with a full stringer, and shutterbugs love the magnificent panoramas. Rocky Mountain sheep, elk, birds and other wildlife live in the spruce, ponderosa and fir forests.

Teton Expeditions, Inc., 427 E. 13 St., Idaho Falls, ID 83401. Att.: Jay Dee Foster. (208) 523-4981 or 3872. Teton Mts., Targhee Natl. Forest (ID). Jul.–Sept. 13–15 riders. 1 day, $30; overnight, $45/day; bring sleeping gear. Arrival: Boise or Idaho Falls, ID. (See also *Float Trips.*)

"No trail. No people. Just you, your horse, your guide and your friends," Jay Dee Foster points out. "You ride in remote wilderness few ever see, go to sleep to the song of a bull elk bugling, awaken to the sound of bacon frying. Guests often get a little sore, but that part of the anatomy heals quickly."

Zeke West's Whitewater Ranch, Air Star Rt., Cascade, ID 83611. (208) 382-4336. Salmon Riv. Breaks Primitive Area. Jul.–Aug. Moving, base camp & drop pack trips. 4–8 riders. 3–6 days. $40/day; ½-price up to 12 yrs. Bring sleeping gear. (See also *Jet Boating.*)

"Scenery and service second to none!" Zeke says. "Take the kids, a few clothes, a fishing rod, and a camera for a trip with spectacular views, pure air, a really blue sky, and the best of mountain cooking." You can ride from 2,500 feet to 8,000 feet, where you'll have a remote mountain lake all to yourself.

MONTANA

Black Tail Ranch, Box 77, Wolf Creek, MT 59648. Att.: Tag & Lyla Rittel. (406) 235-4330. Scapegoat Wilderness, Bob Marshall Wilderness. Jul.–Sept. Moving pack trips. 2–12 riders. 7–14 days. $50/day. Group & youth rates. Bring sleeping gear. Arrival: Helena, MT. (See also *Hiking with Packstock.*)

"Try a wilderness skyline pack trip along the Continental Divide, where every turn in the trail brings something wonderful," invites Tag Rittel. "We ride up where the rivers start, discover hidden, crystal-clear lakes and sleep under the stars or in teepees." Remarks a ranch-raised guest: "The horses and packstock were first class, the equipment very good and the food extra good."

Bob Marshall Wilderness Ranch, Seeley Lake, MT 59868. Att.: Virgil Burns. (406) 754-2285. Bob Marshall Wilderness. Jul.–Sept. Moving, base camp & drop pack trips. 2–15 riders. 5–30 days. $50–$55/day; bring sleeping gear. Arrival: Missoula, MT.

Ecology-minded Virgil Burns features family and group trips for fishing, photography, painting, or just riding and enjoying the unspoiled beauty of the Bob Marshall Wilderness. Riders speak of his capable guides, excellent horses, and practically gourmet food—even a roast turkey dinner on the last night in the wilderness. Lodging and meals at the ranch the night before and after the trip, and transportation to and from Missoula, are included in the rates.

Cheff Guest Ranch, RFD 1, Box 124B, Charlo, MT 59824. Att.: Vern (Bud) Cheff. (406) 644-2557. Mission Mts. Jul.–Aug. Moving, base camp & drop pack trips. 4–15 riders. No time limit. $45–$50/day. Bring sleeping gear. Arrival: Missoula, MT. (See also *Hiking with Packstock.*)

"Beautiful country, rugged and grand," is how Bud Cheff describes this primitive area where he camped with Indians as a boy. To hear him yell "Come 'n' get it" in Flathead dialect is to receive one of the more unique invitations to dine. The trail takes you into the Mission Range, "the Little Alps of America," through groves of tall cedars, across rushing streams, past waterfalls cascading over rocky cliffs, and to breathtaking views of the valley below.

Circle Eight Ranch, PO Box 457-A, Choteau, MT 59422. Att.: K. H. Gleason. (406) 466-2177. Bob Marshall Wilderness. Jun.–Sept. Moving, base camp & drop pack trips. 1–6 riders. 2–30 days. $45/day for 4–6 riders; bring sleeping gear. Arrival: Great Falls, MT.

Ken Gleason paints an inviting picture of his trips: "We ride mountain trails through forests and high meadows and stop for lunch beside a clear stream. In the late afternoon we pitch camp, and someone goes fishing and brings back trout for dinner. In the evening there's singing and story-telling around the campfire." The Gleasons carry on the traditions and hospitality of an old-time outfit, the Circle Eight brand having been registered by Ken's pioneer grandparents.

Double Arrow Outfitters (AG), Box 505, Seeley Lake, MT 59868. Att.: C. B. Rich. (406) 677-2411 or 2467. Bob Marshall Wilderness. Jul.–Nov. Moving, base camp & drop pack trips. 4–15 riders. 3 or more days. $50/day. Group rates. Bring sleeping gear. Arrival: Missoula, MT. (See also *Hiking with Packstock.*)

"We pack in wilderness where man is a visitor, where warmth and fellowship are the rule, and western history overshadows everything you do," writes C. B. Rich. "Following trails through wild valleys, we explore the Chinese Wall of the Continental Divide, the Flathead Alps and Bullet Nose Mountain with its ice caves. Kids from 5 to 80 find enjoyment. There's exceptional fishing."

Dwain Rennaker, Rt. 1, Box 1283-A, Hamilton, MT 59840. (406) 363-1829. Bitterroot & Deer Lodge Natl. Forests. Moving, base camp & drop pack trips. 4–15 riders. 6–15 days. Rates on request. Bring sleeping bag. Arrival: Missoula, MT.

"What could bring a family more together than sharing the natural beauty of Montana's mountains?" asks Dwain Rennaker, who arranges custom trips in the majestic forests of this rugged area. Dwain provides plenty of fresh meat and vegetables—"all you can eat"—and a cook, camp help and packer. "Be prepared to pitch in with camp chores," he says, "and you'll come away from your trip with new skills and a feeling of true accomplishment."

Norm McDonough & Sons, Rural Rt., Wolf Creek, MT 59648. (406) 235-4205. Lincoln back country, Upper Dearborn & Falls creeks. Jun.–Aug. Moving pack trips. 4–6 riders. 5–7 days. $50/day; under 12 yrs., $25/day. Bring sleeping gear. Arrival: Great Falls or Helena, MT.

Ride the Continental Divide, the Lewis and Clark Trail and Indian trails with the McDonoughs. "Our outfit is equipped with the very best pack transportation, competent guides, dependable horses and packstock," Norm says. "We make it a trip the whole family will enjoy. If you can take a 20-mile trip you'll ride to the Valley of the Moon or No Seeum Lakes, and stay in rustic cabins at some mountain camps."

Rogers Guest Ranch, Box 107, Swan Lake, MT 59911. Att.: Orville Rogers. (406) 886-3600 or 3342. Swan & Mission mts., Bob Marshall Wilderness. Jul.–Aug. Moving, base camp & drop pack trips. 2–12 riders. 2–7 days. $50/day. Arrival: Kalispell or Missoula, MT.

The beautiful Swan & Mission mountains form the backdrop for these pack trips led by Orville Rogers and his sons, with many years of experience in mountains which they know so well. They'll take you into an unhurried, carefree world. Their specialty? "Good service."

Seven Lazy P Guest Ranch, Box 193A, Choteau, MT 59422. Att.: Chuck Blixrud. (406) 466-2044. Bob Marshall & Great Bear wilderness areas. Jun.–Sept. Moving, base camp & drop pack trips. 4–15 riders. 5–14 days. Bring sleeping gear. Arrival: Choteau or Great Falls, MT. (See also *Hiking with Packstock.*)

"The grandeur of the Chinese Wall at sunrise, the beargrass blossoms in the high alpine basins, high passes with mountain goats scampering on the ledges above, the solitude of the tall spruce, pine and fir trees—there's so much to be gained from this experience," Chuck Blixrud feels. All his leisurely trips into this spectacular Rocky Mountain wilderness feature fishing, swimming and watching the elk, deer, moose—and sometimes grizzly—in their natural surroundings. "Our gentle horses are as much at home on the rugged trails as on the ranch," he says.

Sixty-Three Ranch, Box 676-AT, Livingston, MT 59047. Att.: Mrs. Paul E. Christensen. (406) 222-0570. Absaroka Mts. of Gallatin Natl. Forest. Jul. & Aug. Moving & base camp trips. 2–8 riders, 3–10 days. $55/day, sleeping gear incl. Arrival: Livingston or Bozeman, MT.

"We take you into some of Montana's most spectacular country," says Mrs. Christensen, "up wooded canyons to rushing waterfalls, snow-capped peaks and mountain lakes. Our longer trips take you to ghost and mining towns, and to a glacier with grasshoppers imbedded in it for thousands of years. You can still catch trout with them!" The ranch features good horses and equipment, good food, guides who love their work and quality trips.

South Fork Ranch, Box 56, Utica, MT 59452. Att.: Ben Steel. (406) 374-2356. Central Montana Belt Mts., Lewis & Clark Natl. Forest. Jun.–Sept. Moving, base camp & drop pack trips. 8–12 riders, 7–10 days. 7 days, $325; 10 days, $450; group & youth rates. Bring sleeping gear. Arrival: Great Falls or Lewiston, MT. (See also *Snowmobiling*.)

Ben Steel bills his trips as true experiences with nature. "We pack over the Great Divide at elevations up to 9,500 feet, where you can see almost forever," he says. "Traveling to our tent camp in the Lost Fork we pass mountain meadows, tumbling streams and crater lakes. Youth groups, family trips or father-son trips—I don't mix one with the other."

Wild Country Outfitters (A), 713 W. Poplar, Helena, MT 59601. Att.: Don & Meg Merritt. (406) 442-7127. Bob Marshall & Scapegoat wilderness. Jun.–Sept. Moving & base camp trips. 8–16 riders. 7–12 days. $40/day. Group & family rates. Bring sleeping gear. Arrival: Helena, MT. (See also *Hiking with Packstock*.)

Don Merritt describes his trips as high-quality, scenic wilderness adventures. "We catch cutthroat trout, look for wildlife and study and interpret nature. Our rides over skyline trails are for everyone—we show beginners how to take the 'bumps' out of trail riding so they can enjoy it!" The pleasures of wilderness living are accented with delicious campstove meals and the exchange of western yarns.

Wildlife Outfitters, Rt. 1, Box 99B-AG, Victor, MT 59875. Att.: Jack & Shirley Wemple. (406) 642-3262. Selway-Bitterroot Wilderness, Bitterroot Natl. Forest. Jun.–Aug. Moving, base camp & drop pack trips. 5–8 riders. 10 days, $600. Group & family rates. Bring sleeping gear. Arrival: Missoula, MT. (See also *Backpacking, Hiking with Packstock*.)

"Discover solitude and a zestful feeling of independence through a return to undisturbed wild America," encourage the Wemples. "We recapture the feeling of the early scouts as we ride in the shadow of lofty peaks through lush green meadows vivid with wildflowers. We use only the best equipment and take it slow and easy so that riders of all ages and experience will enjoy themselves."

NEW YORK

Cold River Trail Rides, Inc., Coreys, Tupper Lake, NY 12986. Att.: John Fontana. (518) 359-9822. [Oct.–Jun.: (914) 476-5368.] Adirondack Mts. Jul.–Sept. Base camp trips. 3–12 riders. 3–5 days. $50/day, sleeping gear incl.; guests with own horses deduct $10/day. Arrival: Saranac Lake, NY.

"Pack trips into the Adirondack wilderness was our hobby—now our specialty," explains John Fontana. "The ride to base camp is 15 miles. We take scenic rides out from there. If you like riding, camping, pure water, fresh air—this is for you!" One guest notes "the excellence of the food: steak, ham and Mrs. Fontanas Italian-style hamburgers." Trips begin every Friday into this "forever wild" area.

NORTH CAROLINA

Cataloochee Ranch, Rt. 1, Box 500-G, Maggie Valley, NC 28751. Att.: Alice Aumen. (704) 926-1401. Great Smoky Mts. Natl. Park. May–Oct. Moving & base camp trips. 8–16 riders. 2–8 days. About $50/day. Bring sleeping gear. Arrival: Asheville or Waynesville, NC.

"The ranch borders the greatest scenic wilderness in eastern America, and no place in the East offers such a variety of riding enjoyment as Cataloochee," the Aumens say. Most trips last a week to 10 days, but 2- to 3-day trips will be arranged for 8 or more people. You ride into high country at 6,000 feet and deep into virgin forests. Camp is set up on a beautiful stream for fishing or dipping. Gentle mounts for novice riders, and spirited ones for the experienced.

OREGON

Cal Henry, Box 26-A, Joseph, OR 97846. (503) 432-3872. Snake Riv. & Eagle Cap Wilderness. May–Sept. Moving, base camp & drop pack trips. 2–8 riders. 1–10 days. 5 days, $250; 7 days, $350; children less. Bring sleeping gear. Arrival: Pendleton, LaGrand or Joseph, OR. (See also *Hiking with Packstock*.)

Cal Henry's trips take you into "the alpine splendor of the Eagle Cap Wilderness and awesome Hells Canyon of the Snake." It's an area rich in wildflowers and animals where you can fish crystal-clear lakes and streams and forget everything but the pleasure of living outdoors. Cal can arrange almost any type of trip that works best for you.

Lute Jerstad Adventures, Inc., PO Box 19527, Portland, OR 97219. (503) 244-4364. Eagle Cap Wilderness. Apr.–Sept. Moving pack trips. 8–20 riders. 5–10 days, $485–$950. Bring sleeping gear. Arrival: Portland, OR. (See also *Mountaineering, Float Trips*.)

The spectacular Eagle Cap Wilderness is the locale for pack trips that are as exciting in their own way as Lute Jerstad's many other adventures. Some combine a float trip, hiking and fishing with riding. You can explore the Imnaha River area and hike to rims at 9,500 feet for a look at mountain goats; travel the wild Minam

Piute Creek Outfitters, UT—Christopher Price.

River area where the fishing is great; or follow the Washboard Trail where even veteran trail riders hang tight to the saddle horn.

Wilderness Pack Trips, PO Box 71-C, Rogue River, OR 97537. Att.: Don Hinton. No tel. May–Nov. Rogue Riv., Siskiyou & Umpqua natl. forests. Moving, base camp & drop pack trips. 1–7 riders. 3–5 days. $35/day; group & family rates. Bring sleeping gear. Arrival: Medford, OR.

"Since we specialize in small groups, the individual doesn't get lost in the crowd," comments Don Hinton. "The high country—5,000 feet plus—is a land born of fire with lakes, rocky ridges, alpine meadows and timbered slopes. With 3 million acres to pick from, we try for solitude. Most any place in southern Oregon and northern California is within our reach." Don is thoroughly experienced—even in first aid and photography.

UTAH

Cache Valley Guide & Outfitters, 268 South 2nd West, Hyrum, UT 84319. Att.: Dean McBride. (801) 245-3896. High Uinta Mts. Jul.–Sept. Moving, base camp & drop pack trips. 5–10 riders, 5–14 days. $40/day; group & youth rates; bring sleeping gear. Arrival: Logan, UT.

In this rugged land of towering mountains (up to 13,000 feet) covered with timber, sheer rock walls and sparkling lakes filled with hungry trout, you'll get to know nature as it really is. The only access to this area is by horse or on foot. Says an appreciative rider, "Dean McBride loves the mountains, nature, his horses and people, and this enthusiasm can't help but rub off on anyone who comes in contact with him."

Horsehead Pack Trips, PO Box 68A, Monticello, UT 84535. Att.: Pete Steele. (801) 587-2929. Canyonlands Natl. Park, Grand Gulch, Dark Canyon, Blue Mt. Apr.–Sept. Moving pack trips. 2–12 riders. 1–6 days. Overnight trips, $50/day, incl. sleeping gear. Arrival: Monticello, UT. (See also *Hiking with Packstock*.)

To really see the unique canyonlands scenery and enjoy a horseback riding experience, Pete Steele recommends these pack trips. His "fantastic cowboy-campfire meals" are a specialty, with sourdough biscuits and Dutch oven potatoes. Trips are designed for exploring and relaxing.

Outlaw Trails, Inc., PO Box 336-F, Green River, UT 84525. Att.: A. C. Ekker. (801) 564-3593. Western Canyonlands Natl. Park. May–Sept. Moving, base camp & drop pack trips. 6–40 riders. 1–14 days. 6 days, $375, incl. sleeping gear. Group rates. Arrival: Grand Junction, UT. (See also *Jeeping, Float Trips*.)

All-out adventurer A. C. Ekker suggests "doing a few miles a day in places only Butch and Sundance knew—through Robbers Roost Canyon, down the Outlaw Trail, into Horsethief Canyon. It's an area of unsurpassed red rock and sandstone formations." Pack trips in this fabulous terrain can be combined with raft trips and jeeping for a total outdoor experience.

Piute Creek Outfitters, Rt. 1-A, Kamas, UT 84036. Att.: Barbara & Arch Arnold. (801) 783-4317 or 486-2607. Western Uinta Mts. & Wasatch Natl. Forest. Jun.–Nov. Moving & base camp trips. 4–10 riders. 3–7 days. $40/day, sleeping gear incl.; group & family rates. Arrival: Salt Lake City, UT.

Piute Creek's base camp in this wilderness of uncharted trails, canyons and peaks is only an hour from the Salt Lake City Airport. Guests can be in camp on a mountain lake the day they arrive, surrounded by impressive scenery familiar to Piute hunters centuries ago. "We're a small, professional, family-style outfit," writes Arch Arnold. "Our college-age wranglers contribute much to the enjoyment of the trips."

WASHINGTON

Cascade Corrals, Box A, Stehekin, WA 98852. Att.: Ray Courtney. (509) 663-1521. North Cascades Natl. Park & Glacier Peak Wilderness. Jun.–Sept. 5–10 riders. Overnight trips, $100; 3 days, $140; 6 days, $290. Also moving, base camp & drop pack custom trips. (See also *Hiking with Packstock, Ski Touring*.)

Ray Courtney takes you on a circle trip that begins with a 12-mile horseback ride through the North Cascades National Park to an overnight camp and a steak dinner. Next morning after a "cowboy breakfast" you have a boat ride down the full 50-mile length of Lake Chelan back to your starting point at his Stehekin headquarters. The trek gives you as scenic a two days as you could ever wish for.

Indian Creek Corral, Star Rt., Box 218-A, Naches, WA 98937. Att.: Edward H. Cristler. No tel. Goat Rocks Wilderness Area, Pacific Crest Trail, Wenatchee Natl. Forest. Jul.–Sept. Moving, base camp & drop pack trips. 2–20 riders. 2–14 days. $35/day up. Bring sleeping gear. Arrival: Yakima, WA. (See also *Hiking with Packstock*.)

"We try to keep our pack trips primitive," notes Ed Cristler, "and most of all we enjoy our riders' reactions when they see the wild high country for the first time. This is truly 'Alps' country, with its glaciers and jagged summits. On our Goat Rocks trip we actually cross Old Snowy, one of the majestic peaks."

Lost Mountain Packing & Guide Service, Rt. 6, Box 920, Sequim, WA 98382. Att.: Mike Jeldness. (206) 683-4331. Olympic Natl. Park. Apr.–Oct. Moving, base camp & drop pack trips. 2–6 riders. 1–10 days. $55/day; $50/day children under 12. Bring sleeping gear. Arrival: Sequim or Port Angeles, WA. (See also *Hiking with Packstock*.)

On a 3-day trip Mike takes riders 12 miles up the Elwha River to his Elkhorn camp for the night. The next day you ride through Press Valley to Hayes River and back to camp—the route of the first expedition (1889) to cross the Olympics. Mike and his wife, Susan, plan whatever kind of trip you want in this ultrascenic area. Even getting to Sequim by car or bus from Seattle is fun. Part of the 2½-hour ride is by ferry. Only 40 inches of rainfall in this region as opposed to 140 inches on the western slope, Mike points out.

WEST VIRGINIA

Honey C Stables, Berkeley Springs, WV 25411. Att.: Ronald L. Clatterbuck. (304) 258-1482. Cacapon Mts. (WV & MD). Apr.–Oct. Moving, base camp & drop pack trips. 10–20 riders. 2–6 days. $40–$45/day; group rates. Bring sleeping gear. Arrival: Berkeley Springs, WV; Hancock or Hagerstown, MD; Winchester, VA.

Teacher Ron Clatterbuck has had much experience with youth and adults. "These are basically walking rides along wooded mountain trails where we often see deer, wild turkey and bobcats. We have well-broken, experienced trail horses and a hospitable, responsible crew who also provide the talent for campfire entertainment." Midway on the 6-day trip Ron plans a day's float on the Cacapon River. Trips begin in Berkeley Springs.

WYOMING

Bar-T-Five Outfitters, Box 2140, Jackson, WY 83001. Att.: Bill Thomas. (307) 733-5386. Jun.–Aug. Gros Ventre Mts. Base-camp trips. 4–10 riders. 5–7 days. 5 days, $305; 7 days, $425; incl. sleeping gear & lodging night before trip. Arrival: Jackson, WY. (See also *Covered Wagons*.)

On pack trips in Jackson Hole country Bill and Joyce Thomas help you experience the thrill known to Bill's great-grandfather when he first passed through this area with the Shoshone Indians. On Bill's special 7-day package, scheduled for Sunday departures and including airport pickup and an overnight in Jackson Hole, you ride to a new camp each day on your way to the headwaters of the Yellowstone River. One guest rating: "An informal, friendly journey into one of the most beautiful places I have ever been. The experience of a lifetime."

Box K Ranch, Moran, WY 83013. Att.: Walt Korn. (307) 543-2407. Yellowstone & Grand Teton Natl. Parks, Teton Wilderness. Jun.–Sept. Moving & base camp. Any size group. 7 days or more, starting Sun. Bring sleeping gear. Arrival: Jackson, WY. (See also *Horse Trekking*—Jackson Hole Trail Rides.)

"We set up camp whenever we find likely-looking spots," Walt explains. "Because we get way back, we see more wildlife, and there's breathtaking scenery. If you've never ridden a horse, we teach you, and we travel at a pace you'll enjoy." He advises hunting with a camera—"you can even capture the appealing beauty of a skunk"—and says you'd think he was spinning a yarn if he told you how good the fishing is.

Box Y Ranch, Box 1172-A, Jackson, WY 83001. Att.: Bud Callahan. (307) 733-4329. Wyoming & Salt Riv. ranges, Bridger-Teton Natl. Forest. Jul.–Aug. Moving, base camp & drop pack trips. 4–12 riders. 3–10 days. Rates on request. Arrival: Jackson, WY. (See also *Hiking with Packstock*.)

Seclusion, an abundance of wildlife and spectacular scenery are the principal ingredients in Bud Callahan's custom-tailored pack trips. Observes one contented vacationer: "The Callahans have a talent for finding the perfect country for your ability. The food they pack is superb. They are very professional and follow good conservation practices. Our group (9 of us) ranged from 5 to 50 years, and it was great fun for all." There's a 3,500-foot runway at the Box Y for experienced mountain pilots. Also charter flights and vehicle pickups in Jackson.

Bridger Wilderness Outfitters, Box 951, Pinedale, WY 82941. Att.: Keith Anderson. (307) 367-2747. Jul.–Aug. 5–10 days. $45/day. Moving, base camp & drop pack trips. Custom & sched. Bring sleeping gear. Arrival: Rock Springs or Jackson, WY.

Keith uses trucks to move horses and equipment to entry points, then the pack string circles into the Bridger Wilderness. "That allows you to see the most in the time you have," he explains. "Crystal-clear streams connect some of the lakes. The variety of scenery and fishing is next to impossible to match anywhere in the world."

Bud Nelson's Big Game Outfitters & Guides, PO Box 409, Jackson, WY 83001. (307) 733-2843. Teton Wilderness Area. Jul. & Aug. Moving, base camp & drop pack trips. 1–6 riders. 2 days, $67.50; 7 days, $345-$650; 10 days, $600-$750; sleeping gear incl.; group & youth rates. Arrival: Jackson, WY.

On Bud Nelson's fully outfitted trips you ride to the headwaters of the Snake and Yellowstone Rivers, high in the magnificent Tetons. Lakes and streams are little changed since the days of Jim Bridger and John Colter. Enjoy Dutch oven chicken and succulent steaks, and swap fish stories around the campfire. Bud provides camp cooks and packers, the most modern camping equipment, tents and immaculate sleeping bags.

Cross Mill Iron Ranch, Crowheart, WY 82512. Att.: Larry Miller. (307) 486-2279. Wind Riv. Mts. & Absaroka Mt. Range. Jun.–Sept. Moving & drop pack trips. 4–10 riders. 3 or more days. $30–$35/day, sleeping gear incl. Arrival: Riverton, WY.

"Rate this four stars," advises a convert to pack tripping. "One of my family's finest vacations. Our cook was expert and the guide very sensitive to the fatigue factor of relative tenderfoots in the wilderness." Large glaciers, rushing streams, rugged mountains and wildflowers make it a most scenic area.

Crossed Sabres Ranch, Box AG, Wapiti, WY 82450. Att.: Rich Marta. (307) 587-3750. Shoshone & Teton Natl. Forests, Yellowstone Natl. Park. Jun.–Sept. Moving pack trips. 1–10 riders. 5–21 days. 6 days, $330, sleeping gear incl. Arrival: Cody, WY.

"Rides average 10 to 15 miles a day over majestic Absaroka Range trails once ridden by 'Jeremiah' Johnson, Jim Bridger and John Colter," remarks Rich Marta. "Wildlife abounds. It's a trip into America's last frontier, a land just as it was 100 years ago."

Diamond D Ranch Outfitters, Jackson Hole, Box 11, Moran, WY 83013. Att.: Rod Doty (307) 543-2479. Teton Wilderness, Yellowstone & Grand Teton natl. parks. Jun.–Aug. Moving, base camp & drop pack trips. 4–10 riders. 5–21 days. 6 days, $300. Bring sleeping gear. Group rates. Arrival: Jackson, WY. (See also *Ski Touring*.)

This small family operation caters to your wishes, whether you'd like to fish, rockhound, spot wildflowers or take pictures. They promise "rare sights, beautiful moments and pleasant times" for a truly memorable vacation in the impressive Yellowstone/Grand Teton Wilderness.

Fall Creek Ranch, Box 181, Pinedale, WY 82941. Att.: Hank Snow. (307) 367-4649. Bridger Wilderness Area. Jun.–Sept. Moving & base camp trips. 6–10 riders. 7–14 days. $65/day; bring sleeping gear. Arrival: Rock Springs, WY.

"Our trips into the Bridger Wilderness offer some of the best trout fishing in the country and by far the most spectacular mountain scenery," asserts Hank Snow. "A day's ride from the ranch you'll camp at the edge of a clear blue mountain lake where you can catch cutthroat and rainbows." There are also golden and brook trout. Hank recommends the 7-day trip with a choice of either one or two base camps.

Game Hill Ranch, Box A, Bondurant, WY 82922. Att.: Pete & Holly Cameron. (307) 733-2015. [Nov.–May: (307) 733-3281.] Gros Ventre Mts., Wyoming Range. Jun.–Oct. Moving pack trips. 2–6 riders. Sample rates: 5 days, $319; 7 days, $431; 10 days, $594. Bring or rent sleeping gear. Arrival: Jackson, WY. (See also *Backpacking, Hiking with Packstock, Ski Touring*.)

Pete and Holly pack in friendly country where a gangly calf moose wading across a bog or a hysterical sandhill crane are common sights. "It's varied terrain—open and rolling, narrow and wooded, high mountain ridges," they say. "In alpine meadows we succumb to the temptation to throw themselves down into the profusion of wildflowers." With small groups, you follow a leisurely pace and have time to familiarize yourself with your gear and horse.

Goosewing Ranch, Inc., PO Box 496, Jackson, WY 83001. Att.: Harold, Claudette or Dan Shervin. (307) 733-2768. Gros Ventre Mts. Jun.–Sept. Moving, base camp & drop pack trips. 2–10 riders. 2–5 days. $45/day, sleeping gear incl. Arrival: Jackson, WY. (See also *Snowmobiling*.)

"A wonderful family experience!" exclaims a vacationer. "The Shervins are interested in seeing that everyone has a good time." On their pack trips riders of every ability ride to high country with lakes, streams, good fishing, waterfalls and wildlife.

Greys River Outfitting, Box 2453, Jackson, WY 83001. Att.: Derrell Roden. (307) 733-6218. N.W. Wyoming. Jun.–Aug. Drop pack custom trips. 4–12 riders. $50/rider for days in & out. Group rates for 6 or more, less for children. Bring camping gear & food. Arrival: Jackson or Afton, WY; Idaho Falls, ID. (See also *Hiking with Packstock*.)

It takes Derrell two days (one in, one out) to pack you into any wilderness area you choose in northwestern Wyoming, where he helps you set up camp. There you are with the lakes and streams, the cutthroat, rainbow and brook trout, the wildlife, birds and scenic trails—until Derrell returns to pack you out again. "Each trip has been well planned and trouble-free," a vacationer remarks.

Grizzly Ranch, North Fork Rt. A, Cody, WY 82414. Att.: Rick Felts. (307) 587-3966. Yellowstone Natl. Park, Teton & Shoshone natl. forests. Jul. & Aug. Moving pack trips. 1–8 riders. 5–30 days. $60/day with 3 or more riders; sleeping gear incl. Arrival: Cody, WY, or Billings, MT.

"We pack into the unspoiled high country of Yellowstone National Park and the wilderness areas of the Teton and Shoshone national forests," comments Rick Felts. "These trips are for the adventurous; they recapture the spirit of the westward movement of yesteryear." Writes one rider: "The beauty and solitude were magnificent. These trips have given our children some of the most memorable experiences of their lives and drawn us close as a family."

High Country Outfitters, Box 941, Cody, WY 82414. Att.: C. O. "Pete" Wheeler, Jr. (307) 587-3071. Shoshone Wilderness Area, Yellowstone Natl. Park. Jul.–Sept. Moving, base camp & drop pack trips. 4–20 riders. 5–21 days. $75/day, 1–4 riders; $60/day, 5 or more riders. Bring sleeping gear. Arrival: Cody, WY.

Pete Wheeler feels justified in bragging a bit: "The outstanding features of my outfit are excellent food, some of the most beautiful country in the world, excellent trout fishing, and lots of elk, moose, bighorn sheep and deer. We pitch horseshoes, teach our guests how to tie hitches for packing, and have a bonfire each evening, complete with a guitar-strumming wrangler." Vacationers have remarked on Pete's knowledge of the area and the varied and good food.

Highland Meadow Guest Ranch, PO Box 774-A, Dubois, WY 82513. Att.: Joe Detimore. (307) 455-2401. Shoshone & Teton Wilderness. Jun.–Sept. Moving & base camp custom trips. 2–12 riders. 5–10 days. $55/day base camp or $60/day moving trip w./4 or more riders. Bring sleeping gear. Arrival: Riverton or Jackson, WY. (See also *Snowmobiling*.)

Hunt for agates, geodes and opalized woods, fish in remote streams and lakes, and photograph wildflowers, trumpeter swans, bald eagles, glaciers and mountain scenes. Joe Detimore's wilderness camps are on the South Fork of the Buffalo River, an 18-mile ride from the last access road. He also plans jeep trips.

Jackson Hole Pack Trips, Box 518, Wilson, WY 83014. Att.: Bob McConaughy. (307) 733-2655. [Nov.–May: 1470 Ute Dr., Salt Lake City, UT 84108. (801) 582-1963.] Yellowstone Natl. Park, Teton Natl. Forest. Jul.–Sept. Moving & drop pack trips. 4–8 riders. 3–7 days. 5 days, $325; 7 days, $450; sleeping bag incl. Arrival: Jackson, WY.

Bob McConaughy believes that "this area is what the beautiful West is all about—Yellowstone, the towering Teton Mountains, wilderness, rivers, streams and lakes aplenty, brimming over with wildflowers, fish and wildlife." To enjoy all this, he gets small groups together, picks his finest strong, gentle horses, loads up his modern gear, takes plenty of good food and heads out. He offers both scheduled trips ahd custom.

Jay Box Dot Guest Ranch, Rt. 1, Box 616-A, Afton, WY 83110. Att.: Everett D. Peterson & Son. (307) 886-5565. [Nov.–May: Box 224, Cokeville, WY 83114. (307) 279-3311.] Teton Wilderness, Headwaters of Yellowstone Riv., Bridger Natl. Forest. 4–14 riders. Moving, base camp & drop pack trips. 1–10 days. $60/day; bring sleeping gear. Arrival: Jackson, WY.

"As you ride across the Continental Divide you can see the parting of the waters at Two Oceans Pass," Everett reports. Trips of any length in these rugged mountains give families a chance to spot game, fish and count the wildflowers. "Come enjoy some real western hospitality."

Sky Line Trail Rides, Alta.

L. D. Frome, Outfitter, Box G, Afton, WY 83110. (307) 886-5240. Teton, Washakie, Gros Ventre & Yellowstone Park wilderness. Jun.–Sept. Moving & base camp trips. 1-20 riders. 4 or more days. $50/day. Bring sleeping gear. Arrival: Jackson or Afton, WY. (See also *Backpacking, Hiking with Packstock, Horse Trekking, Covered Wagons*.)

On L. D. Frome's individually tailored pack trips for families and small groups you begin by riding to a base camp. From there you ride into the surrounding wilderness with a portable camp and deluxe tents, moving camp one day and laying over the next. For added adventure L.D. takes you on cross-country rides into rugged country away from the trails.

Low Gardner, PO Box 107, Smoot, WY 83126. (307) 886-5665. Salt Riv. Range, Wyoming Range in Bridger Natl. Forest. Jul.–Aug. Moving & base camp trips. 5–20 riders. 3–7 days. $33/day or $25/day w./your own horse. Bring sleeping gear. Arrival: Jackson or Afton, WY. (See also *Hiking with Packstock*.)

On the second day of your pack trip from Low Gardner's ranch at the mouth of beautiful Swift Creek Canyon, you'll ride up a rather steep trail to 11,355-foot Wyoming Peak. Stop here and gaze in all directions—north to the Tetons, south to the Uintas, east to the Wind River Mountains and southeast across endless prairie. It's a scene to remember. Then on to camp and a steak dinner and entertainment around the campfire. Each day of your trip with the Gardners will be, as one rider puts it, "a rare opportunity to enjoy the wilderness with a fine group of people."

North Piney Corral, Box 395, Story, WY 82842. Att.: Glenn A. Sorenson. (307) 683-2946. [Oct.–May: Box 156, Arvada, WY 82831.] Big Horn Natl. Forest, Cloud Peak Wilderness Area. Jun.–Sept. Moving, base camp & drop pack trips. 2–25 riders. 2–12 days. $35/day; $25/day without food & equipment; group & youth rates. Bring sleeping gear. Arrival: Sheridan, WY.

"Steady, reliable, experienced and a delightful storyteller," writes one rider of Glenn Sorenson, while another claims that Glenn "taught me to relax and enjoy myself." This should be easy while riding, fishing, learning to take care of your own horse, and camping in a beautiful area of 11,000-foot elevations and snow-capped peaks. Glenn also takes people on overnight rides to a mountain camp, and provides horses for short daytime rides.

Rimrock Dude Ranch, Box FS, Northfork Rt., Cody, WY 82414. Att.: Glenn Fales. (307) 587-3970. Shoshone & Teton natl. forests, Yellowstone Natl. Park. Jul. & Aug. Moving pack trips. 3–10 riders. 5–21 days. $55/day, sleeping gear incl. Arrival: Cody, WY.

"Our 1-week trip with a choice of two itineraries is the best for most families," Glenn Fales advises. He adds that both itineraries offer good fishing, spectacular mountain scenery and country the tourists never get to see. Your mount will be a dependable saddle horse; mules carry the freight. Praise from one packtripper: "Glenn's trips are always well planned from the standpoints of food, comfort and fun."

Rimrock Ranch, Box 485-A, Jackson, WY 83001. Att.: Alice Thompson. (307) 733-3093. Wilson Creek Area near Jackson Hole. Jun.–Sept. Moving, base camp & drop pack trips. 2–6 riders. 2–7 days. $65/day, sleeping gear incl. Arrival: Jackson Hole, WY. (See also *Ski Touring*.)

Remarks one vacationer: "While riding that solid trail horse, keep one eye on the magnificent views and one on your guide, for he may suddenly stop and point out a kingly elk, a doe with twin fawns, or 'ol flat top'—the giant bull moose that roams the area. Alice's home cooking can send you home to diet for three months. The country abounds in fossils and ancient Indian campsites."

SeTeton Pack Ranch, Box 224, Pinedale, WY 82941. Att.: Tom Mollring. (307) 376-4605. Bridger Wilderness, Gros Ventre Mts. All yr. Moving, base camp & drop pack trips. 4–10 riders. 2–14 days. $65/day; bring sleeping gear. Arrival: Rock Springs, Jackson or Pinedale, WY.

You ride by horse into this pack ranch, a 1910 gold mine camp, using it as a base for day trips. Arrangements can also be made for regular pack trips which offer an endless succession of scenic thrills. At the ranch you can try panning for gold in the old sluice boxes. A day's float trip on the Green or New Fork is also yours for the asking.

Sheep Mountain Outfitters, Inc., Box 1365-C, Cody, WY 82414. Att.: R. E. Cole. (307) 587-2026. Shoshone Natl. Forest Wilderness. Jul. & Aug. Moving, base camp & drop pack trips. 1–10 riders. 5–30 days. $65/day, 1–3 riders; $60/day, 4–10 riders; sleeping gear incl. Arrival: Cody, WY.

Thousands of miles of fishing streams, countless lakes, and the snow-topped splendor of the Absaroka Mountains on every side greet the Sheep Mountain packtripper. "Rough it in style in our comfortable tents and enjoy the best of food prepared by an experienced full-time cook," encourages R. E. Cole. "Bring the whole family on a trip they'll never forget."

Siggins Triangle X Ranch, Cody, WY 82414. Att.: Stan & Lila Siggins. (307) 587-2031. Washakie Wilderness, Shoshone Natl. Forest, Yellowstone Natl. Park. May–Nov. Moving, base camp & drop pack trips. 1–25 riders. 3–14 days or longer. $60-$70/day. Bring sleeping gear. Arrival: Cody, WY; Billings, MT. (See also *Youth Adventures*.)

"The ranch borders the largest contiguous and most primitive wilderness area in North America," the Siggins say, "with lush green mountain parks, massive forests in the valleys and mountain passes at 10,000-feet." As one rider describes them, the Siggins are "efficient, painstaking, intelligent outfitters with good equipment who share their vast knowledge of the country, wildflowers, birds, animals, rocks and Indian lore." The third generation of their family to pack in this country, they encourage guests to "relax and enjoy."

Skinner Brothers, Box B-G, Pinedale, WY 82941. Att.: Bob Skinner. (307) 367-4675. Bridger Wilderness. Winter, summer & fall. Moving & base camp trips. Up to 17 riders. 3 or more days. $75/day. Arrival: Pinedale, WY. (See also *Youth Adventures*.)

Courtney, Monte, Quentin, Robert and Sherwood Skinner have spent their lives in the guiding and outfitting business, and they've continued the service their parents started in the 1920s. Each brother earned a degree in an outdoor subject (biology, geology, conservation), and they stress the meaningful, educating aspects of the wilderness on all of their trips.

Teton Trail Rides, Box 183, Moose, WY 83012. Att.: L. L. Rudd. (307) 733-2108. [Oct.–May: PO Box 173, Rt. 2, St. Anthony, ID 83445. (208) 624-7956.] Teton & Yellowstone natl. parks. Jun.–Sept. Moving, base camp & drop pack trips. 4–10 riders. 2–10 days. $50/day; day trips, $15; dinner ride, $10; children, $8. Group rates. Bring or rent sleeping gear. Arrival: Jackson Hole, WY.

A park concessionaire, Teton Trail Rides take you into back country where you can see the awe-inspiring Tetons in their individual grandeur. The 3-day trip circles the Grand Teton Peak over the Skyline Trail. The 10-day trip takes you into more primitive country—"a trip you'll live forever," as L. L. Rudd bills it. A 16-ounce steak (12-ounce for children) is part of the 2½-hour dinner ride.

Triangle R Lodge, PO Box 784 (44), Pinedale, WY 82941. Att.: Harold & Ben Bennett. (307) 367-2121. [Nov.–May: (308) 382-9561.] Bridger Wilderness, Wind Riv. Range. Jul. & Aug. 5-10 riders. 7-14 days. Moving pack trips, $75/day; drop pack trips, $50/day per horse. Group & youth rates. Bring sleeping gear. Arrival: Rock Springs, Jackson or Pinedale, WY.

The beautiful Pinedale area was first roamed by the early mountain men. Explore it yourself on a leisurely moving camp trip or, if you're an experienced outdoorsman, let Triangle R drop pack you into the high lake country, where the fishing and scenery are unbeatable.

Triangle X Ranch, Box 120, Star Rt., Moose, WY 83012. Att.: The Turner Brothers. (307) 733-2183. Grand Teton & Teton wilderness, Yellowstone Natl. Park. Jun.–Aug. Moving & base camp trips. 2–15 riders. 5 or more days. 4–15 riders, $55/day; 2–3 riders, $70–$95/day; sleeping gear incl. Arrival: Jackson, WY. (See also *Float Trips, Ski Touring*.)

Third-generation outfitters, the Turners take you into remote wilderness regions where you'll see hidden river systems, tundra tops, wildlife complexes and jagged ascents. The Turners describe it: "All is as undisturbed as when traveled by the Indians and lonely mountain men." You ride to wilderness camps, and from there take day trips tailored to your interests.

Valley Ranch, Inc., South Fork Rt. Z, Cody, WY 82414. Att.: Dr. Oakleigh Thorne II. (307) 587-4661. Washakie & Teton Wilderness. Jul.–Oct. Moving & base camp trips. 4–15 riders. 5–15 days. $65-$75/day. Bring sleeping gear. Arrival: Cody, WY.

Especially arranged for each group, these trips go from toe ranch's glacial valley into back country south of Yellowstone, "one of the great wilderness areas left in the U.S.," according to the Thornes. Guests have been taking these trips since 1915. A 10-day pack trip is part of the riding program for 10- to-15-year-olds in July ($975 for 1 month).

ALBERTA

Amethyst Lakes Pack Trips Ltd., Box 508, Jasper, Alta. TOE 1EO. Att.: Wald & Lavone Olson. (403) 852-4215. [Sept.–Jun.: Brule, Alta. TOE OCO. (403) 866-3946.] Jasper Natl. Park. Jun.–Sept. Base camp trips. 1–15 riders. 2 or more days. 2 days, $110; 3 days, $130; each addl. day, $25; sleeping gear incl. Group & youth rates. Arrival: Jasper, Alta.

"The Tonquin Valley will awe you," assert the Olsons. "It offers excellent fishing, acres of flowers, mighty glaciers and the main range of the precipitous Ramparts. The Astoria River Trail leads into Tonquin from the highway viewpoint near Mount Edith Cavell over a high alpland trail and down to the cabin camp at Amethyst Lakes. We also will pack in gear for hikers, but otherwise they're on their own."

Holiday on Horseback, The Trail Rider Store, Box 448, Banff, Alta, TOL OCO. Att.: Warner & MacKenzie Guiding & Outfitting Ltd. (403) 762-4551. Banff Natl. Park. Jun.–Sept. Moving & base camp trips. 1–35 riders. 5 nights, 6 days: $330, Jul. & Aug.; $275, Jun. & Sept. Bring sleeping gear. Arrival: Banff, Alta.

You're invited to enjoy "the beauty of nature's best" in the fantastic and majestic mountain scenery of Banff National Park. It all begins in Banff with a bus ride to the Mount Norquay Corral. Once there you mount up, and it's up and over mountain passes, fording streams, crossing alpine meadows and storing up memories.

Jim Simpson Wilderness Pack Trips, PO Box 1175, Jasper, Alta. TOE IEO. (403) 852-3909. Willmore Wilderness Park, wilderness areas & Tonquin Valley of Jasper Natl. Park. Jun.–Sept. 6–12 riders. 5- or 10-day sched. wilderness trips, also custom trips, about $60/day. Bring sleeping gear. Tonquin Valley (base camp) trips, 5 days, $300, incl. sleeping gear. Group & family rates. Arrival: Jasper, Alta.

On a 10-day wilderness trip, moving camp almost every day, you cover over 100 miles of Rocky Mountain splendor. There's great beauty in the remote high country of these parks. On Tonquin Valley trips you ride 14 miles to base camp cabins for 5 days of scenery, fishing, birds, wildlife, hiking, riding, evening campfires and serenity. Jim Simpson is well qualified to introduce you to the wilderness.

Sky Line Trail Rides, Alta.

Skyline Trail Rides Ltd., Box 207, Jasper, Alta. TOE 1EO. Att.: Ron & Lenore Moore. (403) 852-3301. [Oct.–May: Brule, Alta. TOE OCO. (403) 866-3984.] Jasper Natl. Park. Jul.–Aug. Moving pack trips. 1–10 riders. 2–6 days, unless custom trip. 2 days, $90; 3 days, $135; 6 days, $270 for 4 or more riders; sleeping gear incl.; family rates. Arrival: Edmonton or Calgary, Alta.

From Maligne Lake, 2- and 3-day pack trips take you from Jasper Park Lodge over the Skyline Trail to high mountain country (8,000 feet) where alpine flowers, bighorn sheep and truly spectacular panoramas greet you. Six-day trips head into dramatic mountain country via Poboktan Creek, Maligne Pass and Shovel Pass to the beautiful Skyline Trail. Camp at night in cabins, canvas houses or tents; daytime you ride, hike, swim in a mountain stream or slide down a snowbank.

T. Ed McKenzie, Box 971, Rocky Mountain House, Alta. TOM 1TO. (403) 845-6708. Job Valley & Brazeau Riv. area (outside Jasper Natl. Park). Jul.–Sept.

Moving & base camp trips. 4–15 riders. 6–14 days. $60/day; bring sleeping gear. Group rates. Arrival: Calgary or Edmonton, Alta.

"Our 7- and 12-day pack trips offer spectacular beauty and adventure in Alberta's magnificent Rockies," writes Ed McKenzie. "We believe we have one of the most beautiful, unspoiled areas anywhere in Canada. On trips of 10 or more days we travel over 100 miles without seeing other people." The terrain is rugged, but the experienced horses know their way—as do the McKenzies. "They're experts in the mountains," writes a vacationer, "and gave us superb service and great food." Comfortable tent camps.

Tom Vinson, Guide & Outfitter, Brule, Alta. TOE OCO. (403) 866-3746. Jasper Natl. Park & Willmore Wilderness Area. May–Aug. Moving & base camp trips. 6–12 riders. 6–12 days. 6 days, $330; 12 days, $600. Bring sleeping gear. Group rates. Arrival: Edmonton, Alta.

"Experience the thrill of riding 'the rooftop of North America' where three major watersheds originate," urges Tom Vinson. "The unknown and alluring Canadian Rockies are virtually unchanged since the days of the first explorers." People of all ages make these rambling trips with Tom into the vast mountain wilderness of hidden valleys, waterfalls and snowy peaks bathed in summer sunshine. "Probably the best-organized packer I've ever been with," writes an experienced packtripper.

Trail Riders of the Canadian Rockies, Box 6742, Station D, Calgary, Alta. T2P 2E6. (403) 287-1746. Banff Natl. Park. Jul.–Sept. Moving & base camp trips. Max. 30 riders. 6 days. $300/6-day trip. Bring sleeping bag. Arrival: Calgary, Alta.

For 55 years this nonprofit organization has explored and enjoyed the wilderness of Banff National Park. With a base camp and teepees in the shadow of Mt. Assinaboine one year, or in the high majestic Cascade Valley another, they circle the scenic area on rides of about 12 miles each. For trips that begin each Sunday, riders arrive at the Mount Royal Hotel in Banff on Saturday afternoon. Moving camp trips for hardier riders are scheduled during September.

BRITISH COLUMBIA

McCook & Furniss Kechika Range Outfitters, Ltd., Fort Ware, B.C. VOJ 3BO. Att.: Emil McCook & Rick Furniss. Fort Ware via Vancouver radio oper. [Jan.–Apr.: 1515 Orchard Ave., Moscow, ID 83843. (208) 882-7961.] Rocky Mts. of north-central BC. Jun.–Sept. Moving, base camp & drop pack custom trips. 2–10 riders. 3–10 days. Rates on request. Youth rates. Bring sleeping gear. Arrival: Mackenzie, Prince George or Fort St. John, BC. (See also *Float Trips.*)

Between the Tatlatui/Spatsizi Plateau and the Kwadacha Wilderness Provincial Park lies a 2,000-square-mile territory so remote it can be reached only by air charter. This is where McCook and Furniss take small groups of riders. It's a land with 400 miles of trails, thousands of unnamed peaks and more lakes than have been counted; also a fishing paradise and the home of mountain sheep and goats, caribou, grizzly and black bears, wolverines, wolves, elk and mule deer.

ONTARIO

Echo Ridge Riding Ranch, Box 137-A, Kearney, Ont. POA 1MO. Att.: W. Schmidt. (705) 636-5327. Algonquin Park & townships of Bethune & Proudfoot. Jun.–Oct. Moving & base camp trips. 6–8 riders. 5 days, $264; sleeping gear incl. Arrival: Emsdale, Ont.

Echo Ridge is linked by quiet trails to Algonquin Park, one of Canada's largest wilderness preserves. Pack trips wind along old logging roads and trapping trails and through scenic areas of the Almaguin Highlands, a 2,000-square-mile Indian hunting ground until the late 1800s. The ranch makes travel arrangements for guests from the Toronto airport.

Vermont Bicycle Touring—John S. Freidin.

III ON WHEELS

Biking

Are you up to a rugged, hilly 50 to 70 miles a day of riding in the saddle—the bike saddle, that is? Then you meet the requirements for serious cross-country bike touring.

Happily, there are all degrees of two-wheel tours, from rugged to downright slothful. On some, for example, if you don't make it to your night's destination, and if you're not bothered by a desire for outstanding accomplishment, you just pedal along at your own leisurely pace and let the sagwagon pick you up.

But, lackadaisical or not, biking is great fun, a fabulous way to see the country and meet the people, a prolific user of expendable energy—yours—and next to walking, it is among the least expensive forms of touring locomotion (including equipment costs) known to man.

The art of biking and its infinite possibilities would have boggled the mind of the early man who at last discovered the wheel. Cycling, in fact, was not evolved by man for another 6,000 years. But its inexorable progress since the 1700s, when someone figured out how to attach two wheels to a seat (handlebars came later), has been dazzling. Today in the U.S., for example, it is possible to follow specially designated bikeways for 4,500 miles winding across the country from sea to shining sea, 1,500 miles north to south from border to border, and any number of miles you choose on routes that crisscross and loop all through the nation.

In 1976, the summer the TransAmerica Trail was opened, some 4,000 cyclists pedaled its entire length in 80 days or more, logging altogether around 17 million miles. What a distance the huff-and-puffers have come since 1884 when a young man from the West, Tom Stephens, rode, lugged and pushed his bike from San Francisco to Boston across 3,700 miles of roads, mountains and prairie—a route that was roadless one third of the way!

In the 1960s the ten-speed bike became popular and made prolonged long-distance biking feasible. In 1963 a Florida couple started the idea of marking less-trafficked streets for bicycles. Now just about every state in the union has mapped bikeways—from a modest 50 miles to 1,000 (the extent of the north-south route in California). Routes are now posted even in Chicago and New York City, where riding a bike can make you a poor insurance risk.

Traffic, in fact, is regarded by bikers as "the enemy." It is far easier to cope with mountains, rain, snow, sleet and flats. Ideal cycling country has few cars, winding roads, easy grades, small towns and camping spots, hostels or "bike inns"—a chain of which has been established on the TransAmerica Trail.

Bikecentennial, MT.

It is wise to try weekend touring before setting forth on an extended cycling journey. It gives you a chance to test not only your stamina but also your equipment—the basic personal gear to take and the bags to pack it in; and the maps, tools and bike accessories (fenders, lights, carriers and other essentials) you will need.

The start of a two-wheel adventure can be the classified section of the telephone book, where bike dealers and rental services, usually familiar with local routes, are listed. Another source is *Bicycling!* magazine, P.O. Box 330, San Rafael, CA 94902 (subscription, $7.50). A wealth of information on cycling routes and group trips may be found in the American Youth Hostel's *North American Bicycle Atlas* and *Highroad to Adventure*, and in Bikecentennial's publications. Both organizations are listed below.

Also in these pages (and in the chapter "Youth Adventures") are special arrangers of cycling tours. They provide expert guiding, companionship, encouragement (when needed), and handle arrangements for lodging, camping and meals. Some of them add variety to your trek with rafting down a river or climbing up a mountain. They bring wheeling adventures on little-known byways and in spectacular regions into the vacation scope of every adventurer, experienced or not.

How many miles can you cycle a day? To travel 50 miles in 8 hours is an average of 6½ miles per hour, 1-hour lunch break. Does the cycling service provide a sagwagon (a station wagon assigned to pick up sagging riders)? Is there an extra charge for it? Do rates include meals and overnights? Bikes and insurance? Is the route level or hilly? Are you apt to have headwinds? Double-check rates and exactly where the trip begins and ends.

FLORIDA

Davis Islands Community Church, 211 Como, Tampa, FL 33606. Att.: Rev. Edward Earl Hartman. (813) 251-1591 or 3345. All yr. FL & NC. 15–40 cyclists. 1–21 days. $5/day, incl. bicycle. Bring sleeping bag. Arrival: Tampa, FL.

The rolling hills of North Carolina's Blue Ridge Parkway are featured on Rev. Hartman's summer tours and Florida routes both summer and winter. He mixes cycling with some white-water tubing and a bit of sightseeing. Coed groups average 70 miles a day, and all-male groups 90 miles. "The outstanding bonus on these trips," feels Rev. Hartman, "is learning how to work in a group guided by Christian principles."

INDIANA

Out-Spokin' Bike Hikes, Box 370-B, Elkhart, IN 46515. Att.: Stanley Miller. (219) 294-7523. US, Puerto Rico, Canada. All yr. 16–35 people. 2–50 days. About $10/day, incl. bicycle, food, insurance, camping gear. Bring sleeping gear.

Out-Spokin' co-ordinates bike hikes for coeds, families, marrieds and singles. Most trips are from 75 to 300 miles, in the East, Midwest and eastern Canada, with a few in the Far West. One is a 3,600-mile tour from Oregon to New Hampshire pedaling and seeing historic sights for 7 weeks. Sponsored by the Mennonite Church, it's open to all. Goal: "A worthwhile, fun and educational experience in Christian fellowship."

NEW HAMPSHIRE

The Biking Expedition, Inc., RD 2, Box AG, Hillsboro, NH 03244. Att.: Tom Heavey. (603) 478-5783. New Eng. May–Sept. 8–20 cyclists. 2–7 days (or 16 abroad). 2–3 days, $75–$110; 6 days, $220; 7 days camping, $165. (See also *Youth Adventures.*)

This organization, covered basically in the "Youth" chapter, also offers trips especially for adults and families in New England and abroad. They are unhurried excursions on uncrowded back roads and are keyed for the novice, intermediate or experienced. In small groups you pedal through historic Contoocook Valley, New London, Keene, Francestown, Sunapee or Fitzwilliam in New England, covering 5 to 32 miles in a day. There are many enjoyable things to see and do—from rolling across covered bridges to antiquing to refreshing swims. Except for the New Hampshire camping trip, overnights are spent at fine country inns.

OHIO

Men in Motion, PO Box 3568-CC, Mansfield, OH 44907. Att.: Charles Sanger. (419) 589-7981. US, Canada. All yr. 20–40 cyclists. 2–45 days or more. Rates on request. Bring sleeping bag. Arrival: Mansfield or Crestline, OH.

This interdenominational religious group, an offshoot of Wandering Wheels, takes its cycling seriously: all-male trips cover 100–200 miles in a day, and coed groups 80–120 miles, in areas throughtout the Unites States. A sagwagon and trailer follow as support vehicles. Trips are for 14-year-olds and up. Rates include most meals, riding clothes, helmet, repairs, insurance and trail fees. Elevation? "We climb where the road does," Sanger replies. "We allow time for some sightseeing along the way, and Bible study is part of the daily routine."

TEXAS

Bike Dream Tours, Inc., PO Box 20653, Houston, TX 77025. Att.: Wayne G. Alfred. (713) 771-1172. US & abroad. 8–30 cyclists. 7–21 days, 8-day tours, about $250, incl. lodging, 2 meals daily, sagwagon. Group & children's rates.

Families, retirees, singlvs and students hit the road on these tours. Alfred, an experienced bike tour leader, offers daily alternate routes to satisfy both the long- and the short-distance riders. "This is most helpful when one partner likes challenges while the other partner prefers an easy trip," he says. Requirements: good health, a 10-speed bike, and ability to travel the distance for each tour. Texas, Oregon, and Colorado are among the '78 itineraries.

VERMONT

Bike Vermont, Inc., PO Box 75A, Grafton, VT 05146. Att.: Robert R. McElwain. (802) 843-2259. VT. May–Oct. 5–20 cyclists. 2–5 days. Wkends, $64; 4–5 days midwk, $35/day; meals, lodging, leaders incl. Bike rentals.

"Vermont is beautiful, bicycling is fun." And so, concludes Bob McElwain, "We organize bicycle touring trips throughout Vermont." Evenings are spent at friendly

Vermont inns. It's easy-to-moderate biking—the pace is up to you. You know the day's route, and where you'll meet the rest of the group for dinner and a comfortable night. "Ride with friends or get off by yourself to enjoy the beauty that surrounds you," McElwain urges. "It's a low-key, individual, noncompetitive activity."

Vermont Bicycle Touring, Box 123-AG, Bristol, VT 05443. Att.: John S. Freidin. (802) 388-4263. VT. May–Oct. 4–40 cyclists, 2–28 days. 2 days, $72; 5 days, $170; incl. food & lodging. 10-speed bike rentals extra. Arrival: Woodstock, White River Junction, Burlington, Brandon, Rutland, St. Johnsbury, VT.

"Our tours are for adults and families, for beginners to advanced cyclists, with a spirit of adventure and a taste for country hospitality," writes John Freidin. "There are usually two leaders and 10–24 cyclists on each—most cyclists (but not all) are between 25 and 45, and about half are single." Cyclists spend evenings at country inns where the tone is informal and the meals homecooked. Trips range from weekends and 3-day rambles to 24-day tours, and trucks haul luggage on the longer trips. Freidin provides a tour-planning service and a repair clinic. It's a happy way to explore and enjoy Vermont, as some 2,100 riders who took a VBT tour last year will agree.

WISCONSIN

Bicycle Travel Tours, 1025 Green Bay St., Dept. AG, La Crosse, WI 54601. Att.: George Lahue. (608) 784-3325 or 782-6011. WI, MN, IA. 10–30 cyclists. 2–14 days. Approx. rates incl. motels, 2 meals/day, mechanic, sagwagon, airport pickups: 2 days, $62; 3 days, $94; 5 days, $158; 7 days, $213. Arrival: La Crosse, WI.

With the novice and intermediate in mind, the Lahues provide experienced escorts for loop and other tours in their Mississippi Valley area. On some you follow the Wisconsin Bikeway; on others, back roads. And there's some tunnel travel. "Bring a flashlight!" they advise. Bathing suits and cameras are also on their "must" list, and on some excursions a Mississippi paddlewheeler gets into the itinerary.

NATIONAL—U.S.

American Youth Hostels, Inc., National Campus, Delaplane, VA 22025. (703) 592-3271. (See also *Youth Adventures*.)

"Youth" in AYH terms is anyone who enjoys "traveling under their own steam"—be it cycling, backpacking, hiking, canoeing, skiing, sailing, horseback riding—and staying at its chain of 200 inexpensive overnight dorms (around $2 per night) called "hostels." Through its national organization, and through its 29 local councils, AYH offers hundreds of such expeditions to members, with trained leaders and usually with small groups. For addresses of local councils that provide details of their regional excursions, write AYH. Or write for the free *High Road to Adventure* brochure, which details nationally sponsored far-flung trips—such as a 30-day Ghost Town trek in the Old West ($600), a Hawaiian Islands trip (38 days for $790), an Atlantic Seafarer (30 days for $370), or a Transcontinental Expedition (82 days for $845). AYH also puts out *The North American Bike Atlas*, listing approximately 100 cycling routes, which can be ordered for $3.50. A nonprofit organization, AYH has functioned since 1934. Membership fees are from $5 to $11, depending on age, or $12 per family.

Bikecentennial, PO Box 8308, Missoula, MT 59807. Att.: David Prouty. (406) 721-1776. TransAmerica Trail. May–Sept. 7–9 bikers/trip plus leader. 8–90 days. Rates approx. $8–$12/day, depending upon services offered.

Take the ultimate bike tour—the 4,500-mile TransAmerica Trail, stretching from Oregon to Virginia. The route (little-used county and secondary roads) meanders through national forests, parks, prairies, desert, farmlands and rural towns. Not that ambitious? Choose a segment of the trail. Or take one of the new loops in Virginia, Kentucky, Idaho or Oregon which begin and end in the same town—good for limited vacations. Trained group leaders take charge of all excursions, which average 40 to 50 miles each day. Bikecentennial also gives a hand planning private trips. It must be fun. In '76, 4,100 cyclists tried it, logging nearly 10 million miles on a portion or all of the TransAmerica Trail. Write for departure dates and rates for this season's tours.

International Bicycle Touring Society, 846 Prospect St., La Jolla, CA 92037. Att.: Clifford L. Graves. (714) 454-2441. 1- to 2-wk. trips for 25 cyclists, avg. $20–$30/day incl. food & lodging.

"The average cyclist likes the idea of a bicyle tour, but he doesn't know where to go," Clifford Graves remarks. With this premise IBTS offers its members excursions in various parts of this country and abroad. Membership is $7 a year, minimum age 21, and is open to anyone who enjoys the freedom of cycling and is not afraid of an all-day ride. Station wagons lug the luggage.

League of American Wheelman, 19 S. Bothwell, Palatine, IL 60067. (312) 991-1200.

Since the 1880s the League of American Wheelmen has worked to promote bicycling, encourage favorable legislation, and to teach safe, correct riding techniques. It presently includes over 365 affiliated bicycle clubs in all 50 states, and publishes a directory of members and clubs and *The L.A.W. Bulletin*, a monthly magazine. The latter gives details on rallies, events, and year-round invitational bike tours, which range from a half-day's outing to a 700-mile jaunt to extended tours in the U.S. and abroad. Membership dues are $10 for 16 years up, $15 for families.

The Biking Expedition, Inc., NH.

Wandering Wheels, IN.

Covered Wagons

They went with axe and rifle,
     when the trail was still to blaze,
They went with wife and children,
     in the prairie-schooner days,
With banjo and with frying pan—
     Susanna, don't you cry!
For I'm off to California
     to get rich out there or die!

—Stephen Vincent Benét*

The ruts are still visible in western Kansas and the Oklahoma Panhandle. They are deep, grass-covered furrows etched by iron-rimmed, wood wheels, the labored autograph of covered-wagon trains that lumbered across the plains a hundred years ago or more. In Wyoming, there are hewed markings on trees and rocks—work that had to be done to accommodate cumbersome wagons through rugged canyons.

The Mormon pioneers, in the 1880s, cut a steep wagon road down through solid rock in order to reach the Colorado River to make a crossing. It is difficult to believe their accomplishment, but it is there, near Utah's Canyonlands National Park, to marvel at and see.

In Wyoming and in Kansas, you can move from station wagon to covered wagon and jounce over prairie sod or mountain trails. Some of the refurbished prairie schooners are old hay wagons that were retired from use on the farm with the advent of the jeep. Today, hitched to a team of horses or mules, the kind that used to power the plow, the wagons roll on overnight journeys and longer. You sleep under canvas in the wagon itself, or under the stars in a sleeping bag. You'll hear the sounds of years ago—the moan of straining wood, the snorting of mules, the jingling of harnesses—you'll think of the pioneers for whom a covered wagon trip was far from a vacation, but the way to a new life.

Shifting your personal gear from a bulky suitcase to a duffel or lightweight bag is more convenient for wagon trips. Double-check on what to bring, departure dates, where to meet, how to arrange overnight accommodations before and after the trip, what the rates include, if there's a tax and whether sleeping gear is provided. Where

---

Wagons Ho, KS.

will you park your car and your extra luggage? Will you have a chance to fish? What about a license? Happy pioneering!

KANSAS

Wagons Ho, Box 74-A, Main St., Quinter, KS 67752. Att.: Ruth & Frank Hefner. (913) 754-3347. KS. Jun.–Aug. 9–30 wagons. 45–80 people. 3 days, $173–$293 all-incl. Sleeping gear & airport pickup (Hays) extra. Family rates per person; group & day rates. Arrival: Hays, KS.

Each Thursday through Sunday an authentic wagon train follows the still-visible ruts of the original Old Smoky Hill Trail—60 miles of it across the Kansas prairie. Nine covered wagons and a stagecoach form the train by day, and there are also horses to ride. At night up to 30 wagons circle the campfire. You cover 20 miles a day, stop to see a sod house, hunt fossils, ford streams, and have hearty meals and campfire music in the evening. The Hefners themselves are pioneers—first to offer wagon treks for vacationers.

WYOMING

Bar-T-Five Outfitter, Box 2140, Jackson, WY 83001. Att.: Bill Thomas. (307) 733-5386. Targhee Natl. Forest. Jun.–Sept. 20–50 people. 5 days, $215, incl. lodging night before trip & sleeping gear. Group & youth rates. Arrival: Jackson, WY. (See also *Pack Trips.*)

In 1889 "Uncle Nick" Wilson drove the first covered wagon over Teton Pass into Jackson Hole. Today his great grandson Bill Thomas recaptures this experience with covered wagon treks along the back roads of the Targhee National Forest, between Yellowstone and Grand Teton national parks. Wagons move to a new camp each day—two of them on the shores of high mountain lakes. Horseback rides, chuck-wagon-style meals, campfire singing and old-fashioned hoedown square dances round out each day's fun.

Wagons West, L.D. Frome, Outfitter, Box G, Afton, WY 83110. (307) 886-5240. Grand Teton Natl. Park (WY). 1–35 people. 2–6 days. 2 days, $90; 4 days, $165; 6 days, $225; incl. transport to/from motel. Group & youth rates. Bring sleeping bag. Arrival: Jackson, WY. (See also *Backpacking, Hiking with Packstock, Horse Trekking, Pack Trips.*)

There's a lapse of either an hour or a hundred years, depending on how you look at it, from your Jackson Hole motel to a Conestoga wagon at Sagebrush Flat or Skull Creek Meadows. It's modernized with rubber tires and foam-padded seats that convert to deluxe bunks, but it looks like the real thing. Horses or mules pull wagons and chuckwagon over trails or remote back-country roads. Dutch oven cooking, cowboy songs, fishing, riding and spotting wildlife are part of a day's trek.

Wagons West, WY.

Jeeping

"The only difference between a horse and a jeep* is that the jeep doesn't stop for a drink when you cross a creek," says a onetime passenger for the benefit of those who might think that this is a tenderfoot trek, as easy and soft as lolling on a water bed. In fact, a wilderness jeep trip can combine first, second and reverse with the stomach-churning buckboard bounce of a horse and carriage at full gallop.

Some four-wheelers, however, provide the luxury of air-conditioned comfort while they ford shallow streams or lurch along abandoned wagon roads, creekbeds, stagecoach routes, pioneer trails or old railroad grades.

There are jeeping services that offer everything from a scenic breakfast cookout at some remote spot in the back country to week-long excursions with chuckwagon trailers and deluxe camping gear. They trek into deserts and canyons, over remote mountain passes that cross the Continental Divide, along ocean shores and into eerie ghost towns.

Besides their scheduled trips, jeep outfitters custom plan outings of varying length and ruggedness for families and groups. The areas they tour extend all the way from the shores of the Sea of Cortez in Baja California to the remoteness of the Cariboo-Chilcotin country of British Columbia. Whatever trip you choose, the experience will be enriched by driver-guides who know a lot about the history, geology and animal and plant life of the region.

It's an adventurous way to see the land. On a single trip you may spot some wild mustangs, climb into ice caves, examine Indian teepee rings, and find ancient artifacts and fossils. Or follow old mining roads through a magnificent landscape of high peaks, volcanic rocks, tumbling waterfalls and alpine meadows ablaze with wildflowers.

"Since we've begun taking people on jeep trips, we've seen some of our own land for the first time," a Colorado rancher admits. "In several hours our four-wheeler will cover more ground than the mountain men could have traveled in several days."

Although jeeps have the power and traction to take off across open country and up mountain slopes, knowledgeable four-wheeling enthusiasts are well aware of the damage that off-the-road journeying does to fragile areas. "You should be reluctant to leave tire tracks where they haven't been before," says a former jeep racer.

---

* "Jeep" is a registered trademark of American Motors Corporation, but through common usage it has become a generic word for the four-wheel-drive vehicle and is so defined by dictionaries. We have used the term in this way.

Tag-A-Long Tours, UT.

"There are still scars on the mountain I made years ago that I'm ashamed of."

In *Your Land, Your Jeep and You,** Ed Zern gives this graphic picture: "You may have been in parts of Alaska where the tundra rolls like a multicolored carpet to the horizon, and seen tracks made across the Arctic prairie by the tractors of prospecting geologists . . . fresh tracks, it seems, no more than a few days old. And then . . . you learn that the 'fresh tracks' were made five years ago, or 15."

One look at the old mining routes and pioneer trails that are termed "roads" in the West, and you'll not feel that "on-the-road" travel makes your journey any the less adventurous.

Does the trip you're booking provide for camping out or sleeping at a lodge or ranch? Do rates include overnights? Are sleeping bags supplied? Will the outfitter arrange lodging for before and after the trip? What weather will you encounter? Check dates, rates, tax and the rendezvous point. If altitude affects you, find out what elevations you'll experience. Clarify whether you expect to join other travelers, or whether you want your own custom trip.

ARIZONA

Canyoneers, Inc., PO Box 2997, East Flagstaff, AZ 86003. Att.: Gaylord Staveley. (602) 526-0924. All yr. From Flagstaff: 4 hrs., $12; 10 hrs., $28–$30. Indian

---

* Copies of *Your Land, Your Jeep and You* may be obtained free from Dept. JB, American Motors Corporation, Detroit, MI 48322.

country: 7 days, $361. Baja Peninsula: 10 days, $385; 2 wks., $500. Rates incl. sleeping gear or lodging, & meals. Arrival: Flagstaff, AZ. (See also *Backpacking, Float Trips*.)

Canyoneers leads excursions through colorful areas near Flagstaff, and into Navajo and Hopi Indian lands in the mountains, plateaus, deserts and canyons of northern Arizona and southern Utah. In winter they journey through Mexico's Baja Peninsula—driving and camping in the back country with its great Cardon cacti and weird Boojum trees, visiting villages, and setting up camp on the shores of the Sea of Cortez or the Pacific Ocean, where gray whales play offshore.

Wahweap Lodge & Marina, Box 1597, Page, AZ 86040. Att.: A.G.I. (602) 645-2433. Lake Powell area (AZ & UT). All yr. 5 or more persons. 2 hrs., $9; 4 hrs., $18; all day, $30; 20% off, Nov.–Mar. Arrival: Page, AZ.

One of America's water wonderlands, Lake Powell's scenic panoramas include fantastic overlooks, moonscapes and picturesque buttes and canyons. In air-conditioned comfort your jeep maneuvers ravines, dry washes and wagon trails 100 years old and takes you to Indian ruins, ghost towns, fossil beds and old mines. Jeep and boat trips may be combined on 1-day ($33) or 2-day ($68) tours, (children, $30 or $59).

CALIFORNIA

Desert Expeditions, Inc., PO Box 1404, Palm Desert, CA 92260. Att.: George Service. (714) 346-6927. Palm Springs: day trips, $25, Oct.–May; Death Valley: 7 days, $365, fall & spring; Bristlecone Pines & high desert: 8 days, $395, summer. Camping & sleeping gear incl. Arrival: Palm Springs, CA.

Visit the ancient bristlecone pines, the oldest living things on earth. Explore eerie ghost towns, including Bodie, with over 100 buildings standing. Marvel at the desert wildflowers. Drivers for these expeditions are teachers, museum curators and park rangers who know intimately the area's natural history. You drive in air-conditioned vehicles accompanied by custom-built chuckwagon trailers and deluxe camping gear.

COLORADO

Canyon Ranch, Rt. 1, Box 61-A, Olathe, CO 81425. Att.: Bob & Bea Frisch. (303) 323-5288. Black Canyon of the Gunnison. All yr., 2–12 people. 1 day, $29, incl. lunch & supper; overnight w./breakfast, $34. Arrival: Montrose, CO. (See also *Cattle Drives*.)

"The Ute Indians used to winter in our canyon, and we explore their old stomping grounds," the Frisches say. "With jeeps we get into unbelievable high country, with alpine meadows ablaze with wildflowers. We poke around old mining camps and ghost towns, climb into caves, and hunt arrowheads, dinosaur bones and rocks." Accommodations at the guest ranch.

The Mountain Men, 11100 E. Dartmouth, 219-A, Denver, CO 80232. Att.: Burt Green. (303) 750-0090. Mt. Zirkel Wilderness, Pike, Routt & White Riv. natl. forests. Jun.–Oct. 2–12 people. $30 & up, incl. meals & sleeping & camping gear. Arrival: Denver, CO.

"Our first-class four-wheel-drive tours are over remote mountain passes and through ghost towns and historic areas," Burt Green explains. "We drive on old wagon trails through magnificent country across the Continental Divide." His Executive Weekend trip meets your plane at Denver. "A personal experience, not a mass product," he says. Burt also offers pack trips and cross country skiing.

San Juan Scenic Jeep Tours, Box 143, Ouray, CO 81427. Att.: Francis Kuboske. (303) 325-4444. San Juan Range. Jun.–Sept. Up to 150 people. ½ day, $9; full day,

$18; children 12 or under, $6 or $12.50.

"We drive . . . you look," says Francis Kuboske. He and his expert mountain drivers take you into a land of volcanic rock, tumbling waterfalls, fields of flowers and spectacular peaks. "We follow old roads carved by miners into high country. We see old mining towns, sheep grazing above timberline, snowdrifts in late July." So you can really enjoy the view they travel at 5 miles per hour—about right on a road cut into sheer cliff.

Tiger Run, Inc., PO Box 1418, Breckenridge, CO 80424. Att.: Glenn Campbell & Dean Vosburgh. (303) 453-2231. All yr. Arapaho Natl. Forest. Jun–Oct. 3–24 people. 1–4 hrs, $6–$22 adult, $5–$18 for 4–11 yrs. Arrival: Frisco, CO. (See also *Snowmobiling*.)

Join a driver-guide in an open-topped vehicle for "fantastic scenic vistas, deserted mining camps and fields of wildflowers," Tiger Run urges, "some of the most exciting scenery anywhere." You'll jounce along from 9,300- to 13,500-foot elevations in rugged and beautiful back country.

Vail Jeep Guides, PO Box 1474-A, Vail, CO 81657. Att.: Jim Rea. (303) 476-5387. Summer. 3–120 people. 2-hr. min. $3/hr.

You'll get some spectacular views of the Gore Range on these mountain trips with Jim Rea and his qualified guides. Combine a scenic tour with breakfast, lunch or dinner cookouts. Jim also arranges pack trips, rafting, riding, fishing, snowmobiling, ski touring and skibobbing.

UTAH

Kent Frost Canyonlands Tours, Inc., Dept. A78, 180 South 2nd East, Monticello, UT 84535. Att.: Pete Steele. (801) 587-2929. Canyonlands Natl. Park (UT); also canyon & Indian country of AZ, CO, NV & NM. Day trips (all yr.), $25; 2–5 days (Apr.–Nov.), $42.50/day, incl. camping & sleeping gear. Arrival: Monticello, UT.

In comfortable air-conditioned vehicles you ride through this fabulous country of red rock canyons, spires and sandstone formations, and camp in the open each night. On day trips (with lunch provided) you explore the Needles, Angel Arch, the Silver Stairs and other areas. Longer safaris take you to historic and wonderfully scenic areas of Four Corners country. You can arrange custom safaris for your own group, or take one of the 6- or 10-day tours scheduled for Sunday departures.

Outlaw Trails, Inc., PO Box 336-F, Green River, UT 84525. Att.: A.C. Ekker. (801) 564-3593. Canyonlands Natl. Park. All yr. 1–40 people. 1–14 days. 1 day, $30; 2 days, $125; 4 days, $250; 5 days, $310; incl. food & gear. Group rates. Arrival: Grand Junction, UT. (See also *Pack Trips, Float Trips*.)

Wander by jeep through a colorful array of canyons, buttes, mesas, spires and cliffs along secluded, ancient trails. See Butch Cassidy's old hideout at Robbers' Roost. Drive into Horseshoe Canyon with its extensive prehistoric Indian pictographs. Or combine your tour with a 3-day Cataract Canyon float trip.

Tag-A-Long Tours, PO Box 1206-G, 452 N. Main St., Moab, UT 84532. Att.: Mitch Williams. (800) 453-3292 toll-free (except UT, HI & AK) or (801) 259-6690. Canyonlands, Escalante Wilderness. All yr. 6–100 people. 1–7 days. 1 day, $25–$30; 4 days, $192; all-incl. Group & youth rates. Arrival: Grand Junction, CO, or Moab, UT. (See also *Float Trips*.)

Visit a fantasy land of eroded rock and vividly colored canyons in the comfort of an air-conditioned four-wheel-drive station wagon. The leisurely pace allows plenty of time to fully enjoy the awesome landscape. Bring plenty of film. Delicious Dutch oven food on each night's campout.

WYOMING

Red Cliff Marina, 261-A Hampshire, Lovell, WY 82431. Att.: Norman D. Hoffman. (307) 548-7708. Pryor Mts. Apr.–Oct. 4–42 persons, 6–8 per jeep. 1-day trips cover 25–100 mi. 2 hrs., $8; 4 hrs., $16; all day, $30. Arrival: Lovell, WY.

"The Pryor Mountains are the home of the wild mustangs," writes Norm Hoffman. "You'll also see many other sights—ice caves, Indian tepee rings, rustlers' corrals, ancient artifacts, rocks and fossils and much more. But the wild mustangs are number one for most people."

Timber Trails, Box 2473, Jackson, WY 83001. Att.: Larry L. Boyd. (307) 733-5054. [Nov.–May: (307) 733-4956.] Bridger-Teton Natl. Forest, Yellowstone Natl. Park. Jun.–Oct. 1–8 people. ½-day photo safari, $10; all day, $25; supper & sunset, $15; overnight at Tipi Camp, $30. Arrival: Jackson, WY.

Larry Boyd's unique excursions into this scenic area "vary from relatively smooth to pretty rough," he tells us. "The valley floor is at 6,5000 feet, and we go up to 8,000 feet," he says. "We stop whenever you want to take photos or identify flowers or watch the wildlife." He provides refreshments on the ½-day trip, lunch on the day tour, supper on the "Supper & Sunset" special and three meals at the authentic Sioux Indian Tipi Camp. And what meals! Larry describes a typical supper: "Roast sirloin tips and potatoes cooked in the Dutch oven, buried in the ground with hot coals all day, bean hole beans cooked the same way, paper bag tossed salad, sourdough bread from dough started in 1906, coffee or hot chocolate and dessert. Nothing fancy—just good food and plenty of it. Almost everyone comes back for a second helping." He's adding hiking and a float trip to some excursions.

BRITISH COLUMBIA

Western Outdoor Adventures Ltd., 16115 32nd Ave., White Rock, B.C. V4B 4Z5. Att.: Frank Lockwood. (604) 531-3969. Shore, mountains & ranch country, BC. Jun.–Sept. Up to 11 people. 7–15 days. Safari-Bus Tour, 7 days, $340; Western Safari, 15 days, $750; Safari for Cameras, 10 days, $410, or 13 days, $610. Rates incl. accom., transport, guide-driver & meals. Arrival: Vancouver, BC. (See also *Wilderness Living, Ski Touring, Youth Adventures*.)

You ride a maxiwagon, train, plane, ferry, charter boat and helicopter on these safaris to remote back-country roads and shores. Itineraries include such dreamy spots as WOA's Wilderness Camp on Jervis Inlet or Ocean Camp on Vancouver Island, the Cariboo-Chilcotin ranch country, Bella Coola and the Inside Passage, and Alert Bay, with its array of Indian totems and artifacts. Meet cowboys, Indians, loggers and fishermen. Comb the beach. Pan for gold. Hike, swim, fish, climb—relax.

San Juan Scenic Jeep Tours, CO.

Offshore Sailing School, Ltd., NY.

IV BY BOAT

Boat Charters

"Chartering," says one expert, "is like having a moving hotel. One can stay in one place or move on if the scenery is not appealing."

It is possible to charter a boat, expensively or inexpensively, power or sail, with or without captain and crew. It can be forty dollars a day with three meals, or several hundred dollars a day, depending on the degree of luxury.

Yachts chartered without crew are called "bareboat" charters. It is a popular way of defraying expense for the owner, and a wonderful way for the vacationer to be a part-time yachtsman without the responsibility of yacht ownership. You will be asked for a security deposit, references and testimony to your sailing and navigational ability before the charter is yours.

Yachts come in different degrees of bareness, some with air-conditioning and snorkeling equipment included. Bareboat charters are for the experienced sailor who has the ability and know-how to sail the boat with the help of his own experienced sailor guests as crew.

"Too large a party is the mistake most often made in planning charters," warns a yacht broker. "Another is covering too much ground—or water. A tight schedule takes away a great deal of the fun." All charterers have a common fetish about having their boats returned as you found them—clean and undamaged.

Can you picture, for example, cruising in the Caribbean or off New England's coast with a professional skipper and crew doing the navigating, serving the meals, and taking you into and out of whatever ports or anchorages your carefree lives desire? In fact, such luxurious arrangements may be made in coastal waters both East and West.

There are many such charter services. The ones we know the most about are described in the following pages.

There are great variations in what services and equipment are included in rates. Check carefully. You'll also want to be clear on the following details: provisioning and insurance of charters, food and beverages, amount of luggage space and arrangement of sleeping facilities. Also find out what water sports and safety equipment is aboard, fuel and docking charges, weather conditions, fishing licenses required, clothes and equipment you should bring, deposits, refunds and how to obtain maps and charts. Other things to check: whether the radio, heads, showers and lights function properly. Are there any leaks? For sailing ships with regularly scheduled departures, see the section on "Windjammers."

CONNECTICUT

Russell Yacht Charters, 126 Davis Ave., Suite 300, Bridgeport, CT 06605. Att.: Joanne J. Russell. (203) 366-4561. Caribbean, Bahamas, FL, New Eng. Crewed & bareboat charters. Indiv. or groups. All yr. Sample rates: for indiv. on windjammer-type cruise, $325/wk. for everything on board exc. bar; for 4 or more on pvt. yacht, from $390/person/wk. for everything on board incl. food & bar; for bareboat charter, from $680/2 wks., summer, 30-ft. boat, in Bahamas. (See also *Scuba Diving*.)

A group of 2 to 10 may charter their own private, crewed yacht—theirs to command, to go where they wish, with all services provided and a course suggested by skipper and crew. Special air fares and hotel rates are included in a complete travel package. With yachts from 30 feet to 130 feet, RYC will find the right vessel in the desired location for each booking—whether bareboat or crewed, sail or power— or will book a windjammer cruise for an individual.

FLORIDA

Ott's Yachts, 2222 NW 22nd Ct., Miami, FL 33125. (305) 271-1193. Bahamas & FL Keys. Bareboat & skippered charters. All yr. 55-ft. ketch, $1,000/wk.; 65-ft. ketch, $1,200/wk., w./o. crew. Skipper, $65/day plus food. Also Shark VIII, IX & X, 52-ft. Fiberglas boats.

"My boats sleep 16 to 19 people and can take large groups at minimum cost," explains Captain Jack Ott. The Shark VII, a 65-foot ketch, has 8 double staterooms and bunks for 19." Skippers should have their own complete navigation kit. Captain Ott provides a skipper if you need one.

Tampa Bay Sail Charters, Box 20773-AG, St. Petersburg, FL 33742. Att.: Stanley March. (813) 527-6097. Bareboat & skippered charters. All yr. 2–8 persons. Rates by day, wk. or longer. Sample rates: 20-ft. sloop for 2, $225/wk; 45-ft. ketch for 6, $1,400/wk. with skipper; provisions extra.

Your cruise begins with a short sail to determine if your party needs instruction or requires a skipper. Skippered or bareboat, charter party serves as crew. This includes time at the helm, tending the sails, a turn in the galley and anchor watch.

MARYLAND

Chesapeake Bay Charters, Ltd., 2948 Edgewater Dr., Edgewater, MD 21037. Att.: William D. Jones, Jr. (301) 956-3051. Bareboat & crewed sailing charters. Chesapeake Bay. Apr.–Nov. 2–8 people, 2 or more days. $275–$740/wk. per yacht, wkend. & midwk. rates, incl. all but linens & food. Skipper, $35/day extra.

These are bareboat charters on Chesapeake Bay for experienced sailors 21 years or older. The sailing yachts are 26 to 42 feet and sleep 4 to 6 people. Jones also can provide skippers, and claims that here you'll find "the best seafood in the East." Also secluded harbors and hundreds of clean, cool tributaries, historic seaports and an opportunity to observe the last sailing fleet in the U.S. dredging for oysters.

MASSACHUSETTS

V. E. B. Nicholson & Sons, 9 Chauncey St., Suite 50, Cambridge, MA 02138. (617) 661-8174. [Or use Nicholson's West Indies address: Nelsons Dockyard, English Harbour Pay Office, Antigua. Tel.: 31055/31059.] Crewed charters. Caribbean, US East Coast. 36 people max./boat. 7 days min. All-incl. rates $45–$220/day/person.

Nicholson's has operated in the Caribbean since 1948, the oldest established yacht charter broker in the world. It maintains contact with yachts and charter guests through its own radio station at English Harbour, and also has Telex and cable facilities. Its fleet consists of 127 yachts and motor vessels of all kinds, 36 to 150 feet, first-class and fully crewed. "Instruction can be given in sailing, celestial and

V. E. B. Nicholson & Sons, MA.   Offshore Sailing School, Ltd., NY.

coastal navigation and other activities connected with passage-making," points out Manager Peter Baker. "We can arrange any kind of boat charter, anywhere. Guests may be as active or relaxed as they wish." Snorkel, scuba, fishing and skeet equipment is always carried aboard.

NEW YORK

Offshore Sailing School, Ltd., 820 2nd Ave., New York, NY 10017. (212) 986-4570 or toll-free (800) 221-4326. Branches in Sarasota, FL; Edgartown, MA; City Island, NY; Hilton Head, SC; Captive Island, FL; Tortola, Brit. V.I. 1 wk, $199 for basic instruction, $229 for advanced sailing & racing. Refresher, 3-day & other special courses, from $45 up. Also bareboat & crewed charters, New Eng., Caribbean & Europe.

Here's a service for sailing instruction and sailing vacations. You learn sailing techniques from basic to advanced, and when you graduate, OSS displays its confidence by qualifying you for chartering its own bareboats. It's the oldest sailing school in the country, run professionally by knowledgeable sailors, and makes skippers out of hard-core urbanites in less than a week.

World Yacht Enterprises, Ltd., Box A, 14 W. 55th St., New York, NY 10019. Att.: J. Neil Heap. (212) 246-4811. Motor & sailing yacht charters. Coastal US, Canada, Caribbean. Per person rates incl. crew & meals from $40/day up, or $175–$1,000/wk. up.

With a fleet of 1,000 yachts, small enough for 2 passengers and large enough for 200, this charter company arranges a private-yacht vacation adjusted for each group's requirements. All cruises are completely catered, and WYE recommends them as a different twist for conferences and entertaining as well as for a carefree vacation. All yachts carry auxiliary boats for fishing, swimming and going ashore.

WASHINGTON

Northwest Marine Charters, Inc., 2400-G Westlake Ave. N., Seattle, WA 98109. Att.: Phil Simon. (206) 283-3040. U-Drive cruisers, houseboats & sailboats; also skippered yacht charters. Puget Sound, San Juan Is., Gulf Is., Inside Passage to SE Alaska. All yr. Sample rates: $750/wk. for 34-ft. U-Drive cruiser (sleeps up to 6); $750/day for 65-ft. skippered luxury yacht for 6, incl. crew of 2.

"The Pacific Northwest has the finest protected cruising waters anywhere," Phil Simon maintains. "There are driftwood and fossils on the island beaches, fighting King salmon, clams, crabs, oysters, whales and porpoises in the water, tea and crumpets in Victoria—and unbelievable beauty everywhere." He offers a choice of over 100 boats from 26 to 126 feet, each complete for extended cruising.

CARIBBEAN

Blue Water Cruises, Box 758-A, St. Thomas, VI 00801. Att.: Mrs. Nancy H. Stout. (809) 774-3032. US & Brit. Virgin Is. Crewed boats, private charter; also sched. cruise. All yr. 2–10 people, 3 or more days. Winter about $60/day per person all-incl.; summer less.

Blue Water Cruises, a yacht charter brokerage, makes a specialty of matching boat and crew with each client's needs. They also offer scheduled 1-week "join a group" cruises for 14 to 26 passengers out of St. Thomas. "A yachting vacation is a relaxing, informal, barefoot-type get-away-from-it-all holiday," Nancy Stout comments. "You're never out of sight of islands in this idyllic area, and never more than 15 minutes from a beautiful anchorage." All yachts carry snorkeling and fishing gear, and some have scuba gear and water skis.

The Moorings, Ltd., PO Box 50059-A, New Orleans, LA 70150. Att.: E. A. Rainold. (504) 834-0785. Brit. Virgin Is. All yr. Crewed & bareboat charters. 2–6 people per boat, 7 days min. Rates vary w./season, type of boat & service. Discounts for 3 or more boats.

The Moorings' 60 sailboats (sloops and ketches), with complete snorkeling gear and dinghy with outboard, cruise from Tortola through the British Virgin Islands, which Rainold calls one of the world's best sailing areas. "A typical charter lasts 7 to 10 days," he says, "sailing from one island to another and sampling many beautiful beaches and anchorages. With islands about 5 miles apart, you're never more than an hour from a safe anchorage. The sailing conditions are ideal—constant trade winds, beautiful water, fair weather and warm temperature."

Stevens Yachts of Annapolis, Inc., Severn 100, Annapolis, MD 21403. Att.: William H. Stevens. (301) 267-9337 or (800) 638-9150. Windward & Leeward Is. All yr. Crewed & bareboat charters, 7 days min., 2–6 people per yacht. Sample all-incl. rates, Apr.–Dec.: crewed, $1,850/wk. for 6; bareboat, $1,260–$1,600/wk.; Dec.–Apr. rates higher. "Escape to the Grenadines" 1-wk. summer cruise, $425.

With St. Lucia as home port, a fleet of yachts from 43 to 65 feet for up to 6 passengers in each may be chartered with a crew of 2, or without crew, for cruising through the Windward and Leeward Islands year-round. And in summer, individual vacationers may book into scheduled weekly cruises called "Escape to the Grenadines." Charters are tailored for each group's requirements. Generally it's a life of relaxed sailing, fine snorkeling, a barbecue on a secluded beach, a shore excursion, an evening at a "jump up!" party at an island hotel, and sailing to another beautiful anchorage each day. One-way charters arranged anywhere between Antigua and Grenada.

Vernon Charter Yachts, Yacht Nordic, Homeport, St. Thomas, VI 00801. Att.: Capt. Deek Vernon. Yawl charter, crewed. 3 double staterooms, each w./pvt. head & shower. All-incl. luxury charter rate: $3,000–$3,600/wk. for 6 guests.

"The *Nordic* is a yawl (the world's largest Fiberglas sailing vessel), 74 feet on deck, with a 20-foot beam," according to Deek Vernon. "She's the perfect charter vessel, with space to spare for sunbathing, gracious dining, comfortable living quarters. I'm the skipper. My wife, a stewardess and a deckhand complete the crew."

Jet Boating

Jet boating is a noisy way to cruise. It consumes fuel. And on rare occasions an underwater rock will rip a hole in a boat's bottom and it will sink.

Having said that, we have given a complete summary of the negatives. Jetting down the Main Salmon or Hells Canyon or the Rogue River is an exhilarating, scenic, enjoyable, exciting and leisurely ride. In an hour you can cover a distance that could take all day to run on a raft. If you're jetting to a river lodge or fishing camp, you gain vacation time at your destination through the jet approach.

Besides, how else could you get there and then get both yourself and your boat back upriver again? Only the flat-bottomed jet boat can speed back upstream against the current and over the rapids with ease. The alternative, if you should travel by raft (or by kayak, rowboat or canoe), is to continue on downriver with the current and laboriously truck your equipment on a roundabout route back to the starting point. Or fold up an inflatable craft and fly back—frequently done, but a more expensive venture.

Jet boating has opened these strikingly beautiful river canyons for many who want to see them but do not have the time to float, row or paddle through. These are sporty trips, no matter how you do it. Some of the outfitters who can take you by jet boat are listed below. They are expert in navigating the wild white water, and whether for just a day or longer, they will give you a great wilderness experience.

Some trips are scheduled on a daily basis; others (customs trips) may be planned especially for your family or group. Outfitters can arrange overnights at river lodges which in some cases are their own, and can handle logistics for overnight campouts.

IDAHO

Salmon River Lodge, PO Box 58A, Salmon, ID 83467. Att.: Dave & Phyllis Giles. (208) 756-2646. Salmon Riv. (ID). Feb.–Nov. Custom & scheduled. 1–40 people. 1 day, $40, incl. guide, food & lodging. Arrival: Salmon, ID. (See also *Pack Trips, Float Trips.)*

The lodge's powerful jet boats take you leisurely downstream between the rocky cliffs and forested slopes of the Main Salmon Canyon. There are many sandy beaches for camping. This is country for rockhounds, anglers, Indian pictographs and gold panning. Jetting back upstream to the lodge, the boats easily maneuver the river's riffles and rapids.

Court's Rogue River "White Water Trips," OR.

Snake River Outfitters, 811 Snake River Ave., Lewiston, ID 83501. Att.: Norman Riddle. (208) 743-6276 or 746-2232. Snake & Main Salmon Riv. Apr.–Nov. Short day trips, $40; longer, $50; overnight, $120; addl. night, $40; incl. meals & lodging. Arrival: Lewistown, ID. (See also *Float Trips.*)

"The Middle Snake into Hells Canyon is one of the longest white-water trips left—100 miles with more than 100 rapids," says Norman Riddle. There are lots of white sand beaches for swimming, sunning and fishing. On overnight trips you stay at Kirby Creek Lodge. "Come in the fall if your plans include steelhead fishing," Riddle advises. In summer he includes a day of rafting in a 3-day or longer trip.

Zeke West's Whitewater Ranch, Air Star Rt., Cascade, ID 83611. (208) 382-4336. Main Salmon Riv. (ID). Jul.–Aug. Custom trips. 2–6 people, 1–4 days. Rates on request. (See also *Pack Trips.*)

"I cover 100 miles on the Main Salmon," Zeke explains. "The old-timers say, 'Once you drink from the Salmon you'll always return.' We think our stretch of river has the sweetest water of all." It also has abandoned gold mines, wild game and spectacular rapids. You can drive to the main lodge where the road ends and the wilderness begins.

OREGON

Court's Rogue River "White Water Trips," PO Box 1045-CB, Gold Beach, OR 97444. Att.: Court A. Boice. (503) 247-6504. Rogue Riv. May–Oct. Up to 40 people. Round-trip: adult, $25; child, $15; overnight: adult, $37, incl. 4 meals. Arrival: Gold Beach, OR.

Court leaves Jot's Resort every day at 8 A.M. during the season. It takes just 7 hours to jet the 104-mile round-trip on this nationally designated "wild river." You stop at the Barbarian or Paradise Lodge, spend the night if you wish, and return the next day. "The country is exactly as Zane Grey witnessed it over 40 years ago," says Court.

Hellgate Excursions, Box 982, Grants Pass, OR 97526. Att.: Gary Woolsey. (503) 479-7204. Rogue Riv. May–Sept. 15–48 passengers. Trips daily. 2-hr. scenic excursion, $8/adult, $4/child 4–12 yrs.; barbeque excursion, $19 & $10; 5-hr. whitewater excursion, $25 & $15. Arrival: Grants Pass or Medford, OR.

"It's a fun trip for all ages," says Gary Woolsey. "You will ride aboard a safe and comfortable jet boat traveling the untamed Rogue to view the spectacular rock cliffs of Hellgate Canyon, and you'll see abundant wildlife which inhabits the waters and river banks." Trips originate and end at the Riverside Motel.

Hells Canyon Guide Service, PO Box 165, Oxbow, OR 97840. Att.: Gus Garrigus. (503) 785-3305. Hells Canyon (ID). May–Sept. 2-hr. trips, $10; under 16 yrs., $5. Custom rates on request. (See also *Float Trips.*)

On custom trips Gus can jet you up the Snake River to his base camp for camping out a day or so. Or you can cruise up through the riffles and rapids on a 2-hour run, with departures every day at 9:30 A.M., 12:30 P.M. and 3:00 P.M. "The Canyon is 3,000 feet deeper than the Grand Canyon," he points out. "It's where the Nez Perce Indians spent their winters for 120 centuries."

Hells Canyon Navigation, PO Box 145-A, Oxbow, OR 97840. Att.: Jim Zanelli (503) 785-3352. Hells Canyon. White water. Summer. 5–25 passengers. 2-hr. trips. Adult, $12.50, child, $6.25; preschool free. Fishing charter, $25/day. Arrival: Baker, OR, or Boise, ID. (See also *Float Trips.*)

These trips start below Hells Canyon Dam and jet through the wild, untamed Snake River into the isolated, primitive canyon. The beauty of the towering walls, the wildlife and the violent thunder of the river make this a wilderness adventure. You stop to investigate earth mounds of an ancient Indian Village.

Jerry's Rogue Jet-Boat Service, Box 1011-A, Gold Beach, OR 97444. (503) 247-7601. Rogue Riv. May–Oct. 6-hr. round-trips, twice daily. Adult, $10; 4–11 yrs., $5; under 4 yrs., free. Group rates. Also 8-hr. round-trip: adult, $25; child, $12.50. Arrival: Gold Beach, OR.

"Travel 64 miles through the Rogue wilderness," Jerry urges. "You'll experience 100 years of Indian and pioneer history while viewing mother nature at her undisturbed moments." On his longer trip you cruise 104 miles going deeper into the upper Rogue canyons.

WASHINGTON

Held's Canyon Tours, 118 Sycamore, Clarkston, WA 99403. Att.: Floyd F. Held. (509) 758-3445. Snake Riv. May–Nov. 2–24 passengers. 1 day. Adults, $40; under 12 yrs., $15; group rates. Arrival: Lewiston, ID, or Clarkston, WA.

Floyd Held calls his jet boat excursion "the bargain trip of the century." He has logged more than 150,000 miles on this 182-mile run. Trips starting at 7:30 A.M. and back by 5:30 P.M. give passengers a "composite view of the Snake River." A picnic lunch and refreshments are served, and when it's warm enough for swimming, "children have a ball."

Dirigo Cruises, CT.

Windjammers

"Windjammer! Windjammer!" steamer crews once shouted derisively at the old-fashioned silhouette of oak hull and canvas—a 125-foot engineless sailing ship with 6,000 square feet of canvas billowing over her decks. Today the sight of the stately two- or three-masted ships brings only cries of delight, and more than likely the "crew" on board did not know ten days earlier the difference between a halyard and a sheet.

Cruising—and "crewing"—on a windjammer is today a favorite way to spend a vacation, and for some former landlubbers it has become an annual event. Anyone who grew up with Jack London's novels or Errol Flynn's films cannot help but have a secret longing for the sights, sounds and smells of the sea. And anyone who saw the tall ships in New York Harbor on the Bicentennial Fourth of July must have had a similar twinge.

There are many reasons for the appeal of a windjammer vacation. For some it is simply the relaxation. Or the camaraderie that develops on shipboard . . . the fun of exploring out-of-the-way harbors . . . finding satisfaction in the encounter with the wind, sea and sky . . . hearing the waves lap softly against the ship's hull at night . . . participating to the extent that you become a functioning cog in hoisting sails or anchor or taking a turn at the helm . . . or the abundant meals that come out of the ship's galley for ravenous, seagoing appetites.

Rerigged to carry passengers, the windjammers built in the 1800s once hauled lumber from Chesapeake Bay to Maine, or served as carriers for the Hudson River brick trade, or spent years freighting and oystering in Delaware Bay. Others that have been built expressly for passenger service in recent years are modeled after schooners with histories of running contraband during the Civil War or plying Far Eastern waters.

On a windjammer the cabins are not what you would call luxurious, but they are adequate, compact, shipshape and Bristol-fashion—the British Royal Navy term for perfect in every respect—and passengers keep their own cabins more or less that way. Basins with cold-water taps and cold-water showers, with a pail of hot water available for the asking, are standard equipment. Some cabins are equipped with electricity, though the voltage is too low as a rule for electric shavers or hair driers.

Life aboard a windjammer is unhurried and the itinerary unplanned. The captain decides each day's cruise according to the winds and tide. You'll sunbathe on deck on a gentle balmy day, or read a book and swap stories in a New England fog or rain. Or anchor in a blue-green crescent-shaped lagoon in the Caribbean to swim and snorkel. Or sail up a fjord and watch the seals and whales off the British Columbia coast. Anchoring in a snug cove or village harbor, you'll go ashore to explore. And a weekly event on a New England cruise is an old-fashioned clam- and lobsterbake on the beach of some remote island. Yummm!

With summer cruising through the picture-postcard offshore isles of Maine, and winter sailing among the tropical U.S. and British Virgin Islands in the Caribbean, a windjammer cruise can be planned nearly any time of year. The all-inclusive rates of approximately $50 per sailing day are reasonable, indeed, in comparison with many vacations. You generally are invited to board ship at no additional cost the evening before you sail.

And the memories you take away? "It was a quiet, dark sail up the bay under a late September moon," writes a vacationer, "with the northern lights shimmering green above black shapes of islands. The next morning, in predawn darkness, we walked a path through the woods to the eastern shore to watch from the cliffs as the rising sun brought mauve and apricot shadows to the silver blue of the sea—then flooded the sky and the sweep of sea at our feet with glorious light."

Take a paintbrush—and your camera.

Rates, tax, dates and what to bring are among the basic things to check. Be sure to take raingear. You may want to know to what extent you can participate in sailing the ship, or just what the arrangements are for washbasins and running water, cold or hot. No cabins have private heads (toilets). Ports of call, length of time ashore, minimum age limits, car parking and embarkation points are generally noted in brochures.

NEW ENGLAND

Captain Havilah S. Hawkins, Coastal Cruises, Box 798-G, Camden, ME 04843. (207) 236-2750. ME coast. Jun.–Sept. 28 passengers. Cabins for 1–3. $250/wk.

"There's no pushbutton entertainment on board the *Mary Day*," says Captain Hawkins, who has sailed passengers for 29 years. "People have to depend on their own resourses instead of sitting in front of TV. We visit fascinating out-of-the-way places. Our only auxiliary power is a small boat which can be used to push the schooner if there is no wind." Wash water is dipped out of barrels on deck. The captain depends on the help of passengers to cat the anchor and hoist the sail.

Coastwise Packet Company, Inc., Vineyard Haven, MA 02568. Att.: Capt. Robert S. Douglas. (617) 693-1699. 6-day cruises from Martha's Vineyard. 29 passengers. Min. age, 16 yrs. Cabins for 1–4. Jun.–Sept., $275/wk.

The *Shenandoah* is a square-rigged, topsail, engineless schooner built in 1964. She is modeled after the speedy American clipper that plied eastern waters 100 years ago, and on deck you get an idea of what the great American clippers were like. Today, ports of call are from Edgartown and Nantucket to Long Island Sound. The captain welcomes help with halyards and sheets.

Dirigo Cruises, Dept. G, 39 Waterside Lane, Clinton, CT 06413. Att.: Capt. Eben Whitcomb. (203) 669-7068. Jul.–Sept.: ME & East Coast, $275/wk. Dec.–Apr.: Carib., $325/wk. Family rates. May–Jun.: from NYC, $175/3 days. Up to 34 passengers. Also group charters.

The two-masted 95-foot schooner *Harvey Gamage* was built in a famous Maine shipyard and launched in 1973. "She combines the charm of a wooden vessel with the safety and comfort of modern technology," Captain Whitcomb explains. You are welcome aboard Sunday evening for weekly cruises that set sail Monday, returning on Saturday. In summer, cruises leave from Rockland, Maine, visiting coastal villages and islands. Winter cruises through the U.S. and British Virgins start at St. Thomas. May and June "Cruises to Nowhere" sail up the Hudson or around

Dirigo Cruises, CT.

Long Island, depending on wind, weather and tide. Captain Whitcomb also provides details on an accredited fall SeaMester for college students.

Maine Coast Cruises, Box A, Castine, ME 04421. Att.: Capt. Frederick B. Guild. (207) 596-6060. [Oct.–May: (207) 326-8856.] ME coast. Jun.–Sept. Cabins for 2 or 4. 1 wk., $295.

The three-masted, 132-foot *Victory Chimes* is the largest passenger-sailing vessel under the American flag. She carried cargo until 1949. "Visits to Maine's outer islands from Portland to Bar Harbor are very popular," writes her captain, who has sailed passengers for 44 years. "There is swimming over the side from a ladder, or from the beach while at anchor."

Maine Windjammer Cruises, Inc., PO Box 617-CA, Camden, ME 04843. Att.: Capt. Les Bex. (207) 236-2938. ME coast. 27 passengers; min. age, 12 yrs. Cabins for 2–6. 6-day cruises, Jul.–Aug., $225; Jun. & Sept., $205.

"Our ships, the proud *Mattie*, veteran of the West Indies fruit trade, and the doughty *Mercantile* are Yankee merchantmen, clipper-bowed and able, with billowing sails and hempen rigging," writes Captain Bex. He has operated sailing vacations since 1935. "The area we cruise, Penobscot Bay and adjacent waters, is well protected. We do not sail the high seas. For seagoing appetites there are New England family-style meals . . . roasts, ham, chicken, fish, chowders . . . all cooked in the galley on the wood-burning stove. A lobsterbake on shore is a highlight of the cruise."

Schooner *Bill of Rights*, Box 477-A, Newport, RI 02840. Att.: Capt. Joseph M. Davis, Jr. (401) 724-7612. [Nov.–Apr.: 110 Wilcox Ave., Pawtucket, RI 02860.] Southern New Eng. coast. May–Oct. 32 passengers. Cabins for 1–4. $300/wk., (end of Sept., $400/wk.). $100–$150 for 2–3-day wkends.

To Joe Davis, *Bill of Rights'* master, goes credit for the ship's existence. Launched in 1971, it's an engineless, 125-foot replica of a topsail schooner that flew the New York Yacht Club burgee in the 1850s and ran contraband during the Civil War. Under a good breeze, 6,000 square feet of sail will billow over her decks. Her top speed is 14 knots an hour. With a touch of elegance the family-style meals are served on pewter plates. Ports of call are from Maine to southern New England.

Schooner *Isaac H. Evans*, Box 482-G, Rockland, ME 04841. Att.: Capt. Douglas K. Lee. (207) 594-8007. ME coast. Up to 22 passengers. Jul.–Aug., $250/wk.; Jun. & Sept., $225/wk., or charter, $4,200/wk.

"Spend a relaxing week on an old-time sailing vessel," urges Captain Lee. "We sail during the day and find a snug harbor for the night. Lend a hand if you like . . . or just stretch out on deck and enjoy the sun." The *Isaac H. Evans*, built in 1886, spent years freighting and oystering in Delaware Bay. She has recently been rebuilt and rerigged. You may board Sundays for Monday sailings, returning on Saturday.

Schooner *Lewis R. French*, Box 482, Rockland, ME 04841. Att.: Capt. John C. Foss. (207) 594-8007. ME coast. 22 passengers. 6 days, Jun. & Sept., $200; Jul. & Aug., $225.

Built in 1871 as a cargo vessel for Maine ports, the 64-foot *Lewis R. French* is one of the oldest two-masted schooners. She has been gracefully refurbished for *sailing*—there's no inboard engine—with 10 small but comfortable passenger cabins and "a galley forward and potbelly stove back aft in the main cabin." For going ashore, there's a 13-foot motor-powered yawl, also a rowing boat. Rebuilt from keel up in 1976, the *French* is structurally a new vessel.

Schooner *Nathaniel Bowditch*, Res. Dept., Harborside, ME 04642. Att.: Capt. Gib Philbrick. (207) 326-4496 or 4440. ME coast. Jun.–Sept. Up to 24 passengers. $225/wk. Youth rates.

"Discover the glory of Penobscot Bay with some salty characters who make their marvelous vessel yours for a week," encourages an enthusiastic vacationer. The 81-foot schooner, built in East Boothbay in 1922 and completely refitted, 1971–73, sails in Maine's coastal islands where "the air is so clear and the sea so blue that you use up all your film in one day. You can help sail, and the food is terrific and never-ending," continues our vacationer. "The captain tells unbelievable stories that must be true, since no one could make them up." Sunday evening boardings for Monday sailings, returning on Saturday.

Schooner *Richard Robbins, Sr.*, Box 951, Rockland, ME 04841. Att.: David A. Johnson. (207) 354-6865. ME coast. 6–18 passengers. $225, Jul.–mid-Sept.; $200, Jun. & late Sept.; charter, $3,000/wk.

"Every week we have a clam- and lobsterbake on the shores of some remote island. At night we stop in a different port or cove. The passengers soon become a close-knit group with the four crew members, and everyone shares in the voyage.

Evenings are often spent 'yarning' in the main cabin, listening to tall tales of Maine and seafaring life." Guests may board Sunday evening for Monday morning sailings.

Yankee Packet Co., Box 736-AG, Camden, ME 04843. Att.: Capt. Mike Anderson. (207) 236-8873. ME coast. 22 passengers; min. age, 16 yrs. Cabins for 2–4 & Pullman bunks. Wkly. cruises: Jun. & Sept., $200; Jul.–Aug., $225.

   "The *Stephen Taber* is the oldest, active, pure sailing vessel documented as a U.S. merchant vessel," says Captain Anderson. "She is a two-masted gaff schooner, 68 feet long. Built in 1871, she started as a carrier for the Hudson River brick trade. Then she transported pulp wood on the Maine coast, and in 1946 was converted to passengers. On cruises we anchor in some cove or harbor between 4 P.M. and 6 P.M. After dinner people go ashore to hike or explore. Sometime during the week we have a lobster cookout on shore." Passengers board ship Sunday afternoon, and return the following Saturday.

BRITISH COLUMBIA

Whitewater Adventures Ltd., PO Box 46536, Vancouver, B.C. V6R 4G8. Att.: Dan Culver. (604) 736-2135. Coastal waters (BC). Jul.–Sept. 6–15 people, 4–10 days. 4 days, $195; 10 days, $450. Bring sleeping bag. Scheduled trips & charters. Arrival: Vancouver, BC. (See also *Backpacking, Float Trips.*)

   On a luxuriously appointed 51-foot ketch with private and semiprivate staterooms, you'll sail up fjords to glaciers and spectacular waterfalls, and among uninhabited islands of these beautiful coastal waters. Spot whales, porpoises, seals and sea lions. Drop anchor around 3:30 P.M. to fish, swim or explore ashore. It's a carefree life—with "gourmet food."

CARIBBEAN

Dirigo Cruises—see above for Virgin Island winter cruises.

Kimberly Cruises, Box 5086-A, St. Thomas, VI 00801. Att.: Capt. Arthur M. Kimberly. (809) 774-0650. Virgin Is. Nov.–May. 16 passengers in 2- & 4-berth cabins. 8-day cruises, $335.

   Under sail, the 90-foot brigantine *Romance* is a spectacular re-creation in cordage and canvas of a 19th-century vessel. Built by the Danes as a North Sea cargo ship, she was rerigged in 1965 for the filming of James Michener's *Hawaii*. In winter and spring the *Romance* makes leisurely cruises in the Virgin Islands, following no set itinerary. In summer and fall she sails to exotic ports in the South Pacific.

Schooner *Bill of Rights,* RI.

V ON OR IN WATER

Canoeing/Kayaking

When the Indians, French voyageurs, explorers and trappers of past centuries traveled the lakes and rivers of our continent in their birchbark canoes, they could hardly have envisioned a day when some 11,000,000 paddlers would be following their wilderness trails. Yet this is the estimated number of canoeing enthusiasts who each year cruise the canoeable rivers, lakes and coastal channels from Alaska's Alatna or Misty Fjords to North Carolina's Nantahala, California's American, Texas' Rio Grande, Mexico's Usumacinta and thousands of other waterways in between.

The largest canoe region is formed by the Boundary Waters Canoe Area in Minnesota and the Quetico Provincial Park in Ontario, separated by a 100-mile watery boundary. For wilderness travel on smooth water, this is the canoeists's nirvana. It is an area of interlocking lakes—thousands of them—that covers 1,062,000 acres in Minnesota alone with 1,200 miles of canoe trails. "No one can live long enough to explore it all," sighs a Minnesota canoeist.

This is a land of solitude and primeval wilderness beauty, a refuge for the black bear, wild mink and bald eagle, and the last range in the U.S. for the timber wolf. To maintain its pristine beauty, protective laws require that no cans or bottles be taken into the vast area.

The canoeists who enter the region each year pack in all the food and equipment they will need for the duration of their trips. They are aided by outfitters in the region who have developed an ultralight complete outfitting service for as little as $15 to $18 a day (less for families and groups), which includes everything but personal clothing (see Minnesota section). It is possible to drive or fly to a canoe base carrying only a small duffel of clothing, and paddle off for a week in the wilderness totally equipped with food, canoes and camping gear within an hour of your arrival.

Any expert canoeist will tell you that the sporty way to run a white-water river is not in a raft, but in a canoe up to Class II or Class III water, and in a kayak beyond that. But there is no objection to having raft support. For extended trips a raft can carry a longer-lasting food supply, and it provides a floating base if the rapids are too big a challenge.

Favorite white-water trips are down the rugged 92-mile corridor of Maine's Allagash Wilderness Waterway, or in the churning waters of Appalachian rivers, or through the rapids of western rivers the Snake, Salmon, Owyhee, Rogue, to name a few. Outfitters listed in the following pages take kayakers and canoeists on these and many other white-water rivers. The equipment they provide includes the tough,

Grumman Canoes.

hard-to-puncture inflatable canoe and kayak where side-bending rocks are mixed with white water. For flat-water canoeing, boats of aluminum, Fiberglas, canvas-covered wood and a laminate sheet are more common. But gone with the past is the voyageur's birchbark—except for a replica that holds ten paddlers now being used by a Minnesota outfitter.

Not all canoeing is done in remote wilderness or in rugged waters. Throughout the land, from New York to Michigan, the Ozarks and California, there are gently flowing rivers, easy to reach, and serviced by canoe liveries that provide rental canoes and a shuttle service for a river jaunt of a half day or longer.

A complete nationwide directory of canoe liveries is available, free, from Grumman Boats, Marathon, NY 13803. To locate canoe clubs in your area, contact the American Whitewater Affiliation, 264 East Side Drive, Concord, NH 03301, which has about 125 canoe and kayak club affiliates, or the U. S. Canoe Association, 606 Ross St., Middletown, OH 45042, with 42 club affiliates nationwide.

Canoeing is one of the most enjoyable and least expensive sports in the country. To rent a canoe costs from $6 to $10 a day for two or three paddlers. In the Boundary Waters, your total equipment and food for a week or so come to around $16 a day per canoeist—"cheaper than living at home," some say. A guided expedition to a remote wilderness may come to three times that amount. Whatever your preference, except for the rhythmic slap of the paddle and the roar of whitewater rapids, canoeing and kayaking are noiseless relative to the environment—so silent as to surprise a deer or moose at the water's edge, but not so silent as to exclude bird calls, wind in the trees, waves lapping on the shore and other sounds of nature.

What is your outdoorsmanship rating? Can you handle a canoe or kayak safely? Proper safety for white water includes personal flotation, a helmet, a spare paddle, proper clothing (wet suits when water or air temperatures are at 50 degrees), and grab loops. Can you swim? Set up a wilderness camp? If not, remember that guides are available even in areas where most trips are unguided. Check on equipment and food provided in rates and what you should bring. Double-check rates, tax, dates, canoeing skill needed, pre- and posttrip lodging and car parking. Find out about campsite facilities, maps, charts, anticipated weather, fishing license, car or canoe shuttle service, safety equipment and laws concerning wilderness camping in various regions. Novices may want gloves to prevent blisters, especially for lake paddling. On rivers you get help from the current—sometimes too much! And you never throw refuse overboard. Other rules, written or unwritten, on most waterways are: Wear life jackets, don't mix booze with canoeing, and be sure your skill is equal to the water. Let's say that again: life jackets. . . no booze. . . adequate skill. These are the rules. If everyone observed them, the statistics would look better.

ALASKA

Alaska Discovery Enterprises, PO Box 337-AG, Juneau, AK 99802. Att.: Chuck Horner, Ware Hulbert, Gary Cole. (907) 586-6245. Glacier Bay Nalt. Monument, Hubbard Glacier, Granite Fjords, Tracy Arm & Admiralty Is, May–Aug. Smooth water. Usually about 10 canoeists. 7 days, $350–$500; bring or rent sleeping gear. Arrival: Juneau, AK.

Love of the wilderness and wanting to show this remarkable area to others motivate the "magnificent adventures" that Horner, Hulbert and Cole offer. Most of their frequently scheduled trips start by charter flight or boat, and all are for kayakers except for Admiralty Island, where canoeists paddle the lake system. On these excursions you explore glaciers—some "calving" almost constantly with falling towers of ice. You will observe rookeries, the bald eagle, a glacier bear, inquisitive seals, porpoises, spawning salmon and other wildlife. Or visit a picturesque Indian village and mineral hot springs. Or camp in a lush green forest. "Few want to leave," these kayaking specialists say.

Alaska Pioneer Canoers Assn., Box 931-AG, Soldotna, AK 99669. Att.: John A. Stephan. (907) 262-4003. Swanson & Moose riv. Kenai Peninsula, Natl. Moose Range, Swan Lake. Smooth water. May–Oct. 1–60 canoeists, 1–10 days. W./guide & full outfitting: $20–$25/day for 15–35 canoeists; $15 for 36–60. Bring sleeping gear. Canoe only, $15/day. Arrival: Anchorage or Kenai, AK.

"This is primitive camping," explains John Stephan. "Everyone pitches in." He teaches young canoeists to set up camp, cook, pack, portage, prospect or whatever. The area is remote and the canoe system well mapped for those who go alone. John's guide service caters to groups, those who need help portaging, and families who want to expand their camping and canoeing know-how.

Alaska Wilderness Expeditions, Inc., Box 7814, Ketchikan, AK 99901. Att.: Dale Pihlman. (907) 247-8444. Misty Fjords Wilderness. Jun.–Aug. Smooth water. 2–10 canoeists, 4 or more days. 7 days, $400 (addl. days, $50), incl. sleeping gear, tents, transport to/from river, 1 night Ketchikan. Also canoe or kayak rental pkg. Misty Fjords, 7 days, $250; addl. days, $6/person. Arrival: Ketchikan, AK. (See also *Float Trips*.)

Southeast Alaska's jagged 5,000- to 8,000-foot mountains and active glaciers drop sharply into the rivers and fjords of the proposed 2.1 million-acre Misty Fjords Wilderness, scene of AWE's salt-water canoe trips. "It's a young and spectacular land still being shaped by ice and water," as Dale describes it, "a geological drama." His experienced guides lead canoeists through the fjords, and into the rain forests of spruce, hemlock and cedar, the home of mountain goats, eagles, Sitka deer and wolves.

Kenai Guide Service, Box 40-A, Kasilof, AK 99610. Att.: George R. Pollard. (907) 262-5496. Chilikadrotna & Mulchatna riv. (AK). Jun.–Aug. White water. 6–10 kayakers. 12 days, $780, incl. bush flight to/from riv. Bring sleeping gear. Arrival: Homer, AK. (See also *Backpacking*.)

"Paddle an inflatable kayak down 200 miles of wild and scenic river in the tundra-taiga wilderness of southwestern Alaska," urges George Pollard. "There's white-water excitement heightened by the sight of a black wolf disappearing into the willows, a caribou and calf swimming to the opposite bank, harlequin ducks taking flight or a grizzly whuffing at the strange beings on the river. We stop on a gravel bar, early, to catch grayling for supper."

Mountains North Guide Service, 851 University Ave., Fairbanks, AK 99701. Att.: Ev Wenrick. (907) 479-2984. Fortymile, Yukon, Delta, Chena, Birch Creek, Chatanika, Alatna, Wild, John & other AK. riv. Jun.–Aug. Smooth & white water. 3–10 canoeists, 3 or more days. $40/day; fly-in trips, $50/day. Bring or rent sleeping gear. Arrival: Fairbanks, AK. (See also *Backpacking, Mountaineering, Ski Touring*.)

Inflatable canoes and kayaks open Alaska's interior and Brooks Range to Ev Wenrick's modern-day explorers. His small groups follow a flexible schedule, with time to catch "the rhythms of the wilderness through fishing, photography, nature study, berry-picking, panning for gold, relishing the quiet." Camp chores are shared, and basic survival methods are taught.

Sourdough Outfitters, Bettles, AK 99723. Att.: David Ketscher. (907) 692-5252. Wild, John, Alatna, Koyukuk & Kobuk riv. (AK) Jun.–Sept. Smooth & white water. Up to 8 canoeists, 5–30 days. 6–8 days, $35–$500, incl. flight. Bring sleeping gear. Arrival: Bettles, AK. (See also *Backpacking, Float Trips, Ski Touring, Dog Sledding*.)

With mostly easy Class I water and occasional Class II rapids, the paddling is leisurely on these trips through the majestic Brooks Range wilderness. Canada geese and their young dart across the gravel bars. You can sight moose, wolves and black and grizzly bears on shore, and catch grayling, lake trout, pike, salmon and sheefish. The Alatna and Koyukuk trips may be tacked onto scheduled backpacking trips.

CALIFORNIA

W. C. "Bob" Trowbridge Canoe Trips, 625 B St., Santa Rosa, CA 94501. (707) 433-4116 or 542-0598. 6 CA rivers & Lower Colorado Riv. (AZ). All yr. Up to 10 days. 1 day, $9.25; 2 days, $18; transport, $5.25. Bring sleeping gear. Car-top carrier & trailer rates.

Bob Trowbridge pioneered canoeing in California. He has "the world's largest canoe fleet" for trips on the Russian (headquarters in Healdsburg), American and Feather (Fair Oaks), Sacramento (Los Molinas), Eel and Klamath (Santa Rosa) and the Lower Colorado (Lake Havasu City, AZ). He offers special group rates in midweek (4 or 5 days), and at Healdsburg canoeists are treated to a barbecue buffet dinner (about $3).

Zephyr River Expeditions, PO Box 529, Columbia, CA 95310. Att.: Robert Ferguson. (209) 532-6249. Klamath Riv. (CA). Jun.–Sept. White water. Up to 19 canoeists. 2 days wkend, $100; 4 days midwk., $180. Bring sleeping gear. Group & family rates. (See also *Float Trips*.)

Your paddle and life jacket are your companions as you shoot the rapids and cruise the calm water of the Klamath River in an inflatable canoe. No previous white-water experience needed—guides offer individual instruction on techniques of bracing, correct paddle use and reading water, then send you off on your own.

CONNECTICUT

Riverrun Outfitters, Inc., Main St., Falls Village, CT 06031. Att.: Mark Caliendo. (203) 824-5579. Mar.–Oct. Up to 100 people, 1–5 days. Kayak & canoe courses, Housatonic (MA & CT), 2 days, $85, incl. equipment, shuttles, & lunch. Canoe & kayak trips: Upper Hudson (NY), Rio Grande (TX). Group rates. (See also *Ski Touring*.)

Mark Caliendo runs a 2-day course for kayakers every Saturday and Sunday on the Housatonic, with 6 hours of instruction each day. Riverrun has its own slalom course with 9 gates, and an extra day's instruction includes slalom technique, downriver or wild water, and Eskimo roll. With white water from Class I to Class V, Caliendo considers the Housatonic an excellent beginner's river—"not the Class IVs and Vs, of course."

DELAWARE

Wilderness Canoe Trips, Inc., Box 7125, Talleyville, Wilmington, DE 19803. Att.: Jay Dean Poole. (302) 654-2227. [Nov.–Mar.: 1002 Parkside Dr., Oak Lane Manor, Wilmington, DE 19803. (302) 658-0515.] Brandywine Riv. (PA), Algonquin Wilderness (Ont.) & LaVerendrye Provincial Park (PQ). Rentals: canoes, $40/wk.; food, $50/wk.; camp equip., $30/wk.; also daily rates. Complete outfitting: $11/day. Put-in/take-out transport, $.20/mi. Bring sleeping gear.

"We are unique in that we offer both a partial and complete outfitting service on a daily basis," Jay D. Poole explains, "as well as guided trips." His complete outfitting includes ultra lightweight food in burnable, waterproof packages, Grumman or Old Town canoes, tents, life jackets, all camping equipment except sleeping gear and (at a small extra charge) transport to and from river locales. His Algonquin trips are especially for young adults of 18 to 30.

FLORIDA

Canoe Outpost of Florida. 4 locations open all yr. Peace Riv.: Rt. 2, Box 301, Arcadia 33821, (813) 494-1215. Suwannee, Santa Fe & Itchtucknee: PO Box 473, Branford 32008, (904) 935-1226. Withlacochee: PO Box 188, Nobleton 33554, (904) 796-4343. Alafia: Rt. 1, Box 414-K, Valrico 33594, (813) 681-2666. Rentals, half day to overnight, $5–$25; under 12 yrs., half price; under 6, free. Pick-up & load rates. Also guided trips in Everglades (4 days, $90), Okefenokee Swamp (GA), Boundary Waters (MN) & Buffalo Riv. (AR). (See also *Youth Adventures*.)

Florida is one of the places you can go canoeing all year—*freshwater* canoeing on six rivers. Canoe Outpost also guides 4-day trips through the fascinating Everglades and in Georgia's Okefenokee Swamp. They provide all necessary camping equipment—but bring your own camp food.

Tropical Wilderness Outfiters, 15355 S. Dixie Hwy., PO Box 570898, Miami, FL 33157. Att.: Lawrence Keller. (305) 253-8131. Everglades Natl. Park: Oct.–May, up to 12 canoeists, up to 10 days, $28/day incl. food. Suwannee Riv.: summer, up to 40 canoeists, 3–4 wks. Gulf Coast: up to 40 canoeists, 9–10 days. Group & pkg. rates.

On leisurely Everglades trips, you see animals and birds by the thousands—flamingos, storks, even rosette spoonbills (ibis). For a longer excursion, canoe for 3 to 4 weeks down 300 miles of the Suwannee from the Georgia border to the Gulf. Or start in Goodland, canoe through mangrove islands along the Gulf Coast, then on through the Everglades. Canoeing in Central American (also backpacking and rafting) is another guided specialty; rates on request. The longer trips may include college credit courses in ecology, photography, archaeology and anthropology for limited groups.

GEORGIA
Wilderness Southeast, Rt. 3, Box 619-L, Savannah, GA 31406. Att.: Dick Murlless. (912) 355-8008. Okefenokee Swamp & Ogeechee Riv. (GA); Suwanee Riv. & Everglades (FL). All yr. Smooth & white water. 10–20 canoeists. 2–7 days. $20/day incl. sleeping gear. Group & youth rates. (See also *Backpacking, Scuba Diving—FL, Youth Adventures*.)

"A trip in the Okefenokee," Dick Murlless tells us, "is a unique learning experience. No other swamp has its concentration of wildlife and wildflowers. We frequently see large alligators, white ibis, sandhill cranes and osprey." You paddle 5 to 8 hours daily with little or no current. An alternative is the Suwannee. Its banks rise higher, channeling the water and producing a gentle current—wild and yet easy to canoe. "My staff are well qualified professional biologists and ecologists," Murlless notes. "We care about our trippers."

IDAHO
Leonard Expeditions, PO Box 98, Stanley, ID 83278. Att.: Joe Leonard. (208) 774-3325. ID & OR riv. & lakes. Summer. Hrly. lessons: $7.50–$10, pvt. $10–$15. Inquire for trip rates. (See also *Ski Touring, Youth Adventures*.)

"We have established one of the safest and most rapidly learned kayak courses now available," Leonard says of his kayaking school. Fundamental skills are taught in a swimming pool, then on a lake. From there you progress to a gentle section of the Salmon River, then to more difficult white water. Besides hourly lessons

Grumman Canoes.

Leonard offers a 2-day camping package, and 3- to 6-day guided trips down the Owyhee or Main Salmon.

Primitive Area Float Trips, Inc., Box 585-D, Salmon, ID 83467. Att.: Stanton C. Miller. (208) 756-2319. Middle Fork & Main Salmon, Snake & Selway (ID), Owyhee (OR). Apr.–Oct. 4–15 kayakers. 3–10 days. $40/day incl. river support. Group rates. Canoes, kayaks, gear extra. Inflatable U-row trips arranged. Arrival: Salmon, ID. (See also *Float Trips.*)

"We furnish complete logistical support for kayakers," Stan says, "and participants need only bring their own canoes or kayaks, or rent ours." He cautions that you should have some skill before operating the crafts in these waters.

The Wilderness Institute, PO Box 338, Bonners Ferry, ID 83805. Att.: Larry E. Fidler. (208) 267-3013. Yellowstone Lake (WY), Ootsa Lake & Inside Passage (BC), Yukon Riv. (YT). Jun.–Aug. Smooth & white water. 8–12 canoeists. 10–12 days, $235–$250, sleeping gear incl. (See also *Backpacking, Mountaineering, Ski Touring.*)

On the lakes of Yellowstone Park beginning and intermediate canoeists paddle along ever changing shorelines of grassy meadows, marshes, dense forests, thermal pools, geyser basins and steep mountain slopes—a geologic extravaganza with some of the best fishing in the world. The remote Ootsa Lake trip, deep in the massive glaciated peaks of B.C.'s Coastal Range, is for intermediates. For the experienced, there are trips on the Yukon River and the Inside Passage—a remote ocean/mountain wilderness of the British Columbia coast where awesome ice formations hang overhead.

ILLINOIS

Chicagoland Canoe Base, Inc., 4019 N. Narragansett, Chicago, IL 60634. Att.: Ralph Frese. (312) 777-1489. Northeast IL. Quiet water. All yr. Canoes, $10/day, $17/wkend, $30/wk.; double rate for kayaks. Rates incl. paddles, life jackets, tie-down ropes & cartop carrier. Damage deposit required.

The Chicagoland Canoe Base will help paddlers select a suitable river for their time and skill. It has 65 canoes and 10 kayaks (with flotation bag, sprayskirt, etc.) for rent, and 6-canoe trailers. CCB provides a free brochure, *Chicagoland Canoe Trails,* which describes local waterways and lists Illinois canoe clubs, and sells a wide range of canoes, kayaks, accessories, books and maps. "With 21 canoeable waterways we offer variety, historical heritage, wildlife and scenery," comments "Mr. Canoe" Ralph Frese.

INDIANA

Oldfather Canoe & Kayak Center, RR 2, 60390 S.R. 15, Box 451, Goshen, IN 46526. Att.: Russ Oldfather. (219) 533-2295. St. Joseph, Elkhart & Pigeon riv. (IN & MI). Smooth water. May–Sept. 6–50 canoeists. 1–4 days, $10/day/canoe, $12/day/kayak. Group & shuttle rates, & instruc.

Oldfathers, Indiana's largest canoe center, will help you select the craft to fit your needs, teach you how to paddle, and introduce you to paddling clubs. Its headquarters are close to many streams. The Elkhart tumbles through farmland. On the St. Joseph you're apt to see deer and many blue herons. The Pigeon runs through wild wilderness with many pullovers and past fallen trees. And there's the Fawn, Little Elkhart, Trout Creek and many lakes.

Whitewater Valley Canoe Rental, Inc., PO Box 2, Rt. 52 (West), Brookville, IN 47012. Att.: R. T. Ritz. (317) 647-5434. Whitewater Riv. & Whitewater Canal (IN). Smooth & white water. All yr. Unltd. canoeists. Canoes $8–$17/day incl. shuttle. Group & family rates.

Glimpse abundant wildlife and historical landmarks as you wind through the scenic Hoosier countryside. Paddle downstream at your own pace, or swim, picnic and fish. Several wooded riverside sites and islands for camping out.

LOUISIANA

Pack & Paddle Inc., 601 Pinhook Rd. E., Lafayette, LA 70501. Att.: Joan & Dick Williams. (318) 232-5854. Whiskey Chitto Creek (LA). All yr. Smooth water. 1–3 days. Canoes, $10/day; guide, $40/day. Camping gear & maxivan addl. Arrival: Lafayette, LA. (See also *Backpacking*.)

Pack & Paddle trips begin with a 2-hour practice session on a nearby lake, then proceed to "clear, fast-running streams and white sandbars of pristine quality." They also take canoeists into the Atchafalaya Basin, Louisiana's great wilderness swamp.

MAINE

Allagash Canoe Trips, 69 Winchester St., Presque Isle, ME 04769. Att.: Dana Shaw. (207) 764-0494. Allagash & St. John riv. White water. Jun.–Sept. 1–12 canoeists. Guided/outfitted trips, 3–5 days, $50/day.

"Good fishing and wilderness travel," says Dana Shaw. "A canoe trip through the Maine Wilderness is a memorable adventure." Besides trips for families and adults, he also guides canoeing and camping for teens. He has an M.A. in education and can give private white water and camping courses.

Allagash River Canoe Trips, Rt. 5-A, 16 Woodside Rd., Augusta, ME 04330. Att.: Frederick W. King. (207) 623-4429. Allagash Riv. Smooth & white water. May–Sept. 1–5 canoeists. 12 scheduled 8-day guided trips, $450/person incl. food & all exc. sleeping bag. Arrival: Augusta, ME.

Trips start in the Telos Lake area and end at Allagash, with lakes, ponds and plenty of rapids for white water practice. "If you don't already know how, you'll learn to use a setting pole in rapids," advises Fred King. Ask about his two cabins in the Maine woods. "I like to take my people on unusual side trips, such as a visit to a logging camp," he says.

Allagash Wilderness Outfitters, Frost Pond, Star Rt. 76-A, Greenville, ME 04441. Att.: Rick Givens. No tel. Allagash, St. John, Penobscot riv. & Chesuncook, Chamberlain-Eagle-Churchill lakes. Smooth & white water. May–Sept. 2–26 canoeists. 2–14 days. Canoe $6.50/day; w./food & sleeping gear, $15/day. Guides & transport extra.

"The novice or expert can find a unique, beautiful wilderness experience on these waterways," predicts Rick Givens. "For unguided parties we provide transport, route planning and quality equipment—do our best to give you an unforgettable vacation." And with "good meals," adds a Scout leader.

Maine Wilderness Canoe Basin, Springfield, ME 04487. Att.: Carl W. Selin. (207) 989-3636, ext. 631. Grand Lake Chain, ME lakes & riv. May–Oct. Smooth & white water. 1–100 canoeists, 1–30 days. $14/day w./complete outfitting. Bring sleeping gear. Group rates. Also 1–10 kayakers, 3–4 days, $16/day. Arrival: Bangor, ME. (See also *Ski Touring, Snowmobiling, Youth Adventures*.)

Located on the northern shore of 4-mile Pleasant Lake amidst the dense Maine forests, this canoeing base, Captain Selin assures us, is the ideal spot for beginning a canoe trip into the great variety of lakes, streams and rivers of eastern Maine. The entire Grand Lake Chain opens with more than 40 miles of wilderness waterways—white water, placid streams and wilderness islands—for exploration and excellent fishing. A special feature of the operation is kayak outfitting and progressive areas to learn kayaking.

Grumman Canoes.

Saco Bound/Northern Waters, PO, Fryeburg, ME 04037. Att.: Ned McSherry. (603) 447-2177. Saco & Androscoggin riv., Rangeley Lakes region, other NH & ME areas. Smooth & white water. 6–10 on guided trips, unltd. rentals. 1–10 days. Group & youth rates. Arrival: North Conway or Berlin, NH.

Saco Bound and its Northern Waters outpost offer a complete canoe and kayak service. Saco's rental program enables you to launch from convenient racks right at the river's edge for trips of various lengths at any time of year. The Northern Waters outpost is on one of the Androscoggin's rapids, and McSherry calls it "the best summer white water spot in the eastern U.S." The intersecting Rapid and Magalloway are Class IV rivers, suited for closed boat paddling, while much of the 70 miles on the Androscoggin and Connecticut is within the beginner's capacity. Northern Waters' school specializes in kayak instruction, with a 25-gate white water slalom. "Kayaking is a family sport," McSherry maintains, "and can be relaxing as well as challenging."

St. Croix Voyageurs, Box A-197, China, ME 04926. Att.: George L. Dwelley. (207) 968-2434. Allagash, St. John, Penobscot & St. Croix riv. Jul.–Sept. Smooth & white water. Up to 12 canoeists. 7–10 days. 7 days, $325, incl. all but sleeping bag. Group rates. Arrival: Greenville, ME. (See also *Youth Adventures.*)

In August and September George Dwelley schedules Allagash trips which individuals may join. And he arranges custom trips all summer on the Allagash and other rivers. "The northwoods is a lumberman's paradise," he says, "where well-planned multiple use of the land—for both recreation and lumbering—follows the Maine tradition. We give canoeists a good historical, geological and topographical idea of the country."

Sunrise County Canoe Expeditions, Inc., Cathance Lake, Grove PO, ME 04638. Att.: Martin Brown. (207) 454-7708. St. Croix, Machias & St. John riv., Grand Lake Chain (ME). Smooth & white water. May–Oct. 1–25 canoeists. 2–15 days. $35/day w./guide, canoes, gear, food & transportation. Canoe only, $8.50/day. Also 3-wk. teens (11–17 yrs.) trip, $390.

Marty Brown provides the only complete outfitting and guide service in the remote semiwilderness of Washington County—at the northeast tip of the U.S. with forests, meadowlands and hundreds of miles of canoeable waterways. He considers canoe voyaging an art, and will teach you to run rips gracefully in a few days, with both paddle and pole. "Marty is skilled, young and strong, a good instructor interested in carrying on the tradition of the old Maine guide," writes one canoeist. "He also tells a good story and provides excellent food."

MASSACHUSETTS

South Bridge Boat House, Main St. (Rt. 62), Concord, MA 02723. Att.: George F. Rohan. (617) 369-9438. Sudbury, Concord & Assabet riv. Apr.–Nov. Up to 100 canoes. Up to 7 days. $2.50–$3.60/hr., $12–$17/day.

"There's *calm* paddling on 18 miles of river where you'll see lots of ducks, turtles and geese," says George Rohan. Also glimpse old houses and churches, see where the Minutemen stood and go under historic Concord Bridge. Picnic areas along the way. A handy, close-by service for Bostonians.

MICHIGAN

Smooth but swift, flowing through forests and farmlands, Michigan rivers challenge do-it-yourself canoeists with sharp bends, overhanging trees and occasional log jams, stumps and dams. "It's a leisurely and rewarding experience in country still pretty much untouched and full of birds and animals," canoeists say.

Forest campgrounds dot the riverbanks—many accessible only from the streams. Rivers in western Michigan flow into Lake Michigan, and those in the east into Lake Huron. From Grayling, a center for canoeists, you can paddle 240 miles in either direction—west on the Manistee River or east on the AuSable. Several of the waterways—the Pere Marquette, Manistee and AuSable—are being considered for classification in the National Wild and Scenic Rivers system. The smaller Betsie, Boardman, Jordan, Rogue and White rivers already belong to Michigan's own Scenic Rivers System.

Canoe liveries offer an hour's paddle to ten days of canoe-camping from April through October, though the hardy paddle on through the winter as long as the water is liquid. Rentals run from $6 to $10 a day plus shuttle fees. A good source for livery listings is *Carefree Days* (West Michigan Tourist Association, 136 Fulton East, Grand Rapids, MI 49503), or *The East Michigan Travel Guide* (Michigan Tourist Association, Bay City, MI 48706).

Among the livery services for the state's many streams are the following:

AuSable Riv.:   **Carlisle Canoe Rental,** 110 State St., PO Box 150-A, Grayling, MI 49738. (517) 348-2301.

Carr's Pioneer Canoe Livery, 217 Alger St., Grayling, MI 49738. (517) 348-5851.

Jolly Redskin Canoe Livery, PO Box 396, Grayling, MI 49738. (517) 348-5611.

Paddle Brave Canoe Livery Campground, Box 998-A, Rt. 1, Roscommon, MI 48653. (517) 275-5273.

Penrod's AuSable Canoe Trips, 100 Maple St., Grayling, MI 49738. (517) 348-3711.

Betsie Riv.:   **Betsie River Canoe Livery,** RR 1, M-115, Thompsonville, MI 49683. (616) 438-6145.

Big Manistee Riv.:   **Chippewa Landing,** PO Box 234, Cadillac, MI 49601. (616) 775-3441.

Huron Riv.:   **Eco Sports Canoe & Kayak Rental,** 275 W. Liberty, Box 281,

Milford, MI 48042. (313) 685-4310. [Eve. & Nov.-Apr.: 1257 W. Highland Rd., Highland, MI 48031. (313) 887-2521.]

Jordan Riv.:   **Village Inn Canoe Livery,** Box 25, Walloon Lake, MI 49796. (616) 535-2475.

Père Marquette Riv.:   **Baldwin Canoe Rental,** Box 265, Baldwin, MI 49304. (616) 745-4669.

Pine Riv.:   **Marrik's Pine River Canoe Service,** Rt. 1, Wellston, MI 49689. (616) 862-3471.

Rogue Riv.:   **Grand Rogue Campground,** 6400 W. River Dr., Belmont, MI 49306. (616) 361-1053.

St. Joseph Riv.:   **Callman Canoe Center (American Canoe Association),** PO Box 98, Buchanan, MI 49107. (616) 695-3218.

Thunder Bay Riv.:   **Red Lantern Canoe Livery,** Box 285, Rt. 3, Atlanta, MI 49709. (517) 785-3296.

White Riv.:   **Happy Mohawk Canoe Livery,** RR 2, 735 Fruitvale Rd., Montague, MI 49437. (616) 894-4209.

MINNESOTA

In northern Minnesota they'll tell you there's about as much water as land. It makes for some of the best wilderness canoeing in the world. The *Introduction* to this chapter describes this vast Boundary Waters Canoe Area which offers 3 million acres of wilderness canoeing.

There are three gateways from the U.S. side for canoeing the wilderness chains of lakes: the Western Gateway from Crane Lake; Central Gateway from Ely, Winton and Babbitt; and the Eastern Gateway from Grand Marais and Tofte. Although outfitters can provide guides, canoeing parties generally are on their own, an independence made possible by an unusual outfitting service.

If you already have some equipment of your own, the outfitters' *partial outfitting* (or rental) service will supply the rest. But their real specialty is known as *full outfitting,* with the further refinement of *ultralight outfitting.* Rates for this service range from $15 to $18 a day per canoeist, with discounts for children and groups. For this daily rate you receive a canoe, paddles, life jackets, food (freeze-dried or dehydrated), tent, sleeping gear, cooking and camping equipment, maps, route recommendations, canoeing instruction (if needed), and a place to park your car if that's the way you arrived.

Many outfitters, for an extra fee, provide cabin accommodations and meals at the start or end of your trip; a store for clothing, tackle or other gear; a towboat or float plane for put-in or take-out deep in the wilderness, and pickup in Duluth or Hibbing.

Most outfitters are open from May to October. With few exceptions, three days is the minimum for fully outfitted trips, but rentals (partial outfitting) can be arranged for a day.

ARTA North Country, 5375 Eureka Rd., Shorewood, MN 55331. Att.: Duncan Storlie. (612) 474-5190. MN & WI riv. & lakes. Smooth & white water. 8–25 canoeists, 2–7 days. Lake Superior, 7 days, $270; Flambeau Riv., 4 days, $155. Bring sleeping gear. (See also *Float Trips*—CA.)

In giant Voyageur Fur Trade 34-foot canoes, replicas of the original ones of birchbark, 10 paddlers island-hop in Lake Superior's south shore Apostle Islands area. ARTA's interpreter-guides discuss the folklore of the voyageur routes and frontier life. Also shorter outings on Lake Superior's north shore in Canada, and white water canoeing and kayaking on Wiscoinsin's Flambeau River in the clean, clear North Country.

Bear Track Outfitting Co., Box 51, Grand Marais, MN 55604. Att.: David & Cathi Williams. (218) 387-1162. Boundary Waters. May–Oct. Smooth water. Up to 40 canoeists. 1 or more days. Complete outfitting, $15/day, less after 3 days. Group rates & rentals. Arrival: Grand Marais, MN. (See also *Backpacking, Ski Touring, Youth Adventures.*)

Stressing personalized service and an ecological approach to the wilderness, Cathi and Dave Williams will plan a route through the BWCA to fit your capabilities. They provide ultralight meal units and show you how to use the equipment and handle the canoe.

Bill Rom's Canoe Country Outfitters, Inc., Dept. AT, Box 30, Ely, MN 55731. Att.: Bob Olson. (218) 365-4046. Boundary Waters. May–Oct. Complete outfitting: adult $18/day; under 16 yrs. & groups, $14.50/day. Also partial outfitting, fly-ins & outpost cabins.

"Outfitting canoe trips is our main business, and our entire attention is directed toward assuring joyful, pleasant and properly outfitted trips," writes Bob Olson. "No other outfitter can match us in our knowledge of the canoe country and wilderness outfitting. We're one of the oldest and largest in the country."

Border Lakes Outfitters, Dept. AG, PO Box 158, Winton, MN 55796. Att.: Jack Niemi. (218) 365-3783. Boundary Waters. May–Oct. Complete outfitting: $15.50/day, $100/wk.; (under 13 yrs., $12/day, $80/wk.). 10% off for over 10 days. Also Scout, church & other youth group rates.

This outfitter has offered complete and partial outfits for canoe trips into the heart of the Quetico-Superior wilderness since 1929. Sigurd F. Olson, famed author and wilderness preservationist, was part owner and chief guide here during the '30s and '40s. Located on Fall Lake, 3 miles east of Ely.

Canadian Waters, Inc., Box ATG, 111 E. Sheridan St., Ely, MN 55731. Att.: Jon Waters. (218) 365-3202. Any no. canoeists. $20/day, $14.50 under 16 yrs. or for 8 or more canoeists. Free transport to 5 put-in points. Guide rates. Arrival: Duluth or Ely, MN.

Jon Waters claims he is the world's largest canoe outfitter and the first to offer ultralightweight equipment and provisions. His brochure describes a canoe trip as an "adventure in living" and clarifies how to arrange one.

Crane Lake Outfitters, Box 74, Crane Lake, MN 55725. Att.: Robert K. Anderson. (218) 993-2287. May–Sept. Boundary Waters. 1-100 canoeists. 3-14 days. Complete outfitting: $15/day, $10.50/day w./10 or more people, $95/wk. Also partial out-fitting.

This is the first total outfitting service at Crane Lake, western entrance to the Boundary Waters, with guides, pickup at Duluth, Hibbing and Orr, and tow and fly-in service to remote lakes. They specialize in ultralight equipment and food— "nutritious, delicious and easy to prepare"—with 18 suggested menus from which to choose.

Duane's Outfitters, St. Hwy. 21, Box 145, Dept. A, Babbitt, MN 55706. Att.: Duane S. Arvola. (218) 827-2710. Boundary Waters. May–Sept. Canoes, $6/day. Complete outfitting: $45/3 days, $93/wk.; longer trips, $90/wk. plus $12/extra day. Rates for Scouts, religious groups, etc., leader free for every 9 canoeists under 19 yrs. Partial outfitting, $6/day.

Duane's is a family-run business specializing in personal service which aims to send campers home happy. "A canoe trip has a special magic to help people understand each other better," he explains. He can outfit more than 400 campers at a time and offers hot showers and a sauna at trip's end.

Gunflint Northwoods Outfitters, Box 100-AD, Grand Marais, MN 55604. Att.: Bruce Kerfoot. (218) 388-2296. Gunflint Trail, Boundary Waters, Quetico & Canada's North Country. May–Oct. Up to 80 canoeists. 3–30 days. Complete outfitting, $16.50–$21.50/day, $8–$10/day for child.

"Paddle the route of the voyageur and enjoy the largest canoeing wilderness in the world," urges Bruce Kerfoot. He speaks of being known for "the quality and quantity" of his food supply. He arranges fly-ins and towboats, and, for before and after the trip, a choice of rustic or deluxe lodge accommodations with meals and sauna.

Huntersville Outfitters, Rt. 4, Box 308-A, Menahga, MN 56464. Att.: Turk Kennelly. (218) 564-4279. Crow Wing & Shell riv. May–Sept. Smooth water. Up to 100 canoeists. 1–14 days. Complete outfitting: $6/day. Guide rates. Shuttle service. Arrival: Menahga, MN.

Canoe the comparatively mild rapids of the Crow Wing, passing old Hudsons Bay Co. boat landings on the sandy beaches. Then, after 3 or 4 days, take one of the Kennellys' horses overland along the same stretch of river. The Kennellys say the Crow Wing has a wilderness image—it's great for families.

Irv Funk Outfitting, Rt. 2, Box 51-A, Sebeka, MN 56477. (218) 472-3272. Crow Wing Lake Chain & Crow Wing, Shell & Mississippi riv. May–Oct. Smooth water. Up to 150 canoeists. 1–8 days. $5/day ea. for 2 or more, incl. all but food. Group & guide rates. Canoe only, $5/day. Arrival: Sebeka, MN.

"This heavily forested country is very beautiful," writes Irv Funk. "There's abundant wildlife, fine swimming and fishing, and campsites along the trail. The rapids are not dangerous, but still exciting."

Pigeon River Expeditions, PO Box 547, Hovland, MN 55606. Att.: H. F. Drabik. (218) 475-2359. Boundary Waters (MN), Quetico Provincial Park (Ont.). Jun.–Aug. Smooth water. 5–8 canoeists. 5–12 days. 6 days, about $100, incl. sleeping gear; less w./own equip. Group & youth rates. Arrival: Hovland, MN.

"We run a quality approach," says Barry Drabik, "and our services have been used by two TV shows for instruction and public service programs." His specialty trips include canoeing, camping, fishing, fur trade history, Indian history, wildlife, birds, plants, photography, geology, camp cooking, survival and anthropology. Routes begin on Canadian lakes and rivers, ending on the Pigeon River. "We stress keeping our people away from the more traveled routes," Harry notes. "Each trip is an individualized affair that helps people learn the ropes. Novices have nothing to fear."

Quetico-Superior Canoe Outfitters, Dept. AG, Box 89, Ely, MN 55731. Att.: Bernie Carlson. (218) 365-5480. 2–30 canoeists. $16.50/day, $12.50 for 10 or more. Guide rates.

"You'll find solitude and stillness in the vast outdoors. The only sounds are the roar of a waterfall, an outcry from a wild inhabitant of this forest land, movements of your own party . . ." is Bernie Carlson's description of a canoe trip here. His base is on Moose Lake, 20 miles northeast of Ely, and your trip begins at his dock.

Tip of the Trail, Box 147-GT, Grand Marais, MN 55604. Att.: Bill Douglas. (218) 388-2225. Boundary Waters (MN), Quetico Provincial Park (Ont.). May–Oct. Smooth & white water. 2–200 people. 3–30 days. $17/day, $12/day under 16 yrs. Sleeping gear incl. Group rates. Arrival: Grand Marais, MN.

Joe M. Clark—Ozark Society, AR.

"Just outside our door," say Bill and Sue Douglas, "lies the established wilderness." Their base on Saganaga Lake, 60 miles out of Grand Marais at the end of the famed Gunflint Trail, is the jumping off point for canoe trails in the wilderness areas of Minnesota's BWCA and Canada's Quetico Park. The Douglases specialize solely in canoe outfitting, "Because we are not a large, pretentious outfitter, and own and operate our own business, we are eager and able to provide you with more personal service," they say.

Tom & Woods' Moose Lake Wilderness Canoe Trips, Box 358, Ely, MN 55731. Att.: Woods Davis. (218) 365-5837. Boundary Waters. May–Oct. Up to 75 canoeists, 3–30 days. Complete outfitting: $18–$19/day, $120–$126/wk.: under 16 yrs., $13/day. Rates for groups, guides, partial outfitting, pickup in Duluth, tow service & fly-ins.

Formerly known as Beland's, this outfitting headquarters is on Moose Lake, 20 miles northeast of Ely and 5 miles by water from Canadian customs. Tom and Woods consider it the most strategic jumping-off point for trips into Quetico-Superior wilderness area, starting from their very doorstep. They offer both light and ultralight outfitting rates, and lakeside overnight accommodations at the start or end of your trip. They help you select routes as long and as easy or hard as you want.

Way of Wilderness, Grand Marais, MN 55604. Att.: Bud Darling. (218) 388-2212. [Oct.–May: (312) 534-0557.] Boundary Waters. 12–15 canoeists. Group rates, $12/day up.

Located between Seagull and Saganaga lakes, endmost of the Gunflint Trail, Bud Darling can start you off on one lake for a circle route back through the other. Complete outfitting into the Minnesota-Canadian wilderness is his specialty— "rediscovering the simplicities of life."

Wild Places, Inc., Box 758, Ely, MN 55731. Att.: Tom Dayton. (218) 365-5884. [Sept.–May: 942 N. 12 St., Dekalb, IL 60115.] Boundary Waters. May–Oct. 2–40 canoeists. From $10/day for 10, to $16 for 2. Guide, $40/day.

Personalized service for families and individuals is a specialty, Dayton says. "We like to see people return from our canoe trips refreshed." Wild Places, Inc., has a lodge and base on secluded Jasper Lake. A new program offers a humanistic approach to the wilderness experience to improve outdoor skills or pursue academic studies such as biology or geology, with college credit. Special wilderness adventures introduce the wilderness to the mentally, socially and physically disabled, and to the elderly.

Wilderness Outfitters, Inc., 1 E. Camp St. Ely, MN 55731. Att.: Jim Pascoe. (218) 365-3211. Boundary Waters. $18/day incl. canoe, food & light equipment. Child & group rates.

"Our many years of canoe trip outfitting assure all of a successful and rewarding experience," Jim Pascoe promises. He offers fishing trips at remote tent cabins on beautiful Basswood Lake and fly-ins to Canadian outpost cabins. His company has been operating since 1921—"the world's oldest canoe outfitting firm," he says.

MISSISSIPPI

Bogue Chitto Water Park, Rt. 2, Box 223-A, McComb, MS 39648. (601) 684-9568. Bogue Chitto Riv. (MS). All yr. Smooth water. 6–60 canoeists. 1–3 days. Canoe, $12/day. Put-in & pickup extra. Group rates. Arrival: McComb, MS.

One-day canoe trips along the Bogue Chitto offer good fishing—an abundance of black bass, catfish, crappie and other game fish waiting to be caught. You can also camp overnight at one of the five Pearl River Boatway Parks, where you might encounter deer, raccoon, squirrel, possum, beaver, turkey, armadillo or even a small (vegetarian) bear.

MISSOURI

The Ozark Mountains of southeast Missouri have become "canoe country" for midwesterners in recent years. It's leisurely canoeing on the crystal clear waters, with just enough riffles and chutes to keep you alert.

This is a land of high limestone bluffs, springs and caves, of blue heron and wild turkey, beaver and bass, pools and eddies and gravel bars for river camping.

On some rivers outfitters provide equipment year-round, though most floating is done from spring through fall. Parts of the Current and Jacks Fork rivers are now protected in the Ozark National Scenic Riverways, and the Eleven Point is included in the National Wild and Scenic Rivers system.

Among those who specialize in canoe outfitting are the following:

Akers Ferry Canoe Rental, Cedar Grove Rt.-E, Salem, MO 65560. Att.: G. E. Maggard. (314) 858-3224. Current Riv. All yr. Up to 400 canoeists, 1–8 days. Canoe, $9/day. Hauling & guide service extra. Arrival: Salem, MO.

Before you set out, Maggard fills you in with details on the numerous caves and springs you'll run across on your trip on the Current.

Big M Resort, Success Rt., Box 124, Licking, MO 65542. (314) 674-3488. Big Piney Riv. in Clark Natl. Forest. 1–100 canoeists. 1–10 days. Canoe, $7/day. Lodging. Arrival: Licking, MO.

"We offer trips from 5 to 50 miles long," the Big M reports. "To the observing canoeist each mile has some unique features named by tie and lumber rafters at the turn of the century—such as Horseshoe Bend, Turkeyneck Eddy and Ritz Rock."

Gunwhale Canoe Rentals, 2527 Oepts, Jennings, MO 63136. Att.: Anthony Denatale & William Kallaos. (314) 388-0125. Black Riv. (MO). Apr.–Oct. Smooth water. 2–80 canoeists. 1–3 days. Canoe, $6.50/day per person incl. put-in & pickup. Arrival: Lesterville, MO.

Anthony tells us that he's most often complimented on the "beautiful bluffs and the clarity of the water" along his scenic routes. Other features on his Black River excursions are "a small cave for spelunkers, several springs, and many sand and gravel bars for picnicking and camping."

Jadwin Canoe Rental, Box 28, Jadwin, MO 65501. Att.: Darrel Blackwell. (314) 729-5529. Current Riv., Ozark Natl. Scenic Riverways. All yr. Up to 150 canoeists. 2 hrs.–12 days. Canoe, $9/day. Pickups. Arrival: Rolls or Salem, MO.

On "K" Highway, 15 miles south of Salem near the headwaters of the Current, Jadwin aims "to give you the best possible service." It's for people of all ages, with plenty of camping spots along the riverbanks.

Neil Canoe & Jon Boat Rental, PO Box 396, Van Buren, MO 63965. Att.: Roy Gossett. (314) 323-4447 or 8330. Current, Jacks Fork & Eleven Point riv. All yr. 2 hrs.–8 days. Canoe, $9/day. Transport rates. Arrival: Van Buren, MO.

Begin at the headwaters of the Current for an 8-day float. Paddle to picturesque towns—Akers Ferry, Log Yard, Paint Rock, Cataract Landing or Doniphan. Best months are April through October, Roy says, but he'll take reservations anytime.

Silver Arrow Canoe Rental, Gladden Star Route (DP), Salem, MO 65560. Att.: George or Dennis Purcell. (314) 729-5770. Current Riv. All yr. Up to 150 canoeists, 1–10 days. Canoes, $9/day; hauling extra. Arrival: Salem or Rolla, MO.

The Current is tops for fishermen in May and June, great for families in July and August, and in October ideal for fall foliage fans, say the Purcells. They are flexible in put-ins and pickups and guarantee that the customer never waits.

Twin Bridges Canoe Rental, Dept. AG, SS Rt. Box 230, West Plains, MO 65775. Att.: Wendell & Jan Olmsted. (417) 256-7507. North Fork of White Riv. & Bryant Creek (MO). All yr. White water. 1–320 canoeists, 2½ hrs.–5 days. Canoe, $9/day; life jackets & hauling extra. Arrival: West Plains, MO.

Jan describes the North Fork River and Bryant Creek: "These are clear, spring-fed streams that flow through forested hills and along high bluffs, with wildlife caves and springs along the river. The flow of water varies from mild rapids to quiet, deep pools. There are old active grist mills—one on each stream—that are both interesting and scenic."

Wild River Canoe Rental, Cedar Grove Rt., Salem, MO 65560. Att.: Jack Patton. (314) 858-3230. Current Riv. All yr. Up to 175 canoeists, 1–8 days. Canoes, $9/day; hauling extra. 10% discount Nov.–Mar. for 3 or more canoes. Arrival: Salem, MO.

Wild River Canoe Rental is located 25 miles from the headwaters of the Current River in the heart of the beautiful Big Springs country. They offer free camping and bus service to and from the river for their customers.

MONTANA

Missouri River Cruises, Box 1212-A, Fort Benton, MT 59442. Att.: Bob Singer. (406) 622-3295. Missouri Riv. May–Sept. Up to 18 canoeists, 3–8 days. Canoe, $9/day. Guided trips incl. all but sleeping bag, $30/day. Arrival: Great Falls or Havre, MT. (See also *Float Trips*.)

This 160-mile historic wilderness waterway, now part of the National Wild and Scenic Rivers System, is gentle enough for families to canoe. The area is much the same as when Lewis and Clark journeyed through it in 1805. You observe wildlife, deserted cabins, wilderness badlands, white cliffs and lava dikes, and hike to scenic vantage points.

NEBRASKA

Wilson Outfitters—Nebraska, 6211 Sunrise Road, Lincoln, NB 68510. Att.: Loren W. Wilson. (402) 489-6241. Niobrara, Missouri & other riv. Mar.–Oct. Smooth & white water. 16–55 canoeists, 2–7 days. $25–$45/day, according to distance, size of group; youth, off-season & midwk. discounts. Sleeping gear incl.

Loren Wilson has a way with words. "We are cruisers, not racers," he says. "We want people to return home feeling 'recreated,' and not 'wreckreated.' " Toward this end he aims for a happy balance of canoeing, camping, beachcombing, fellowship and excellent food such as "rib-eye steak, corn on the cob, sausages, pancakes with *hot* syrup and even ice cream." With a sizable canoe service, Wilson offers a number of specialty trips including observation of the sandhill crane migration (March), edible foods, folklore, blue grass and a combo backpack/canoe trip. With a state-wide livery service, he blends a 2-day trip into any itinerary.

NEW JERSEY

The River School, South Branch Canoe Cruises, PO Box 173, Lebanon, NJ 08833. Att.: Jay Langley & Peter Buell. (201) 782-9700. Eastern riv. Smooth & white water. Up to 20 canoeists, 1–10 days. 1 day, $15; 2-day wkends, $45; 3 1-day courses, $50; 3–7 day trips, $65–$145. Group, children & midwk. discounts. Arrival: Flemington, NJ.

"We're the river people," say Peter and Jay. "We're the people who guide you and teach you the tricks of river canoeing, who camp and eat and work beside you because we like it that way." All trips include some white water, but are graded for experience. One is a weekend canoe/hiking combination through New Jersey's famed pine barrens. Now teaching classes at three colleges, they have produced a river canoeing textbook. And Peter adds, "Be sure to ask Jay for his campfire onion soup recipe."

NEW YORK

Gordon Adventours, Box 414, Gracie Station, New York, NY 10028. Att.: I. Herbert Gordon. (212) 535-8472. Delaware Riv. (NY), Le Domaine, Ottawa & Megiscane riv. (PQ). May–Sept. Smooth & white water. 6–10 canoeists, 2–14 days, $70–$460. Bring sleeping gear.

"Participation" is the key word in Herb Gordon's Adventours canoe trips on the Delaware and in Canada. "While there are especially qualified leaders," he explains, "all camp chores, from cooking to cleaning to erecting tents, are co-operative activities. You may not know a bang plate from an Optimus 111B before a trip, but you'll return filled with knowledge about how to handle a canoe, and perhaps even some exciting new facts about camping." Herb also offers a weekend Delaware trip with pickup in Manhattan on Friday evenings, and back to the city late Sunday. His 1- and 2-week Canadian trips start in Montreal.

Jerry's Canoe Rentals, Rt. 97, Pond Eddy, NY 12770. Att.: Jerry Lovelace. (914) 956-6078. Delaware Riv. Smooth & white water. Apr.–Oct. Up to 200 canoeists, 1–5 days. Wkdays, $12/day; wkends, $14/day. Rates for outfitting, transport, car carrier, guide & campsite.

"We try to plan for each group's needs," Jerry says. "Our trips have enough rapids to be exciting, and still water for relaxing."

Saddles and Paddles, Outdoor Adventures, Ltd., Box 331, Callicoon, NY 12723. Att.: Dick Freda. (914) 887-5100. Delaware Riv. Smooth & white water. Up to 1,000

South Branch Canoe Cruises, NJ.

canoeists. Canoe, $11/day, or $12/day w./transport & horseback ride. Midwk. & group rates.

You can ride a horse to the put-in point, or paddle first and then have a trailride—"unique on the Delaware," says Dick Freda. "Our 75-mile stretch is great for novice and expert alike."

Ten Mile River Lodge, RD 2, Narrowsburg, NY 12764. Att.: Bob Lander. (914) 252-7101. Delaware Riv. from Hancock to Port Jervis. Smooth & white water. Apr.–Oct. 3 hrs.–1 wk. Canoe, $13/day wkend, $11/wkday, $50/wk. Also lodging, restaurant, 2 campgrounds, transport, car shuttle.

"With 700 canoes and 6 convenient river locations, we're the largest livery on the Delaware," says Bob Lander. You can paddle for 75 miles downriver.

Timberlock Canoe Trips, Adirondacks, Sabael, NY 12864. Att.: C. R. Catlin. (518) 648-5494. [Sept.–May: Sugar Hill Farm, RD 2, Woodstock, VT 05091. (802) 457-1621.] Adirondack Chain Lakes. Smooth water. Jul.–Aug. 6–9 canoeists. 2–5-day guided trips, $26/day. Bring sleeping gear. Group & family rates. Arrival: Indian Lake, NY. (See also *Backpacking*.)

Canoeists arrive Saturday for Sunday training and packing, for their Monday to Friday trip. Timberlock features flexibility to group needs. "Some want to keep moving, some to dawdle," Catlin explains. "Guides size up the group and pace things accordingly." Or you can book a week at Timberlock and have a 3- or 4-day trip.

NORTH CAROLINA

Nantahala Outdoor Center, Inc., Star Rt., Box 68, Bryson City, NC 28713. Att.: Payson Kennedy. (704) 488-6407. Nantahala, Chattooga & Little Tennessee riv. in Smoky Mts. (NC). Mar.–Nov. 1–15 canoeists or kayakers; 1–5 days. Rentals: 1st day, $15; $10/day thereafter. Wkend canoe or kayak clinic, $75, incl. food & equip. 5-day clinic, $175 w./lodging. Arrival: Asheville, NC, or Chattanooga, TN. (See also *Backpacking, Mountaineering, Float Trips*.)

"Our outstanding service is high-quality white-water instruction for all levels of canoeists and kayakers—beginner to competition," says Payson Kennedy. Specialties include 2- and 5-day clinics and trips, group training programs, a decked boat clinic for (and by) women, and ACA instructor certification programs. Gentler sections of the Nantahala, Little Tennessee and French break in beginners, while advanced paddlers challenge the wild Chattooga, which drops 275 feet in 6 miles. Kennedy was the canoeing double in the film *Deliverance*.

OREGON

Northwest Waters, Box 212, Portland, OR 97212. Att.: R. Herman. No tel. West coast Vancouver Is. (BC). Jun.–Oct. Smooth water. 10–24 canoeists, 12 or more days. 2 wks., $185. Bring sleeping gear & food.

Northwest Waters explores the sea islands of Canada's "wild shore," which is described as "a coastal wilderness of steep mountains, dense forests and deep, glacier-carved inlets; an intricate maze of offshore islands and reefs. The sheltering arms of Esperanza Inlet break the force of the open Pacific to provide calm, protected canoe passages for exploration of the area's trackless beaches and uninhabited islands." All essential equipment is provided except sleeping bags, foam pads and food. The trip begins at Gold River with a 6-hour voyage on a small coastal freighter to the Esperanza base camp.

Sundance Expeditions, Inc., 14894 Galice Rd., Merlin, OR 97532. Att.: Michael Saul & James Koons. (503) 479-8508. Rogue & Umpqua riv. (OR). May–Sept. White water. 8–12 kayakers, 1–10 days. School: 10 days, $425; 5 days, $225; incl. equip., lodging, food & transport. Group rates & charters. Arrival: Medford or Grants

Pass, OR. (See also *Float Trips*.)

Having become the West's largest and most comprehensive kayak school, Sundance teaches white-water reconnoitering, boat handling and wilderness camping in an intensive 10-day program on the Rogue. There's an instructor to every 4 students, and accommodations, dorm-style or private, are in the sauna-equipped Riverhouse, just 200 feet from one of the best "playing" rapids on the Rogue.

PENNSYLVANIA

Kittatinny Canoes, Dept. AT, Silver Lake Rd., Dingmans Ferry, PA 18328. Att.: Frank & Ruth Jones. (717) 828-2700 or 2338. Delaware Riv. Smooth & white water. Apr.–Oct. 1,500 canoeists, 1–7 days. Canoe, $11/wkday, $13/day wkend, $45/wk. Transport rates or base to base trips.

Operating on the 135-mile stretch between Hancock (NY) and Martins Creek (PA) with 750 canoes and 5 bases, Ruth and Frank have "the best-equipped livery on the Delaware." They plan white-water trips for experts or quiet trips for beginners. Camp along the river, pitch a tent in a wild spot, or stay at the Kittatinny Campgrounds in the heart of the white-water section. The Delaware is lined with forested mountains and rocky cliffs.

TENNESSEE

Buffalo River Canoe Rental Co., Flatwoods, TN 38458. Att.: Alf Ashton, Jr. (901) 398-8885 or (615) 589-2755. Buffalo Riv. Smooth & white water. Mar.–Nov. Up to 300 canoeists, up to 9 days. Canoe, $11/day, incl. shuttle & campground.

Eighteen access points dot this 110-mile section of the Buffalo River, with choice campsites nearby—including Alf Ashton's "beautiful, primitive campground at Slink Shoals on the water's edge." It's a scenic river, with wildlife, waterfalls, caves, springs and rapids—really turbulent in the upper sections. It is accessible via Interstate 40 and state highways 13 (where Alf's "fast, efficient selvice" is based), 50, 100 and 6.

Hiwassee Float Service, Inc., Delano, TN 37325. Att.: H. C. Sartin. (615) 263-5581 or 2524 (eve.). Hiwassee Riv. (TN). Apr.–Oct. Smooth & white water. 6- & 12-mi. trips, $20 w./shuttle; guide, $15 extra. (See also *Float Trips*.)

Don't try this in a canoe unless you're a really good paddler. If you are, it's great fun.

TEXAS

Texas Canoe Trails, Inc., 1008 Wirt Rd., #160, Houston, TX 77055. Att.: Wayne Walls. (713) 688-3741. Rio Grande, Guadalupe (TX); Balsas, Moctezuma & Usumacinta (Mexico). Smooth & white water. All yr. 6–14 canoeists or 4 kayakers on guided trips. Also charters, rentals, shuttles. 2–14 days, $30–$40/day. Bring sleeping gear. Youth rates. Arrival: San Antonio. (See also *Float Trips*.)

Canoeing the Guadalupe above and below Canyon Lake is a favorite pastime for water people. TCT has a fleet of canoes and guides for custom trips to make it possible. Also weekend training trips. On the Rio Grande, canoeists paddle with raft support (depending on water conditions), or the trip is made with a mixture of rafts and canoes for this run through Big Bend National Park. The same holds true for runs on Mexican rivers.

VIRGINIA

Downriver Canoe Co., Rt. 1, Box 214, Front Royal, VA 22630. Att.: John Gibson. (703) 635-5526. South Fork Shenandoah Riv. Apr.–Oct. Smooth & white water. 2–100 canoeists, 1–7 days. Canoe, $15–$18/day. Group & youth rates.

John Gibson loves the South Fork of the Shenandoah. "The river," he says, "is legendary not only for its beauty. The fishing is some of the best in Virginia." He offers trips from several hours, paddling 8 miles, to 3 days and 44 miles. On hikes you can find Indian artifacts and explore limestone caves. Downriver is located just 1½ hours from Washington, DC.

4 River Canoe Trips, Little River Leisure Enterprises, PO Box 83, Dept. AT, Doswell, VA 23047. Att.: Chuck & Nancy Martin. (804) 227-3401. Little Riv., South Anna, North Anna & Pamunkey (VA). Apr.–Nov. Smooth & white water. 2–28 canoeists, 1–3 days. Canoe, $12/1st day, $9/ea. addl. day. Trip pkgs.: 1 day, $11.50–$18; 2 days, $29–$32.50; incl. shuttle. Arrival: Richmond, VA.

Canoeing through "primitive, undeveloped country that will look to you much as it did to the Indians when they first canoed these rivers"—that's what Chuck Martin promises on his trips down these four quaintly named rivers. Chuck will rent you tents, camping, fishing and almost any other equipment you may need.

Shenandoah River Outfitters, Dept. AT, RFD 3, Luray, VA 22835. Att.: Joe Sottosanti. (703) 743-4159. Shenandoah, Cacapon & Potomac riv. All yr. Up to 300 canoeists, up to 14 days. Canoe, $16/day for 2 days; $8/day thereafter. Complete outfitting: $25/day, $60/2 days, $80/3 days. Guide & group rates.

The oldest and largest outfitter in the Mid-Atlantic states, Shenandoah has established a base in Maryland for trips through both the calm and the white water of the Cacapon and the scenic calm water of the Potomac in western Maryland. These as well as the Shenandoah offer beautiful wilderness only 2 hours from DC. Joe Sottosanti is continuing his "help preserve the Shenandoah" offer: free canoeing in exchange for two filled trash bags. And he has designed and built a sturdy canoe of flexible vinyl rubber (Royalex) for white-water canoeing—named the *Shenandoah* after the river that has damaged many a canoe with its tough white water and side-bending rocks.

WASHINGTON

Discovery Islands Canoe Trips, 2615 N.E. 140th St., Seattle, WA 98125. Att.: Linda Johnson & Terry Humes. (206) 364-0054. Discovery Is. near Campbell Riv. (BC). Jun.–Oct. 4–9 canoeists. 7 days, $345, incl. flight from/to Seattle. Bring sleeping gear. Arrival: Seattle, WA.

A scenic float-plane trip from Seattle to Quadra Island begins this expedition into the Discovery Islands. From there you paddle decked touring canoes in waters where you'll see whales, porpoises and seals at close hand, as well as eagles, deer, osprey, otter—and maybe even Big Foot. You stop at places accessible only by boat and spend each of the 7 nights at a different selected campsite. Trips begin and end on Saturdays.

Northwest Alpine Guide Service, Inc., 1628 Ninth Ave. #2, Seattle, WA 98101. Att.: Linda Bradley Miller. (206) 622-6074. Ross Lake, Lake Chelan, Columbia Riv. (WA), 2–7 days. Wild, Alatna & Koyukuk Riv. (AK), 7–14 days, about $75/day. Sched. Jul.–Aug. Custom all yr. Smooth water. 2–8 canoeists or kayakers. Bring or rent sleeping gear. (See also *Backpacking, Mountaineering, Float Trips, Ski Touring, Wilderness Living, Youth Adventures.*)

"We can arrange both salt- and white-water tours on request year-round," says Brad Bradley. His Alaska trips follow a leisurely pace with layover days—"ideal for the novice."

WISCONSIN

Blackhawk Ridge Recreation Area, Box 92-A, Sauk City, WI 53582. Att.: Larrie & Diana Isenring. (608) 643-3775. Wisconsin Riv. (WI). Summer. 1–5 days. $14/day incl. shuttles and all equip. Overnights: canoe, $5–$6/day; transport extra. Arrival: Madison, WI. (See also *Ski Touring.*)

From Blackhawk Ridge's canoe base right on the Wisconsin River, canoeists have 80 miles of flowing water with no dams or towns, before it reaches the Mississippi. There are plenty of sandbars for overnight camping. The base provides rentals, shelter and campsites for early starters, and a put-in and pickup service.

Brule River Canoe Rental, PO Box 90-A, Brule, WI 54820. Att.: Brian Carlson. (715) 372-4983. Brule Riv. (WI). Smooth & white water. May–Oct. 1–3 days. Up to 100 canoeists & 40 kayakers, $12–$18/day for 2, incl. shuttle. Also guided trips.

"Our novice 12-mile canoe trip has a dozen small rapids through a cedar swamp and pine forest," says Brian Carlson. "Shoot some intermediate rapids on an 18-mile trip or try our kayak run of 4 hours through continuous rapids, with a drop of 200 feet in 12 miles." Spot bald eagles and the world's largest white pines.

Sauk Prairie Canoe Rental, 106 Polk St., Sauk City, WI 53585. Att.: James Staff. (608) 643-6589. Wisconsin Riv. Smooth water. Apr.–Oct. Up to 120 canoeists, 1–5 days. Canoes, $5/day; shuttle rates.

"As you leave Sauk City there's nearly 100 miles of wilderness river ahead, with scenic islands and sandbars for camping, yet you're never more than half a mile from a paralleling highway. It's ideal for beginners, with all flat water. We tailor each trip for the length the customer wants."

BRITISH COLUMBIA

Adventure Unlimited, Box 1881, Golden, B.C. VOA 1HO. Att.: Pete Austen. (604) 344-2380. Columbia, Blaeberry & Kicking Horse riv. in Yoho Park & hidden wilderness lakes. Jun.–Sept. Smooth & white water. 2–12 canoeists, 1–7 days. 6–7 days, $220. Bring sleeping gear. Arrival: Golden, BC. (See also *Mountaineering, Ski Touring.*)

For a "happy, relaxed holiday" Pete Austen offers a week's trip where the scenery is superb and the navigating easy, a weekend of white water with Class II and III rapids, and combo trips mixing smooth water and white water. Hike, fish, observe the eagle nesting sites and lumbering bear and moose, or just drift along with the current. Overnight camps on the riverbanks.

Canadian Wilderness Experiences Ltd., Box 46304, Vancouver, B.C. V6R 4G6. Att.: Rand Rudland or Jim Millar. (604) 325-9118. BC lakes. Jun.–Sept. Smooth water. 4–10 people. 7 days, Symphony Lake, $485–$645; 11 days, Turner & Symphony lakes, $830. Custom & sched. Arrival: Vancouver, BC.

"These tours," Jim tells us, "are aimed at providing a well-balanced mixture of flying, canoeing, hiking, fishing, photography, swimming and any other relevant outdoor activity the group can dream up." He offers an 11-day trip to the Turner Lakes and Symphony Lake, or 7 days to Symphony Lake alone. The Turner Lakes comprise seven beautiful, clear-water mountain lakes, streams and waterfalls. Symphony Lake is a total alpine wilderness surrounded by four glaciers where you canoe through floating statues of ice, and hike and explore the glacial terrain. Says Jim, "Our clients are often urban professionals who want to get back to basics." Air transport is by float and amphibious craft. One nice touch—all trips begin with dinner at a fine Vancouver restaurant.

Interior Canoe Outfitters, Ltd., 751 Athabaska East (AG), Kamloops, B.C. V2H 1C7. Att.: Adolf Teufele. (604) 374-9434. BC, Alta., Yukon. May-Sept. White water. 4–10 canoeists or kayakers. 1–14 days. Sample rates: 2 days, $141; 3 days, $232; 5 days, $240–$316; 14 days (Liard Riv.), $1,500. Rates incl. all exc. sleeping bag. Group & youth rates.

There's good and exciting water, from Class I to Class III+, on the wilderness rivers which you travel with ICO guides and instructors. Among the rivers are the North Thompson, Vermilion, Kootenay, North Saskatchewan, Barriere, Nicola and

Grumman Canoes on the Colorado.

the spectacularly beautiful Grand Canyon of the Liard. Intermediate canoeing is required for some trips. On others you learn to paddle an inflatable kayak that will "challenge your stamina, reflection and wits," Teufele advises. A canoe school for instructors also is part of his program.

North Country Travelers, Box 14, Atlin, B.C. V0W 1A0. Att.: Bruce Johnson. No tel. Atlin Lake (BC). Jun.–Sept. Smooth water. 1–14 days. $95/day. Bring sleeping gear. Family & youth rates. Arrival: Atlin, BC. (See also *Dog Sledding.*)

The Johnsons travel between Atlin and their cabin, 30 miles down Atlin Lake, in a 20-foot motor canoe, a trip of about 5 hours. "This is gorgeous mountain and lake country," one of their vacationers writes. "It's a real wilderness experience. Bruce, a former biologist from Fairbanks, takes guests to see a glacier, a placer gold claim deep in black bear country, a hidden emerald lake, a forgotten trapper's cabin, a fossil beach." The Johnsons' desire is to "incorporate the guest into the northern feel for things . . . an inside, patient but exciting exposure to the North Country and its people and places."

MANITOBA

Northern Outfitters Ltd., 514 McKeen Ave., Flin Flon, Man. R8A 1A4. Att.: Don Wright. (204) 687-4098. Churchill, Nelson & other Arctic riv. May–Oct. Smooth & white water. 2–40 canoeists, 1–90 days. $6–$25/day, sleeping gear incl. Arrival: Flin Flon, Man.

"From the 54th parallel north to the Arctic Circle," Don Wright will outfit you for your canoe trip. He calls the Churchill and the Nelson "the mightiest rivers of them all," and contends, "You haven't canoed until you've paddled with our voyageurs."

ONTARIO

Adventure Canoe Trails, Box 208, Atikokan, Ont. POT 1C0. Att.: Alan Kerr. (807) 597-6467. Quetico Provincial Park. May–Sept. Smooth water. 1–20 canoeists, 3–21 days. $18/day, incl. sleeping gear. Group, youth & partial outfitting rates. Arrival: Atikokan, Ont.

"Our special interest," Alan tells us, "is in personally working with our customers, to help them enjoy the finest wilderness canoeing in the world. I always enjoy equipping and trading notes with our expert customers, but some of our most pleasant experiences have been with people who have never before canoe-camped."

Algonquin Waterways Wilderness Trips, 21 Parkwood Ave., Toronto, Ont. M6J 2W9. Att.: John D. McRuer. Algonquin & Killarney parks, Madawaska, French & Missinaibi riv. (Ont.). Flat & white water. 5–18 canoeists, 3–15 days. Sched. trips, about $25–$33/day, incl. all but sleeping gear. Group rates.

AW's canoeing parties venture far into the lonely northern wilderness where Indians have lived and hunted. "So great is the Indian competence—their knowledge of weather, wind, water and land—that we have copied them, and we share their reverence for the awesome forest and gleaming land," writes John McRuer. His service has been running wilderness adventures since 1969. Leaders have logged thousands of miles by canoe. Pretrip training is an essential part of the program, and a day or more of training is included in the cost of each trip.

Canadian Quetico Outfitters Ltd., PO Box 910, Atikokan, Ont. POT 1CO. Att.: Roger Thew. (807) 929-2177. Nov.–Apr.: (807) 929-2141. Quetico Park (Ont.). May–Oct. Smooth & white water. Up to 20 canoeists, 3–30 days. Complete outfitting, $14/day. Group rates & rentals. Arrival: by air to Thunder Bay or Int'l. Falls, bus to Atikokan, Ont.

Since 1955 CQO has outfitted canoeists. Its base is on Highway 11 at the Quetico Trading Post, 3 miles west of the park entrance at French Lake. "Quetico is a primitive area," Thew explains, "in which logging, mining, fly-ins, roads, buildings and motors are banned. There are good long hiking trails with big game sightings. We provide the best and lightest of equipment." Fly-in trips to a lake outside the park boundary, paddling back to French Lake downstream most of the way, are featured.

Canoe Algoma, RR 2, Sault Ste. Marie, Ont. P6A 5K7. Att.: Oskar Mahlmann. (705) 777-2426. No. Ont. May–Oct. Smooth & white water. Up to 40 canoeists, up to 21 days. Completely outfitted & guided trips: 20 days, $273, incl. 1 night hotel, plus $3/day for food. Also partial outfitting rates; canoe/kayak, $5–$6/day.

The District of Algoma is at the junction of Lakes Huron and Superior, with woodlands, clear waters and sparse population. Here Mahlmann guides canoe groups from Sault Ste. Marie eastward along the historic voyageur canoe route. There are scenic, lonesome islands, rugged shoreline and deserted beaches, and villages where fresh food can be purchased every 3 or 4 days. Canoe Algoma is a division of Heyden Crafts, builders and suppliers of canoes and other equipment.

Canoe Arctic, Inc., 9 John Beck Crescent, Brampton, Ont. L6W 2T2. Att.: Alex M. Hall. (416) 451-0290. NWT. Jun.–Sept. 1–6 canoeists, 12 or more days. $48/day, complete outfitting & guide service. Bring sleeping gear. Arrival: Yellowknife or Fort Smith, NWT.

Alex Hall calls the Northwest Territories "North America's last great wilderness." His trips emphasize wildlife viewing and photography, wilderness adventure and fishing, and are customized to special interests. "It's an opportunity," he says, "to photograph white Arctic wolves and muskox, walk through herds of migrating caribou that have never seen man, and travel great rivers where few have ever gone before." Hall has canoed thousands of miles in the Northwest Territories, has an M.S. degree in animal ecology, and has been a biologist for the Ontario government and an environmental consultant for private enterprise. For married couples or singles who wish to share a trip, he will find others in their age group with compatible interests.

Canoe Canada Outfitters, PO Box 1810-A, Atikokan, Ont. POT 1CO. Att.: Bud Dickson or Jim Clark. (807) 597-6418. Quetico Park & White Otter Wilderness. May-Sept. Smooth & white water. 2–40 canoeists. 3–21 days. Rates for ultralight complete outfitting: $18/day; 7-day trip, $119. Youth & group rate: $14/day; 7 days, $91. Arrival: Atikokan, Ont., or International Falls, MN.

CCO will start you off, fully equipped, on a variety of wilderness canoe routes— from a 5-day trip over 30 miles of canoe trails with 5 portages, to 10 days of paddling over 75 miles with 20 portages. They also offer a fly-in-paddle-out service in this vast canoe country, and "top quality young college men" if you want guides for part or all of your trip. They meet planes at the International Falls Airport. CCO considers itself tops in trail food, wilderness know-how, careful planning and excellent equipment.

Madawaska Kanu Camp, Box 635, Barry's Bay, Ont. KOJ 1BO. Att.: Herman & Christie Kerckhoff. (613) 756-3620. [Sept.–May: 2 Tuna Ct., Don Mills, Ont. M3A 3L1. (416) 477-8845] Madawaska, Petwawa & Ottawa riv. Jun.–Aug. White water. 10–40 canoeists or kayakers, 1 or more days. 6-day course, $98–$180.

MKC specializes in teaching white-water paddling to kayak and canoe enthusiasts. Located on the roaring Madawaska, they offer 5 slalom training courses with more than 80 gates, long stretches of challenging rapid runs up to Class III, safe pools dividing the rapids, daily videotape and movies, rentals and a gourmet kitchen. It's for recreational paddlers or serious racers, in dam-overflow water that remains a comfortable 70 degrees. The Kerckhoffs were Canadian national canoeing champions from 1969 to 1971, and their daughter Claudia won the North American Cup in 1976 at age 15.

Northern Wilderness Outfitters, Box 89, South River, Ont. Att.: Peter Robertson. (416) 794-0441. Algonquin Park. May–Oct. Smooth water. 2–120 canoeists, 2–14 days. Complete outfitting, $13–$14/day. Group & youth rates. Canoe rentals only $7/day. 10-day workshops, $100.

With a base including tenting sites on Round Lake, NWO outfits campers, fishermen, photographers and school groups "with the finest equipment and food available for a canoeing adventure." There is immediate access from their base to dozens of wilderness canoe routes through Algonquin Provincial Park. They also offer canoe tripping qualification workshops with instruction and certification.

Ontario Canoe Trip Outfitters, Algonquin Outfitters Div., RR-1, Box T, Dwight, Ont. POA 1HO. Att.: Bill Swift. Algonquin base: (705) 635-2243. Temagami base: (705) 569-3770. [Nov.–Apr.: c/o Bill Swift, 402 Bonnie Brae Ave., Rochester, NY 14618. (716) 473-7690.] Algonquin Park & NE Ont. Apr.–Oct. Mostly smooth water. 2–100 canoeists, 2–30 days. Complete outfitting: $13–$14/day. Rates for under 12 yrs., long trips, groups, guides, shuttle, partial outfitting.

Established since 1961, this is the oldest complete outfitting service in the Algonquin Park area. In 1977 a new base was opened in Temagami, 150 miles farther north. Both areas offer hundreds of lakes for wilderness canoeing. In Algonquin Park canoeists can select trips that start or end at any of more than 25 access points or at the base. The Temagami base is the jumping-off spot for a vast and beautiful area—Maple Mountain, the Troutstreams, Lady Evelyn Lake, and the Montreal and Sturgeon River systems—and canoeists can paddle more than 40 miles without making a portage. On the long list of groups OCTO has outfitted is the royal family of Luxembourg.

Paddle & Portage, RR 1, Hanover, Ont. N4N 3B8. Att.: Elden & Murray Cathers. (519) 364-1657. Canadian lakes & riv. Jun.–Sept. Smooth & white water. 1–12 canoeists, 4–90 days. Custom guided trips w./complete outfitting (exc. sleeping gear): 1 wk., $200; 2 wks., $330; 3 wks, $450. Yukon & NWT: 2 wks., $550; 3 wks., $745. Air charters extra. Also partial outfitting & group & family rates.

"Hopelessly afflicted with canoe fever, we are unable to resist the rocking motion of a canoe on a gently wind-blown lake, or the silent glide past sheltered evergreen shores," write the Cathers. They would like you to catch that fever on one of their trips to Canada's major canoeing areas anywhere from Quebec to the Yukon. Activities and/or instruction may include retracing fur trade routes, gold panning, Indian pictographs, wildlife study, photography, fishing, canoe handling and relaxing. They'll also guide kayak trips (but do not supply kayak equipment). Their telephone is not always manned. Write if there's no answer.

Portage Store, Algonquin Park, Ont. POA 1BO. Att.: Sven & Eric Miglin. (705) 633-5622. Algonquin Park. May–Oct. Smooth water. 1–100 canoeists, 1–28 days. Complete outfitting, $83–$90/wk., $13–$14/day. Partial outfitting, group & family rates. Arrival: Huntsville, Ont.

The Miglins supply everything you need for canoeing the secluded lakes and meandering rivers of Algonquin Park, 1,800,000 acres of wilderness. Their portage store and Openego Store are on Highway 60, near the west and east entrances, respectively. "The largest and most complete outfitting service in the park," they say.

Quetico Wilderness Outfitters, Box 1390-CA, Atikokan, Ont. POT 1CO. Att.: Ben & Vi Eyton. (807) 597-6888. Quetico Park. May–Oct. Smooth water. 2–40 canoeists. 5 or more days. Complete lightweight outfitting: $14/day, $10–$12 for groups. Also rentals, guides. Arrival: Thunder Bay or Intl. Falls, bus to Atikokan, Ont.

"Very personal service and our own special food packing" are features of the Eytons' canoe trips through Quetico Park. For an excellent circle trip, start at Lerome (10 miles from their base) and finish at Nym, 2 miles away. But there are many routes, which they'll discuss to find the best one for you.

Temagami Outfitters, Box 444F, Temagami, Ont. POH 2HO. Att.: Ed Schroeder. (705) 569-3872. Temagami Provincial Forest. May-Oct. Smooth water. 2–50 canoeists, 2 or more days. Complete outfitting: $13–$15/day. Also rentals, group rates, shuttle. Arrival: air to North Bay, bus to Temagami.

Over 4,200,000 acres of virgin forest dotted with crystal-clear lakes, rivers and streams is where Ed Schroeder offers 68 different canoe routes of varying distance and terrain. The Temagami Forest Reserve is in northern Ontario just west of the Quebec boder. "Refresh yourself away from the rush of everyday life. Take a canoe trip!" Schroeder urges. He'll give expert advice on route selection and outfit you completely or partially from his base on Highway 11 in the heart of the forest.

Voyageur Wilderness Programme Ltd., Box 1210, Atikokan, Ont. P0T 1C0. Att.: Charlie Ericksen. (807) 597-2450. Quetico Provincial Park & Far North. Jun.–Oct. Smooth & white water. Any no. of canoeists or kayakers, 1 or more days. Complete outfitting: $17.50/day. Group & youth rates. Arrival: Thunder River or Intl. Falls, bus to Atikokan, Ont.

"Ecology oriented" is how Charlie Ericksen sums up his trips, and that perspective prevails. He says, "Breathing pure air and drinking from crystal-clear lakes make our trips a unique experience."

Wanapitei, 7 Engleburn Pl., Peterborough, Ont. K9H 1C4. (705) 743-3774. Anywhere in Canada. May–Sept. Smooth & white water. 6–10 people, 3–22 days. Sample rates: 3 days, $80; 8 days, $140; 14 days, $370; 21 days, $780. Bring sleeping gear. Family rates. (See also *Ski Touring.*)

Camp Wanapitei on Lake Temagami, 300 miles north of Toronto, is the starting point for canoeing the Eagle Lakes and Lady Evelyn River. Wanapitei also offers trips on the Missinaibi River to Moosonee on James Bay, on the Churchill River in Saskatchewan, and the Nahanni in the Northwest Territories. For spring training there's a weekend on the Mississauga, north of Peterborough. The camp is known also for its canoe trips for youth.

SASKATCHEWAN

Churchill River Canoe Outfitters, c/o Box 26, La Ronge, Sask. S0J 1L0. Att.: Tom Jones. (306) 425-2762. [Sept.–May: Peter Whitehead, 509 Douglas Park Crescent East, Regina, Sask. (306) 522-9589.] Churchill Riv. system. May–Sept. Smooth & white water. 2–50 canoeists, 1–28 days. Complete outfitting: $16/day. Group & family rates, rentals, fly-ins. Arrival: La Ronge or Otter Lake, Sask.

On Otter Lake in the heart of the famous Churchill River system, CRCO, the only complete canoe outfitting operation in Saskatchewan, offers more than 50 canoe trip routes, most for 5 to 10 days. "Our trips include a variety of lake and river travel," writes Tom Jones, CRCO manager. Providing a bit of background, he says, "The river system was the heart of fur trading in the old days. The Frobisher brothers used it in exploring the area, and Sir Alexander MacKenzie used it on his two famous voyages into the Arctic and the Pacific." White-water canoeists, take note: There are about 50 rapids and falls within 20 miles of CRCO's base camp.

YUKON TERRITORY

Yukon Expeditions, 2 Kluhini Crescent, Whitehorse, Y.T. Y1A 3P3. Att.: Monty Alford. (402) 667-7960. Tributaries of Yukon & Peel riv. Jul.–Aug. Smooth & white water. 1–4 kayakers, 4–30 days. About $110/day for 2. Bring sleeping gear. Arrival: Whitehorse, YT. (See also *Mountaineering.*)

Monty Alford guides custom trips mostly on tributaries of the Yukon River and Peel River systems. The pace in these remote areas is leisurely, with side trips into the hills, gold panning, and hiking and climbing. He expects participants to have had some experience in handling kayaks. For these journeys he has designed expedition kayaks that are "comfortable tourers."

Float Trips

Drifting serenely with the current, you watch the morning sun slide down the canyon walls, lighting grotesque rock formations and craggy trees on narrow ledges, until at last its rays flood the canyon bottom with sunlight. A distant rumble warns that the river's calm will soon abruptly end. Closer, louder, then a glimpse of white water ahead. Passengers in bulging life jackets grip the ropes that crisscross the boat. Now it is caught in fast current, moving irresistibly toward a thunderous roar. Down the tongue, gliding swiftly toward a jumble of waves—a mad, turbulent, frothy boil. Then . . . crashing, rising, floating, flying, pounding, twisting in the drenching, cascading water! Roaring, tumultuous, exhilarating moments! And just as suddenly it's over and, thoroughly drenched and tingling with excitement, you drift smoothly on.

For the joys of running tempestuous rivers, thousands trek each year to streams as distant as the Usumacinta in Mexico, the Chattooga and Nantahala in North Carolina, the Cheat and New in West Virginia, the upper Kennebec in Maine, the Wolf in Wisconsin, the Salmon and Snake in Idaho, the Fraser and Thompson in British Columbia and dozens of other turbulent waterways.

Thousands more each year float placidly on quieter waters—such as the calm stretches of the Yukon in Alaska, the Upper Missouri in Montana, or the Snake above Jackson, Wyoming, where more than 70,000 people each summer coast quietly through a lush, scenic valley below the jagged Teton peaks.

But the classic run, and the best known, is through the Grand Canyon of the Colorado River from Lees Ferry, Arizona, to a take-out point near the Nevada border north of Lake Mead, a distance of nearly 300 miles. In 1869 John Wesley Powell made the first exploratory journey down the Colorado. By 1949 only 100 people had duplicated his feat. Now some 15,000 hardy vacationers run it each year.

The exploding popularity of float trips has been aided by professional outfitters and guides.* Their service and the challenging logistics of a single expedition boggle the mind. A trip that involves, say, 20 to 30 participants, will require camping and sleeping gear, duffels with each one's personal gear, food (during seven days, 30 people will require 630 individual meals, plus snacks), waterproof containers for everything, basic tools, a two-way radio, a first-aid kit, and several inflatable neoprene or rubber rafts (some are 33 feet long) and perhaps a 40-horsepower motor for

---

* Some 150 different river runs in the U.S. and across the borders, provisioned and guided by outfitters, are noted in the *River Runs and Outfitters* section of this book, page 232. Details on each outfitter's service start on page 134.

each. On some trips outfitters provide Sportyaks, kayaks, canoes, paddle boats or dories for sporty riders who firmly believe that oar or paddle power, rather than motor power, is the way to go.

Depending upon the remoteness of the river, vehicles or airplanes are needed for transporting rafters and crew as well as the gear to the put-in point. And transport back from the take-out point must also be arranged.

The wonder of it is that not only do the outfitters accomplish their gargantuan tasks in an organized way, but they accept a heavy load of responsibility for land-lubbers who may never have been on a river, and they have a good time in the process—or so it seems. Outfitters and their boatmen are, indeed, an unusually responsible and jolly lot.

They are counted upon to look out for the needs of the float trippers and teach them all the things they should know. This can include the basics of camping as well as floating, and a thorough briefing on safety measures to be observed. The boatmen also are expected to be knowledgeable on the flora and fauna of the region, the geology and archaeology, and the history and ecology. They become cooks at meal-time, sometimes with an assist from the passengers. They are expert at handling their craft and "reading" the river to plot their course through rapids with walls of converging water, holes, and boulders the size of a house. They lead canyon hikes, join water fights and swap stories.

A rafter tells of a boatman on one trip who was a Ph.D. in nuclear chemistry. "He wasn't there for the pay—he was there for the ride." Another rafter sums it up: "Boatmen are great river chefs and also slightly crazy, which helps—a group to trust and enjoy."

Riding the rapids has an appeal that few who have tried it can deny. "The sheer enjoyment of the thrill, spiced with fear, is a 'high' unlike any other," explains a repeater. But it's not the thrill alone that is the magnet. Perhaps it's the challenge and the adventure that floaters enjoy the most, or the camaraderie that develops when they share hardships together, or seeing a wilderness that seems untouchd by man, or a magnificent canyon that puts you and your world in proper perspective.

For many the lure is the total escape from the confines of day-to-day life, as expressed by a river runner on the Gauley in West Virginia: "While hanging on to a rubber raft for dear life, with waves breaking ten feet over your head, there is little time to mull over the cares of the workaday routine."

While a float trip is a vacation, it is not at all times relaxed. Trippers are apt to join wholeheartedly in whatever is going on. This can be helping to set up camp or hauling and packing gear. They will lug fallen tree trunks to serve as benches around the campfire. They will smash empty cans with rocks to take less space in the refuse bag, which is carried out of the wilderness and back to civilization. They will bail furiously when their raft fills with water. On a windy day they will form a human screen to shield the cooking pots from the swirling sand. And they will help clean their campsite of any trace that they've been there so it will be wilderness-fresh for the next group of floaters.

As one outfitter succinctly explains, "It is a participation sport, where you pay big money to work."

Not only do you work. You also experience heat, cold, bugs, mosquitoes, drench-ings, bruises, scratches, rain, wind, lightning, dunking and exhaustion. With your raft hung up on rocks in low water, you get out to push, lift, jump on it or stumble over it to get it floating again. But no matter. To a dedicated river rat each trip is a success, whether it's a sun-filled ecstatic run or a cold, soggy bummer.

Even droughts do not dull the ardor of rafters, as evidenced during the summer of 1977, though some of their favorite runs closed for part or all of the season. Once the sluices opened in mid-June for water to flow through the Grand Canyon, more floaters than ever flocked to the river and reported terrific trips. On the Salmon the outfitters used their short rigs instead of the longer high-water rafts, and it was "as great as ever." But the swiftness of high water, especially during spring and early summer runoffs, provides the sportiest runs and no one hopes for a drought.

Reading up on the history and geology of a region, its plant and animal life and the river lore, enriches a trip through unfamiliar territory. And studying a map can help. "What's the difference between the Salmon and the Colorado?" an Easterner recently asked. To begin with, about 1,000 miles, is the answer, and forested craggy cliffs with snow-covered peaks in the distance instead of the Grand Canyon's red-orange-pink walls and sparse greenery.

For more specifics such as weather, water temperature, rafting and camping equipment, length of trip, minimum age for participants (usually 12 on rugged trips), logistics of getting to and from the river and a checklist of what to bring, outfitters' brochures are usually practical sources of information. An outfitter will also answer your questions by phone or by mail, and will provide references if talking with someone who has made the trip gives you added confidence.

It's important also to understand what the rates include. If a day's float is priced at $25 and an overnight trip on a slightly longer stretch of the same stream is $75, this is neither a misprint nor an overcharge. It simply reflects the difference between a trip with a picnic lunch and no camping gear, and one that requires provisions for four or five meals and all the paraphernalia for cooking them and setting up camp, to say nothing of a longer haul to put-in and take-out points.

Expedition rates reflect a variety of factors—quality of meals (simple stews and hamburgers or lavish hors d'oeuvres and steaks grilled to order), whether shuttle by vehicle or by air is included, type of floating and camping equipment used, relative difficulty of river runs and getting in and out of each area, and whether you or the outfitter provides the sleeping gear, duffels, waterproof camera containers and other items. In some cases, rates include overnights at river lodges instead of primitive camping (as on some Rogue River trips), and in others they reflect the added expense of fresh food airdrops, a high ratio of guides to passengers, and helicopter take-out or other variations in this complex and diverse sport.

Is river running for everyone? The choice of trip is wide—from a few hours to ten days or more, from a gentle float with hardly a ripple to rollercoastering over rambunctious, cresting waves.

But there are basic requirements, especially for the more ambitious trips. They include good health, enthusiasm about active outdoor life, a sense of humor and a willingness to cope with whatever conditions present themselves, whether they concern weather, hygiene or an overturned boat.

"Lillydippers should stay home," advises an experienced tripper, referring to those who complain about exerting effort or doing more than their share.

Appreciation of natural beauty is another essential. An unhappy companion, indeed, would be the one overheard to remark, "What did they bring us way out here for? There's nothing to look at but the damn trees!"

All will agree that the white-water sport makes unique demands of participants. "We had our boat ripped badly going down the Middle Fork," a western rafter reports, "and another raft in our party got hung up on a rock, and the people and gear were dumped into the river. So we did have adventure, but no one was hurt or anything of value lost. Later, though, my husband and I were both thrown out of our paddleboat, and he did lose the watch he was wearing. But even with being uncomfortable at times, this trip will be a lasting, happy experience, and our entire group wants to go again soon."

"Being uncomfortable at times" is the typical understatement of most river runners, and it does not dampen their enthusiasm one whit. Battered or not, "the best trip we ever had" is invariably their comment. "Just hang loose and roll with the punches and you'll have the time of your life," an experienced floater advises. "To anyone who has ever considered this crazy sport as a possible holiday, I have only this to say: DO IT!"

The details that follow tell whether boats are oar-powered or motor-powered. Which kind of trip do you want? Check carefully what rates include—whether or not you pay extra for transport to and from the river, car shuttle, waterproof duffel or camera container, sleeping gear, accommodations for before or after the trip, or whatever. Is this a guided or an unguided trip?

Choose the type of float and length of trip you really want—a scenic pleasant run, or a rugged white-water adventure. Either way, it's rewarding. Check limits on weight or bulk of personal gear, minimum age for taking the trip, physical fitness required, anticipated weather and fishing regulations. (We do not include information about float trips primarily for fishing, as that is a specialty better covered by other sources.) For float trips especially for young people, see the chapter, "Youth Adventures."

ALASKA

Alaska Raft Adventures, Box 73264, Fairbanks, AK 99707. Att.: Gary W. Kroll. (907) 456-6610. AK rivers. Jun.–Jul. Kobuk, 12 days, $1,200; Chilikadrotna, 11 days, $1,000; Alagnak, 8 days, $800; Copper, 5 days, $500. Rates incl. charter flights, sleeping gear & all equip.

Each trip begins and ends in Anchorage or Fairbanks, with charter flights into the wilderness. Each involves "white water excitement, fantastic fishing and great photography that only Alaska can offer," according to enthusiastic Gary Kroll. He refers to the Kobuk River trip as "150 miles of pure Alaska," and describes the Chilikadrotna as an area that yields a truly wilderness Alaska experience. As for the Alagnak, "Hang onto your rod once we hit the river," he advises. And hang onto the raft too, as you hit Class III white water with a waterfall. "More Class III on the Copper River, with three waterfalls to boot," Gary says. "These trips look so good that I'm going. Won't you join me?"

Grand Canyon Dories, CA, by Patricia Caulfield.

Alaska Wilderness Expeditions, Inc., Box 882, Wrangell, AK 99929. Att.: Dale Pihlman. (907) 874-3784. Jun.–Aug. 6 AK rivers. 7 days, Stikine, $750; 7 days Alsek/Tatshensheni, $850; 6 days, Copper, $600; 10 days, Kobuk, $1,000. Rates incl. sleeping gear, transport & some lodging. Raft rental pkg. for unguided Stikine trip: 6 days, $475 for 2; addl. days, $24; incl. transport to/from Ketchikan. (See also *Canoeing.*)

In their attempt to get people and land together in a meaningful way, AWE features "quality river-oriented wilderness trips" in paddle- and oar-powered rafts to primitive areas that they feel should be left intact. The Stikine River is one, with its steep canyons, snow-capped mountains, glaciers and "the most spectacular calm, fast-running water wilderness in North America." For moderate white water the ultimate, they say, is the Alsek and Tatshensheni trip—a primordial atmosphere, with glaciers and geologic forces at work. They also outfit climbing parties, and exploratories on other rivers.

Alaska Wilderness River Trips, Inc., Float Dept., PO Box 1143, Eagle River, AK 99577. Att.: John Ginsberg. (907) 694-2194. Yukon, Chilikadrotna, Mulchatna & Talchulitna (AK). May–Sept. Up to 16 people. Scheduled & custom trips. 14 days, $1,090–$1,230; 7–8 days, $610–$660; 1 day, $50; incl. bush flight & all but personal gear. Arrival: Anchorage, AK.

For all but his Yukon River trip, John Ginsberg flies people into remote wilderness rivers by float-equipped aircraft. In these beautiful areas, each "a photographer's delight," you see the nesting ground of the whistling swan, miners working claims staked out in the gold rush of '89, an Eskimo village—and plenty of rainbow trout and salmon. The 16-foot inflatable rubber boats, oared by well-trained guides, carry 3 to 4 people by these "last frontier" journeys.

Klondike Safaris, PO Box 1898, Skagway, AK 99840. Att.: Skip Burns. (907) 983-2496. [Oct.–May: 823 6th St., Juneau, AK 99801. (907) 586-3924.] 6–8 people. 8 days on Bennett, Tagish & Atlin lakes, $550, incl. sleeping gear, Skagway & Atlin lodging & transport. Arrival: Skagway, AK. (See also *Backpacking, Youth Adventures.*)

"The most beautiful lake country in the Northland" is where Skip Burns guides small groups exploring the headwaters of the Yukon River. The trip begins with a narrow-gauge train ride to Bennett. Traveling in inflatable boats on wilderness lakes, you visit ghost settlements and spend 2 days in log cabins of Atlin, "a beautiful little gold rush town," where you ride horseback to a warm springs for a dip in 78-degree water.

Sourdough Outfitters, Bettles, AK 99726. Att.: David Ketscher. (807) 692-5252. Noatak (AK). Jul–Aug. 8 people. 22 days, $995, incl. air charter Fairbanks to wilderness; air back to Fairbanks extra. Bring sleeping gear. Arrival: Fairbanks, AK. (See also *Backpacking, Canoeing, Ski Touring, Dog Sledding.*)

Your trip begins with a charter flight from Fairbanks to a lake near the remote headwaters of the Noatak River. Spot moose, Dall sheep and golden eagles on hikes, float downstream past exciting rapids, tundra and the steep-walled Noatak Canyon. Catch chum salmon and Arctic char on the Kelly River. The expedition ends in the all-Eskimo village of Noatak.

ARIZONA

Canyoneers, Inc., PO Box 2997, East Flagstaff, AZ 86003. Att.: Gayord Staveley. (602) 526-0924. May–Sept. Grand Canyon (AZ), Upper Colorado (CO), Desolation/Gray canyons & San Juan Riv. (UT). 1–12 days. 1 day, San Juan, $55; 5 days, Desolation/Gray, $280; 7 days, Grand Canyon, $460, 12 days, $670. Bring or rent sleeping gear. Family & group rates. Arrival: Flagstaff, AZ. (See also *Backpacking, Jeeping.*)

Trips begin and end in Flagstaff for 2, 7, 10 or 12 days in the Grand Canyon, or for a 7-day combination hike/float trip. Canyoneers offers many Grand Canyon departure dates as well as 1- and 2-day floats on the San Juan and 5 days on the Green. Remarks Gaylord Staveley, "We cover canyon history, lore, geology and ecology, and use motor-powered pontoon boats or smaller oar-powered vessels."

Georgie's Royal River Rats, PO Box 12489, Las Vegas, NV 89112. (702) 451-5588. Att.: "Woman of the Rivers," Grand Canyon (AZ). May–Sept. Group size varies. 4 days, $125; 6 days, $250; 9 days, $375. Bringing sleeping gear. Arrival: Las Vegas, NV.

"See the Grand Canyon from the bottom by boat," Georgie urges. "There are rapids, thrills and excitement. I have a small river quota and many repeaters." Boats are tied in sets of 3 to form a large raft 27 feet by 35 feet with Johnson motors. Three small boats tied together form a smaller raft—"our thrill boat"—equipped with oars and motors. Georgie, a pioneer river-runner on the Colorado, goes on all her trips.

Grand Canyon Youth Expeditions, RR 4, Box 755, Flagstaff, AZ 86001. Att.: Dick & Susan McCallum. (602) 774-8176. 12–24 people. Mar.–Aug. Grand Canyon (AZ), 5–18 days, $285–$575. San Juan (UT), 2 days, $55. Dolores (CO), 3 days, $75. Bring sleeping gear. (See also *Backpacking, Ski Touring, Youth Adventures.*)

Family vacation trips through the Grand Canyon are a specialty with the McCallums. These are oar-powered journeys in boats that Dick has designed. He also supplies raft support for kayakers running the rapids. "I've been down the Canyon 75 times in everything from a kayak to a 30-foot raft," he says. "Each trip is a rich, rewarding new adventure." Some of his Grand Canyon and Dolores River trips are planned for the Museum of Northern Arizona, with a geologist providing educational interpretation.

Sanderson River Expeditions, 148 Sixth Ave., PO Box 1535, Page, AZ 86040. (602) 645-2587. Grand Canyon (AZ). Apr.–Sept. Up to 15 people (12 yrs. & older) on oar-powered trips: 5 days, $260; 7 days, $360; 11 days, $535. Up to 28 on motorized trips: 4-, 6-, 7-, 8- or 10-day trips, $225–$490; 7 days, incl. 1st night in motel & charter flight, $460. All equip. incl. Arrival: Page, AZ.

"All hardy, outdoor-loving people are welcome to explore with us the most rugged and spectacular canyons in the world. It's truly the experience of a lifetime!" Jerry Sanderson and Bill Diamond promise. You ride either 33-foot motorized or 22-foot oar-powered neoprene rubber boats.

Sundance River Expeditions, Inc., PO Box 1658, Flagstaff, AZ 86002. Att.: Russell Sullivan. (602) 635-2354. Dolores (CO). Apr.–Jun., 6–15 people. 3–8 days, $125–$300, incl. pickup in Moab. Bring sleeping gear. Group rates. Arrival: Moab, UT.

"We pick you up in Moab," says Russell Sullivan. "Soon we're floating the Dolores through ranch bottoms into canyons where deer come for a drink at river's edge and tanagers and western goldfinch fly overhead. With small groups everyone gets acquainted and shares in the boatmen's knowledge of ecology, outdoor cooking the river lore. We camp early to explore, swim and enjoy wilderness sounds—the breeze in the trees, a steak sizzling over the fire." The trip ends in the rounded dome country near Arches National Park at the confluence with the mighty Colorado.

CALIFORNIA

Adventours—Wet and Wild, Inc., Box B-AG, Woodland, CA 95695. Att.: Loren L. Smith. (916) 662-6824 or 3168. 8 CA rivers, Rogue (OR), Rio Grande (TX), Dinosaur Natl. Monument (UT). Apr.–Sept. Up to 25 people. 1 or more days. Sample rates: Sacramento, 1 day, $20; American, 2 days, $60; Rogue, 5 days, $210; Snake, 6 days, $285. Bring sleeping gear. Group rates.

"An inflatable boat is a magic carpet into otherwise inaccessible wilderness," says Loren Smith. His oar-powered trips stress variety. Feel free to hike while others fish or explore a cave, or take advantage of the guides' willingness to teach rowing and camping techniques. A vacationer comments: "Excellent, well-planned trips with good equipment and superior food." Adventours also organizes pack trips, backpacking, canoeing and other outdoor expeditions.

American River Touring Association, 1016-B Jackson St., Oakland, CA 94607. Att.: Lou Elliott. (415) 465-9355. 14 western riv.; also Midwest & BC. Apr.–Sept. 1–19 days. Sample rates: 4 days, Lodore Canyon & Green Riv. (UT), $180; 8 days, Grand Canyon, $475; 10 days, Chilcotin & Fraser riv. (BC), $785. Bring or rent sleeping gear. (See also *Canoeing*—MN.)

ARTA is staffed with more than 100 professional guides for dozens of oar-powered and some motorized trips on rivers throughout the West and Northwest and in British Columbia and the Midwest. With trips of varying length and many starting dates, they fit most vacation schedules. Besides river runs, ARTA conducts a white-water school for people interested in the techniques of white-water navigation and river expeditioning.

ECHO: The Wilderness Company, AG, 6505 Telegraph Ave., Oakland, CA 94609. Att.: Joseph Daly or Richard Linford. (415) 658-5075. Apr.–Oct. Up to 25 people, 1–14 days. 4 rivers in AK, 6 in CA, 3 in ID, Dolores (CO), Owyhee & Rogue (OR), Desolation/Gray & Westwater canyons (UT), 4 BC rivers. Sample rates: 6 days, Main Salmon, $350; Lower Salmon, $265; incl. pretrip motel & shuttles. CA rivers, $37/day, incl. shuttle. Cariboo riv. (BC), 14 days, $850. Koyukuk or Alatna 12-day backpack/raft combo, $799. Bring sleeping gear. Group & youth rates. Charters.

A typical ECHO fleet consists of 4 or 5 boats, 4 to 6 people in each, and sometimes a kayak or two. Oars or paddles provide the power, and passengers can develop white-water skills, instructed by guides who win kudos for being "alert, able and intelligent." With chartered and scheduled trips on many western rivers, ECHO has ventured north to four rivers of the Cariboo region in British Columbia and to the Alatna, Kobuk, Koyukuk and Noatak rivers in Alaska, where they sometimes combine backpacking with rafting in this awesome wilderness.

Grand Canyon Dories, Box 3029, Stanford, CA 94305. Att.: Martin Litton. (415) 851-0411. Grand Canyon (AZ); Hells Canyon, Main & Lower Salman (ID); Owyhee, Grand Ronde (OR); Desolation/Gray canyons (UT). May–Sept. Up to 22 people. 5–22 days. Sample rates: Grand Canyon, 18 days, $864; Main Salmon, 13 days, $650; Hells Canyon, 6 days, $360; Lower Salmon, 5 days, $280; Green, 6 days, $320. Bring or rent sleeping gear. Rates for groups, charters & under 15 yrs.

For all his river trips, Martin Litton uses the motorless dory—a compartmented rough-water boat of aluminum, Fiberglas or taut marine plywood. "It rides higher and drier than a raft, and does not bend or buckle in the waves or get soft when it's cool," he explains. There's an oarsman in each boat, but passengers (4 per boat) may take the oars and learn to run the rapids. Litton's Grand Canyon trips of 18 to 22 days are for those who want a slower, quieter voyage, with guided hikes along the way.

Henry & Grace Falany's White Water River Expeditions, PO Box 1249-D, Turlock, CA 95380. (209) 634-1133. Grand Canyon (AZ), May–Sept. Up to 36 people. 6–7 days, $475–$550. Bring sleeping gear. Children's rates. (See also *Scuba Diving*—Caribbean.)

Henry Falany believes that other things are involved in a river trip besides shooting the rapids and singing around the campfire—great as these are. His motor-powered trips include oral and visual orientation to instill respect for the ecology of wilderness areas. "We pay special attention to our younger river rats," he says, "as their ecological attitudes are important to the future of our society." Features of his service? "Excellent crew, food, safety record and equipment."

O.A.R.S., Inc., PO Box, 67-G, Angels Camp, CA 95222. Att.: George Wendt. (209) 736-2924. Tatshensheni (AK), Grand Canyon (AZ), 7 CA rivers, Dolores (CO), Middle Fork, Main Salmon & Lochsa (ID), Rogue, Owyhee & Grande Ronde (OR), Rio Grande (TX), San Juan, Green & Cataract (UT). Most trips Mar.–Oct., Rio Grande in Dec. 16–25 people, 2–19 days. Sample rates: 5 days, Rogue, $235; 7 days, San Juan, $385; Grand Canyon, 5 days, $345; 13 days, $675. Bring sleeping gear. Youth rates. (See also *Youth Adventures.*)

Oars only on these trips—no motors to destroy the serenity. George Wendt also believes in small groups. Sixteen is maximum in the Grand Canyon, where he plans plenty of time for leisurely canyon hikes to explore rare natural wonders and Indian ruins. "Floats on Utah's San Juan River, Oregon's Rogue and Idaho's Salmon are geared especially for families," he says, "while young adults enjoy the exciting rapids of the California rivers and the Middle Fork."

Outdoors Unlimited, Dept. A, 2500 5th Ave., Sacramento, CA 95818. Att.: John Vail. (916) 452-1081. Grand Canyon (AZ), 6 CA rivers, Main Salmon (ID), Rogue (OR). Apr.–Oct. Up to 25 people. 2–12 days, $60–$530. Sample rates: Rogue, 3–4 days, $115–$145; Main Salmon, 6 days, $325; Grand Canyon, 5–12 days $295–$530. Everything provided. Discounts for charters & children under 13 yrs.

"Each day brings delights," says John Vail, "the splash, spray and tumult of rapids, and the tranquil, reflective stillness that only the wild places can provide." His boats carry 5 people and are manned by qualified oarsmen who double as trail chefs and guides on these pleasureable trips. He also runs the Chilcotin in British Columbia through an affiliate.

River Adventures West, PO Box 5219-A, Santa Monica, CA 90405. Att.: John W. Dorr, Jr. (213) 396-2333. Mar.–Sept. 1–30 people. Stanislaus, Merced, Tuolumne, American & East Carson riv. (CA): 1–3 days, $31–$155. Middle Fork & Main Salmon riv. (ID): 3–10 days, $255–$395. Bring sleeping gear. Group & children's rates.

"Running the Middle Fork of the Salmon River is a perfect family adventure," John Dorr says of his oar-powered trips. "There are 106 thrill-packed miles and time to swim, fish, explore, make camp and eat." Trips start on scheduled dates. "It's an experience all should have," writes a vacationer. "The food was very good, the boatmen competent and companionable."

River Rat Raft Rentals, 4053 Pennsylvania Ave., Fair Oaks, CA 95628. Att.: Robert N. DeVisscher. (916) 966-6555. [Oct.–Mar.: RAFT, 3632 Waynart Ct., Carmichael, CA 95608.] American Riv. (CA). Apr.–Sept. Any number of people. 1 day, $25. Bring sleeping gear.

With "the finest of river equipment," the enthusiastic DeVisscher family runs the American River exclusively. Believing their guests should have a chance to participate, they offer paddle options whenever conditions allow, the paddle boats being the same as the rafts they use for guided tours. On the upper section of the river you float through gold country. The lower American, a family favorite, is a do-it-yourself run, "an ideal introduction to the experience of river running."

Wilderness Water Ways, Inc., 33-A Canyon Lake Dr., Port Costa, CA 94569. Att.: Bryce Whitmore. (415) 787-2820. [Or 12260 Galice Rd., Merlin, OR 97532. (503) 479-2021.] 6 CA riv., Rogue & Illinois (OR). Mar.–Oct. 8–25 people. 2 days, $55–$70; 3–4 days, $130–$200. Group & youth rates. Bring sleeping gear.

Bryce Whitmore's rafts are "Huck Finn" style—"more fun, more maneuverable, and self-bailing," he claims. "The river is the heart of the wilderness, and river running is the best way to enjoy it." Choice of lodges or camping on Rogue trips.

Wilderness World, 1342 Jewell Ave., Pacific Grove, CA 93950. Att.: Vladimir Kovalik. (408) 373-5882. Grand Canyon (AZ); 4 CA rivers; Hells Canyon, Middle Fork & Main Salmon (ID); Rogue, Owyhee & John Day (OR); Rio Grande (TX); Usumacinta (Mexico). Apr.–Oct. Up to 25 people. Sample rates: Tuolumne, 2–3 days, $125–$155; Owyhee, 5 days, $260; Hells Canyon, 6 days, $285. Bring sleeping gear. Group & youth discounts.

"The best float trippers," remarks Vladimir Kovalik, "are the people with open eyes, who see the beauty of light patterns on water, fresh spring sorrel or wild mint at creekside, the softly rounded indentation in a flat rock where Indian maids once ground acorn seeds." His neoprene rafts, oar-powered, carry 4 to 5 passengers. He also offers a 5-day white-water course on the Stanislaus or Rogue ($205 for 18 years and up) to teach how to handle small rafts, prepare gear and preserve the river environment.

William McGinnis' Whitewater Voyages/River Exploration Ltd., Dept. AGI, 1225 Liberty St., El Cerrito, CA 94530. Att.: William McGinnis. (415) 236-7219. Most rivers Apr.–Sept.; Rio Grande also Dec. 6–25 people. American, Carson, Eel, Klamath & Merced (CA): 1 day, $38; 2 days, $70; 3 days, $100. Owyhee & Grande Ronde (OR): 5 days, $180. Rio Grande (TX): 5–6 days, $200. Bring sleeping gear. Group & family rates.

Bill McGinnis' small outfit offers a broad range of river voyages, from 1- and 2-day trips near San Francisco to extended expeditions. He uses paddle boats, inflatable kayaks and oar-powered rafts, with everyone getting into the action. There's time to poke around the beaches, pools and caves, and the skilled, friendly guides turn out sumptuous meals. Bill feels his expeditions are "the best available—and at

Grand Canyon Expeditions, UT, by Patricia Caulfield.

very reasonable prices.'' His book *Whitewater Rafting* graphically describes the art of running rivers.

Zephyr River Expeditions, PO Box 529, Columbia, CA 95310. Att.: Robert Ferguson. (209) 532-6249. American, Carson, Eel, Kern, Klamath & Merced (CA). Mar.–Oct. 4–25 people. 1 day, $35; 2 days, $75–$80; 4 days (Eel), $125. River study program, $17/day. Bring sleeping gear. Group & family rates. Charters. (See also *Canoeing*.)

"Mid-May to mid-June has the highest water level for the ultimate ride,'' says Robert Ferguson. "Mid-June to August is ideal for swimming and exploring, while early fall is beautiful in this land of canyons and limestone cliffs.'' Your choice of oar-powered or paddle boats. The multitalented guides prepare meals "designed for hungry adventurers'' and share their knowledge of natural history, folklore, wildlife and rafting. For educational groups, a river study program includes controlling a raft, reading water, cooking, geology, botany, river lore and gold panning.

COLORADO

Adventure Bound, Inc., 6179 S. Adams Dr., Box S, Littleton, CO 80121. Att.: Jerry Wischmeyer. (303) 771-3752. Desolation/Gray, Cataract & Westwater canyons, Dinosaur Natl. Monument (UT); North Platte & Upper Colorado riv. (CO). May–Sept. 6–40 people. Avg. rates, 1–4 days, $23–$180. Westwater Canyon, 2 days, $90; Lodore Canyon, 3 days, $150; Desolation/Gray Canyons, 4 days, $180. Bring sleeping gear. Group & family discounts.

Adventure Bound's oar-powered river runs through Dinosaur Natl. Monument (Lodore or Yampa Canyons) start and end in Steamboat Springs, CO, and the Westwater Canyon trip in Grand Junction. For Cataract Canyon you meet in Moab, and for Desolation/Gray Canyons in the town of Green River. Upper Colorado trips (1 day) begin at Steamboat. Dozens of scheduled trips to choose from.

American Wilderness Company, Box 9397, Aspen, CO 81611. Att.: Larry Edwards. (303) 925-1934. [Oct.–Apr.: (303) 925-6093.] Arkansas, Upper Colorado, Dolores, Roaring Fork (CO); Main Salmon (ID); Rogue (OR); Cataract, Desolation/Gray, Westwater canyons, Dinosaur Natl. Monument (UT). May–Sept. 15–35 people. 1–6 days. Simple rates: Arkansas, 2 days, $60; Roaring Fork, $23/day; Dolores, 6 days, $225; incl. shuttle. Bring or rent sleeping gear. Youth rates.

Get ready for excitement, wildflower walks, bird watching, good fellowship and sumptuous meals (most boatmen have cooked for restaurants) on AWC trips. What's white water like? "Serenity, anticipation, apprehension, a growing roar, increasing speed, the first wave, spume, spray . . . hang on, lifting up, plunging down, the last crest, exhaustion, exultation, serenity.'' Dedicated to excellence and using "the best of oar and paddle boats,'' AWC also stresses low rates.

Anderson River Expeditions, Gypsum, CO 81637. Att.: Travis Anderson. (303) 524-7766. Upper Colorado (CO), ½ day, $15; 1 day, $25; 2 days, $50; 3 days, $80; incl. transport to/from Vail. Bring or rent sleeping gear. Under 12 yrs., less. Arrival: Vail, CO.

Anderson's specialty is running the Upper Colorado in 15-foot oar-powered Avon rafts, with 6 passengers in each. You intermittentently shoot rapids and float lazily through low alpine and high desert country to towering rock formations, with overnight camping on a beautiful island. All trips start from Dotsero—an unmarked village at the junction of the Eagle and Colorado rivers. Don't fret about finding it: ARE takes you there from Vail.

Colorado Rivers, Box 1386, Durango, CO 81301. Att.: Preston Ellsworth (303) 259-0708. [Sept.–May: (303) 247-0834.] Animas, Dolores (CO), Rio Grande (NM & TX), San Juan (UT). May–Sept. 8 or more people. 2–5 days, $50/day; 1 day, $25–$35; ½ day, $15; incl. shuttle. Bring sleeping gear.

With day floats on the Animas, scene of Colorado's frenetic silver rush 100 years ago, Pres Ellsworth has expanded his service (through Rio Bravo Tours and Canyon Tours) to the Rio Grande, where Anasazi and Pueblo civilizations once flourished; and to the San Juan, archaeologically and geologically as interesting as the Grand Canyon but tamer—a good choice for families; and to the Dolores, under consideration for inclusion in the Wild and Scenic Rivers Act—a superb wilderness experience and interesting white water.

Four Corners Expeditions, PO Box 1032-AG, Buena Vista, CO 81211. Att.: Reed & Karen Dils. (303) 395-8949. Dolores, Arkansas, Upper Colorado, Animas, San Juan, Roaring Fork (CO). Apr.–Aug. 2–30 people. 1–6 days. Dolores, 4 days, $165. Arkansas, ½ day $16. 6 day pkg. on 5 riv., $315. Bring sleeping gear. Group & family rates.

From April to June, Reed and Karen recommend the Dolores for an exciting white-water wilderness experience for environmentally concerned people. They run the Arkansas River on ½- and 2-day trips from June through August—including Brown's Canyon, the most thrilling ½-day trip in Colorado. Their 6-day package (June only) starts at Durango and takes you on 5 Colorado rivers. With overnights in scenic mountain towns, it's "for those who want daytime excitement and nighttime comfort."

International Aquatic Adventures, Inc., 2047 Broadway, Boulder, CO 80302. Att.: John Sanker & Tim Hervey. (303) 449-4620. Dolores, Upper Colorado, Arkansas, Cache la Poudre (CO); North Platte (CO & WY). May–Sept. 4–40 people. 1–6 days. Sample rates: Cache la Poudre, ½ day, $10; North Platte, 2 days, $75; Dolores, 3 days, $120, 6 days, $215. Bring or rent sleeping gear. (See also *Scuba Diving/Snorkeling*—HI.)

IAA believes in involving you in the total river experience, whether it's rowing a boat or helping with the campsite chores. "The more you're involved, the more you'll bring home from a river adventure," they say. There are exciting rapids on each of their runs, some more intense than others. On fall trips (at lower rates) you view the wildlife and changing aspens with few other boaters on the river. IAA offers 7-day white-water rafting schools in spring.

Mountain Guides and Outfitters, Inc., PO Box 2001, Aspen, CO 81611. Att.: Kenneth R. Wyrick. (303) 925-6680. Dolores & Upper Colorado (CO), Desolation/Gray & Stillwater/Labyrinth canyons (UT). Custom trips. Mar.–Jun. 4–15 people, 4–10 days. $75/day, also ½- & 1-day rates. Rates incl. transport to/from Aspen or Grand Junction. Bring or rent sleeping gear. Sept.–Oct., Togiak (AK), $125/day. (See also *Backpacking, Mountaineering, Ski Touring*—Aspen Ski Touring School, *Dog Sledding*.)

"We cater to those interested in the quiet and exhilaration of river and desert," says Ken Wyrick, "and customize each trip. With small groups you can decide where to camp, when to lay over, which canyons to hike." Ken uses oars mostly, with a small motor for windy days, and he plans fresh food on trips of up to 7 days. He also arranges fly-ins for those needing to save time.

Rancho del Rio, Bond, CO 80423. Att.: Bud Wilcox. (303) 926-3631. Upper Colorado (CO). May–Sept. 2–20 people. Adult, $15/day, $12.50/half day; under 13 yrs., $12.50 or $10.

Ideal family trips, these scenic floats travel rapids and calm water through 10 or 15 miles of the Lower Gore Canyon. You'll investigate prehistoric dinosaur tracks at one stop. Bring tennis shoes, rain gear and lunch.

River Runners, Ltd., Salida, CO 81201. Att.: Pam & Dave Smith. (303) 539-2144. Arkansas (CO), May–Sept. 3–35 people. Adult, $25/day, $12/half day; child, $20

Grand Canyon Dories, CA.

or $10; incl. lunch on all-day trip.

"Our ½-day run on the Arkansas is an excellent, affordable introduction to white-water rafting," comments Dave Smith. "The river is an ever-changing source of adventure, filled with gigantic boulders, calm pools and rapids as it tumbles through the breathtaking scenery of the Sangre de Cristo Mountains and the Royal Gorge."

Rocky Mountain Expeditions, Inc., PO Box CC-AG, Buena Vista, CO 81211. Att.: Al McClelland. (303) 395-8466. Arkansas (CO). May–Sept. 3–6 people per raft, 8 yrs. min. ½ day, $15–$20. Longer trips & group rates. (See also *Backpacking, Ski Touring, Wilderness Living*.)

"The Arkansas offers the wildest little raft ride in Colorado," Al says. "Kayakers come from around the world to try it. Our floats go through the Upper Arkansas Valley from Buena Vista to Salida and beyond."

Rocky Mountain River Expeditions, Inc., PO Box 1394, Denver, CO 80201. Att.: Greg Young. (303) 289-5959. Arkansas, Dolores, Upper Colorado, North Platte (CO); Desolation/Gray & Westwater canyons (UT). May–Sept. Up to 21 people, 1–5 days. Sample rates: 1 day, $30; 2 days, $85–$95; 3 days, $85–$105; adult & youth group rates. Bring sleeping gear.

"Outdoor adventure in the Rocky Mountain Region" is what Greg Young considers the outstanding feature of his service, plus years of experience. He also combines oar-powered river trips with backpacking treks (for 6–12 people, 3–5 days, $35/day) in the Eagles Nest Wilderness area of the Gore Range. With many departure dates, his trips, according to vacationers, are "educational excursions of quality and genuine fun."

Snowmass Whitewater, Box 5566, Snowmass Village, CO 81615. Att.: Bob Harris. (303) 923-2000. Jun.–Sept. 4 or more people. Upper Colorado & Roaring Fork

(CO): adult, $22/day; under 16 yrs. $15. Arkansas (CO): $35/day; rates incl. lunch & shuttle.

Looking for something to do near Aspen? All three Snowmass river trips are conveniently nearby, and Bob Harris shuttles you to and from the river. Bob takes large groups as well as families with small children on these 1-day scenic floats through the canyons of the Upper Colorado and Roaring Fork and the more adventurous white-water trips on the Arkansas.

Timber Travels, Inc., PO Box 344, Wheat Ridge, CO 80033. Att.: Kent Cluck. (303) 420-6089. Upper Colorado & near Glenwood Springs (CO): May–Sept. 10–60 people, 1–2 days, $30–$75, incl. shuttle. Bring sleeping gear.

"It's thrills and chills on these fun-filled 1- and 2-day trips amid froth and foam," raves a float tripper. "And all within easy driving distance of Denver." The 2-day mini-adventures pack in a lot—shooting the rapids of narrow, steep-walled Gore Canyon, watching bald eagles soar overhead, eating as much hand-cranked ice cream as you can, and finally, floating into open, smooth water through the White River National Forest. You do the paddling, under the direction of the skilled, fun-loving guides. "Our trips are great starters for bigger rivers," remarks Kent Cluck. "Join us—and leave your problems behind!"

Viking River Expeditions, PO Box 383, Greeley, CO 80631. Att.: Brian & Sandy Hanson. (303) 351-6796. May–Sept. 5–35 people. North Platte (WY & CO) & Upper Colorado & Arkansas (CO): 1 day, $25; 2 days, $75; 3 days, $95. Cache La Poudre (CO): 1 hr., $6.50. Bring or rent sleeping gear.

The North Platte challenges float trippers with some of the most intense white water in Colorado and Wyoming as it flows through primitive Northgate Canyon and Medicine Bow National Forest. Pine and spruce line the banks, and you'll spot deer, eagles and bighorn sheep. Outstanding mountain scenery also on the Upper Colorado and lots of white water on the Arkansas, both "real fun weekend outings," as the outfitter rates them. For an introduction to river running, the Poudre provides a wet and wild 1-hour thrill. Your choice of oar-powered (try your hand) or paddle boat (*everyone* participates.)

Wild Water West River Excursions, 8240A Queen St., Arvada, CO 80005. Att.: Jim Temple. (303) 421-2102. May–Sept. 8–32 people. Upper Colorado (CO): 1 day, $25; 2 days, $75. North Platte (WY & CO): 2 days, $82.50. Arkansas (CO): 1 day, $35. Incl. lunch on 1-day trips, 5 meals on 2-day trips. Bring or rent sleeping gear. Also arr. longer custom trips on other rivers.

"Our main base of operation is the Upper Colorado River," explains Jim Temple. "And our stretch through the beautiful Gore Range is one of the most popular runs in Colorado. You travel through picturesque canyons and ranchland with the ever-present snow-capped peaks in the background." More advanced but equally spectacular are trips on the North Platte through alpine mountains with canyon walls soaring to 500 feet. Also trips on the churning white water of the Arkansas as it descends through the Sangre de Cristo Range—"the ultimate rafting adventure." Some guests ride the oar-driven rafts, but most prefer the fun on a paddle boat.

Wilderness Aware, PO Box 401A, Colorado Springs, CO 80901. Att.: Bill Alexander. (303) 687-9662. 6–18 people. May–Aug. 1–6 days. Arkansas, Cache La Poudre, Upper Colorado, Dolores (CO); North Platte (WY & CO). 1 day, $30; 2 days, $85; 3 days, $120; 6 days, $240. Also Rio Grande (TX) Dec.–Jan., 7 days, $300. Bring sleeping gear. Group rates.

Bill Alexander's popular 2-day adventures on the Arkansas start south of Buena Vista. These are small, personalized trips—oar-powered the first day in difficult white water, and paddle-powered the second day, with everybody paddling. In fact, there's white-water excitement on all the rivers Bill runs. "We use only the best equipment," he says, "and safety is our primary concern. Our qualified guides are a storehouse of river know-how. We pull into camp in time for a hike before a delicious meal."

Wilderness Sports, Ltd., PO Box 36A, Bond, CO 80423. Att.: Ed Peterson. (303) 926-3774. [Oct.–May: 8828 E. Florida Ave., #218, Denver, CO 80231. Same tel.] Upper Colorado (CO) May–Sept. Up to 100 people. 1–2 days. $44/day; $39 under 16 yrs.; incl. lodging & meals. Bring sleeping gear. Group rates.

"Check in at our Pour House Lounge the night before for dancing and entertainment, use the volleyball court and bathhouse, and stay in preset tents," invites Ed Peterson. "After a hearty breakfast we drive to the put-in point upriver, and we're off for a full day on the Colorado." The second day's put-in is downriver. Wilderness Sports accommodates singles, clubs, business groups, Scout troops, individuals and families. Each raft holds 8 paddlers and a boatman.

GEORGIA

Southeastern Expeditions, Inc., 2220 Parkdale Dr. N.E., Suite 330, Atlanta, GA 30345. Att.: Claude Terry. (404) 491-9439. 2 GA rivers, Apr.–Oct. Chattooga, 30 people max., 1 day, $25; $75 overnight. Bring sleeping gear. (Also day hikes, $40.) Cattahoochee, 40 people max., ½ day, $10–$12. Group charters.

"Our most popular and challenging trip is Section IV of the Chattooga, with over 40 rapids (Class III +) in a 6-mile stretch," Claude Terry explains. "This is where most of the *Deliverance* movie was filmed." In fact, it was this film, for which Terry was technical director, that launched him into the river-running business. The tamer Section III of the river is for 9-year-olds and up; 11-year-olds and up on the Section IV. "No experience necessary—we train you on the river," Terry says. These all-day trips, with a smorgasbord lunch, or 2 days with a wilderness campout, start at his base camp near Clayton and can be combined with an extra day's guided hike. Also ½-day float trips on the scenic Chattahoochee outside of Atlanta, and a canoe and kayak service.

IDAHO

Bob Smith's Salmon River Boat Tours, Box 1185, North Fork, ID 83466. (208) 865-2525 or 2512. Main Salmon (ID). Mar.–Oct. 4–20 people. 1 or more days. Avg. rates, $50–$60/day. Bring sleeping gear. Family & group rates. Arrival: Salmon or North Fork, ID.

On these river trips you stop to pan for gold, visit old homesteads, find Indian artifacts, and fish and swim in the granite-walled Salmon River Canyon—⅕ mile deeper than the Grand Canyon. Besides raft trips, Bob offers excursions in 24-foot or 30-foot aluminum jet boats, with overnights at China Bar Lodge (1 day, $25–$40; 2 or more days, $35–$50/day). Or try a combination float-jet boat trip with your choice of a lodge or camping out at night. Bob was boatman for a *National Geographic* expedition on the river.

Eldon Handy River Expeditions, Box 15-A, Jerome, ID 83338. (208) 324-4339. Middle Fork & Main Salmon (ID). May–Sept. Up to 40 people, up to 6 days. Middle Fork, 6 days, $395; Main Salmon, 6 days, $360. Bring or rent sleeping gear. Family discounts.

"My first oar-powered trips were for my own enjoyment," recalls Eldon Handy. "But I soon found I was sharing these experiences with others." According to one float tripper who shared the experience, it was a particularly great family trip. "We took all our children, seven being girls. Our float down the Middle Fork had to be the most memorable family vacation we've ever had."

Frontier Expeditions, Inc., Box 839, Dept. 201, North Fork, ID 83466. Att.: Woodrow & Linda Hassinger. (208) 865-2200. [Sept.–May: 3921 S. Helena St., Aurora, CO 80013. (303) 693-0349.] Main Salmon (ID). May–Sept. 2–25 people, 1–6 days. 4 days, $390; 5 days, $450. Sleeping gear and shuttle to Salmon incl. Family rates.

"Come share an adventure on the legendary Salmon the whole family will enjoy," invite the Hassingers. "We navigate calm-flowing pools laced with powerful rapids in our oar-powered neoprene and nylon boats." The 5-day trip runs through 90 miles of primitive mountain country. You can fish for trout, salmon and steelhead in what the Shoshone called the "big fish water;" splash in the hotsprings; poke around deserted cabins—and satisfy first-class river appetites with first-class meals. The 4-day trip stops at the China Bar Lodge for the third night. And both trips claim an exciting finale: a jet boat ride back to the put-in at Corn Creek.

Happy Hollow Camps, Box 694-A, Salmon, ID 83467. Att.: Martin R. Capps. (208) 756-3954. Middle Fork & Main Salmon (ID). Jun.–Sept. Up to 20 people, 3–12 days. About $50/day. Bring or rent sleeping gear. Arrival: Salmon, ID. (See also *Pack Trips.*)

Marty Capps, who has run these rivers for 20 years, believes you haven't had a real western vacation until you've floated the beautiful Salmon. He uses sturdy nylon neoprene boats, oar-powered, designed for Idaho's wild rivers. His trips feature panning for gold, visiting Indian caves, spotting wildlife, swimming, fishing, experienced guides and good, wholesome meals. Middle Fork trips put in at Dagger Falls on Indian Creek.

Idaho Adventures, Inc., PO Box 834-C7, Salmon, ID 83467. Att.: Hank Miller. (208) 756-2986. Hells Canyon, & Main & Middle Fork of Salmon (ID); Owyhee (OR). Apr.–Oct. 4–20 persons. 6-day trips: Middle Fork, $465; Hells Canyon & Main Salmon, $435. 5-day trips: Owyhee Riv., $357; Lower Salmon, $345. Bring or rent sleeping gear. Group & family rates.

All trips start and end in Boise, Idaho, which is served by major airlines, and Hank's rates include charter flights over the beautiful Idaho mountains to the put-in point. "This eliminates the problems people have had in getting to and from the river," Hank writes. "Once in Boise you receive our complete guide service with no hidden expenses, and Sharon and I get personally involved with the trips."

Ken Smith's Middle Fork River Expeditions, Box 1122A, North Fork, ID 83466. (208) 865-2498. Middle Fork of Salmon (ID), Jun.–Sept. Up to 16 people, 5 days. Private trip, $400, incl. charter flight & sleeping gear. Volume trip, $375 + flight to put-in; bring or rent sleeping gear. Child & group rates. Arrival: Salmon, ID.

Ken Smith is a third-generation outfitter and guide. His grandfather hauled freight in wooden scows on the Main Salmon to the gold mines. His father started hauling passengers, and Ken specializes in 5-day custom float trips on the Middle Fork in 20-foot oar-powered boats. "Our trips are restful and tranquil," he says. "You can hike, swim, find Shoshone petroglyphs, photograph wildlife—or just enjoy the savory, crystal like mountain air. See you on the river!"

Nez Perce Outfitters & Guides, Box 1454-S, Salmon, ID 83467. Att.: Val B. Johnson. (208) 756-3912. Middle Fork of Salmon (ID). Jul.–Sept. 2–10 people. 3-day trips, $325; 5-day trips, $425. Bring or rent sleeping gear. Arrival: Salmon, ID. (See also *Hiking with Packstock, Pack Trips.*)

"We stay at Forest Service campsites at night and spend about 4 hours each day actually floating the river under oar power," Val Johnson tells us. "This allows time to enjoy all aspects of life on the river—camping, fishing, swimming, hiking, picture-taking." He will tailor trips for groups and arrange charter flights, car shuttles and other services. "A remote and beautiful area and an excellent service," say vacationers.

Nicholson & Sons Float Trips Inc., Rt. 4, Twin Falls, ID 83301. Att.: Roy L. Nicholson. (208) 733-6139. Middle Fork of Salmon (ID). Jul.–Aug. Up to 15 people, 3–6 days. 6 days, $395. Bring sleeping gear. Family & group rates. Arrival: Stanley, ID.

From Stanley the Nicholsons drive you to the put-in spot on the Middle Fork. Their guides have chalked up a total of 10,000 miles on this 106-mile run—an oar-powered trip with over 80 rapids. It's both peaceful and wildly exciting. Starting in rich virgin forest land at about 6,600 feet, you float through constantly changing scenery and finish at 3,000 feet in a spectacular sheer rocky gorge. "These are marvelously knowledgeable, dedicated and safety-conscious guides," one of their guests writes, "who know the lore and history of the region. The campfire cooking and sourdough recipes are excellent."

Norm and Bill Guth, Box 705, Salmon, ID 83467. (208) 756-3279. Apr.–Aug. Up to 30 people, 5 days. Middle Fork of Salmon (ID), $400 + transport to put-in. Main Salmon (ID), $375. Return to Salmon incl. Bring or rent sleeping gear. Custom trips.

"Ride your air mattress behind the mother boat, swim, fish, pan gold, and ride the big pontoons through the Main Salmon's famous rapids," invite the Guths. Or you can float downstream 4 days, then jet-boat back upstream—no need for a car shuttle or charter flight. For the 5-day Middle Fork trip you fly to the put-in point, and camp where night overtakes you. "Our trips are easy to make," note the Guths. "They're ideal for adults of all ages—and great fun for small fry!" Vacationers write, "A tremendous trip!"

Primitive Area Float Trips, Inc., Box 585-D, Salmon, ID 83467. Att.: Stanton C. Miller. (208) 756-2319. Hells Canyon, Middle Fork & Main Salmon, & Selway (ID); Owyhee (OR). Mar.–Nov. 4–15 people. 3 days, $234; 11 days, $522. Group discounts. Arrival: Salmon, ID. (See also *Canoeing.*)

Stan Miller writes: "Custom trips for families and small groups are based on group interests—fishing, photography, archaeology, Indian habitat." He offers both custom and scheduled trips, some combined with backpacking, horse packing or overnight jet boat trips on the Salmon. For those who love river-running and yen to go pro, Stan also runs the Idaho Outfitters School for Professional Guides.

Salmon River Lodge, PO Box 58A, Salmon, ID 83467. Att.: Dave & Phyllis Giles. (208) 756-2646. Main Salmon (ID). Jul.–Aug. 1–5 days, $40–$375. Group rates. Arrival: Salmon, ID. (See also *Pack Trips, Jet Boating.*)

The Giles' lodge is across the river from where the road ends. Crank the roadside phone and they'll jet over to pick you up. "They are warm and friendly hosts," vacationers say, "and everything is topnotch on these trips. It's heaven on earth if you love the outdoors." Floats can be combined with jet boat cruises or pack trips on horseback.

Snake River Outfitters, 811 Snake River Ave., Lewiston, ID 83501. Att.: Norman Riddle. (208) 743-6276 or 746-2232. Jun.–Sept. Hells Canyon, 4 days, $235; Lower Salmon, 3 days, $165; incl. sleeping gear. Arrival: Lewiston, ID. (See also *Jet Boating.*)

Besides his scheduled Hells Canyon trips, Norman Riddle provides raft support for "do-it-yourselfers" and arranges custom trips of 5 days or longer for groups of 8 or more. On the Lower Canyon of the Main Salmon River his trips run from Whitebird (ID) to the mouth of the Grand Ronde. Raft and jet boat combinations are one of his specialties.

Sun Valley River Tours, Box 354-A, Ketchum, ID 83340. Att.: Al Beam. (208) 726-5218. Middle Fork & Main Salmon (ID) Owyhee & Bruneau (OR). May–Sept. Up to

15 people. Middle Fork, Jun.–Aug.: 3 days, $300; 6 days, $500; less in May & Sept; charter flights extra when required; Owyhee, May, 5 days, $350; Main Salmon day trip, $30; 6-day river tour package, $449. Group & children's rates. Bring sleeping gear.

On these trips you spend about 5 hours a day on the water, with frequent stops to hike, explore and swim. Veteran guides explain local history and geology, and also can give kayak instruction to raft passengers adventurous enough to try it. Kayakers may accompany trips for a nominal fee. Beam's new 6-day Main Salmon package includes 2 nights at Sun Valley, 3 on the river, 1 at a river lodge, and 2 air charter flights.

Teton Expeditions, Inc., 427 E. 13 St., Idaho Falls, ID 83401. Att.: Jay Dee Foster. (208) 523-4981. Mar.–Oct. 5–20 people, up to 12 days. Middle Fork & Main Salmon (ID). 5–6 days, $325. Day trips on Blackfoot, Teton & Snake (ID & WY), $20. Bring sleeping gear. (See also *Pack Trips.*)

"Our family company started over a quarter century ago, when my uncle and I explored trapping possibilities on Henry's Fork," Jay Dee says. "Every one of us is a fully qualified river boatman today. You'll have fun, excitement, rapids and good food on these trips."

Wilderness River Outfitters & Trail Expeditions, PO Box 871-AG, Salmon, ID 83467. Att.: the Tonsmeires. (208) 756-3959. Main Salmon & Hells Canyon (ID), Bruneau & Owyhee (OR), Desolation/Gray canyons (UT). Mar.–Nov. 3–13 people, 2–14 days (longer for charters). Sample rates: Bruneau, 5 days, $775; Main Salmon, 6 days, $400; Hells Canyon, 4 days, $310. (See also *Backpacking, Ski Touring.*)

"These are more than just outdoor trips," the Tonsmeires explain. "They're adventures with small groups in which each person can contribute to—as well as receive from—a learning experience. We try to create an increased awareness of the challenge, and the beauty and fragility of the wilderness."

Grand Canyon Expeditions, UT, by Patricia Caulfield.

MAINE

Maine Whitewater Expeditions, West Forks, ME 04985. Att.: Jim Ernst. (207) 663-2214. May–Oct. Up to 30 people. Upper Kennebec Gorge, (ME). Wkdays & Sat., $30; Sun., $20. Dead Riv. (ME), $35/day. Group & youth rates.

"After over 20,000 miles of white-water guiding in the West, I've returned to Maine," writes Jim Ernst, "to introduce people to a true white-water experience in the beautiful Maine wilderness." His day trip on the Upper Kennebec River begins with a short hike to spectacular 90-foot Moxie Falls ("worth the day in itself," writes a guest). From there you run some of the East Coast's roughest white-water in an inflatable raft.

Northern Whitewater Expeditions, PO Box 57, Rockwood, ME 04478. Att.: Wayne Hockmeyer. (207) 534-7355. May–Oct. 1–60 people. Kennebec (ME) wkdays, $42.50. West Branch of Penobscot (ME) wkends, $47.50.

It's your choice on these Kennebec River trips: take the upper portion, an easy run and a cruise across Indian Pond. Or if you're over 12, continue on the lower section as the river plummets through deep canyons on the longest, steepest drop of any river in the East. Even more challenging is the West Branch of the Penobscot— "easily the most spectacular river in the East," claims Wayne Hockmeyer. With steep drops, then calmer water under Mount Katahdin, keep alert for the cry, "Paddles to hand, white-water ahead!" (Over 15 years only on this trip.) NWE was first with the white-water rafts on these rivers.

MONTANA

Halter Ranch, Box 50, Big Sandy, MT 59520. Att.: Jerry Halter. (406) 386-2464. Upper Missouri & Judith (MT). May–Oct. 2 or more people, 1–6 days. $100/day per group of 2–4. Sleeping gear incl.

"Jerry Halter's love for this Lewis and Clark area and his intense interest in its history make every day a pleasurable lesson in Americana," writes a vacationer. "Jerry is a fantastic host and good company." His motorized boat trips, beginning at his ranch, take you past the river's White Rocks area. Strange formations— castles, cathedrals, fortresses—rise from the riverbanks like the ruins of an ancient civilization. You'll see wildlife, explore abandoned homesteads and forts in this primitive area, and dig for artifacts.

Missouri River Cruises, Box 1212-A, Fort Benton, MT 59442. Att.: Bob Singer. (406) 622-3295. Upper Missouri Riv. May–Sept. 8–18 people, 1–5 days. About $40–$45/day; under 16 yrs; $30; incl. all but sleeping bag. Car ferrying extra (See also *Canoeing*.)

Where the deer and the antelope still roam, canopied riverboats lazily wend their way through 160 miles from Fort Benton's Main Street levee to Fort Peck Reservoir. Read the Lewis and Clark journal of May 31, 1805, for a compelling description of this untouched, primitive land. You float past rock formations, white cliffs and abandoned cabins whose inhabitants serviced the bygone steamboat route—a delightful return to the past. The more adventuresome paddle the route in canoes.

NEW YORK

Big Apple Expeditions, 17 Hatfield Place, Staten Island, NY 10302. Att.: Michael Notarfrancesco. (212) 981-1017. Lower Hudson & Long Island Sound (NY), Delaware & Barnegat Bay (NJ). Apr.–Oct. 6–24 people, 1–7 days. $20–$60/day, incl. sleeping gear.

"Ours are the only trips in the U.S. exploring salt-water marsh areas," states Mike Notarfrancesco. And they're something new for the Big Apple area. On motorized rafts you navigate New York/New Jersey tidal waters and crab, clam and fish—feasting on your catch. Mike's nature-oriented trips and paddle floats on the

Upper Delaware emphasize hiking, birdwatching and conservation. "Our routes are planned," he adds, "but our itinerary is flexible."

NORTH CAROLINA

Nantahala Outdoor Center, Inc., Star Rt., Box 68, Bryson City, NC 28713. Att.: Payson Kennedy. (704) 488-6407. Chattooga & Nantahala riv. (NC): all yr., 2–48 people, ½ day–3 days, $10 & up. Usumacinta (Mexico): Jan.–Feb., 12 people, 16 days, $1,000 from New Orleans. Bring sleeping gear. Group rates. (See also *Backpacking, Mountaineering, Canoeing.*)

This center is operated by outdoor people who provide equipment, instruction, and guides to help others enjoy mountains and rivers. Explains Payson Kennedy: "We offer rafting trips on three different rivers: a ½-day trip on the Nantahala (Class II and III rapids) for first-timers; 1-, 2-, or 3-day trips on the Chattooga (Class IV and V rapids) for thrill-seekers; and a 16-day River of Ruins Expedition on the Usumacinta in Mexico for adventurers who'd like to explore ancient Mayan ruins."

Smoky Mountain River Expeditions, Inc., PO Box 398-AG, Hot Springs, NC 28743. Att.: Rich Wist. (704) 622-7260. French & Broad Riv. (NC). May–Oct. Up to 75 people. 1-day trips, $20, incl. all equip.

"Neither dangerous nor difficult, our trips can be enjoyed by anyone 12 years or older," says Rich Wist. He provides a picnic lunch midway in the 5 or 6 hours of floating. The French Broad River is one of the finest white-water streams in the East, and most of the float is through Pisgah National Forest, spectacular with huge boulders and wooded mountains above the frothing river.

OREGON

Dean Helfrich Guide & Outfitter, 2722 Harvest Lane, Springfield, OR 97477. (503) 747-8401. Middle Fork & Main Salmon (ID); Bruneau, Owyhee, Rogue & 8 other Oregon rivers. Coastal riv., Nov.–Mar.; others, May–Nov. 2–16 people, 1–6 days. Sample rates: coastal riv., $40/day; Middle Fork & Main Salmon, 6 days, $400-$750. Deschutes, 4 days, $290. Bring sleeping gear.

"We specialize in family and fishing float trips," remarks Dean Helfrich. He uses only full-time professional guides, well qualified in river running and guiding operations, on his oar-powered rafts, pontoons and dories. A vacationer speaks of Dean's service as "tops—excellent food, great guides, beautiful scenery."

Don Merrell's Northwest Whitewater Expeditions, PO Box 3765, Portland, OR 97208. (503) 236-9706. 5 OR riv., Hells Canyon (ID). Apr.–Sept. Up to 25 people, 2–6 days. Sample rates: Deschutes & John Day, 3 days, $140; Owyhee, 6 days, $300; Snake, 4 days, $235. Sleeping gear incl. Group, family & repeat rates.

"While a dash through rapids may be the highlight of your trip," says Don Merrell, "the excitement of white water is only part of the story. There's excellent fishing, and great rock and driftwood hunting—and photographers have a field day." Each of Don's trips is distinct: The turbulent Deschutes offers thrills, the Grande Ronde mountain scenery, the Owyhee isolated wilderness. The tamer John Day is perfect as an outdoor geology lab with its fossil-laden bluffs and buttes. And the Snake is magnificent. On each vacationers testify that "the pace is unhurried, the food heavenly, and the hospitality unfailing."

Hells Canyon Guide Service, PO Box 165, Oxbow, OR 97840. Att.: Gus Garrigus. (503) 785-3305. 5–14 people. Hells Canyon (ID): May–Oct., 3 days, $195; 5 days, $300. Owyhee (OR): May, 5 days, $300. Sleeping gear incl. (See also *Jet Boating.*)

A pleased vacationer says it all: "Hells Canyon is beautiful, remote and rugged, and this service is well equipped to make it a memorable experience. They use roomy, self-righting dories and good boatmen who know the river and its geology and history. Besides his regular trips, Gus can drop you off either a his base camp or in more remote areas by jet boat. Incidentally, the fishing is excellent—smallmouth bass, rainbow trout, fighting steelhead.''

Hells Canyon Navigation, PO Box 145-A, Oxbow, OR 97840. Att.: Jim Zanelli. (503) 785-3352. Hells Canyon (OR). May–Sept. 5–25 people. 5 days, $340, incl. flyback to Oxbow; $295 w./o. flyback. Arrival: Baker, OR, or Boise, ID. (See also *Jet Boating*.)

Jim Zanelli invites you to join his ''River Devil'' clan floating the 107 miles of the Snake from Hells Canyon Dam to Lewiston on 27-foot and 33-foot oar-powered pontoons. ''this deepest gorge in North America is the last stronghold of the white sturgeon,'' he says. Campfire cooking includes sizzling steaks, spuds baked on the coals, canyon stew, dumplings and cherry cobbler. ''We carry along inflatable kayaks for those who want to exercise their skill in white water,'' Jim adds.

Lute Jerstad Adventures, Inc., PO Box 19527, Portland, OR 97219. (503) 244-4364. OR riv. Apr.–Sept. 5 days. Rogue, $275; Snake or Owyhee, $295; 3 days, Grande Ronde, $165; Deschutes or John Day, $145. Bring sleeping gear. (See also *Mountaineering, Pack Trips*.)

Lute thinks each of his rivers is special and unique. The Rogue ''cuts through solid rock, alternating quiet stretches with sudden, chutelike rapids.'' The Snake flows through the deep Hells Canyon gorge. On the remote Owyhee you see herds of wild mustangs roaming the canyon rim. The Grande Ronde (with some Class III water) cuts through the ancestral hunting grounds of Chief Joseph and his Nez Perce Indians. The Deschutes is ''world-renowned for steelhead and trout.'' And the John Day is ''a geologist's and archaeologist's dream.''

Northwest Whitewater Excursions, 1726 Mill St., Eugene, OR 97401. Att.: Galand Haas. (503) 343-0450. 9 OR riv., Hells Canyon & Main Salmon (ID). May–Oct. 2–24 people, 1–5 days. Sample rates: Deschutes, 2 days, $95–$110; 5 days, $215; Hells Canyon or Main Salmon, 5 days, $245–$295. Bring sleeping gear. Group & family rates. Charters. (See also *Youth Adventures.)*

''Our most outstanding and popular trip is through the Central Oregon Desert on the Deschutes River,'' explains Galand Haas. ''It's one of the wildest, most scenic and historic trips on any western river.'' He uses 17-foot rubber rafts and brings inflatable 1-man kayaks for people to challenge the lesser rapids on their own, and explains the local geology, history, plant life and wildlife. And for anglers—some of the finest fly fishing west of the Rockies. ''Relaxing and fantastic,'' reports a vacationer.

Orange Torpedo Trips, PO Box, 1111-A, Grants Pass, OR 97526. Att.: Jerry & Helen Bentley. (503) 479-5061. Sched. trips Jun.–Sept. 10–21 people, min. age, 10 yrs. Rogue (OR), 1–3 days, $30–$195. Deschutes (OR), 3 days, $200. Klamath (CA), 3 days, $175. Lower Salmon (ID), 4 days, $275. Sleeping gear incl.

These are paddle-yourself adventures in comfortable, easy-to-maneuver, inflatable kayaks. The Bentleys have pioneered running white-water rivers in the tough vinyl inflatable boats, 9½ to 11 feet long. Even if you've never boated any kind of river before, you'll soon be paddling and controlling your ''orange torpedo.'' Expert guides give instruction at the start of and during each trip, and your confidence grows with each river mile. Overnights are spent at river lodges on Rogue trips. For nonpaddlers, the Bentleys have ''raft options'' on the Rogue River.

Prince E. Helfrich & Sons, 47685 McKenzie Hwy., Vida, OR 97488. Att.: Dave Helfrich. (503) 896-3786 or 822-3582. Middle Fork & Main Salmon (ID); Bruneau, Owyhee, Rogue & other Oregon riv. Apr.–Oct. 6–20 people. 4–6 days, $250–$700. Sample rates: Main Salmon, 5 days, $250; Bruneau, 5 days, $600; Owyhee, 5 days,

$250. Bring sleeping gear. Group & family rates.

Prince Helfrich's sons carry on their father's tradition of 50 years of guiding on Northwest white-water rivers. They use rubber pontoon boats, McKenzie drift boats and, on the rugged Bruneau, specially designed neoprene boats. On most trips there's time to swim, fish, and explore desert canyons and ancient Indian campgrounds. Featured are "deluxe camping and the finest in outdoor cooking." As one guest writes, "Anyone who is fortunate enough to spend time with the Helfrichs will have an unforgettable experience."

River Trips Unlimited, 900 Murphy Rd., Medford, OR 97501. Att.: Irv Urie. (503) 779-3798. Klamath & Smith (CA), Middle Fork of Salmon (ID), Rogue & other OR riv. 2-20 people, 1-6 days. Rogue, 1 day, $45; 3-4 days, $180-$390. Coastal streams, $60/day. Middle Fork of Salmon, 6 days, $800. Rates incl. overnights at lodges.

Running wild rapids with a "pro" is unforgettable, according to Irv Urie. He uses both deluxe rubber rafts and McKenzie River drift boats, and assures you that his trips offer the highest-quality wild river experience—"the vacation of a lifetime." Swimming, inner-tube riding, rock hunting, gold panning and wildlife sighting round out your day. Good food, hot showers and comfortable beds await you at each evening's lodge.

Rogue Excursions Unlimited, PO Box 855, Medford, OR 97501. Att.: Paul E. Brown. (503) 773-5983. Rogue (OR). May-Nov. Up to 20 people, 2-5 days. Rubber raft, $140-$200; hard-shell drift boat, $140-$350; incl. lodging & meals.

After a day of shooting the Rogue's thrilling rapids, rock hunting and swimming, relax at a rustic riverside lodge to enjoy a sumptuous meal and hot shower before sinking into bed. Paul Brown's trips offer all this and more—a pace leisurely enough to let you absorb the quiet beauty of your surroundings. His boats and equipment are "the best money can buy." Says a repeat guest, "An absolutely perfect trip. Fishing was great, food super and the guide service could not have been better."

Rogue River Raft Trips, Box AT, 8500 Galice Rd., Merlin, OR 97532. Att.: B. A. Hanten. (503) 476-3852 or 3027. Rogue (OR). May-Nov. Up to 20 people, 1-4 days. For 4 or more w./overnights at lodges, 2 days, $135; 3 days, $170; w./overnight camping, 4 days, $180. Bring sleeping gear. Day trips, $95/raft up to 6 people. Morrison's Lodge before & after trips, $22/day, incl. 2 meals. Pickup at Grants Pass, no chg.

Plunge through Galice Shoot, Wildcat, Devil's Staircase and other Rogue rapids on Hanten's oar-powered boats—or an inflatable kayak. After the excitement, take a leisurely hike, pan for gold, watch the wildlife or swim. On the 3-day trip, you're treated to fine food and lodging each night at the Black Bar and Marial river lodges. On the 4-day camping trip meals are Dutch oven specialties. Pack a collapsible rod—there's great steelhead fishing during the fall season.

Snake River Packers, Rt. 1, Box R, Enterprise, OR 97828. Att.: Jim Walker. (503) 426-3307. May-Sept. 4-24 people. Hells Canyon (OR), 1 day, $75; 4-5 days, $235-$295; Lower Main Salmon (ID), 4 days, $245. Rates incl. flying in & out by float plane. Bring or rent sleeping gear. Arrival: Lewiston, ID.

"The Snake River in Hells Canyon has three distinct personalities in the 80-mile stretch we travel," notes Jim Walker. "The upper third contains the most challenging rapids, the middle third is more open with evidence of the pioneers' struggle to eke out a living from the steep slopes, and the lower third closes in again to steep-walled sides." He uses rubber rafts and inflatable kayaks on all trips, and will fly in to the starting point.

Sundance Expeditions, Inc., 14894 Galice Rd., Merlin, OR 97532. Att.: Michael, Saul & James Koons. (503) 479-8508. Rogue, Illinois & Umpqua riv. (OR). Charters on 5 other OR riv. & Klamath (CA). 4 days: $210 on Rogue, 15 people, Jun.-Sept.; $200 on Illinois, 8 people, May only. 3 days: $150 on Umpqua, 12 people, Jun.-Sept. Bring sleeping gear. Group, family & repeat rates. Arrival: Grants Pass, OR. (See also *Kayaking*.)

Traditional oar-powered rafts, paddle boats with everyone paddling, and banana boats—inflatable, stable, one to a boat—are all part of a Sundance flotilla on the Rogue. With emphasis on learning and a personable staff, Sundance has become Oregon's foremost educational river touring company, according to Mike Saul. "Our downstream pace is leisurely," he says. "We choose a beautiful spot near a sparkling creek to camp, with time to hike, sunbathe, swim, and fish before dinner. The cuisine crushes the notion that river food is simple and uninvolved." At the end of the 40-mile run a shuttle bus takes you back to the Almeda Bar put-in or to Grants Pass.

Whitewater Guide Trips, Inc., 12120 S.W. Douglas St., Portland, OR 97225. Att: Mike Carey. (503) 646-8849. Hells Canyon, Main Salmon (ID), Owyhee, Rogue, Deschutes & 5 other OR riv. All yr. 2-20 persons. 1-6 days. Hells Canyon, 6 days, $365; Main Salmon, 5 days, $310; Deschutes, 2-4 days, $90-$160; Rogue, 4 days, $250. Bring or rent sleeping gear. (See also *Youth Adventures*—Whitewater Youth Camps, Inc.)

"The rivers we run expose you to the serenity, purity and clean environment that still exists here," Mike Carey promises. Some are white-water trips through deep canyons, others a relaxing drift in calm water past basalt rock formations, pastel canyons, red clay cliffs and pinnacle thrones. For an easy day trip from Portland, Mike recommends a 10-mile drift on the Clackamas.

Whitewater Challengers, PA.

PENNSYLVANIA

Canyon Cruises, The Antlers Inn, RD #4, Wellsboro, PA 16901. Att.: John & Ed McCarthy. (814) 435-6300. Pine Creek (PA), Upper Hudson (NY). Mar.-Jun. 4-50 people. Lodging incl.: $25/day w./4 meals & 20 mi. on riv.; $50 for 2 days, 7 meals & 34 mi. on riv. Discounts for youth groups & midwk. cruises.

"These trips are ideal for school or youth groups, Scouts, environmentalists—anyone who loves the outdoors," write the McCarthys. Paddling Pine Creek in the spring through the scenic "Grand Canyon" is one of the East's most interesting outdoor adventures, they say. Lodging and meals are at the Antlers Inn. Large youth groups—bring sleeping bags.

Laurel Highlands River Tours, Inc., Box 107, Ohiopyle, PA 15470. Att.: Ed Coleman. (412) 455-3703. [Sept.–May: 1286 Washington St., Indiana, PA 15701. (412) 465-2987.] Youghiogheny (PA), daily Jun.–Aug., up to 240 people (80 max. per trip). $20–$25/day. Arrival: Ohiopyle, PA.

One of the two original pioneers of guided white-water rafting in the East, Coleman has been shooting the rapids along the exciting 8 miles of the wild and beautiful Youghiogheny for more than 15 years. "Make this your year to challenge and conquer the incomparable Yough," he urges. For people staying overnight or longer he offers complete packages that include raft trip, meals, and accommodations at lodge, motel or campground.

Mountain Streams & Trails Outfitters, Box 106G, Ohiopyle, PA 15470. [or Box 144G, Albright, WV 26519.] Att.: Ralph W. McCarty. (412) 329-8810. Youghiogheny (PA): May–Oct., $20/wkday; $25/wkend; up to 80/trip; 3 trips/day. Cheat (WV): Apr.–May, $25/wkday; $30/wkend; up to 40/trip; 8 trips/day. Gauley (WV): Oct.–Nov., wkends only by arrangement. Rates incl. lunch. (See also *Backpacking.*)

"Come on weekdays for the best trips and least congestion," urges Ralph McCarty. Also on weekdays he can give special attention to handicapped groups. He sends floaters down the churning rivers in 4-place and sporty 6-place rafts. "The 'Yough' is still *numero uno*. Things haven't changed in the Cheat since George Washington wrote in his journal that it is 'impassable. . . full of grt bowlders & trech. rifts.' But the Gauley—that's only for those of sound wind and limb. It's a rugged 2-day trip on which guides use proven safety precautions."

Pocono Whitewater, Ltd., PO Box 44, Jim Thorpe, PA 18229. Att.: Doug Fogal. (201) 774-6965 or (717) 325-4097. [Nov.–Mar.: PO Box 25, Ocean Grove, NJ 07756.] Lehigh Riv. (PA), Mar.–Nov. Up to 150 people. $15-$20/wkdays; $20-$25/wkends. Bring lunch. Group rates. Charters.

"Just two hours away from New York's George Washington Bridge you can be on the rapids of the spectacular Lehigh River," Doug Fogal points out. The 12-mile route cascades through the southern Lehigh River Gorge—a scenic and primitive area of the Poconos. "An exciting introduction to white-water rafting for families, club groups, anyone," Doug continues. "You paddle your 5- or 6-place raft, but expert guides are there to offer quick assistance." Breaks for lunch, resting and swimming before the trip ends in Jim Thorpe. Rates include all equipment, briefing and shuttle service.

White Water Adventurers, Box 31-A, Ohiopyle, PA 15470. Att.: Bob Marietta or Wendall Holt. (412) 329-8850 or 5986. Youghiogheny (PA): May–Oct. Up to 80 people. $20 wkdays; $25 wkends. Min age, 12 yrs. Pickup in Ohiopyle, PA. Cheat Canyon (WV): Apr.–May. Up to 40 people. $25 wkdays, $30 wkends. Min. age 16 yrs. Pickup in Kingwood, WV.

"These trips are full of adventure and fun," writes a float tripper. "With 4 to 10 persons to a raft you're so busy that all of life's cares are forgotten. Many people come back for repeat trips and bring their friends along." Each trip lasts about 6 hours, with time out for lunch, swimming and splash fights.

Whitewater Challengers, Inc., Box AG, Star Rt. #6A1, White Haven PA 18661. Att.: Ken Powley. (717) 443-9532. Lehigh Riv. (PA). Mar.–Jun., Sept.–Oct. 2-88 people. $15 wkdays, $20/day wkends. Bring lunch. Group rates.

"An excellent introduction to white water," remarks Ken Powley. "The numerous class III rapids can be handled comfortably by first-timers, yet provide plenty of excitement for more experienced paddlers. We have a lot of repeaters." Acres of rhododendron surround this isolated river gorge, and deer, beaver and red fox can be seen on the banks. "Beautiful virgin terrain, and only a short drive from

New York or Philadelphia," writes a float tripper. "A memorable experience. The people at Whitewater Challengers are all very friendly and positive."

Wilderness Voyageurs, PO Box 97, Dept. AT, Ohiopyle, PA 15470. Att.: Lance Martin. (412) 329-4752 or 5517. Youghiogheny (PA). Apr.–Oct.

"Our guided white water river trips are on the beautiful 'Wild and Scenic' Youghiogheny River in southwestern Pennsylvania," write the Wilderness Voyageurs. "We provide experienced guides, rafts, life jackets, paddles, lunch and bus transport to and from the river. The 6-hour trip covers 8 miles of river. Our office is open from 9 A.M. to 5 P.M. weekdays in season, but we'll take telephone or mail reservations as early as January."

SOUTH CAROLINA

Wildwater, Ltd., Dept. A, Long Creek, SC 29658. Att.: James C. Greiner. (803) 647-5336. [Nov.–Mar.: Dept. A, 400 West Rd., Portsmouth, VA 23707. (804) 397-6658.] Chattooga (SC), Nolichucky & Ocoee (TN). Apr.–Oct. 1-30 people, 1-2 days. $16 wkdays, $20–$25 wkends & holidays; overnights, $40.

People learn about conservation on these trips, according to Jim Greiner. "We start with a short hike down a mountain. During the day we pass only one spot where man has intruded—a bridge. The canyons, falls, rapids, huge rocks, virgin timber and wildlife are our companions." Any active person will enjoy navigating the Chattooga, a National Wild and Scenic River. Previous experience is recommended for rapids of the Nolichucky.

TENNESSEE

Hiwassee Float Service, Inc., Delano, TN 37325. Att.: H. C. Sartin. (615) 263-5581 or 2524 (eve.). Hiwassee & Ocoee (TN). Apr.–Oct. 2-135 people. 3-6 hrs. 2 people in 4-man raft, $16; 4 in 6-man raft, $32. Rates for groups, guide, transport, pickup & delivery. (See also *Canoeing*.)

When the TVA built a dam just inside North Carolina, rafting on the Hiwassee became possible. Now it's rocky, rough, and challenging. For a smoother float, try the lower Hiwassee. This outfitter says there are ideal trips for all ages, "from two to grandmother." And along the way you can stop to hike, loaf or fish for blue-ribbon rainbow trout. Nearby are campgrounds, food and fishing supplies.

TEXAS

Texas Canoe Trails, Inc., 1008 Wirt Rd., #160, Houston, TX 77055. Att.: Wayne Walls. (713) 688-3741. Jun.–Mar.: Balsas, Moctezuma & Usumacinta (Mexico). Feb.–Oct.: Guadalupe (TX). Aug.–Apr.: Rio Grande (TX). 6-14 on guided trips, 2-14 days. Sample rates: 3 days, $110; 5 days, $180; 10 days, $500. Also charters, rentals. Bring sleeping gear. Arrival: San Antonio or Mexico City. (See also *Canoeing*.)

For a popular run on the Guadalupe near San Antonio, rafters can rent TCT equipment and float it alone, but on the Rio Grande TCT generally guides and outfits the trips. Its most exotic runs, though, start at the Mexico City Airport for weekends on the Balsas, 5 days on the Moctezuma or 10 on the Usumacinta. "We observe ancient ruins, jungles, tropical fruit trees, parrots and villages of people living in another age," Walls says. Canoes and kayaks are frequently included on these trips.

Villa de la Miña Rio Grande River Trips, PO Box 470-G, Terlinqua, TX 79852. Att.: Glen Pepper. (915) 364-2466. Rio Grande (TX). All yr. 2 or more people. ½-5-day trips. $35–$75/day, group rates. Bring sleeping gear. Arrival: El Paso, Odessa or Alpine, TX.

The Rio Grande borders Big Bend National Park for 107 miles, with put-in points for floating Santa Elena, Mariscal and Boquillas canyons. Or start upriver through the scenic Colorado Canyon, or run the Lower Canyon from 3 to 5 days, depending on river level. Each canyon has its own personality, with rockslide barriers, sheer walls and calm or bumpy currents. The Villa de la Miña Lodge is 10 miles west of the park.

UTAH

Adventure River Expedition, Dept. AR, 4211 Mars Way, Salt Lake City, UT 84117. Att.: Lee R. Richmond. (801) 278-1867 or 564-8190. Apr.–Sept. Riv. in UT. 7–50 people. Desolation/Gray canyons: 3–5 days, $140-$180. Canyonlands (Colorado Riv.): 2–3 days, $50 up. Green Riv. 1–2 days; $20 up. U-row trips, 3–5 days, $90 $220. Bring sleeping gear. Group & youth rates.

"Adventure-Beauty-Challenge" is Lee Richmond's motto. His specialty is the magnificent canyon and red rock country of Utah's canyonlands, with dozens of scheduled trips. On U-row adventures you learn boat-handling techniques in calm water and rapids. Overnight trips in Castle Country or Canyonlands combine rafting with hiking. Lee features "expertise, reasonable rates, first-class meals and congenial, knowledgeable guides."

Canyon Country River Adventures, Inc., 3580 Winesap Rd., Salt Lake City, UT 84121. Att.: Bill George. (801) 943-1013 or 1026. Grand Canyon, (AZ); Desolation/Gray, Cataract & Westwater canyons, San Juan, Upper Colorado (UT); Middle Fork & Main Salmon (ID). May–Sept. 10–80 people. Sample rates: Grand Canyon, 5–7 days, $487-$545, Middle Fork, 5 days, $465; Desolation/Gray, 3 5 days, $225-$295, incl. flight to/from Grand Junction, CO, or Salt Lake City, UT. Westwater Canyon, 2 days, $100. Sleeping gear incl. Charters.

Bill George's guided oar-powered trips take rafters on some of the West's most fabulous river runs—Desolation and Gray canyons on the Green, the Middle Fork of the Salmon, Flaming Gorge and Westwater Canyon. He runs motor-powered trips on the Main Salmon and through the Grand Canyon and Cataract Canyon. You won't go hungry. The river menu includes steaks, lobster, melon and homemade ice cream. Bill is also known for his raft rental service for "do-it-yer-sef nuts."

Colorado River & Trail Expeditions, Inc. 5058-N So. 300 West, Salt Lake City, UT 84107. Att.: David Mackay. (801) 485-8572, 825-0364 or 261-1789. Noatak Riv. (AK); Grand Canyon (AZ); Cataract, Desolation/Gray & Westwater canyons & Dinosaur Natl. Monument (UT); Dolores (CO). Apr.–Oct. 6–30 people, 2–14 days. Sample rates: 2 days, Westwater, $80; 4 days, Cataract, $195; 9 days, Grand Canyon, $440. Sleeping gear incl. Family & group rates.

"We stress off-river hiking and exploration on every trip," says David Mackay. During the course of the day you frequently leave the excitement of the river to explore Indian ruins and old mines, hike intriguing side canyons and frolic in natural pools. Dinner is a three-course meal over driftwood coals in the light of a spectacular sunset.

Fastwater Expeditions, Box 365-A, Boulder City, NV 89005. Att.: Bill & Fran Belknap. (702) 293-1406. May–Oct. Up to 16 people. Desolation/Gray canyons (UT), 9 days, $440; 14-day exploration special, $640; San Juan (UT) or Dolores (CO), 6 days, $335. Sleeping gear incl.

"Why should river guides have all the fun?" the Belknaps ask. "If you love water, try our Sportyak trips for doers who'd rather row than ride." With one to a boat, the fleet of Sportyaks glides, splashes and careens through the rapids and ever-changing beauty on the 100-mile stretch of the winding Green River. It's exciting, challenging and a real thrill to navigate thundering rapids without flipping. On canyon hikes you discover Indian petroglyphs and turtle fossils, and poke around an abandoned ranch where Butch Cassidy used to stop. Bill (photographer and writer) adds a photo seminar to some trips. "It was superb guiding and supervision," writes a Sportyakker. "Learning to 'read' the river and run the rapids is a great experience."

Grand Canyon Expeditions, Inc., Dept. AG, PO Box O, Kanab, UT 84741. Att.: Ron & Sheila Smith. (801) 644-2691. May–Sept. Up to 14 people. Grand Canyon (AZ), 9 days, $505. Sleeping gear incl. Arrival: Las Vegas.

"Through years of Grand Canyon expeditions we've found that people running it all the way from Lees Ferry to Lake Mead have a more meaningful and enjoyable trip," Ron Smith says. "It's a once-in-a-lifetime vacation and should be unhurried. Our specially designed neoprene boats have proved so successful they are used by the National Park Service for the river patrols," he adds.

Harris Boat Trips, Inc., Box 521, Kanab, UT 84741. Att.: David Kloepfer. (801) 644-5635. Apr.–Nov. 12–28 people. Grand Canyon (AZ): motor-powered, 9 days, $525, 12 days, $625; 4- & 6-day charters, $300 & $400; oar-powered, 14 days, $700; 6- & 8-day charters, $450 & $550. Desolation/Gray canyons (UT): oar-powered, 9 days, $400. Sleeping gear incl.

"The guides are probably the most important part of any river trip," says David

Grand Canyon Expeditions, UT.

Kloepfer. "We feel ours are the best partly because we are a small outfit, but mostly because we care. Our trips are longer than most. We feel it takes time to relax, enjoy off-river hiking and exploring, and everything that adds up to a real wilderness experience." Their shorter Grand Canyon trips put-in or take-out at Phantom Ranch.

Hatch River Expeditions, Dept. B, 411 E. 2nd North, Vernal, UT 84078. Att.: Don & Ted Hatch. (801) 789-3813. Grand Canyon (AZ), Middle Fork & Main Salmon & Selway (ID), Catarct & Desolation/Gray canyons, Dinosaur Natl. Monument (UT). Up to 45 people, 3–6 days. Sample rates: Grand Canyon, 6½ days, $425; Dinosaur, 3–4 days, $120; Cataract, 4 days, $190; Selway Riv., 5 days, $440. Also custom trips. Bring or rent sleeping gear.

The Hatches started their operations in 1928—"for fun." They wanted to conquer the rapids, so they built their own special motorized boats. Three generations of Hatches have been white-water boaters, and have developed the many scheduled trips they offer each year. Their Grand Canyon trips include helicopter service out of the Canyon at Whitmore Wash, then by air to Las Vegas, Marble Canyon or the South Rim.

Holiday River Expeditions, 519 Malibu Dr. ATG, Salt Lake City, UT 84107. Att.: Dee Holladay. (801) 266-2087. Cataract, Desolation/Gray & Westwater canyons, & Dinosaur Natl. Monument (UT); Dolores (CO). Apr.–Oct. Up to 20 people, 2–7 days. Sample rates: Westwater, 2 days, $100; Cataract, 6 days, $300. Bring or rent sleeping gear. Group & family rates.

For the greatest wilderness experience, Dee Holladay prefers oars to motors, keeps his groups small, and is on most expeditions himself. "Ride a rubber raft into a wilderness wonderland," he urges. He offers a wide selection of trip dates, especially in Cataract Canyon. He knows his business thoroughly, according to float trippers, and his boatmen are knowledgeable about the geology and history of the rivers.

Moki Mac River Expeditions, 6829 Bella Vista Dr., Salt Lake City, UT 84121. Att.: Richard M. Quist. (801) 943-6707 or 564-3361. Grand Canyon (AZ), Cataract, Desolation/Gray & Westwater canyons (UT). Apr.–Sept. Up to 24 people, 10–12 per boat, 1–14 days. Sample rates: Desolation, 5 days, $250; Grand Canyon, 4 days, $200; Cataract, 6 days, $250.

"Our service is small and personalized, with a 'wilderness experience' orientation," emphasizes Richard Quist. There are 13 different trips, some motor, some rowing. "The smaller 16-foot to 20-foot rafts that we use on a rowing trip make navigating big rapids more strenuous, more exhilarating and most wet!"

Outlaw Trails, Inc., PO Box 336-F, Green River, UT 84525. Att.: A. C. Ekker. (801) 564-3593. Cataract, Desolation/Gray & Westwater canyons (UT), Dolores (CO), May–Sept. Rio Grande (TX), Oct.–May. 1–10 days. Sample rates: Cataract, 6 days, $375; Green, 7-day Sportyak trip, $435; Westwater, 2 days, $125. Rates incl. sleeping gear, pickup & return to Grand Junction or other central point. (See also *Pack Trips, Jeeping.*)

Whether in an oar-powered raft or (on the Green) a row-yourself Sportyak, these white-water trips are described as "unsinkable excitement" by A. C. Ekker, who wants everyone to love this land of sandstone canyons and high grassy plateaus as he does. For a land-and-water adventure, A.C. offers combination pack/float excursions.

Red Rock River Runners, PO Box 31, Moab, UT 84532. Att.: Skeeter Irish. (801) 259-6019 or 7660. Westwater & Cataract canyons, Colorado above Moab (UT). May–Sept. 3–70 people, 1 or more days. Westwater, 2 days, $95; Colorado above

Moab, 1 day, $20. Bring sleeping gear. Youth rates. Charters.

"Of the handful of outfitters running oar-powered trips in the Canyonlands area, I am the smallest, which is the way I like it," notes Skeeter Irish proudly. His personalized service gives river runners a chance to participate, no more than 8 per boat on day trips, 5 on overnights. Vacationers cite Skeeter's expertise, knowledge of geology, history and ecology, and above all his good-natured personality on trips stressing "good, clean family fun." Also charters "anywhere, anytime."

Tag-A-Long Tours, PO Box 1206-X, 452 N. Main St., Moab, UT 84532. Att.: Mitch Williams. (800) 453-3292 toll-free (exc. in UT, HI & AK) or (801) 259-6690. Cataract, Westwater, Desolation/Gray canyons, San Juan (UT) & Dolores (CO). Apr.–Oct. 2–7 days, $115–$392. Sample rates: Desolation/Gray, 4 days, $225; Cataract, 4 days, $225; Canyonlands float/jeep combo, 4 days, $130; 7 days, $369. Bring or rent sleeping gear. Group & family rates. (See also *Jeeping.*)

Mitch and his team show you the highlights of this fantastic red rock country from the naturalist's view—flora, fauna, geology and history. They float motorized neoprene and nylon boats through rapids sporting such names as "Capsize," "Mile Long" and "The Big Drop." The rafting trip can be combined with jeeping in an air-conditioned vehicle, with campouts each night.

Tour West, Inc., PO Box 333, Orem, UT 84057. Att.: Russell H. Hansen or Frank Stratton. (800) 453-9107. Main Salmon (ID) & Colorado (UT & AZ). Apr.–Sept. Up to 40 people, 3–7 days. Sample rates: Grand Canyon (AZ): 4 days, $249; 6 days, $489; 8 days, $609; combo 6-day backpack/float, $295. Main Salmon (ID): 7 days, $359. Cataract Canyon (UT): 4 days, $235. Rates incl. sleeping gear & 1 motel night.

Tour West trips begin in Boise for the Salmon, in Moab for Cataract Canyon, and in Page, Grand Canyon Airport or St. George for Grand Canyon trips. Back-packing-float trip combinations give you either rugged Grand Canyon hiking, or camping near the Havasupai Indian Village, plus one or more days on the river. On a "river running introduction" in the Lower Grand Canyon Rapids, you have 2 days of camping and floating. Tour West considers the guides for its many departure dates "the outstanding feature of our service—the majority of them are schoolteachers, highly trained in river skills and knowledgeable in geology, history and ecology."

Western River Expeditions, PO Box 6339, Salt Lake City, UT 84106. (801) 486-2323. Grand Canyon (AZ); Cataract & Westwater canyons (UT); Selway, Middle Fork & Main Salmon (ID). Apr.–Oct. Up to 36 people, 1–7 days. Sample rates: Grand Canyon, 5–7 days, $487–$545; Middle Fork, 5 days, $465; Westwater, 2 days, $123; Cataract, 4 days, $300. Bring or rent sleeping gear.

Veteran guide and outfitter Jack Currey selects his boatmen for "character, congeniality and competence." Each expedition is filled with adventure, hiking, fishing and relaxing in some of the most scenic and primitive areas in America.

Wild & Scenic, Inc., PO Box 2123-A, Marble Canyon, AZ 86036. Att.: Patrick & Susan Conley. (602) 355-2222. Desolation/Gray canyons, San Juan (UT). Apr.–Oct. 10–15 people. 6–9 days, $295–$395, incl. sleeping gear. Arrival: Green River, Bluff or Mexican Hat, UT.

The Conleys give one-to-a-boat Sportyak adventures for anyone who likes water, hiking, personal challenge, small-group participation—and fun! Bring your sense of adventure—people do get dumped in the rapids. "This trip provides a chance to relate to the out-of-doors on your own terms," writes a vacationer. "The Conleys love the wilderness and take a great deal of time interpreting it for their guests. The food is excellent. Memorable are the evenings on soft, warm ledges of river sand; a hike to an overlook and discovering a whole bed of fossilized sea shells; swimming in a small, hidden pool."

Wonderland Expeditions, PO Box 338, Green River, UT 84525. Att.: Ken Sleight. (801) 564-3656. May–Oct. 10–20 people. Grand Canyon (AZ); Cataract & Desolation/Gray canyons, Dinosaur Natl. Monument & San Juan (UT); Rio Grande (TX); AK riv. Grand Canyon 8-day motor trip, $400; 12-day oar trip, $550. Canyonlands, 6 days, $225. Desolation Canyon, 5 days, $175. Dinosaur, 5 days, $200. Bring sleeping gear. Custom trips.

"Our trips are really wilderness oriented," states Ken Sleight. "They're not for those who wish to be pampered. We offer as much off-river hiking as time allows, and want our people to experience the total environment of a particular area." This includes sighting wildlife and investigating historical and archaeological sites. Ken offers some special hiking trips in Grand Gulch, Escalante and Waterpocket Fold.

World Wide River Expeditions, Inc., 445 East Scott Ave., Salt Lake City, UT 84115. Att.: Richard Jones. (801) 467-6426. Cataract, Desolation/Gray & Westwater canyons & Dinosaur Natl. Monument (UT), Main Salmon (ID). May–Sept. Dinosaur, 5 days, $165; Cataract, 6 days, $290; Westwater, 4 days, $135; Green, 7 days by Sportyak, $285; Canyonlands by raft, jeep and air, $310; Main Salmon, 7 days by Sportyak, $359; by raft, $349. Rates incl. motel before & after. Bring or rent sleeping gear. Family rates.

"Would you like to explore some of the most rugged and remote canyons of the West?" If your answer is "Yes!" Richard Jones invites you to join one of his many river expeditions to swim, fill up on Dutch oven cooking, and feel the cold spray in your face. For the more daring he offers Sportyak trips on the Green or Main Salmon. You navigate your own 7-foot polyethylene plastic craft through thundering rapids. The rewards are challenge, excitement and self-esteem.

WASHINGTON

Northwest Alpine Guide Service, Inc., 1628 Ninth Ave., #2, Seattle, WA 98101. Att.: Linda Bradley Miller. (206) 622-6074. 9 WA riv. Also 7 & 14 days on Wild, Alatna & Koyukuk (AK), about $75/day. (See also *Backpacking, Mountaineering, Canoeing, Ski Touring, Wilderness Living, Youth Adventures.*)

Most of the NAGS float trips on Washington rivers (more than 9 of them) are for 1 or 2 days. "We don't have any Grand Canyon," Brad Bradley says, "but we do have spectacular scenery, with snow-capped mountains rising above the lush green of our famous forests." He runs 7- or 14-day trips on rivers of Alaska's Brooks Range with rafts or canoes or both.

Pacific Northwest Float Trips, 829 Waldron St., Sedro Woolley, WA 98284. Att.: David E. Button. (206) 855-0535. Methow, Nooksack, Sauk, Skagit & Wenatchee (WA). Wkends all yr., wkdays Jun.–Sept. 1–5 days, 5–35 people. 1 day, $20–$30. Bring sleeping gear. Group rates. (See also *Backpacking.*)

"The Washington rivers we run are relatively unknown to travelers," writes Dave Button. "We chose them for their variety, scenic beauty, smooth or white water, and good fishing. They're for all ages. We see eagle and deer, hunt for gold and driftwood, and explore old cabins and Indian burial grounds." Overnight trips on request.

Rivers Northwest, c/o Adventure Tours, 19415 Pacific Highway South, Suite 414, Seattle, WA 98188. (206) 824-2192, also toll-free no. Queets, Hoh & Quinault (WA), 5 OR rivers, Cataract Canyon (UT). Apr.–Sept. 3–15 people, 1–7 days. 1 day, WA rivers, $25; child, $20; incl. lunch & shuttle. OR rivers, 3–7 days, $180–$270. Bring or rent sleeping gear. Also charter trips.

"Splashing down the Queets, the Hoh, or the Quinault in Olympic National Park—what better way to experience the lushness of the rain forest?" queries this service. It provides a hearty afternoon meal on these oar-powered float trips, and also offers longer guided trips on Oregon's Owyhee, Deschutes, Grande Ronde, John Day and Minan rivers.

WEST VIRGINIA
(See also Pennsylvania outfitters who run West Virginia rivers.)

Appalachian Wildwaters, Inc., PO Box 3234-P, Columbus, OH 43210. Att.: Imre Szilagyi. (614) 268-4427. Up to 45 people, 1–2 days. 3 WV rivers: Cheat, Apr.–Jun., $30/day. New, May–Nov., $35/day; $70, 2 days. Gauley, Setp.–Oct., $35–$45/day; $95, 2 days. Lunch incl. on day trips. For 2 days bring sleeping gear. Group rates Tues. & Thurs. Custom family trips on Upper New.

For the Cheat River, head for Albright (east of Morgantown). "This is Class IV to V water in early spring—bring a wetsuit, and experience," advises Imre Szilagyi. "By June it's for first-timers." Imre's headquarters for the New and Gauley rivers are in Minden, southeast of Charleston. Besides day runs, he provides 2-day trips on both with steak dinners and hearty breakfasts added to the luncheon fare. "The rapids are big through the majestic canyon of the New," he says. "Beginners should wait until August." On the Upper Gauley he takes only those who have had other trips with him. The Lower Gauley—"a delightful run."

Blue Ridge Outfitters, PO Box 456, Dept. AG, Harpers Ferry, WV 25425. Att.: Herb & Tom Soles. (304) 725-3444. Shenandoah (WV). May–Oct. $14/day wkdays; $16 wkends; incl. lunch. Arrival: Harpers Ferry, WV.

Everybody paddles and everybody wears a helmet on these bouncy river rides down the "Shenandoah Staircase" from Millville Dam to Harpers Ferry. With both big and small rapids and many boulders, the 8-mile stretch is an exciting run. The Soles brothers started their program with white-water canoe instruction. "But parents kept asking if they could come, too," Herb recalls. So his participants now are families with middle-aged children—and Easterners who lack the time, money or gasoline to challenge the wild rivers of the West.

Cheat River Outfitters, Box 196-AG, Albright, WV 26519. Att.: Eric Neilson. (304) 329-9816. Cheat Riv. (WV). Up to 40 people, 4 trips a day. $25 in Apr., $30 in May & Jun. Also Sept. & Oct. trips.

"We give you 13 miles of some of the best white water in the eastern U.S.," says Eric Neilson. "There are at least 38 major rapids of Class III, IV and V difficulty. You'll shoot Big Nasty, High Falls, Even Nastier, Cue Ball and Coliseum—and lurch to the top of exploding 10-foot waves. We take anyone from 14 years up willing to challenge this fantastic river." They use top-quality 8-man rafts with an experienced river guide in each.

Mountain River Tours, Inc., PO Box 88CA, Hico, WV 25854. Att.: Paul W. Breuer. (304) 658-5817. New, Gauley (WV). Apr.–Nov. 6–96 people, 15 yrs. min. Day trips, $37. 2 days on New, $95; on Gauley, $125. Bring sleeping gear. Group rates. Arrival: Hico, WV.

"There you are, paddling along in a big rubber raft and enjoying the incredible beauty of the Appalachians," writes Paul Breuer. "Then you hear the rumbling of churning water, see froth ahead, and suddenly you're flying, rising, floating, bouncing, shooting through the rapids." With a team of white-water experts he offers these adventures on the New River from April to mid-November, and spring and fall only on the Gauley, using 16-foot rafts.

New River Adventures, Star Route, Box 25A, Thurmond, WV 25936. Att.: Barry & Sarah O'Mahony. (304) 469-9627. New, Bluestone & Gauley riv. (WV). Apr.–Oct. 10–60 people. $40/day, incl. lunch; $100 for 2-day trip, incl. 5 meals. Primitive camping; bring sleeping gear.

The O'Mahonys remind you that the New River, with Class IV and V rapids

Grand Canyon Expeditions, UT, by Patricia Caulfield.

through an awesome gorge, is the biggest run on the East Coast. They offer 1- or 2-day trips on the New, with camping at their base. In spring the snow runoff provides water for 1-day floats on the Bluestone, and trips on the Gauley are determined by dam runoff.

Wildwater Expeditions Unlimited, Inc., Dept AT, PO Box 55, Thurmond, WV 25936. Att.: Jon A. Dragan. (304) 469-2551. Gauley & New riv. (WV). Mar.–Oct. Up to 65 people, 1–2 days. $40–$60 per day, depending on service, river & time of year.

On the overnight raft trips through untamed Appalachian Foothills, you pitch in with the paddling as you bounce over foaming rapids between sheer cliffs on the New River trips. "Some of the best white water in the East," says this experienced outfitter.

WISCONSIN

Herb's Wolf River Raft Rental, Wild Wolf Inn, Box B, White Lake, WI 54491. Att.: Herb Buettner. (715) 882-8612. Wolf Riv. (WI). May–Oct. 2–300 people. 2½–6-hr. trips, $7.50–$15. Guides available. (See also *Ski Touring.*)

Herb Buettner claims that rafting is the only way to go through this 10-mile white-water section of the Wolf. His Wild Wolf Inn, open all year, is on Gilmore's Mistake rapids. "Most people manage a raft without prior experience, and everyone makes it—not *because of* how they paddle, but *in spite of* how they paddle," he says.

River Forest Rafts & Campground, Star Rt., White Lake, WI 54491. Att.: James R. Stecher. (715) 882-3351. [Sept.–May: 1032 Cameron St., Green Bay, WI 54304. (414) 499-7587.] Wolf (WI). May–Oct. Up to 300 people, 1–3 days. $10–$20/day. Group rates.

Jim Stecher provides the campground, the parking space, the shuttle, the raft—and the shove-off. Beyond that, you're on your own for a wild ride on the beautiful Wolf River. Although there are no falls on this run, and prior rafting experience is not at all necessary, Jim asks children under 12 to remain ashore. Bring your own food—and some dry clothes. You're bound to get wet.

Roaring Rapids Raft Co., Star Rt., Box 53A, Athelstane, WI 54104. Att.: Donald Percy. (715) 757-3300. [Sept.–Feb.: 2016 E. Windsor Pl., Milwaukee, WI 53202.] Peshtigo, Menomonee (WI). Apr.–Aug. 2–100 people. 1 day, $8.50–$18, incl. wetsuits, helmets, meal & sauna.

"We are the only guided operation running the Peshtigo in April and May," says Don Percy. "This Class IV river (in high-water periods) has the longest, most challenging continuous stretch of white water in the Midwest— the Roaring Rapids. White-water rafters are in for the time of their lives!" And Pieres Gorge on the Menominee he calls "absolutely wild." On both rivers Don offers five types of rafts for all levels of experience. During low-water periods he won't lead you on— he closes operations.

Wolf River Lodge, Inc., Box AGI, White Lake, WI 54491. Att.: George W. Steed. (715) 882-2182. Wolf (WI). May–Oct. 2–100 persons, 1–2 days. Wkdays, $7.50/day; wkends, $10/day; wkend package, $65/person, lodging, meals. Campgrounds, $1.75/person/night. (See also *Ski Touring*.)

The Wolf is a good, high-quality boating river. George Steed writes, "There's white water that's tough in a canoe, but reasonably safe and exciting in a rubber raft. And it's runnable at all water levels, though less exciting when low. We advise *honestly* what the level is. Don't want people expecting Niagara and getting molasses!" For $2.50 George will issue you a ticket for river travel through parts of the Menominee Indian Reservation. He also runs a school for white-water canoeing and kayaking.

WYOMING

Richard Brothers, Inc., 2215 Rangeview Lane, Laramie, WY 82070. Att.: Paul & Jim Richard. (307) 742-4872. Upper Colorado (CO), North Platte (CO & WY), any WY riv. Custom trips. May–Aug. 2–60 people, 1–7 days. $40–$55/day. Bring sleeping gear. Group rates. Arrival: Laramie, WY. (See also *Backpacking*.)

In the canyons and thundering rapids of the North Platte, wild enough to satisfy ardent white-water buffs, you float through 4 major life zones. Each has its own unique plant and animal life, about which the Richard brothers, biology teachers, are authoritative sources of information. They use oar-powered inflatable boats, provide well-prepared meals and share background on the area's history.

Shoshone River Float, Inc., Cody, WY 82414. Att.: Kit Cody & Glenn Rice. (307) 587-3535. Shoshone (WY). May–Sept. 2-hr. trips. Adults, $7.50; under 16 yrs., $5. Group rates.

Float through the Shoshone River's red rock canyon with a great-grandson of Buffalo Bill. Kit Cody informs us that his trip is "not rough, although we do hit some good white water."

The Snake River, flowing from headwaters in Yellowstone National Park into Jackson Lake and beyond, winds serenely through a scenic stretch between Moran and Moose just north of Jackson Hole. The jagged Teton peaks tower above lush banks of aspen, cottonwood and spruce where moose, elk, deer and other wildlife graze. Each year, from May through September, more than 70,000 visitors float the gentle Snake on trips of 5, 10 or 21 miles. Rates for the scenic half-day run vary from around $5 to $12, less for children. They include transportation to the put-in point and back to Jackson, and sometimes a snack or lunch.

But for some 30,000 white-water enthusiasts, the Snake River Canyon south of Jackson, between Hoback Junction and Alpine, is the stretch to run. Here the twisted limestone gorge creates churning rapids that give rafters a drenching and some roller-coasting they'll remember, especially in high-water season. Trips vary from about $10 to $20 for a half-day trip and $20 to $30 for a full day, usually with shuttle between Jackson and the river included.

The following are among the local outfitters with whom trips may be arranged:

† **Barker-Ewing, Inc.,** Box 124-J, Jackson, WY 83001. (307) 733-3410.

† **Fort Jackson Float Trips,** 310 West Broadway, Jackson, WY 83001. (307) 733-2583.

* **Grand Teton Lodge Co.,** PO Box 250, Moran, WY 83013. (307) 543-2811.

* **Heart Six Guest Ranch,** Moran, WY 83013. (307) 543-2477 or 733-6650.

† **Jack Dennis Sports,** Box 286, Jackson, WY 83001. (307) 733-3273.

† **Lewis & Clark Expeditions,** Box 720, Jackson, WY 83001. (307) 733-4022.

† **National Park Float Trips,** PO Box 411, Jackson, WY 83001. (307) 733-4325.

* **Osprey Float Trips,** Box 1903, Jackson, WY 83001. (307) 733-4486.

‡ **Parklands Whitewater Expeditions,** Box 525-A, Wilson, WY 83014. (307) 733-6203 or 2421. On the O'Neills' overnight white-water trips through the Snake River Canyon, everyone takes part—from pulling oars to setting up camp. The rate is $35, or $30 for 6–17-year-olds, including shuttle, sleeping gear and "the best food on the river." They feature photo stops and a box lunch on their day white-water trips.

† **Sands/Walker Wild Water River Trips,** Box 290, Jackson, WY 83001. (307) 733-4410 or 543-2545.

† **Snake River Park,** Jackson, WY 83001. (307) 733-9929.

† **Solitude Float Trips,** Box 112, Moose, WY 83012. (307) 733-2871 or 543-2522.

‡ **The Triangle X Ranch,** Box 120, Star Rt., Moose, WY 83012. (307) 733-2183. The Turners run the gentle stretch north of Jackson. On their overnight trip you float to an isolated camp for a hearty cookout supper and sleep in an Indian tepee. Next day, a campfire breakfast and a morning float. The rate including 2 meals and shuttle is $30, or $18 for children.

ALBERTA

North-West Expeditions Ltd., PO Box 1551, Edmonton, Alta. T5J 2N7. Att.: David W. Rowe. (403) 452-4433. Jun.–Aug. 8–16 people. Coppermine, Nahanni (NWT). Sample rates: 14 days, Coppermine from Yellowknife, $1,650. 14 days, Nahanni from Watson Lake, $1,500. Rates incl. all equip. & transport. Sched. trips in NWT only. Group charters & pvt. trips in Alta. & NWT by special arrangement.

On a float-plane flight to the put-in point you cross the Arctic Circle into the Barrenlands near the Arctic Ocean for the Coppermine River trip, or across the Continental Divide and over ice-capped peaks for the Nahanni River tour in the southwest area of the Northwest Territories. Both trips provide outstanding wilderness experiences for active participants. From the motorless inflatable rafts you'll spot Arctic wildlife and birds, drift through spectacular canyons, and run (sometimes portage around) exciting rapids. The Coppermine tour offers excellent fishing: char, grayling and trout.

---

* Offers half-day trips above Jackson.
† Offers white-water trips below Jackson, and in most cases, scenic trips above Jackson as well.
‡ Offers overnight trips, and also half- or full-day trips.

BRITISH COLUMBIA

Canadian River Expeditions, Ltd., 845 Hornby St., Vancouver, B.C. Att.: John H. Mikes. (604) 926-4436. BC riv. Jun.–Sept. 20–24 people. Chilcotin/Fraser, 10 days, $785. Stikine, 12 days, $850. Bring or rent sleeping gear. Family rates.

Starting in Vancouver, the Chilcotin and Fraser river adventure progresses by bus, ferry, cruiser and float plane to Chilko Lake, deep in virgin forests surrounded by snow-capped peaks. From there it's 240 miles of rafting and portaging on these swift rivers, with thrilling rides down narrow chutes and into beautiful canyons. The take-out is at Lillooet, with a train ride back to Vancouver. The fly-in for the Stikine River trip starts in Terrace. Fast-flowing water, no big rapids, and 320 miles of "the most magnificent scenery anywhere on this continent," says John Mikes. "It's scenery, scenery, scenery—glaciers reaching right into the river, wild, green valleys of untouched forests, bears, moose, beavers, seals, birds. Wild, remote, eerie and beautiful." The trip ends at Prince Rupert or Skagway.

Cascade River Holidays, Ltd., Box 65, Yale, B.C. V0K 2S0. Att.: Rob Sims. (604) 863-2332. BC riv. Apr.–Sept. 4–22 people, 1–12 days. Fraser: 12 days, $950; 6 days, $280; 1 day, $45. Thompson: 2 days, $80. Chilcotin: 5 days, $290. Bring or rent sleeping gear.

If you think a lot of water flows through the Grand Canyon of the Colorado, try the Fraser. The volume is 10 times larger during spring runoff in June! Rob Sims runs it even then, challenging huge rapids and whirlpools—especially at Hell's Gate—in 33-foot inflatable rafts with 40-horsepower outboards. It's not for timid float trippers. His 12-day Fraser run (Prince George to Vancouver) covers 600 miles of the river—longest raft trip in North America. And there's exciting white water on his overnight Thompson River and 5-day Chilcotin trips. On the latter you have one layover day for horseback riding at a dude ranch. Magnificent wilderness scenes and canyons characterize all of these trips, as does Rob's personalized service and his insistence on small groups for the long runs. He was the first outfitter to offer trips on the Fraser, and is the first to use 33-foot rafts.

Kumsheen Raft Adventures, Ltd., Suite 121, 470 Granville St., Vancouver, B.C. V6C 1V5. Att.: Bernie Fandrich. (604) 683-2381. Thompson & Fraser (BC). May–Oct. 8–60 people, min. age 10. 1–7 days. Thompson: 2 days, $99; 3 days, $150. Fraser (Hell's Gate): 1 day, $45. Both rivers: 5 days, $258; 7 days, $357. Bring or rent sleeping bag. Arrival: Lytton, BC (or Yale for Hell's Gate trip).

The fast-flowing water of the mighty Thompson and Fraser, two of Canada's most powerful rivers, provides some the biggest white-water thrills on the continent. Add to that the area's beauty—craggy mountains, vast ranches, Indian settlements, wooden bridges, waterfalls, canyons, birds, wildlife—and you have "an outdoor experience that will enrich your life." Bernie's headquarters are at Lytton, where the two rivers converge, and "Kumsheen" is the Indian word for "joining of the rivers." The village, known as the oldest continuously inhabited settlement in North America, once was called the "belly button of the world." Bernie recommends his trips for "all outdoor enthusiasts, the young and young at heart, swimmers or nonswimmers, experienced or first-time river runners."

McCook & Furniss Kechika Range Outfitters, Ltd., Fort Ware, B.C. V0J 3B0. Att.: Emil McCook & Rick Furniss. Tel.: Fort Ware via Vancouver radio oper. [Jan.–Apr.: 1515 Orchard Ave., Moscow, ID 83843. (208) 882-7961.] Upper Peace (BC). Jun.–Sept. 2 or more people, 5 or more days. Rates on request. Bring sleeping gear. (See also *Pack Trips.*)

Emil McCook and Rick Furniss outfit charter trips on the Upper Peace River, one of the wildest, most remote rivers in British Columbia. Skilled pilots guide the rubber rafts through scenic canyons and moderate white water, portaging around large falls. Excellent fishing and frequent sightings of moose, caribou, sheep, elk, eagles and other wildlife, as well as a visit to an Indian village. The charter service is for both large and small groups, for trips of any length; tents and log cabins for overnights.

Western Tours Ltd., 3651 Elgin Rd., White Rock, B.C. V4A 2Y8. Att.: John Seppi. (604) 536-2527. Chilko, Chilcotin & Fraser (BC). Jun.–Sept. 6–14 people. 6 days, $475; 12 days, $780. Air to put-in & train back to Vancouver incl. Bring or rent sleeping gear. Family & group rates. Arrival: Vancouver.

All of John Seppi's trips start with a scenic 1½-hour flight from Vancouver to Lake Chilko—"the only raft trip that starts at a headwater lake and runs continuously into the confluence of one of the world's major rivers (the Fraser)," he says. Your oar-powered rafts drift noiselessly past wildlife and birds in this area of high mountains and glacial rivers and lakes. "A classical waterway," John calls it, "with spirited but safe rapids through deep canyon gorges, and calm stretches." Food? "The best."

Whitewater Adventures, Ltd., PO Box 46536, Vancouver, B.C. V6R 4G8. Att.: Dan Culver. (604) 736-2135. Fraser & Thompson (BC), Apr.–Oct., 6–25 people. 1 day, $40; 2 days, $115; 3 days, $150; 7 days, $295. Transport to/from Vancouver incl. Bring sleeping gear. Group, family & early-payment discounts. Arrival: Vancouver, BC. (See also *Backpacking, Windjammers.*)

"This is outdoor adventure made easy," says Dan Culver of his weekend trips on the mighty Thompson and Fraser rivers. On the Thompson you float past sand beaches and rolling hills to startling white canyons and breathtaking waterfalls. Towering rock faces and cascading streams form spectacular scenery on the Fraser. The many huge rapids on both rivers produce cries for "more!" Dan offers a weekend sing-along on the Thompson ("bring your instrument—but please, no pianos") and a geology float to find jade and other gemstones.

MANITOBA

North Country River Trips, Berens River, Man. R0B 0A0. Att.: Jack & Georgia Clarkson. (204) 382-2284 or 2379. Pigeon, Berens & Poplar riv. (Man). May–Sept. Min. age, 12. 6 days, $360, incl. sleeping gear, bush flight & pickup. Air round-trip, Winnipeg-Berens Riv., $80, or drive to Pine Dock for bush plane pickup.

The Clarksons don't run just rapids. They also run waterfalls! Their guests are encouraged to walk around those with 15-to-20-foot drops within 50 yards. And then, there are the double waterfalls! Until 1976 no one had floated the Pigeon River in a raft, and almost no one thought it could be done. But after a thrill-packed maiden voyage, the trip was regarded as a smash hit, and NCRT has been dousing its guests in the roaring stream ever since. At last count, the rapids/waterfalls numbered well over 40 on the 106-mile stretch—all but a few still to be named. You fly from Winnipeg to Berens River, where Jack, a bush pilot, flies you to the put-in. The rubber rafts are "virtually unsinkable." Hang on!

YUKON TERRITORY

Yukon Rafting & Wilderness Travel, Ltd., Box 23, Dawson City, Y.T. Y0B 1G0. (403) 993-5391. Yukon, Fortymile, Klondike, Stewart, Sixtymile (YT). Jun.–Sept. 4–30 people, 2–14 days. Yukon: 14 days, $560; 5 days, $215; 2 days, $90; ½ day, $6. Rates incl. sleeping gear. Group rates. Arrival: Dawson City, YT.

"Roads and rails are newcomers. The river has always tied Yukon's history together." So say Caroline Kennard, Alan Dennis and Greg Caple, who explore the Yukon and its tributaries in Zodiac inflatable rafts. You follow the routes of trappers, prospectors, Indians and the men of '98 through spectacular country rich in history. The 14-day trip starts at Bennett Lake near the B.C. border, where the Klondike stampeders built their crude rafts, and you stop for "one luxury night" at

Whitehorse. "The Yukon Rafting people have done very well by us," writes a river explorer and history buff. "I can't speak loudly enough in their praise," says another vactioner.

Yukon Wilderness Unlimited, PO Box 4126, Whitehorse, Y.T. Y1A 3S9. Att.: John Lammers. Tel.: 2 M 3908 (via Whitehorse mobile operator). Any suitable riv. in YT. May–Oct. 8 people max. Average: 10 days, 8 people, $596. Bring sleeping bag. Custom trips. Rates incl. charter transport to/from riv. Arrival: Whitehorse, YT. (See also *Wilderness Living.*)

John and Polly Lammers, long-time Yukon residents and life-long naturalists, specialize in "gentle adventures"—in-depth experiences in the wilderness environment. "On motorless rubber boats we float quietly with the current, camping nightly along the way and laying over for a day or 2 as the mood strikes," the Lammers explain. "We stop for hikes in a rambling way, enjoying the freedom and beauty of the land. In 10 days, the length of trip we usually plan—though they vary—we float about 250 river miles." The Lammers have operated these trips since 1965.

MEXICO AND CENTRAL AMERICA

Mexican & Central American Expeditions by Wayne Hussing, 11120 Raphael Rd., Upper Falls, MD 21156. (301) 592-7247. Mexico, Guatemala, Honduras, Nicaragua, Costa Rica. Oct.–Apr. 1–8 people, 14 days, $435 plus air fare.

Wayne Hussing tells us his Mexican and Central American rafting adventures are "expeditions" and that all who participate will truly share in a wilderness experience that isn't crowded. He rafts rivers such as the Rio Grande de Santiago, Usumacinta, Lacatum, Ixcan, Negro, Cahabon, Patuca, Coco and others. Wayne says, "With small groups we are able to meet local people on an intimate relationship. Those interested must have the urge to explore and be able to meet nature on its own terms. During our travels we seek new and exciting areas to explore—it's not a preset tour. The expeditions are for hardy souls who can accept the unexpected." Parts of some routes are covered by 4-wheel-drive vehicle and backpacking.

Scuba Diving/Snorkeling

A boat is anchored inside the reef, and the student, having previously learned a back roll and four important hand signals, rolls over into the crystal-clear tropical water. The temperature is comfortable, the surf relatively calm, the depths shallow, and visibility extends as much as 70 feet.

To the student it is unforgettable. He is engulfed in color—the blue of the water, the pure white-sand bottom sprinkled with waving yellow and purple sea fans, fat pink conches, the unworldly formation of coral in a liquid world. Under the instructor's watchful eye, the student flippers silently with multicolored parrot fish, red snapper, yellow tails, bright jewel fish, angel fish and butterfly fish.

As the dive comes to a close, the instructor gathers the length of rope attached to the safety float and diver's flag, and heads back to the boat. The student's first 30-minute dive over a Virgin Island reef is over. He has become aware of the existence of a surrealistic world in which man, as yet, is only a visitor.

The term "scuba" is an acronym for "self-contained underwater breathing apparatus." The introduction of a relatively simple, low-cost diving lung by Emile Gagnan and Jacques-Yves Cousteau in 1943 is responsible for the tremendous rise in popularity of scuba. Today about three million divers are enjoying the sport.

Many insurance companies now require certification of national recognition for diving, and certain areas require that only certified divers engage in the sport. Training is available regularly through the YMCA, YWCA, and local dive shops and schools that offer certified courses. These are taught by competent instructors accredited by national organizations such as the National Association of Skin Diving Schools (NASDS), the National Association of Underwater Instructors (NAUI), and the Professional Association of Diving Instructors (PADI) or the YMCA. Each sets up its own guidelines for scuba instruction but covers the same basic training.

Total training time ranges from 24 to 30 hours or more, spread out over a number of weeks and divided into pool training, classroom time and several open-water dives. In resort areas, accelerated and intensive courses of several days or a week are often given to vacationers. In the classroom, students are taught about equipment, first aid, emergency procedures, and the physics of air and water and how they affect the diver's body. In the pool, training begins with snorkeling and progresses to full scuba practice. Then the student makes several open-water dives and, upon successful completion, receives a certification card. With c-card in hand, the student may progress to more advanced scuba courses, such as search and recovery, cave

Earthwatch, MA.

Dave McLeod's Skin Diving Adventures, Bermuda.

diving, and light salvage. Basic courses usually range from $120 to $150, with advanced courses the same or somewhat higher.

Of course, before a diver is ready to make the plunge, he must be properly equipped. Scuba divers—some of them hanging 12 or more pieces of gear on themselves—resemble creatures from outer space in their black wet suits, fins worn over neoprene foam boots, masks, weight belts, insulated gloves, heavy-duty vests, and backpacks or harnesses with air tanks. Then there are the assorted diving tools and instruments: a waterproof watch, depth gauge, compass, decompression meter, knife, prying tool and an underwater camera. Indeed, completely outfitting yourself with your own equipment can easily cost $2,000 or more. Reasonably priced rentals are available in most diving areas, however, including air fills for your tank.

Once a diver receives his certification card, he's advised always to dive with another. In unfamiliar waters a guide is a great help, not only to handle the boat and anchor but also to choose the best diving area.

While some scuba initiates take lessons in a pool or fresh-water lake, many will travel long distances to train directly in the ocean. The Caribbean, Hawaii, the Florida Keys and a hundred other colorful warm-water areas are ideal. A favorite locale for many is the only living coral reef in North America, which runs parallel to the Florida Keys about 10 or 12 miles offshore for over 200 miles. Three beautiful underwater reefs with a multitude of marine animals and coral just south of Miami are marked by the Biscayne National Monument. Farther south, 20 miles of reef, from four to five miles wide, is known as the John Pennekamp Coral Reef State Park. Both areas are protected from coral collectors.

Divers are apt to take their sport seriously, and they will spend large sums to become acquainted with diving in various areas. In conversations they speak of how diving in Hawaii, for example, differs from dives they have made in the Mediterranean, the Florida Keys, Eleuthera, Cozumel, the Great Barrier Reef and other favorite diving haunts all over the world.

And they are dedicated to their sport. A Chicago advertising executive we know spent so many weekends flying to the Florida Keys to dive that he finally moved there, opened a dive shop, and has been doubling its business each year for seven years. How does he spend his time? Diving, of course, and doing reef-guiding for busy executives who fly down from Chicago every weekend to dive.

Snorkeling and skin diving, without the benefit of an aqualung—just with mask, snorkel and fins—is a more carefree and much less expensive way to gain fish and coral as your friends. You remain close to, usually on, the surface to view the fish and the scenery below. One of the most famous snorkeling meccas, Buck Island National Monument off St. Croix in the Virgin Islands, actually boasts a specially marked nature trail for snorkelers. Traveling in pairs, they dive at above-surface markers to examine coral formations below, and they read concrete subtitles, so to speak, which explain what they are seeing.

Although you need not be an Olympic champ to be a diver, you should have moderate stamina and swimming ability, and should feel at ease in the winter. Snorkeling and skin diving in shallow waters are good introductions for the more demanding scuba.

Once you're beneath the blue, there's much to do—collect marine species or shells, take fascinating photographs, explore old shipwrecks, follow a school of fish or swim away while they follow you. A few of the hundreds of diving services are listed below. Other diving opportunities are mentioned in the chapter on boat charters.

The equipment supplied varies. Double-check what rates include and what you should bring or rent. You'll also want to know the length of the scuba instruction period, how much time you'll have underwater, and whether the course culminates in certification. When you arrange for a diving excursion, be sure your experience qualifies you for it. The cost of shuttle to and from the embarkation point is some-times included in rates.

CALIFORNIA

Baja Expeditions, Inc., AGI, PO Box 3725, San Diego, CA 92103. Att.: Tim Means. (714) 297-0506. Sea of Cortez, Gulf of Mexico (Mex.). Oct.–Jun. 12–18 people. 8 days, $575, incl. equip., lodging and transport aboard boat. (See also *Wilderness Living*.)

"The underwater world of the Sea of Cortez," says Tim Means, "is one of the world's few remaining virgin places to dive." His diving expeditions in these Mexican waters emphasize the total Baja environment, both on land and in the "crystal-clear sea." From San Diego you travel by bus to San Felipe, then cruise on the 75-foot *Poseidon,* which is equipped with a scuba air-compressor system. Each day you stop to explore island and coastline beaches and observe the desert flora and fauna. Fun and excitement on this exotic trip.

Olympic Scuba School, Dive & Travel, 2595 N. Main St., Walnut Creek, CA 94596. Att.: David E. Olson. (415) 935-1076. All yr.

The California coast, Baja California, Hawaii, the Caribbean and Honduras are the exotic areas you can explore with Dave Olson and his staff of professional educators and tour directors. Calling his school "diving's largest educational program," he offers a 6-week course for certification (NASDS, NAUI, PADI) in each area—basic training, which includes 7 lectures, 5 practical pool sessions, 3 ocean classes and an equipment counseling session. The course will familiarize you with underwater navigation, understanding waves and beaches, diving physics and physiology, marine life and safe habits. His instruction also covers advanced training, a resort course for travelers and one in underwater photography.

CONNECTICUT

Russell Yacht Charters, 126 Davis Ave., Suite 300, Bridgeport, CT 06605. Att.: Joanne J. Russell (203) 366-4561. Caribbean, Bahamas, FL, New Eng. 8 people. 12-day pkg., $690/person; 7 days for 4 or more, $400 ea. incl. food,open bar, wine w./meals, scuba gear, lessons, air. (See also *Boat Charters*.)

This charter service offers special scuba tours on the *Bonaventure,* a refitted Gulfstar LOA 49, for exploration of underwater caves, shallow reefs, deep reefs and sunken Spanish galleons. Divers also receive lessons in identification of flora and fauna. With a layout comfortable for family as well as adult groups, and a 13-foot dory with a 6-horsepower engine for recreation fun, the yacht can accommodate up to 8 people.

FLORIDA

Dive Aboard *The Dropout,* 227 Tavernier Dr., Tavernier, FL 33070. Att.: Clifford King. (305) 852-5616. Nov.–Apr., Jun.–Sept.

The Dropout is a fast, 26-foot dive boat offering daily dives off the Florida Keys, including underwater Pennekamp Park. "If your interests run to photography, I will be glad to share my years of experience with you," says Captain King, who prefers "small, unregimented fun groups" of up to 7. He's been a commercial and sport diver since 1954, and a licensed captain since 1962. The trips are for certified divers, or snorkelers of any age, at $13 a day each.

Holiday Isle Dive Shop, PO Box 482-A, Islamorada, FL 33036. Att.: Ed Armstrong. (305) 664-4145. All yr.

Ed Armstrong offers "a relaxed, personalized dive trip with a maximum of 6 divers to insure individualized attention." He also arranges special snorkel and night dives, "and the nondivers may want to come along just for the ride!" Major reefs in the area range in depth from 15 to 30 feet, and advanced divers can explore ledges and canyons at 50 feet and deeper. Half-day trips are $17 per diver; basic scuba instruction is $115 in a group or $165 private with everything provided but mask, fins, snorkel and textbook. He also arranges trips for the serious-minded diver—2 to 7 days in Cay Sal, Andros Island or anywhere in the Bahamas at rates that "aren't nearly as high as you'd expect."

Key West Pro Dive Shop, 1605 N. Roosevelt Blvd., Key West, FL 33040. Att.: Bob Holston. (305) 296-3823. All yr.

The oldest dive shop in the Lower Keys guarantees you a "safe, happy and friendly introduction to a whole new world beneath the sea where the living coral reefs swarm with every variety of underwater life." The *Key Comber* leaves the dock at 10:30 each morning with up to 34 passengers on dive and snorkel trips to 2 reefs ($15/person plus equipment, or $10 just for the ride.). Custom-tailored groups trips are offered at package rates that include motel reservations, meals and island tours. Also NASDS scuba instruction.

The Reef Shop Pro Dive Center, Rt. #1, Box 7A, Islamorada, FL 33036. Att.: Capt. Jim Williams. (305) 664-4385. All yr.

Captain Jim Williams was permanently lured away from being an advertising executive by the crystal-clear warm waters and the beautiful scenes of "the only living reef in North America." His dive center is 14 miles south of Pennekamp Park, and just down the road from Coral Reef Resort, which supplies its guests with free air. "There are over 600 species of colorful fish and tropicals to photograph," he says. He provides PADI and Florida Scuba Divers Association instruction to anyone 15 years or older, and requires certification for dives. Half-day trips are $15 each.

Sunshine Key Aqua Center, Inc., RR 1, Box 790-L, Holiday Inn Trav-1 Park, Sunshine Key, FL 33043. Att.: Capt. Ed Davidson. (305) 872-2400. All yr.

Captain Ed Davidson recommends diving in the emerald waters of Looe Key, with 50- to 100-foot visibility, on the biggest living coral reef formations in North America. Or spending a weekend or a week in the virtually untried waters of the Dry Tortugas Islands, or on the Cay Sal banks of the Bahamas. He uses 25-foot dive boats for 5 or 6 divers in the shallow waters of the Keys, and on longer excursions the 65-foot twin-diesel *Reef Rover* accommodates 15 to 40 people, while his 60-foot replica galleon serves 6 divers in comfort and style. Captain Davidson also gives diving instruction for PADI certification. A private course, including the use of all gear, is $96. A day's diving trip is $13.50 per diver.

Wilderness Southeast, Rt. 3, Box 619-L, Savannah, GA 31406. Att.: Dick Murlless. (912) 355-8008. Looe Key & Dry Tortugas (FL). All yr. 10–20 divers, 5–7 days. $25/day. Arrival: Marathon, FL. (See also *Backpacking, Canoeing, Youth Adventures* —GA.)

The emphasis on these explorations on the Dry Tortugas, 65 miles from the Florida Keys, is on learning about reef biology. Instruction is given in the use of snorkel equipment. Says Dick, "Our programs are wilderness camping trips with minimal facilities and minimal impact on the environment. The snorkeling over coral reefs in these crystal-clear waters is incredible! The Tortugas have the most pristine coral reefs in the U.S. today."

HAWAII
Dan's Dive Shop, 1382 Makoloa St., Honolulu, HI 96814. Att.: Mike Owens. (808) 946-7333. All yr.

"If you've never been scuba diving or snorkeling before, instructors will accompany you on a safe, highly controlled tour of a shallow reef," writes Mike Owens. "More experienced divers will want to explore deeper waters. To see Hawaii's real beauty, look beneath the surface. It's quiet, uncrowded, beautiful—a land of multicolored fish and living coral reefs. You won't believe it until you're there!" Half-day programs with instructor/guides are $30 including equipment, pickup and dropoff at your hotel.

Divin' Hawaii, 5085 Likini St., B306, Honolulu, HI 96818. Att.: Marvin E. Farthing. (808) 833-2298. All yr.

"We specialize in taking people scuba diving for the first time," says Marvin. "Our guides and instructors are friendly, informative and very safety-minded." Divin' Hawaii offers a half-day tour ($28) that includes basic scuba instruction and one dive for people with no experience, or a half-day snorkel course ($13). Hanauma Bay, which is a protected underwater park, is one of their dive sites. They also have a 5-day scuba course that results in NAUI or PADI certification, and they take certified divers on special tours—mostly in the coral reefs around Oahu. Rates include transportation to and from hotels.

International Aquatic Adventures, Inc., 2047 Broadway, Boulder, CO 80302. Att.: John Sanker & Tim Hervey. (303) 449-4620. Nov.–Dec. (See also *Float Trips*—CO.)

Diving and snorkeling on coral reefs teeming with life, and sailing and exploring—all are part of what IAA calls "the most unique tour program in Hawaii." From a base camp on a secluded beach on the island of Lanai, you'll try your hand at navigating a 2-passenger sailboat or venture forth on Avon rafts to the reefs, ancient villages or old shipwrecks. Or board the brigantine *Rendezvous* for a day of poking around Lahaina on the island of Maui. Divers: Bring dive card, regulator and weight belt, and request rental tanks. For 5 days and 4 nights, $275 per person (family rates less) covers tent accommodations, meals and daily excursions. Also 1- and 2-week interisland sailings.

Skin Diving Hawaii, Inc., 1651 Ala Moana Blvd., Honolulu, HI 96815. Att.: John Frederick. (808) 941-0548. All yr.

Operating since 1958, this is the oldest dive shop in the islands, and one that offers complete dive-shop services, scuba and snorkeling instruction, and charters in Honolulu and Kailua-Kona. Packages with transportation to and from hotels include: a beach snorkel tour ($15), boat snorkel tour ($20), introduction to scuba ($30), beach scuba dive ($30), and boat scuba dive ($30). Certification cards are required for divers not involved in the basic scuba course. Skin Diving's specialty is introducing divers to the colorful marine life and coral reefs.

PENNSYLVANIA

Diving Bell, Inc., 681 North Broad St., Philadelphia, PA 19123. Att.: Howard Pruyn. (215) 763-6868. Apr.–Oct. in NJ; Dec.–Mar. in Caribbean.

Diving Bell offers year-round PADI open-water certification, with 5 classes each week at various locations in Philadelphia, and open-water training dives on Sundays, spring through fall, in Sea Isle City, New Jersey. In the winter they travel to the Bahamas, Virgin Islands and British West Indies, where students may make their open-water dives. Rates for pool and class sessions are $80; open-water dives, including boat and instructors, are $50. Caribbean trips, $600 to $700.

WISCONSIN

On The Rocks, Rt. 1, Box 164 AG, Ellison Bay, WI 54210. Att.: Gene Shastal. (414) 854-2808. May–Oct.

This is a lodge for divers where shallow water is at the doorstep and 110 feet of water with spectacular dropoffs are within 150 yards of shore. To the west is Hedgehog Harbor, with at least 4 known wrecks. Complete scuba facilities include a specially equipped charter boat with daily excursions through the upper islands. Scuba divers must have certification cards, and for some difficult dives open-water training is required. Boat trips are from $4; accommodations start at $5 for dorms.

BERMUDA AND CARIBBEAN

Adventure Cruises, Inc., PO Box 22284-A, Fort Lauderdale, FL 33316. Att.: Capt. "Skeet" La Chance. (305) 735-4045. Jan.–Oct.

Visit at least a dozen top diving spots in the Bahamas on 1- to 2-week excursions. "We try to give each diver what he wants," writes Captain La Chance. "Therefore, we offer shelf diving, wrecks, blue holes, ocean holes and reefs ranging from 10 to 100 feet." Rates are about $57/day, including meals, air refills, tanks, weights and belts, and a minimum amount of masks, fins, snorkels and regulators. You cruise aboard the *Highlander IV,* which provides comfortable quarters for up to 10. "Dive all day, then enjoy cocktails and dinner, and in the evening perhaps an onshore adventure," the captain urges.

Aqua-Action, Inc., Wintberg Peak, St. Thomas, VI 00801. Att.: Palmer Williams. (809) 775-3275. All yr.

Whatever age, Palmer Williams likes to get people off the beach and into the incomparable beauty of the underwater world—coral reefs and unusual tropical fish. "Lots of hand-holding for beginners," writes Williams. "We have a very gentle and conservative approach to teaching—*no* video: Real people teach." On advanced guided tours, dives are planned according to divers' interests—from night dives to ship-wreck exploration. Basic NASDS certification is $175; open water, $150. Scuba lesson tours are $30; night dives, $35. Also group rates.

Dave McLeod's Skin Diving Adventures, The Gables Guest House, Harbour Rd., Paget, Bermuda. Att.: Dave McLeod. 809 (29) 1-6207.

Mainly shallow-water diving, with plenty of time to photograph a variety of reef fish. "We have lots of wrecks," writes Dave McLeod—and he'll lead you through them on dives from his specially equipped boats. A PADI instructor, McLeod starts with snorkel instruction and graduates to scuba. Lesson and dive are $35; single-tank dive with your equipment, $20; with theirs, $25. 35mm Nikonos and Super 8 cameras in underwater housing can be rented.

Henry & Grace Falany's White Water River Expeditions, PO Box 1249-D, Turlock, CA 95380. (209) 634-1133. Jan.–Apr. (See also *Float Trips*—CA.)

On an island paradise off the coast of Belize (formerly British Honduras), the Falanys set up a tropical camp for a 7-day scuba and snorkeling adventure. You'll recognize their boats—the same 35- to 40-foot inflatable rigs they use in the Grand Canyon, but with a sunshade and glass-bottom section added and an air compressor on board. There are endless miles of shallow coral gardens, deep dives both inside and outside the reef, and 200-foot visibility in the 80-degree water. Divers must be certified and bring all but tank, tank pack and weight belt. Snorkelers bring snorkel, mask and fins. Other diversions: water skiing, fishing, a sailing rig, exploring, cocktails at 4:30, campfire after dinner. From Belize: adult, $495; child, $300.

Underwater Safaris, PO Box 291-A, Back Bay Annex, Boston, MA 02117. Att.: Fred Calhoun. (617) 283-4933. July.

Off Andros Island in the Bahamas you can dive on the largest living coal reef in the Atlantic, atop a mile-high plateau called Grand Bahama Bank. Fred Calhoun guides divers to the best possible dive sites—Smuggler's Run, Duke's Wreck, The Wall and others. He *encourages* exploration, photography and marine life study, and *discourages* coral reef destruction—no coral harvesting, shell collecting or spear fishing on these trips. It's $350 for a week's excursion, including scuba gear, all meals and overnight accommodations at Small Hope Bay Lodge—no TV, telephones or radios, but a ground-to-air transceiver and nearby radiotelephone.

VI   IN SNOW

Dog Sledding

Mush! Or in the less colorful though more explicit language used today to give instructions to sled dog teams: Gee, haw, woah, go ahead, no!

If you've always wanted to answer the call of the wild in a Jack London setting, dog sledding tours may be just the excitement you're looking for. This classic means of wilderness transportation in the frozen North has been largely replaced by aircraft and the snowmobile for everyday travel and for hauling freight. But the sled pulled by an excited team of tail-wagging huskies still slides through frozen landscapes to carry gear or to give hardy adventurers a snowy ride just for the fun of it.

There are a few outfitters who will take you on frosty excursions by sled and dog team for an hour or two, or overnight or longer. "Sights and sounds are heightened in the still atmosphere," recalls a TV producer from Fairbanks who ventured into the wilderness of McKinley National Park. "There is nothing quite so exhilarating as swishing along in back of twelve panting dogs, with the only sounds being their breathing, your breathing and the sliding of the sled runners. Then to look up through a break in the clouds to see a panorama of the Alaska Range! It makes it a cinch to fantasize yourself as the main character of all those Northland adventure stories."

The more adventuresome may choose a ski touring or snowshoe trek with dog sled support into white Arctic mountain fastnesses, or the frozen Boundary Waters Area along the Minnesota-Ontario border. You can take turns standing on the runners and "helping" to handle the team. It's a rugged adventure for the physically fit and active. Some winterize themselves for an arduous trek in a wilderness school where winter camping and survival skills are taught by experts.

On the short or long treks open to vacationers, rather than breaking new trails each time, the dog sled team frequently follow their own tracks, made on previous trips. Note to ski tourers: Should you come upon their tracks, kindly cross at a right angle. If you slant across, making a "Y," when the dogs came to it they'll get confused and sit down and howl!

ALASKA

Denali Dog Tours and Wilderness Freighters, Box 1, McKinley Park, AK 99755. Att.: Dennis Kogl. (907) 683-2266. Oct.–Apr.

Dennis Kogl leads the way on the pole skis in front of the sled not behind the dogs on these strenuous trips in Mt. McKinley National Park. With 2 persons per team of

8 huskies, one rides the runner tails of the sled while the other sits in the basket. "This can be endured only a short while," Dennis says. "You must jog along with the sled when necessary to warm up, or push with one foot. I take snowshoes on all trips, but we don't usually use them, since the trail is broken, or else we are traveling in an area of light snowfall or on a river system. Everyone helps on hills by running or walking as the team ascends the grade." One of his specialties is sled-dog support ski tourers and mountaineers who don't want to carry heavy gear. Day tours are $80 per person or $100 for 2. Overnight tours to cabins are $200 ($300 per 2) up.

Sourdough Outfitters, Bettles, AK 99726. Att.: David Ketscher. (907) 692-5252. Arrival: Bettles, AK, via Fairbanks. (See also *Backpacking, Canoeing, Float Trips, Ski Touring.*)

You're a part of the wilderness, not an intruder, when you travel the good old way through the Brooks Range. "It involves a lot more than sitting on a sled," writes David Ketscher. "You help make camp, care for the dogs and take turns snowshoeing to break trail if necessary." These are trips for small groups, scheduled by special arrangement. Good physical condition is a must, as is an expedition-quality sleeping bag.

COLORADO

Krabloonik, PO Box 5517, Snowmass Village, CO 81615. Att.: Dan MacEachen. (303) 923-3953. Dec.-Apr.

"Come to Krabloonik for a traditional Alaskan dog sled ride in a hand-crafted sled pulled by 13 huskies through beautiful woods and past magnificent views," Dan MacEachen urges. It's a scenic and exciting way to see the Snowmass area for 2 hours or for 1 or 2 days. Lodging and meals are provided on the longer excursion ($90 per person), and luncheon on the day trip ($40). A 2-hour ride is $20.

Mountain Guides and Outfitters, Inc., PO Box 2001, Aspen CO 81611. Att.: Kenneth R. Wyrick. (303) 925-6680. Nov.-Apr. (See also *Backpacking, Mountaineering, Float Trips, Ski Touring*—Aspen Ski Touring School.)

Tucked onto a sled, a blanket across your legs, you skim down an old railbed trail paralleling the Roaring Fork River at 4 to 5 miles per hour with 8 bushy tails waving in front of your face. The huge Alaskan malamutes are urged into action by your guides standing on the sled behind you, sometimes cursing, sometimes praising his enthusiastic dogs as they race through the woods, along a red-rock cliff, and cautiously slip by an almost iced-over waterfall. You, too, are part of the action. "Lean left," you're told as the sled skirts a large boulder. "Keep wiggling your toes" is another directive, shortly before pausing for hot spiced wine from a thermos. A full day with hot lunch is $45 per person, and half price for children.

BRITISH COLUMBIA

North Country Travelers, Box 14, Atlin, B.C. V0W 1A0. Att.: Bruce Johnson. No tel. Mar.-Apr. (See also *Canoeing.*)

First you fly to Whitehorse, then take a bus to Atlin (110 miles), and notify the Johnsons by CB radio that you are there. (It's a town of 350 people with a nice hotel, which had no road leading to it until 1959.) The Johnsons will come in from their cabin to pick you up—a 30-mile trip by dog sled, 7 miles of it across frozen Atlin Lake. "Transportation here is still the same as during the Gold Rush days," Bruce Johnson writes. "We use dogs because they are a dependable and exciting way to travel." Guests must be able to adapt to the living conditions and unpredictable time schedules of North Country travel, and able to use cross-country skis and snowshoes if trails cross snowed-over areas. Trips for 1 to 6 people, 3 to 10 days, are $125 per day, completely outfitted except for down sleeping bags.

Ski Touring/Snowshoeing

Push, glide, push, glide. The cross-country tourer moves through a calm, white landscape in graceful arabesques, the cold air stinging his lungs. He is setting off through untracked forest and glen to visit areas normally remote until the spring thaws. He may follow a hiking trail, bridle path, logging road, or a trail especially maintained and "groomed" for ski touring. Unlike the extensive development required for the downhill skier, for the tourer any more or less level area with several inches of snow covering will do.

Although ski touring will never replace downhill skiing, touring extends skiing's possibilities and offers many advantages. The techniques are less intimidating, safer, and easier to master, and total outfitting is much cheaper. The terms "cross-country skiing" and "ski touring" are interchangeable in common usage, though technically "cross-country" refers to the competitive rather than recreational aspects of the sport.

Whole families can enjoy ski touring together—mother, father and the kiddies. Everyone follows his own pace. That can be from one to five miles per hour for the practiced skier. If there is a toddler involved, some families bring him along in the backpack. Touring is hiking—hiking in fields or woods on skis. Most skiers just poking along, following animal tracks or listening to the silence of the winter woods.

Some ski tourers, however, seek out the exciting and the unusual, and they have much to choose from. Special ghost town tours are offered by a ski-touring school near Vail, Colorado. On leisurely paced moonlight outings, skiers are outfitted with miners' headlamps and tote wine and cheese if they like. Other sturdy souls include winter bivouac in their touring—spending nights in a tent or snow cave or igloo. Or they trek behind teams of huskies in Minnesota's Boundary Waters Area or Alaska's Mt. McKinley National Park. The dogs break trails and pull sleds loaded with the camping gear. History, also, shapes ski touring treks—such as the 32-mile tour along Lake George arranged annually by the Ski Touring Council of Troy, Vermont, to commemorate the famous retreat of Major Robert Rogers in 1757 during the French and Indian Wars. Indeed, there is something for everyone.

Information on tours, workshops, orienteering trips, Citizen Races and cross-country races is given in the *Ski Touring Schedule* ($2.75) and its companion *Ski Touring Guide* ($3), which describe all aspects of touring—trail marking, technique, equipment, safety precautions, orienteering, organizing workshops, and trails. Both can be ordered from Rudi Mattesich, President, Ski Touring Council, West Hill Road, Troy, VT 05868.

Northern Lights Alpine Recreation, B.C., by Arnör Larson.

Another way of hiking in the snow is on snowshoes. Like ski touring, snow-shoeing resembles walking, but anyone who tries it soon discovers some differences. The main one is the ease with which you step on top of one snowshoe with the other and quickly find yourself horizontal on the snow. You'll soon catch onto the technique of keeping your feet wider apart and lifting them higher, and before long you'll be rhythmically clump, clump, clumping along on a blanket of snow, leaving parallel trackmarks behind. It's a delicious way of walking in the winter country-side.

Ski touring centers throughout the nation not only teach *beginners* how to get started, but they provide marked trails for intermediates and experts as well. Many rent or sell equipment, guide tours and provide food and accomodations.

The descriptions below tell the areas in which some of these services operate, during what months, how long their guided tours last (a few hours to a week or longer), how many skiers they can take on each tour, and average rates per skier. Call them for further details, or write for their brochures.

Check rates, tax, dates, equipment provided and equipment for rent. Are lodging and meals included in rates? Brochures tell what clothing and equipment are best, and listings indicate whether overnight and longer tours are arranged. Find out what degree of skill is a prerequisite for tours, and where it is safe to go unguided. As a rule, the number of skiers noted in listings refers to the size of groups for guided trips, not the total number for whom there are facilities. Listings do not include all the other snow activities that each service offers. Instruction rates pertain to one skier in group instruction, though private lessons at higher rates are usually avail-able. Trail fees are given, though they generally are included in a rental package rate.

ALASKA

Alaska Mountain Expeditions, Talkeetna, AK 99676. Att.: Ray Genet. (907) 733-2306. Feb.–Apr. Arrival: Air to Anchorage; train to Talkeetna. (See also *Moun-taineering.*)

At Pirate Lake Wilderness Camp at the base of Mt. McKinley, you'll ski or snowshoe over frozen rivers and wilderness of the Alaska Range foothills. Over-nights are in rustic log cabins and tents. Or fly in to the Mountain House on magnificent Ruth Glacier and ski tour in the expansive Amphitheatre beneath the shadow of Mt. McKinley. Rentals; guided tours for up to 12.

Mountains North Guide Service, 851 University Ave., Fairbanks, AK 99701. Att.: Ev Wenrick. (907) 479-2984. Nov.–Apr. & summer on ice fields. (See also *Back-packing, Mountaineering, Canoeing.*)

These hardy tours average 8 to 10 miles per day and last from 1 day to 2 weeks or longer. "Participants should be in good physical shape, have good endurance and be able to ski with a 40- to 50-pound pack," writes Ev Wenrick. Rates range from $35 to $40/day; group instruction, $20/day. In summer, you can ski on the Harding Icefield near Seward. Choose either a 10-day crossing, or a 3- to 5-day fly-in or climb-in trip. Another feature: 1-, 2- or 3-day workshops in snow and glacier travel and wilderness skiing techniques ($40/day). A special tour, 2 to 5 days, involves living in a tepee, with a log fire, and carrying only clothes and sleeping bag.

Sourdough Outfitters, Bettles, AK 99723. Att.: David Ketscher. (807) 692-5252. Apr. Arrival: Bettles, via Fairbanks, AK. (See also *Backpacking, Canoeing, Float Trips, Dog Sledding.*)

Fairly high temperatures and long daylight hours make the wilderness of the Brooks Range a skier's paradise in April, when winter scenery beckons and powder snow starts to firm up. "We can provide logistical support with a dog team to allow skiers freedom from carrying heavy, bulky packs," writes David Ketscher, who describes his outfit as the only resident wilderness guide in the area.

Tokosho Mountain Lodge, S.R.B. Box 323, Willow, AK 99688. Att.: John & Sue Neill. No tel. Tokositna Riv. Dec.–Mar. Arrival: Talkeetna, AK.

It's a 20-minute flight by bush plane from Talkeetna to the Tokosho Mountain Lodge, where you tour within view of Mt. McKinley to your heart's content. There are 30 miles of marked and 20 miles of groomed trails for all-day tours, and guides for off-trail touring, snowshoeing treks and overnight excursions. The Lodge, designed especially for those who want a rustic wilderness experience, offers a 3-day stay for $225, meals included, or 5 days for $355.

Wildernorth, Inc., Mile 102 Glenn Hwy., SRC Box 92E, via Palmer, AK 99645. Att.: Joe & Suzi LaBelle & Stu Ashley. No. tel. Nov.–Mar. (See also *Backpacking, Mountaineering.*)

Snowshoeing is the specialty here, with day and weekend trips in the Chugach and Talkeetna Mountains. "We provide snowshoes, lunches and first-aid gear on day trips, and generally cover about 10 miles," Joe explains. "On weekend introductory trips we teach winter camping and cover 15 to 25 miles on marked trails and across open country. For experienced winter travelers the treks are more rigorous." He supplies all but sleeping and personal gear. Day trips are $20; weekend trips, $60.

ARIZONA

Grand Canyon Youth Expeditions, RR 4, Box 755, Flagstaff, AZ 86001. Att.: Dick & Susan McCallum. (602) 774-8176. Flagstaff area, San Francisco Peaks, North Rim of Grand Canyon. Dec.–Jan. (See also *Backpacking, Float Trips, Youth Adventures.*)

In cooperation with the Museum of Northern Arizona, the McCallums offer ski touring of the San Francisco Peaks and the North Rim of the Grand Canyon. These weekend overnight excursions cost $15 (bring your own equipment), with a museum biologist providing educational interpretation.

CALIFORNIA

Mammoth Ski Touring Center, PO Box 102, Mammoth Lakes, CA 93546. Att.: Per Fostvedt. (714) 934-6955. Sierras (Inyo Natl. Forest). Oct.–Jun.

Tamarack Lodge at Twin Lakes and VI Mall in the village offer 40 miles of marked trails for beginners to experts, maintained and patrolled, with no trail fee. Norwegian instructors hold classes morning and afternoon ($6.50 each), and conduct all-day tours ($10 including lunch) and moonlight ski tours with cheese and wine around a fire ($5). Basic winter survival classes ($15), expedition tours to Yosemite with overnights in a snow cave or tent ($35), and an FWSIA instructor certification program round out the activities. Also provided: a ski touring shop, rentals ($6.50/day), repairs, waxing clinics, reasonable lodging, and rates for groups, schools and the like. It's a personalized and "mammoth" service they give.

Mountain People School, 157 Oak Spring Dr., San Anselmo, CA 94960. Att.: Terry Halbert. (415) 457-3664. (See also *Mountaineering.*)

Mountain People offers a weekend snowshoe trek in the Sierra Nevada that they call a "winter wonderland, with high peaks blanketed in white, snow banners streaming from corniced ridges, making faint and feathery trails across a deep blue sky, which glows brilliantly." The trip, teaching the basics of winter camping and survival, begins in San Rafael early on Saturday; $35 includes all.

Royal Gorge Ski Touring, PO Box 178, Soda Springs, CA 95728. Att.: John S. Slouber. (916) 426-3793. Donner Pass area. Nov.–May. Arrival: Reno or Truckee (by air), Soda Springs (by bus).

On the crest of the Sierra in a major touring region, Royal Gorge offers just about everything for the cross-country skier. "It's the largest maintained trail system in the West," John Slouber points out, "with 75 miles of marked, groomed and patrolled track.'' Trail fee, $3/day; rentals, $7.50/day package; lessons, $7/2 hours. Also a unique Wilderness Lodge, open weekends, holidays and ski weeks, which you reach on Friday night by sleigh, wrapped in fur robes. Royal Gorge offers beautiful surroundings, touring instruction, French cuisine, open-loft style sleeping, sauna and hot tub, and warmth and relaxation. Also a 3-race series with prizes, and trips abroad.

Snowshoe Schwarzman, 620 W. Lake Blvd., PO Box 784, Tahoe City, CA 95730. Att.: Jim Schwarzman. (916) 583-3062. Nov.–Apr.

All lessons are tours—even for beginners—here at North Tahoe's oldest touring school, with no trail fee for open and wooded marked trails. Up to 20 skiers can enjoy spectacular views of the Sierra Ridge on part- or all-day guided tours ($6–$10), no matter what their expertise. Rentals, $6.

Squaw Valley Nordic Ski Center, Box 2288-B, Olympic Valley, CA 95730. Att.: Skip Reedy or Jerry Smeltzer. (916) 583-9858. Nov.–Apr. (See also *Backpacking, Youth Adventures.*)

Certified instructors and experienced mountaineers lead lessons and day or overnight tours for skiers of all levels. No fee for 50 miles of trails (15 marked). Extras include nature photography, snow safety, orienteering, full moon tours, races and an avalanche course. Tours are $6 a day; $25 overnight. Rentals are $7, and group instruction, $6. Other Nordic Ski Centers are located at Tahoe, where well-maintained marked and groomed trails wind through rolling terrain; and Alpine Meadows, an intimate cross-country area with trails connecting to Squaw Valley and Lake Tahoe.

COLORADO

Aspen Ski Touring School, Mountain Guides and Outfitters, Inc., Box 2001-A, Aspen, CO 81611. Att.: Ken Wyrick. (303) 925-6680. Nov.–Apr. (See also *Backpacking, Mountaineering, Float Trips, Dog Sledding*—Mountain Guides and Outfitters.)

Experienced guides instruct and lead all ages in ski touring and snowshoeing in Aspen's magnificent surroundings. Beginners ski at elevations up to 9,000 feet, while advanced skiers may reach elevations of 12,000 feet, crossing high passes on overnight tours. There's no fee for the 100 miles of marked trails. Rentals are $6.50, snowshoes $3, and instruction $7.50 for 3 hours. "Each tour is custom-planned to the group's ability and current weather conditions,'' writes Ken Wyrick.

Playing Bear Ranch, Silverton Star Rt. 100, Durango, CO 81301. Att.: Ruedi & Leith Bear. (313) 247-0111. Dec.–Apr.

Tourers glide across 10 miles of marked and groomed trails in the Animas Valley near Durango. Half- and full-day tours start at the clubhouse, and the fee includes lunch and a guide. Instructors with years of Nordic experience teach technical skills. Also rentals, ski shop and snack bar.

Rocky Mountain Expeditions, Nordic Ski Shop, PO Box CC-AG, Buena Vista, CO 81211. Att.: Al McClelland. (303) 395-8466. Oct.–Mar. (See also *Backpacking, Float Trips, Wilderness Living.*)

Follow 18 miles of well marked trails and 100 miles of maintained trails into pristine Colorado back country. There are guided day trips deep into the wilderness and overnight tours to heated cabins. Or take a 4-day Rockies Tour ($150/person)—ideal for families, beginners and intermediates—or custom trips, tailor-made for groups of 2 or more. Instruction is $2/hour; rentals, $5. Snowshoes can be rented, too.

Rocky Mountain Ski Tours & Backpack Adventures, 156 Elkhorn Ave., Box 413P, Estes Park, CO 80517. Att.: Bill Evans, Peter & Rick Marsh. (303) 586-2114. [Off-

season: 130 E. Riverside Dr., Box 413-P, Estes Park, CO 80517. (303) 586-3553.]
Nov.–Apr. (See also *Backpacking.*)

The specialty here is ski touring courses. Tours take you on marked trails in
Rocky Mountain National Park—high, glacially cut areas with lakes, dense forests
and steep mountain walls. "Intermediate ability is required for most trails in the
more spectacular areas of the park," writes Peter Marsh. There's a $1 park entrance
fee; rentals, $5.50; instruction, $9.50/day, $37.50 for 5 days.

St. Paul Cross Country Ski Lodge, Box 463, Silverton, CO 81433. Att.: Chris & Barbara George. (303) 387-5494. Dec.–Apr. Arrival: Montrose or Grand Junction, CO.

The Georges' rustic lodge is snowbound most of the winter, so they meet drivers
at the top of Red Mountain Pass with skis (or snowshoes, if you prefer) for the 1-
mile trek in. "Don't worry," Chris says, "if you're unfamiliar with skis, this is an
easy introduction." Besides lodging and food, rentals are provided ($5), and daily
instruction and guided tours ($25–$30) over 10 miles of marked trails through
breathtaking San Juan Mountain terrain. Both Georges have instructed for Outward
Bound and have climbed extensively.

Vista Verde Ranch, Box 465, Steamboat Springs, CO 80477. Att.: Frank & Winton
Brophy. (303) 879-3858. Nov.–Apr. Arrival: Steamboat Springs or Hayden, CO.

Vista Verde, at 7,800 feet, is near the Mt. Zirkel Wilderness Area and surrounded
by Routt National Forest. There are miles of well-groomed trails on the ranch, or
pack your own in the forest. Snowshoeing, ice fishing, sleigh rides and wine and
cheese parties also are part of the activity. The rate for snug log cabins with fireplaces and cooking facilities is $30/night for 1 or 2, $10 for 3rd person, $5 each addl.
Lessons: 1½ hours, $8. Guided tours, $5 to $9. Rentals in Steamboat.

CONNECTICUT

Riverrun Touring Center, Main St., Falls Village, CT 06031. Att.: Mark Caliendo.
(203) 824-5579. Dec.–Feb. (See also *Canoeing.*)

Ski along 12 miles of marked and groomed, gently rolling trails or glide through
the pines in the neighboring state parks, then schuss down old logging roads. The
mixed terrain is best for beginners and intermediates, while guided tours exploring
the Falls Village area are for intermediate and experts. Instruction is $5/hour,
rentals are $7.50, and a donation is requested for trail use.

IDAHO

Leonard Expeditions, PO Box 98, Stanley, ID 83278. Att.: Joe Leonard. (208) 774-
3325. Nov.–May. (See also *Kayaking, Youth Adventures.*)

Leonard has developed a unique system of huts from 5 to 7 miles apart, "each in
the midst of the magical splendor and beauty of the Sawtooths." The terrain varies
from flat meadows to 1,500-foot powder bowls, and fits the needs of beginner to
expert. Lessons explain route selection, terrain and wildlife, and include climbing,
downhill skiing and Telemark turn on touring skis. Rates range from do-it-yourself
at $10/day to a Helper Tour at $45.

Sun Valley Nordic Ski School, Box 272, Sun Valley, ID 83353. Att.: Leif Odmark.
(208) 622-4111, ext. 2454 or 2455. Dec.–Apr.

Anything can be arranged in the way of guided ski tours here. Six-hour tours
($12–$15, including rentals and lunch), bus or helicopter tours to back country
($23–$56), night tours along torchlit courses for dinner at Trail Creek Cabin, and
overnight tours with cabin accommodations. Instruction ($8/1½ hours) for any
level of skier. Full-day rentals, $6; half-day, $4.

Timber Ridge Ranch Ski-Touring, PO Box 34S, Harrison, ID 83833. Att.: Stan
Gootrad. (208) 689-3422 or 689-3315. Dec.–Apr.

International Alpine School, CO.

In addition to the 104 miles of marked trails, there is open country for ski touring in the Coeur d'Alene National Forest. "It would take the whole winter to cover it all," Stan says. A great log lodge with a massive fireplace is the center of after-ski activities. Rates ($9/day, $25–$36/weekend) include meals, lodging, instruction and guided tours for up to 35 skiers. Rentals are $5/day.

Wilderness Institute, PO Box 338, Bonners Ferry, ID 83805. Att.: Larry E. Fidler. (208) 267-3013. Dec.–Mar. (See also *Backpacking, Mountaineering, Canoeing.*)

On 5- and 7-day excursions, this nonprofit organization studies the winter wilderness of Yellowstone, Colorado high country and the Canadian Rockies. The sights range from the geyser-sprayed "ghost trees" of Yellowstone to historical old ghost towns. You experience exhilarating skiing daytimes, and spend nights in warm cabins and lodges. Five-day trips are $195; 7 days, $225.

Wilderness River Outfitters & Trail Expeditions, PO Box 871-AG, Salmon, ID 83467. Att.: Joe Tonsmeire. (208) 756-3959. Jan.–Apr. (See also *Backpacking, Float Trips.*)

Deep in the heart of the national forest, Salmon is a favorite starting point for ski touring the Continental Divide and Salmon River country. Joe tailors each trip to the group's ability: Most tours vary from 1 to 5 days over fairly gentle terrain. For beginners he recommends a 5-day ski camp—2 days of instruction, plus 1 day and 1 overnight tour ($60/day includes meals, lodging, gear). Overnighters stay in tents, in snow caves in spring, or in huts. Daily rentals are $6; group instruction, $3/hour.

IOWA

Iowa Mountaineers, Inc., 30 Prospect Pl., Iowa City, IA 52240. Att.: John & Jim Ebert. (319) 337-7163. Jan. (See also *Backpacking, Mountaineering.*)

Jim Ebert, former Army ski instructor, and a staff of professional skiers and guides teach cross-country skiing and survival techniques from their base camp at 10,500 feet in the Colorado Rockies. High alpine touring trails (50 miles) for beginners to advanced. Academic credit is offered for this week's course in January.

MAINE

Maine Wilderness Canoe Basin, Springfield, ME 04487. Att.: Carl W. Selin. (207) 989-3636, ext. 631. (See also *Canoeing, Snowmobiling, Youth Adventures.*)

Sporting activities do not cease at the canoe basin during winter months. For ski tourers there are hundreds of miles of unplowed logging roads and trails over frozen lakes—marvelous terrain for all abilities. And housekeeping cabins to stay in. Complete ski touring rentals here in the heart of Maine's ski country.

Sunday River Ski Touring Center, Sunday River Inn DC, Bethel, ME 04217. Att.: Steve Wight. (207) 824-2410. Nov.–Apr.

There's solitude on 25 miles of marked, 20 miles of maintained, and 15 miles of groomed trails ($2 fee) in this high mountain terrain. A covered bridge makes a cozy rest or lunch stop, whether you're on your own or on a 5-skier guided tour ($5–$7). Rentals are $6; group lessons, $4/hour; and there's snowshoeing or dog sledding for kids and inn guests. "Come back to a friendly, family-style lodge and super home-cooked meals," Steve urges.

MICHIGAN

Boardman Valley Outfitting Co., PO Box 587, Traverse City, MI 49684. Att.: Eugene Power. (616) 946-5410, ext. 7126. Dec.–Mar.

Ski deep within Fife Lake State Forest on Boardman's 5 miles of marked and groomed trails or on 9 miles of state forest trails. Up to 10 skiers of all levels take guided tours through the southern valley trails and more challenging northern slopes. Group instruction is $5; rentals, $7. A full range of other snow activities—winter camping, husky dog sledding and sleigh rides pulled by Belgian horses—add to the fun.

Schuss Mountain, Mancelona, MI 49659. Att.: Laurie Schultz. (800) 632-7170; in MI, (616) 587-9162. Dec.–Apr.

There are 5 miles of marked trails at this ski resort, or you can take off over miles of untouched back country, gliding through the silent beauty of the Enchanted Forest. Midweek Ski Touring Packages from 3 to 5 days include lodging, trails and lessons. Also family rates.

MINNESOTA

Bald Eagle Center, Cass Lake, MN 56633. Att.: Tom Yahraes. (218) 665-2241. Dec.–Mar.

Bald Eagle is the outdoor branch of Bemidji State University, but scholar or not, their 20 miles of marked trails in the Chippewa National Forest are for you. Cross-country programs include touring instruction and winter campng. Also in the outdoor curriculum are snowshoeing, winter safety, outdoor cookery, orienteering and evening tours. Bald Eagle also offers summer programs in canoe camping.

Bear Track Outfitting Co., Box 51, Grand Marais, MN 55604. Att.: David & Cathi Williams. (218) 387-1162. Dec.–Mar. (See also *Backpacking, Canoeing, Youth Adventures.*)

David Williams guides you through the solitude of the Superior National Forest and the Boundary Waters Canoe Area on 3- to 7-day tours. A dog team and sled carry camping gear and plow ahead to break trails. Tours are open to all levels of skiers who are in top physical condition. Rates start at $98 and include food and camping gear, with wood-heated tents.

Lynx Track Winter Travel, 5375 Eureka Rd. AG, Excelsior, MN 55331. Att.: Duncan Storlie.

Promoting quiet winter travel is the purpose of this nonprofit organization. Participants, including beginners, learn the skills of cross-country skiing, snowshoeing, dog sledding, winter camping, winter dress, map and compass, igloo building, winter nature lore and safety. Lynx offers weekend seminars near Lake Minnetonka ($48) and 7-day wilderness travel courses in the Boundary Waters Canoe Area ($175–$225). Also 10 days in the BWCA for the more advanced, and in April a 6-day tour with dog sled support in the Big Horns of Wyoming. With scheduled departure dates (also charter arrangements), most courses are limited to 12 to 16 skiers; minimum age, from 9 to 16.

Radisson Inn, Grand Portage, MN 55605. Att.: W. J. Bauman. (218) 475-2401. Nov.–Mar.

There are 60 miles of marked and groomed trails—3 trail systems—in ideal terrain for ski touring. Most are loop trails, from 3 to 18 miles, for intermediate to expert. At the Ski Center: rentals, informal instruction for beginners, and tours with an expert guide of this northern region. Overnight tours also can be prearranged, using cabins. No trail fee for Inn guests, and special rates for Ski Nordic weekends or midweeks.

MONTANA

Izaak Walton Inn, Box 675, Essex, MT 59916. Att.: Sid Goodrich. Ask operator for Essex No. 1. Dec.–Apr.

From this pleasant mountain inn, glide straight from the door into the proposed Great Bear Wilderness Area or Glacier National Park, on 120 miles of marked trails. Intermediates or over take guided tours that last from 1 to 3 days, and venture into remote areas of the park and Flathead National Forest, with 4,000 to 6,000-foot elevations.

Three Bear Lodge, 217 Yellowstone Ave., West Yellowstone, MT 59758. Att.: Clyde G. Seely. (406) 646-7353. Dec.–Mar. (See also *Snowmobiling.*)

A 6-night package with 5 days of ski touring in Yellowstone National Park—some of the most impressive country you'll ever cross—is offered jointly by the Ambassador Motor Inn, Big Western Pine Motel and Three Bear Lodge. They provide a prime rib dinner on arrival, hot lunches on the trail, a "toasty room," transport to and from trailheads, certified instruction when appropriate, park entrance fees (3 days) and winter ecology discussions. You have use of more than 200 miles of marked trails in the awesome area of boiling caldrons and steaming rivers, buffalo, moose and other wildlife. And you can arrange overnight accommodations at a snowlodge in the park ($3 extra) and rides to and from it via snowcoach ($22 round trip) or snowmobile ($40/day for 2 persons). The 6-night package is $186, double occupancy.

NEW HAMPSHIRE

Bretton Woods Touring Center, Dept. AG, Bretton Woods, NH 03575. Att.: Francis Arena. (603) 278-5000. Dec.–Mar.

Beautiful trails at the foot of Mt. Washington and the Presidential Mountain Range—52 marked and 37 groomed—served as Eastern Training Center for the U.S. Nordic team in '73 and '74. Rentals are $5.50, trail fee $2.50, and you can take a scenic guided tour no matter what your skiing prowess. Races and snowshoeing add to the fun.

International Mountain Equipment, Box 494, North Conway, NH 03860. Att.: Paul Ross. (603) 356-5287. Dec.–Mar. (See also *Mountaineering*.)

By special arrangement IME arranges private treks (they recommend 2 to 5 days) of a touring and mountaineering nature through the scenic winter wilderness of the White Mountains in New Hampshire. Cross-country experience is required, but no previous winter camping. Their basic service is rentals.

Jackson Ski Touring Foundation, Box 90C, Jackson, NH 03846. Att.: Thomas Perkins. (603) 383-9355. Dec.–Mar.

This nonprofit organization devotes itself solely to cutting, clearing and grooming the 80-plus miles of marked trails that wind through the splendor of the White Mountains. Nordic shops provide rentals and instruction, while the Foundation offers guided tours. Since the diversified trail system connects every major inn, motel and point of interest in the valley, touring Jackson is both a mode of transportation and an exciting sport. (Trail fee donation, $2.)

Pole & Pedal, Bridge St., Henniker, NH 03242. Att.: Alan Johnson or Jeff Jacobs. (603) 428-3242. Dec.–Mar.

Twenty miles of marked trails follow the banks of the Contoocook River and wind through the surrounding lightly wooded hills. At the top of Proctor Hill, skiers glide through stands of tall pines and pass 200-year-old stone walls; other trails are old logging roads. Day, night and extended overnight guided tours. No trail fee. Rentals are $7; instruction, $6. "Our outstanding feature is that we all ski and love it!" say the Pole & Pedal people.

Sargent Ski Touring Center, Boston Univ. Environmental Studies, RFD #2, Peterborough, NH 03458. Att.: Bob Blair & Doug Richardson. (617) 353-3202 or (603) 525-3311.

Sargent's 16 miles of finely groomed, well-marked trails are well suited to beginners and intermediates. On guided tours past old homesteads you glimpse rural New Hampshire as it once was. Extended tours through the entire Monadnock region are arranged for all abilities. "We offer one of the finest touring centers in New England," write Blair and Richardson, "and are dedicated to providing the most enjoyable time possible in a wide range of outdoor activities." Trail fee is $1.50; rentals including trail use, $7.50; instruction, $3.

Temple Mt. Ski Area, Rt. 101, Dept. A, Peterborough, NH 03458. Att.: Mike Beebe. (603) 924-6949. Dec.–Apr.

Along the Wapack Trail you can tour on 35 miles of marked and maintained

Vermont Development Department.

trails, with 10 miles groomed. They lead across high mountain ridges to fields and brooks. Tours from 1 to 15 miles are planned for skiers of varying ability. Lessons are $5.50; rentals, $6.50. Touring packages, evening tours, free touring clinics and special events.

Waterville Valley Ski Touring Center, Box T8, Waterville Valley, NH 03223. Att.: Chuck Maeser. (603) 236-8311. Dec.–Mar.

Follow 50 miles of graded trails (23 marked and groomed with many loops) through the scenic White Mountain National Forest. A resident naturalist provides guided tours, sometimes to beaver ponds, deer yards or a fox run. Waterville is the 1978 Eastern Training Center for the U.S. cross-country ski team. Trail fee $2. Rentals and lessons are $7 each, or $12 for both; children's rates.

Windblown, Rt. 124, New Ipswich, NH 03071. Att.: Al Jenks. (603) 878-2869. Nov.–Apr.

Eighteen miles of meandering trails (of which 10 are groomed), a snug warming hut deep in the woods (for overnight stays, too), and a well-equipped ski shop. Trail fees for adults are $2; under 20, $1; children, free. Rentals are $6.50 to $7; instruction, $3/hour. "Come early and stay late," Al Jenks writes, "and leave your tracks with us."

NEW JERSEY

Odyssey Ltd., Outdoor Adventures, 26 Hilltop Ave., Dept. AG, Berkeley Heights, NJ 07922. Att.: Art Fitch. (201) 322-8414. Dec.–Mar. (See also *Backpacking, Mountaineering*—Northeast School of.)

Weekend cross-country trips in New England and the Adirondacks—Jackson, Stowe, Lake Placid—and week-long tours in the West—Yellowstone, Aspen and the Canadian Rockies—are Odyssey's specialty, along with ski vacations in Europe. Everyone from beginner to expert is welcome. Their objective is "to teach you the skills necessary for getting along in these quiet and gorgeous places, and to see to it that you're having fun." Package costs include instruction, food and lodging—from inns in New England to tents and cabins in the Rockies.

NEW YORK

Adirondack Mountain Club, 172 Ridge St., Dept. 51, Glens Falls, NY 12801. Att.: Mrs. Doris Herwig. (518) 793-7737. Dec.–Mar. (See also *Mountaineering*.)

At Adirondack Loj near Lake Placid, this nonprofit corporation has varied touring trails and promotes ski touring and snowshoeing. Its free-of-charge system connects to the Mt. Van Hoevenburg ski touring complex. There are dorm accommodations at the Loj ($8 up) and snowshoe rentals.

Bark Eater Lodge & Cross Country Ski Center, Box 1, Keene, NY 12942. Att.: Joe-Pete Wilson. (518) 576-2221. Dec.–Apr.

Glide through the Adirondacks on 25 miles of mostly marked trails, and miles of untracked wilderness. You can take a guided day or overnight tour ($4 & up) and lessons ($5). $1 trail fee donation. A complete cross-country shop provides rentals—and friendly and knowledgeable service that reflects the wide experience of Joe-Pete Wilson, cross-country author and former Olympian.

Country Hills Farm Touring Center, North Rd., Tully, NY 13159. Att.: D. R. Aungier. (315) 696-8774. Dec.–Mar.

Country Hills boasts the longest lighted cross-country trail network in the country and 18 miles of marked, groomed trails. Take guided tours from 2 hours to 2 days over rolling terrain, through a pine forest and past a maple sugar shack. Rentals are $6/day; instruction, $5/hour; trail fee, $2. Each December, there's a 4-day teaching camp for ski touring, winter camping and racing, plus a snowshoe-making clinic. Lodging and meals at the farm.

Garnet Hill Lodges & Ski Touring Center, North River, NY 12856. Att.: Paul M. Cormack. (518) 998-2821. Nov.–Apr.

Enjoy 12 miles of wooded groomed trails ($1) on this 600-acre resort, as well as direct access to unlimited trails in adjoining Adirondack Forest Preserve. EPSTI-certified instruction is $5/hour; rentals are $6.50. Home cooking at the lodge, magnificent views of Thirteenth Lake and the mountains, plus tobogganing and snowshoeing. Lodge, $18.50 up, with 2 meals.

Erie Bridge Inn, Florence Hill Rd., Camden, NY 13316. Att.: Chas. & Joyce Maley. (315) 245-1555. Nov.–Apr.

Skiers at Erie Bridge use 15 miles of maintained trails ($2) or brave the unlimited truck trails of adjoining Mad River State Park. Guided tours for beginners and intermediates explore the Tug Hill Plateau. Rentals are $6, lessons $3/hour. A cabin in the woods provides a cozy rest stop. The Inn's guests can sample Mrs. Maley's "Tug Hill cooking—simple, old-fashioned style."

Outdoor Inns, Inc., Hidden Valley Lake, CPO Box 190, Kingston, NY 13401. Att.: Mickey Duncan. (914) 338-4616. Dec.-Mar. (See also *Snowmobiling*.)

You can take a guided tour through 12 miles of well-maintained, marked and groomed trails, both hilly and flat. The lake is lit for night skiing. "We are a learning center for all ages and levels of ability," writes Mickey Duncan. "We are a full-service, beautiful 200-acre recreation area." Instruction weekends, $5/hour or longer. Rentals are $8/day; trail fee is $2 adult, $1 child. Workshops and events. Ski dorm facilities at the inn are $8; $30 with meals, 20 persons minimum.

Podunk Cross-Country Center, Trumansburg, NY 14886. Att.: Osmo O. Heila. (607) 387-6716. Nov.–Mar.

Ski up to 12 miles of marked trails (no charge)—or use free maps to tour nearby state and federal lands. You can rent equipment and take day and overnight guided tours. Group instruction is $3.50/hour. The Ski Center lodge features a roaring fire, snacks and hot drinks—you're welcome to enjoy your own bag lunch.

Williams Lake Hotel, Rosendale, NY 12472. Att.: Walter G. Williams. (914) 658-3101. Dec.-Feb.

Ten miles of leisurely marked trails ($3) wind through deep forests. Hourly group instruction is $2, and rentals are $7.50. Major competitions are held each year on racing trails. Tobogganing and skating round out the winter fun . . . or try polar bear swimming or snow rolling after a hot sauna.

OHIO

Wilderness Trails, 728 Prospect Ave., Cleveland, OH 44115. Att.: Gary Newman. (216) 696-5222 or 543-8639. Dec.-Mar. (See also *Backpacking, Wilderness Living*.)

Wilderness Trails offers day, evening and weekend instruction in cross-country skiing for groups and individuals in the Cleveland area, and the national forests of West Virginia or New York's Adirondacks. Rates vary from $12 to $30/person, depending on trip length.

PENNSYLVANIA

Raven Rocks Mt. Institute, Ltd., Box G, Ligonier, PA 15658. Att.: Jamie A. & E. Kay Myers. (412) 238-5190. Nov.–Apr.

Guided ski tours varying in time and terrain—depending on ability and number of skiers—begin at Laurel Hill Nordic Patrol Hut, but are organized at Ligonier Mt. Outfitters on Rt. 30 in Laughlintown. Skiers tour on 35 miles of marked trails through Laurel Mt. State Park, State Gamelands and Chestnut Ridge. No trail fee. Rentals are $6 weekdays, $7 weekends; group instruction, $3/hour. The Institute also has winter camping ski treks, and snow and ice climbing in its outdoor curriculum.

VERMONT

Ski touring centers in Vermont offer a guided tour from one country inn to the next. From north to south, participating hosts listed below are: Blueberry Hill Farm, Churchill House Inn, Mountain Top Inn and Mountain Meadows Lodge. Whether you tour all or just a section of the trail, at each stop you'll be provided with lodging, dinner, breakfast, a guide and trail lunch for the next day's tour, and ferrying service for your luggage. Contact your first night's choice for details.

Blueberry Hill Farm Ski Touring Center, Goshen, VT 05733. Att.: Tony Clark. (802) 247-6735. Dec.–Apr.

Soup is always bubbling on the potbellied stove in the ski shop where you can warm up, wax your skis and swap tales. You follow marked trails—42 miles of them—or make your own tracks in unspoiled New England wilderness. The farm, which dates back to 1813, is famous also for its antiques, homemade quilts, gourmet meals and candlelight dining. The ski center provides rentals, instruction and day and overnight guided tours; trail fee, $2.

Burke Mt. Touring Center, E. Burke, VT 05832. Att.: Katy Richardson. (802) 626-3305. Dec.–Apr.

This complete cross-country and alpine resort in northernmost Vermont has over 30 miles of maintained touring trials for all skiing skills. You can request a guided tour. EPSTI-certified instruction is $6, and there's a $2 trail fee, ski weeks and group rates. Warm up or stay overnight in a cabin or lodge within walking distance of trails. Nursery, rentals, repair and retail shops, cafeteria and bar at area.

Churchill House Inn Ski Touring Centre, RD #3, Brandon, VT 05733. Att.: Mike & Marion Shonstrom. (802) 247-3300. Dec.–Apr.

This 19th century inn maintains 40 kilometers of its own touring trails (trail fee, $2), operates a ski shop (rentals, $6), and offers instruction (2 hours, $4) and 5- to 8-hour guided tours for 4 to 12 skiers. It is located at midpoint on the 50-mile Vermont Ski Touring Trail, which links a succession of inns. No chance of going hungry here. Marion excels in country foods like pot roast simmered in cranberry and horseradish sauce, or roast lamb marinated in yogurt with barley pilaf.

Cross Country Outfitters, Box 1308A, Stowe, VT 05672. Att.: Joe-Pete Wilson. (802) 253-4582. Dec.–Apr.

Trails that start right outside the door are ideal for beginners. They're flat, well maintained and linked with all the Stowe area trails. Joe-Pete, a former Olympian, is co-author of *Complete Cross-Country Skiing and Ski Touring*. His guided day or overnight tours takes you all through the Stowe area ($4 up), and can include instruction, lunch and lean-tos. Group instruction is $5, and there are rentals.

Darion Inn Ski Touring Center, East Burke, VT 05832. Att.: John G. Hibschman. (802) 626-5641. Dec.–Apr.

"We pride ourselves in maintaining 30 miles of trails to perfection with 2 expensive track-setting machines," John writes. "We don't know of any other area with such elaborate equipment." The old farm is also noted for its enormous barns, and old sugaring and logging roads. Trail fees, $2. There's snowshoeing off the cross-country trails.

Edson Hill Ski Touring Center, Stowe AG., VT 05672. Att.: Laurence P. Heath. (802) 253-7371. Dec.–Apr.

The Inn's 400 acres of woodland offer a skier's paradise with cleared trails (40 marked, 20 groomed) for all skiing levels and endless Green Mountain views. You can request a guided tour. Instruction is $4/hour; rentals, $7; trail fee, $1. There's a fireplace in every room at the Inn. Also: snowshoe rentals, with full use of all trails on tracks other than skiers'.

Green Trails, Dept. A, Brookfield, VT 05036. Att.: Chris Williams or Ed Taylor. (802) 276-2012. Dec.–Mar.

Twenty-five miles of marked trails up to 6 miles long loop out from the Floating Bridge in historic Brookfield Village. Or blaze your own on 75 acres of rolling meadows, evergreen and maple woods, frozen ponds and a beaver bog. You can join the 3-hour guided tours for $6 with instruction. Rentals are $6, and there's no trail fee. "We welcome skiers of all proficiencies," say the hosts. Hot toddies by the fire, country meals and cozy rooms.

The Hermitage, Box AG, Coldbrook Rd., Wilmington, VT 05363. Att.: Jim McGovern. (802) 464-3759. Dec.–Mar.

Located on 26 acres of fields and picturesque woodlands, The Hermitage offers the finest in cross-country touring, with 20 miles of maintained and groomed trails ($2), plus hundreds of acres of untouched woodlands. Certified instruction ($5/hour) and full rentals, plus guided tours. Ski through sugarbush in spring and see the sugaring process. Superior accommodations and Continental cuisine at this charming inn.

Mountain Meadows, 30 Thundering Brook Rd., Killington, VT 05751. Att.: J. Tidd. (802) 775-7077. [May–Dec.: (802) 775-1010.] Dec.–Apr.

Snugly nestled in a magnificent, high-mountain valley, the lodge has 15 miles of well-groomed trails, 40 miles marked, spreading across 100-acre Kent Lake and surrounding hills. Guided day tours are $10, while evening tours ($5) include rental, lesson and a wine party. Rentals are $6; certified professional instruction, $5/hour. There's a $2.50 trail fee. Lodging for 90 skiers, from private rooms to dorms.

Mountain Top Ski Touring Center, Mountain Top Inn, Chittenden, VT 05737. Att.: Dundonald Cochrane. (802) 483-2311. Dec.–Mar.

Choose according to your ability from the 55 miles of trails (35 marked) around the inn, which features Green Mountains touring from 2 hours to 2 days. Also, there's a moonlight tour and wine party, a "fun race" every Sunday, overnight camping treks and ski mountaineering for strong intermediates and advanced. Tours are $4 to $34; instruction, $4/hour; rentals with area use, $7.50; trail fee alone, $2.50.

Ski Tours of Vermont, RFD 1-A, Chester, VT 05143. Att.: Anne Mausolff. (802) 875-3631 or 824-3793. Jan.–Apr. (See also *Wilderness Living*.)

Every weekend, and sometimes during the week, this organization has beginners, intermediates and advanced skiers touring all kinds of trails in the Green Mountains of central and southern Vermont. With instructors and/or Nordic ski patrollers they explore unmarked wilderness where they would not usually go on their own. They spend nights at comfortable Vermont inns, or in "a snug Indian tepee," or set up their own tent camp—which allows plenty of choice for all ages and all degrees of ruggedness. The emphasis is on enjoyment and safety. For an all-expense weekend with lodging and meals at inns, the fee is $98.

Woodstock Ski Touring Center, Woodstock, VT 05091. Att.: John Wiggin. (802) 457-2114. Dec.–Mar.

The Center, associated with the beautiful Woodstock Inn, has 45 miles of maintained trails (20 miles groomed). Guide yourself on a nature trail, or join a guided tour through managed forests and rolling hills. More winter fun:

snowshoeing, sleigh rides and races. Trail fee is $2; EPSTI-certified instruction, $6 for 1½ hours; rentals, $6.50.

WASHINGTON

Cascade Corrals, Box A, Stehekin, WA 98852. Att.: Ray Courtney. (509) 663-1521. (See also *Hiking with Packstock, Pack Trips*.)

With the North Cascade's Lodge as your base you'll have warmup tours and/or lessons, and will participate in easy or challenging tours and snow camping in the upper valleys—according to your ability and wishes. Spend a night in the snug rustic ski hut, 7 miles up the trail. The Courtneys mention excellent food and cheerful surroundings in these fabulous North Cascades. A weekend package is $112; 5 weekdays, including boat trip from Chelan, lodging, food, instruction and tours, is $136. Float plane instead of boat is $35 extra. Also rentals.

Northwest Alpine Guide Service, Inc., 1628 Ninth Ave. #2, Seattle, WA 98101. Att.: Linda Bradley Miller. (206) 622-6074. WA, western Canada. Nov.–Apr. (See also *Backpacking, Mountaineering, Canoeing, Float Trips, Wilderness Living, Youth Adventures*.)

Director Brad Bradley operates his ski-touring expeditions out of 2 locations: Seattle and Quesnel, B. C. With "the largest teaching staff in the Northwest" he offers instruction and tours by the day, weekend and week. West of Quesnel he operates wilderness day tours from "rustic cabins, with family-style meals and excellent touring terrain."

WEST VIRGINIA

Snowshoe Ski Resort, Slatyfork, WV 26291. Att.: Manyon Millican. (304) 799-6600. Nov.–Mar.

There are 10 miles of marked and maintained trails in this 7,000-acre ski area, beginning at the summit of Cheat Mountain (4,848 feet) and winding into the valley. Lifts take you back up. Gentle trails lead deep into the silence of snow-filled woods. Warming huts, several lodges, a gourmet restaurant, cafeteria, burger shack and lounge complete the extensive facilities. Trail fee is $3; rentals, $7; instruction, $6. Weekend with instruction, 2 nights, trail fee and rentals is $46 to $62.

West Virginia Department of Commerce.

WISCONSIN

Blackhawk Ridge Recreation Area, Box 92-A, Sauk City, WI 53582. Att.: Laurie & Diana Isenring. (608) 643-3775. Dec.–Mar. (See also *Canoeing*.)

There are over 40 miles of marked trails, some of them softly lighted for night touring, at this year-round sports-recreation center. Cross-country skiing is the winter highlight. Trails loop through open meadows, wooded areas and scenic overlooks of the Wisconsin River Valley, as well as past a totem pole, windmill and old trappers' cabins. Rentals are $6/day adult; $4.50/day junior; trail fees, $2 to $3; instruction, $5/lesson.

Bobby Schmidt's Indian Hills, Stone Lake, WI 54876. Att.: Robert W. Schmidt. (715) 865-2801. Jan.–Mar.

Indian Hills, in the heart of 27,000 acres of forestland in northwestern Wisconsin, has over 200 miles of wilderness and 16 miles of marked and groomed trails at its doorstep. They are for beginners to intermediates, through beautiful wooded areas and over frozen lakes. Guided tours for up to 25 skiers follow trails through the Nordic Woods area, 4,000 acres set aside for ski touring. Rentals and instruction; no trail fees. Accomodations and meals at the lodge with weekend, midweek and group rates.

Green Lake Winter Sports Center, Hwy. 23, Green Lake, WI 54941. Att.: Doug Wildes. (414) 294-3323. Dec.–Mar.

Twenty-two miles of marked, groomed trails ($2.50) range from rank beginner to expert, winding through 1,100 acres with woods, stone fences, old estate homes, and panoramic views of the lake. Full-day rentals are $8; instruction, $5 for 2 hours. There's also snowshoeing, dog sledding and other sports, and—for skiers who like to swim—there's a competition-size indoor pool.

Wild Wolf Inn, Box B, White Lake, WI 54491. Att.: Herb & Genie Buettner. (715) 882-8612 or 882-8611. Dec.–Mar. (See also *Float Trips*.)

Skiers start from the inn's door on well-marked trails that lead through towering pines and evergreens in the Nicollet National Forest. The gentle, meandering trails continue on to the National Wild and Scenic Wolf River. On guided tours for 20 or more skiers, Herb explains the terrain and identifies trees and birds. He also offers workshops, rentals, lodging for 38 guests and meals. And there are 25 miles of marked and groomed trails for snowmobilers.

Wolf River Lodge, Inc., White Lake, WI 54491. Att.: George & Helen Steed. (715) 882-2182. Dec.–Mar. (See also *Float Trips*.)

"We are not a ski-touring center; we are a ski-touring lodge!" emphasizes George Steed. Surrounding the lodge are 100 miles of maintained trails to test experts and encourage beginners, with guides or without. You can ski the Ice Age Trail, the Old Military Road or logging roads in evergreen and hardwood forests. Trail fee is $2.50/day; instruction, $5; rentals, $7.50-$10. Lodge rates with meals are $140/couple weekends.

WYOMING

American Avalanche Institute, Box 308-A, Wilson, WY 83014. Att.: Rod Newcomb. (307) 733-3315. Dec.–Mar.

Anyone who goes into the back country when there's snow on the ground is a likely candidate for the 4-day tourer's course in snow and avalanches offered by the Institute. Limited to 24 participants divided into groups of 6 for field sessions, more than half the course is spent on cross-country skis in the mountains. Basic instruction is in stability evaluation, route finding, slab recognition and such, and advanced courses deal in snow physics. Tourer's course in either Jackson Hole or Silverton, CO, $125; professional's 5-day course in Jackson Hole, $185.

Diamond D Ranch Outfitters, Jackson Hole, Box 11, Moran, WY 83013. Att.: Rod Doty. (307) 543-2479. Dec.–Mar. (See also *Pack Trips*.)

"We try to learn the experience and needs of our guests, then plan a trip to suit them," writes Rod Doty. Guided tours for up to 10 skiers through the Teton Wilderness and Yellowstone and Grand Teton National Parks on 1- to 5-day trips. It's $20 for the guide, plus $5 per person. No fee for the 30 miles of marked trails. Snowshoeing is also popular around the ranch.

Game Hill Ranch, Box A, Bondurant, WY 82922. Att.: Pete & Holly Cameron. (307) 733-3281. [May–Nov.: (307) 733-2015.] Dec.–Apr. (See also *Backpacking, Hiking with Packstock, Pack Trips*.)

From the road it's a short ski trek into the ranch, which becomes your base. From there you'll penetrate isolated regions of high aspen groves, windswept ridges and sun-filled valleys. It's ideal country for the cross-country skier. With experienced guides, instruction, lodging and meals at the ranch, rates are $35 per day or $200 per week.

Jackson Hole Ski School, Box 269, Teton Village, WY 83025. Att.: Pepi Stiegler. (307) 733-2026. Dec.–Apr.

Join a guided tour through miles of diversified terrain: from flat-bottom lands of the Jackson Hole valley to the spectacular Granite Canyon of Grand Teton National Park. The base elevation of the valley is 6,300 feet, and tours start at Teton Village. Instruction for groups of 4 is $5 each for 2 hours. Rentals are $5.

National Outdoor Leadership School, PO Box AA, Dept. K, Lander, WY 82520. (307) 332-4381. (See also *Mountaineering, Wilderness Living, Youth Adventures*.)

"It's a spooky place," says the NOLS people about Yellowstone in winter, the scene of their 15- and 21-day ski-touring expeditions. "Steam rises from underground fumaroles, geysers spout, mud springs bubble." According to one instructor, "You expect to see Dracula come skiing out of the woods any minute." Less spooky and more challenging are expeditions (15 or 21 days) across the Wind River, Teton, Absaroka and Snake River ranges, including mountaineering instruction as well.

PowderHound Ski Tours, Box 286, Wilson, WY 83014. Att.: Bruce Simon. (307) 733-2208. Dec.–Apr.

Touring terrain galore, with 30 miles of marked and hundreds of miles of unmarked trails. A Grand Teton National Park approved guide, who's also a naturalist, takes you through breathtaking winter scenes. There's also a fascinating wildlife and winter ecology tour. Instruction is $8/half day; rentals, $6. No trail fee. These tours are for everyone—no experience necessary!

Rimrock Ranch, Box 485, Jackson, WY 83001. Att.: Alice Thompson. (307) 733-3093. Jan.–Mar. (See also *Pack Trips*.)

Deep in the wilderness, Rimrock is reached by a 6-mile private-access road that runs through the 3.4 million-acre Bridger-Teton National Forest. At 7,000 feet, the ranch is a superb base for ski touring, and you can request guides or rentals. "Our area is vast and roadless and virtually untouched, with unlimited miles of touring," writes Alice Thompson. The central lodge and redwood cabins accommodate up to 20 guests.

Triangle X Ranch, Box 120, Star Rt., Moose, WY 83012. Att.: The Turner Bros. (307) 733-2183. Jan.–Apr. (See also *Pack Trips, Float Trips*.)

There are many miles of marked trails through Grand Teton National Park and Teton National Forest. The Turners offer 3 day guided tours for up to 20 skiers or snowshoers. If you're adventurous, you'll have a memorable time touring the spectacular Teton Range, Snake River bottom or national forest lands that surround this ranch. $30/day, including lodging and meals.

White Pine Lodge, PO Box 833, Pinedale, WY 82941. Att.: Terry Pollard & Ron Lundberg. (307) 367-2913. Nov.–May.

Lodge visitors can set out on their own across the 5 marked, groomed trails (no charge) or join a tour ranging from 2 hours to 5 days through spectacular terrain in the Bridger Wilderness Area and National Forest.

Yellowstone Park Co., Room 371, Yellowstone National Park, WY 82190. (307) 344-7311. Dec.–Mar.

Yellowstone's high, flat plateau country provides some of the best ski touring in the West. Follow well-marked trails on your own and have the "secluded wild heart of the park" to yourself. Or let an expert guide point out wildlife and a fascinating array of geysers, hot springs, mud pots and fumaroles. Guided tours from an hour to a day or longer. Instruction: $5.20 for 2 hours, or $7.28 with rental equipment.

ALBERTA

Skoki Lodge, Box 5, Lake Louise, Alta. TOL 1EO. Att.: John M. Worrall. (403) 522-3555. Feb.–Apr.

At 7,200 feet, Skoki, a primitive log lodge 7 miles beyond the nearest road access, offers scenic marked trails. Guided tours can be arranged from Lake Louise. "Not recommended for absolute beginners, though the trails aren't difficult for middle levels of experience," writes John Worrall. Rentals are $8.25; group instruction, $45 for a half day; no trail fee. Overnight with meals, $35.

Northern Lights Alpine Recreation, B.C., by Arnör Larson.

Terratima, Cross Country Ski Hostel, Box 1636, Rocky Mountain House, Alta. TOM 1TO. Att.: Claire & Larry Kennedy. (403) 845-6786. Dec.–Mar.

Over 30 miles of marked and 10 miles of maintained trails take you along creeks—and over the hills if you dare—through the mixed-wood Clearwater/Rocky Forest. The Kennedys will guide tours on their trails or off. Enjoy moonlight treks complete with singing and hot drinks. The hostel has a main ranch house and cabins. "The log saunahouse is heated up every Saturday night—so bring your towel," the Kennedys write. Also bring your bedrolls food and equipment.

BRITISH COLUMBIA

Adventure Unlimited, Box 1881, Golden, B.C. VOA 1HO. Att.: Pete Austen. Dec.–Apr. (See also *Mountaineering, Canoeing*.)

Pete Austen guides cross-country ski tours, beginners to experts, on miles of rolling terrain at 3,000 to 5,000 feet. For ski mountaineering he goes up to 9,000 feet or higher. "There's usually superb snow on all tours," he says, "and we give personal attention to each skier." Instruction is $100 for 6 hours for a group, or $25 for an individual. From 4 to 16 skiers go on a guided tour.

Northern Lights Alpine Recreation, Box 399, Invermere, B.C. VOA 1KO. Att.: Arnör Larson. (604) 342-6042. Nov.–May. (See also *Mountaineering*.)

Northern Lights can arrange anything from a half-day outing in easy terrain in the Invernere area to a 2-week or longer expeditionary trip. They also offer package ski weeks, which include 7 days of Nordic ski touring, guiding, instruction, and lodging at the unique Delphene Lodge, with gourmet meals; or a week at The Hermitage, "a small log cabin in the midst of some of the finest mountain touring to be found."

Western Outdoor Adventures, Ltd., 16115 32nd Ave., White Rock, B.C. V4B 4Z5. Att.: Frank Lockwood. (604) 531-3969. Dec.–Apr. Arrival: Vancouver, BC. (See also *Jeeping, Wilderness Living, Youth Adventures*.)

On a 7-day package that includes transportation to and from Vancouver and cabin or hotel accommodations, WOA takes skiers on guided daily tours of the historic Barkeville and Bowron Lakes area. Or choose their 12-day "Cariboo High" ski tour, on which you camp out in very remote country. The tours are for 12 to 35 skiers, and rentals, instruction and workshops are also provided. 7 days, $400, 12 days, $500.

ONTARIO

Headwaters, Box 288, Temagami, Ont. POH 2HO. Att.: Hugh & Carin Stewart. No tel.; send telegram. Northern Ont. Jan.–Mar. 7–21 days. 1 wk., $205; 2 wks., $355; 3 wks., $500. Rates incl. Temagami flight to/from base & winter clothing & equipment. Arrival: Temagami, Ont. (See also *Wilderness Living, Youth Adventures*.)

There are daily outings from the Headwaters base on touring skis and snowshoes. You'll consider safety and comfort in the winter environment, examine snow and ice conditions, and discuss equipment and techniques for winter camping. Each program involves an expedition, from 2 to 7 days. For further details turn to the chapter on wilderness living.

Wanapitei, 7 Engleburn Pl., Peterborough, Ont. K9H 1C4. (705) 743-3774. Jan.–Mar. (See also *Canoeing*.)

On touring skis or snowshoes, small groups follow abandoned logging roads and portages on both hilly and level terrain in the northern forests at Wanapitei's base in the Temagami area. There are over 100 miles of marked and 20 miles of maintained trails. Single and shared cabins (bring sleeping gear), meals, and someone always on hand to lead tours. The best way to get there is from Temagami village: ski-equipped plane or 18-mile access road. Weekly all-inclusive rate: adult, $110; child, $70; also daily, group and family rates.

196

Three Bear Lodge, MT.

Snowmobiling

Basically, snowmobiling is for outdoor enthusiasts who do not snowshoe or tour on skis. The machines skim along the surface of the snow, transporting riders into wilderness, high mountains, deep valleys and snow-covered lakes. With little physical exertion, they can get way back into areas previously accessible only to the snowshoer or ski tourer. Indeed, snowmobilers sometimes perform a rescue operation for stranded hikers.

But the sport has become controversial, with reason. Some riders have bashed ahead with little regard for ecological damage to young trees and bushtops, or have chased wild animals to the point of exhaustion. Damage to private property is another regrettable by-product. Still another offensive aspect is the machines' terrific clatter. And not to be disregarded are the number of serious accidents that could be prevented by proper safety practices and good judgment.

Manufacturers are heeding the criticism in an effort to muffle the engines, at least to some extent. And snowmobilers themselves are beginning to grapple with the ecological and sociological problems of an otherwise exhilarating and adventurous sport.

Still, snowmobilers are welcomed on thousands of miles of trails that have been laid out over state, federal and private lands in the northern states and in Canada. In the Rocky Mountains the machines zoom over millions of acres of national forests, and in among the geysers of Yellowstone National Park. (In Utah, for example, there are 6,500 miles of trails; in Wyoming, 5,000 miles.) Minnesota, Wisconsin and Michigan (where more people own snowmobiles than in any other state) provide extensive facilities that reflect the sport's popularity. In Maine the trails are so abundant that no one can say how many miles they cover, and to the north the Province of Quebec is crisscrossed by some 28,000 miles of trails.

The sport has spawned hundreds of clubs,* and the snowmobile safari has become a popular expedition. Members plan outings that take them anywhere from a hundred to several thousand miles from home for a weekend to two weeks or more. They will charter a bus for themselves, hire a truck for their machines and equipment, and set out for a headquarters location that provides lodging, meals, trail lunches and guides for riding different trails each day.

"They have a wonderful time," says a western rancher who hosts these winter groups. "They come all the way from the Midwest and even from Maine. They

---

* For names and addresses of clubs, write the state or provincial travel department.

arrive Sunday afternoon and leave the next Sunday morning after a week of seeing the country. Maybe they'll try something different each year . . . or maybe come back again after two or three years."

Exploring the wilderness with people who have a common bond is one of the joys of snowmobiling. "Until you have sat on top of a mountain under the stars on a clear, crisp night with your fellow snowmobilers, you do not begin to appreciate this great country of ours," exclaims a New Englander whose outings are generally in New Hampshire. "It's a thrill to watch the headlights of another group wind and twist up the trail, and visit with them for a while when they reach the top."

The advice of a veteran snowmobiler may well be heeded: "Don't destroy property. Stay on the trails, and leave the wildlife alone. Don't be a noisy nuisance around people's farms and homes. Carry a spare belt and extra plugs for your machine, and the owner's manual. Don't drive in a reckless manner that endangers others or their property. Know your machine and its limits. Wear a loose-fitting snowmobile suit (you'll stay warmer) and boots loose enough to allow for heavy socks. Warm gloves should cover the cuff of your snowsuit. Wear a helmet—even if it's clumsy, it's a much-needed protection. Whether or not you're athletically inclined, enjoy this sport. It will bring fun, excitement and wondrous wilderness exploring into your life."

Where is the rendezvous point? Is there an age limit for participants? Is there a guide (or trail master) who accompanies the group? A mechanic to service the machines? Gasoline supply nearby? Are the trails well marked and groomed? If not, are you experienced enough for off-trail snowmobiling? Double-check rates, whether tax is extra, and whether they include lodging, meals, guide, clothing and other equipment.

COLORADO

Seven-W-Ranch, Gypsum, CO 81637. Att.: Burt & Claudia George. (303) 524-9328. Dec.–Apr. (See also *Pack Trips*.)

The Seven-W has a special weekend safari for up to 15 snowmobilers. On Saturday you meet in Rifle for the 60-mile ride to the ranch. Spend the night and return the next day. The route is through the Flat Top area of the White River National Forest. The safari is $45/day, or $20 with your machine. For snowmobiling around the ranch, $25/day with room, meals, machine and guide; $20 with your machine.

Tiger Run, Inc., PO Box 1418, Breckenridge, CO 80424. Att.: Glenn Campbell & Dean Vosburgh. (303) 453-2231. (See also *Jeeping*.)

Tiger Run guides exciting snowmobile tours on back-country trails in the Rockies past gold camps and ghost towns of bygone eras, and over alpine meadows and forests up to 11,500-foot elevations. It's breathtaking! Tours include machine, clothing and guide: 2 hours, $24; children, $12 double on machine. Also Sno-cat tours with driver.

Wilderness Adventures, Moon Valley Resort, Box 265-CA, South Fork, CO 81154. Att.: Larry Ehardt. (303) 873-5331. Rio Grande Natl. Forest. Dec.–Apr. (See also *Backpacking, Hiking with Packstock, Pack Trips*.)

Snow excursions at Moon Valley range from a day's ride into this winter wonderland with lunch, a machine and a guide ($35) to an overnight excursion or longer, sleeping in snow caves or igloos ($40/day), or with lodging at trip destination ($60/day). On the overnight treks everyone starts out on cross-country skis or snowshoes. Snowmobiles or sleds transport the gear and return midday to give lagging tourers a ride to camp. On the wilderness treks a heated Quonset-type hut provides shelter for meals, story-telling, and lectures on wilderness skills, winter survival, environmental science and—listen well for this is where you'll sleep—igloo or snow-cave building. It's a total winter experience. "Snow fun is all around you," Larry says. College credit and discounts for educational groups.

MAINE

Maine Wilderness Canoe Basin, Springfield, ME 04487. Att.: Carl W. Selin. (207) 989-3636, ext. 631. (See also *Canoeing, Ski Touring, Youth Adventures*.)

Carl Selin promises 300 miles of unplowed logging roads for snowmobilers in the vicinity of his base. The terrain, he says, is a series of lakes and "wood roads" through wilderness terrain. Tents are provided if desired, but most groups return to the main lodge for overnight. Rates: $30/day for guided tour, plus snowmobile expenses, $10 to $15.

Sebago Lake Camps, North Sebago, ME 04029. Att.: Ray & Fran Nelson. (207) 787-3211.

In the rugged western Maine lake region, Sebago offers unlimited "wood trails" through hard- and softwood timber stands. You can follow a vast trail system connecting with remote lakes, ponds and rivers. Safaris may be arranged to any accessible restaurant or lodge in the region, with price depending on group size and trip length. Snowmobile rentals begin at $30/day. Package rates for weekends include housekeeping cottages.

MICHIGAN

Double H Ranch, Pecos River Trail, Brevort, MI 49760. Att.: Carl & Beth Avery. (906) 292-5454.

Snowmobile treks in Michigan's Upper Peninsula are arranged by the Double H all through the winter. Their weekend package (or any 2 nights) includes 6 meals, lodging and guided safaris ($45), and they feature moonlight safaris, lumberjack meals and trail guides.

MINNESOTA

Kohl's Last Resort, Rt. 5 Box 247-A, Bemidji, MN 56601. Robert Kohl. (218) 586-2251.

On guided excursions (primarily for resort guests), snowmobilers ride over rolling terrain, frozen lakes and steams, and through heavily wooded areas with pine and birch. There are 60 miles of marked and groomed trails and 100 miles of connecting trails. Guided trips for 4 to 15 people are $20; rentals, $9/hour.

MONTANA

Lakeview Guest Ranch, 2905 Harrison, Butte, MT 59701. Att.: Kevin Rush. (406) 494-2585. [Jun.–Sept.: (406) 276-3300.]

"Informality is the keynote," say the Rushes of their dorm-style, affordable accommodations in Montana's Centennial Valley. They offer well-marked trails, a heated indoor pool and a mountain chalet, serve dinner family style and arrange guided excursions. Overnight package with meals, lodging, facilities: $20; rentals, $35 to $40/day.

Montana Sports Ranch, Box 501, Hwy. 209, Condon, MT 59826. Att.: Ron Hummel. (406) 754-2351. (See also *Hiking with Packstock*.)

"Arrive at the ranch, unload your machine, and each day travel into spectacular snow-covered beauty," Ron Hummel advises. "Travel into different areas each day in the breathtaking Swan Valley and Mission Mountains. You don't have to load your machine until you leave." He provides cookouts for lunch on the trail, with breakfast and dinner at the ranch and the Western Bar evenings. 500 miles of marked trails. 4 days, 3 nights, $88–$98 with meals, lodging and guide. Group, youth and weekend rates. Machine rentals. Gas available.

South Fork Ranch, Box 56, Utica, MT 59452. Att.: Ben Steel. (406) 374-2356. (See also *Pack Trips*.)

Here is a special service for snowmobile groups. Ben Steel arranges guided tours over high snow-capped mountain ridges where you can see for 100 miles, and in open meadows and side hill climbs where riders can romp and play. "Fine meals will be served at the lodge," Ben says, "with lunches and steak fries served out in the mountains every day. We top off each group's stay with live music and dancing for a royal farewell. It's service that can't be matched." Rates: $30–$35/day with food, lodging, guides and evening entertainment.

Stage Coach Inn, 209 Madison Ave., Box 160, West Yellowstone, MT 59758. Att.: Howard T. Kelsey. (406) 646-7381.

You ride snow toboggans for 2 or 3 people, or 12-passenger heated snowmobiles, into Yellowstone Park. Warm geysers are surrounded by green grass and wild animals feeding. Or you'll drive caravan-style to Two Top on the Continental Divide, where freak moisture and wind sculpture the snow-weighted pine trees into a grotesque winter wonderland. Rentals, $32/day with fuel; guides free with 6 or more rentals. Guided trips, $21–$26; 6 days, 12–60 people, $118 with food, lodging and fees. Also weekend package.

Three Bear Lodge 217 Yellowstone Ave., West Yellowstone, MT 59758. Att.: Clyde G. Seely. (406) 646-7353. Dec.-Mar. (See also *Ski Touring*.)

Three West Yellowstone motels—Ambassador Motor Inn, Big Western Pine Motel and Three Bear Lodge—jointly offer packages for 3 to 5 days of snowmobiling through Yellowstone National Park. The scenes are of fantasyland shrouded in white—grazing buffalo, gigantic ghost trees, brilliant earth colors of jagged river canyons and Old Faithful shooting steam skyward against a backdrop of frozen solitude. Packages include lodging (double occupancy), arrival dinner, snowmobile, clothing (suit, boots, gloves, goggles, face mask) and guide; 4 nights, $176; 6 nights, $280, or $85 with own machine. Daily rentals, $35–$40; clothing, $6.

NEW HAMPSHIRE

The Inn at East Hill Farm, Troy, NH 03465. Att.: Dave & Sally Adams. (603) 242-6495.

Many individuals and clubs come to East Hill Farm to snowmobile on its 300 acres with unplowed dirt roads and a pond. Dave Adams gives them maps for hours of enjoyable riding in the picturesque Monadnock region. And he takes guests on guided trail rides whenever a group is interested. A winter weekend costs $58 with meals ($45 per child). Also 10 miles of ski touring trails.

The Resort at Lake Shore Farm, 4 Jenness Pond Rd., Northwood, NH 03261. Att.: Mrs. Eloise Ring. (603) 942-5921 or 5521.

"Start at our door," says Eloise Ring, "for many miles of scenic, well-marked trails and 300 acres of open area for romping and cruising about." A trailmaster guides safaris. Trails wind through mountain vistas, rolling hills and wooded areas. Weekend package: $34 Modified American Plan.

Tall Timber Lodge, Pittsburgh, NH 03592. Att.: Barbara & Harold Webster. (603) 538-6651. Dec.-Apr.

Skim over 800 miles of marked trails and miles of logging roads in northernmost New Hampshire, northwestern Maine and Quebec, with border crossings near U.S. and Canadian customs. The Websters provide meals at the lodge and trail lunches or cookouts. The terrain is rolling mountains and valleys, lakes in hardwoods of fir and spruce, and good scenery, they say. They'll guide tours in the 1,200-square-mile area, or ride on your own. Lodging, $8/day, or $17–$18 with meals.

NEW YORK

Outdoor Inns, Inc., Hidden Valley Lake, CPO Box 190, Kingston, NY 13401. Att.: Mickey Duncan. (914) 338-4616. Dec.–Mar. (See also *Ski Touring*.)

Twelve miles of marked trails bring snowmobilers to this 200-acre scenic recreation center 85 miles north of New York City. Trail fee is $2.50/day; rentals, $12.50/hour. Also ice skating, ice fishing, sledding, winter camping, clubhouse, snackbar and 10-acre riding area.

WISCONSIN

Greiner's Highlands Resort, Rt. 2, Box 81, Hayward, WI 54843. Att.: Richard F. Greiner. (715) 634-4260. Dec.–Mar.

The Greiners take their resort guests on tours across frozen lakes to woodlands and gently rolling hills, and on nature excursions. "Snowmobile trails lead in all directions, and ice fishing is superb."

WYOMING

Goosewing Ranch, Inc., PO Box 496, Jackson, WY 83001. Att.: Harold, Claudette or Dan Shervin. (307) 733-2768. Dec.–Mar. (See also *Pack Trips*).

"Snowmobilers get to watch moose in the yard, see elk feeding grounds at close-hand, even glimpse bighorn mountain sheep," writes Harold Shervin. Besides 200 miles of marked trails in this Gros Ventre country, there are open hillsides for maneuvering. Guided tours, 5 to 6 hours: $24/person with lodging and meals.

Highland Meadow Guest Ranch, PO Box 774-A, Dubois, WY 82513. Att.: Joe Detimore. (307) 455-2401. (See also *Pack Trips*.)

You go where once only determined outdoorsmen on skis or snowshoes would venture. It's an inspiring experience to see these majestic Wind River Mountains and Yellowstone wilderness in winter. With the Detimores your trip will have conservation significance. 200 miles of trails, some marked. Machine rentals, $40/day. Yellowstone tour: 4 days, $400 for 8–12 people with snowmobile rental ($300 with own machine).

Togwotee Mountain Lodge, Moran, WY 83013. Att.: David Helgeson or Larry Owens. (307) 543-2847. Nov.–Jun.

The Teton National Forest near Jackson Hole is noted for snowmobiling, and 4 lodges in the area have developed a 6-night, 5-day-package for snowmobilers. The Togwotee Trek starts at Togwotee Mountain Lodge. The package includes guided trips over Wyoming's spectacular and variable terrain, to Brooks Lake Lodge, Sawmill Lodge and Goosewing Ranch, with an overnight stay at each, and return to Togwotee on the final day. The tour covers approximately 130 miles. Bring your own machine or rent one at Togwotee.

Schweizer Aircraft Corp., Elmira, NY.

Marian Emrich of Seattle Sky Sports, WA.

Wyoming Travel Commission.

VII   IN THE AIR

Seagull Aircraft, Inc., Santa Monica, CA.

Balloon Excelsior, CA.

Ballooning

Since the day the Wizard of Oz started out from Kansas in a balloon, more and more Americans have been tucking themselves into human picnic baskets to be lofted into the air by giant nylon bubbles.

And there's nothing else like it. As one licensed balloonist says, "The ride is very gentle, not unlike a boat ride in a very calm sea, only in a sea of air."

The first to enjoy the pleasure of ballooning were a duck, a rooster and a sheep—launched into the air for eight minutes by brothers Joseph and Etienne Montgolfier in France in 1783. A century later, balloonists successfully crossed the English Channel and unsuccessfully attempted to fly over the North Pole. The early 1960s saw a rekindled interest in the sport due to a heightened propensity to leisure and an improvement in hot air ballooning—using blasts from propane gas burners for uplift.

Perversely, one of the most appealing attractions about ballooning is that the balloonist really doesn't know where he's heading. This alone makes the sport unique. The wind is the sole determinant of direction (except in the case of some new "steerable" balloons—see below), and it may be surprising to know that ballooning is probably the smoothest and safest form of air transportation. Air sickness is almost unheard of among flyers, and those prone to the syndrome may find ballooning a pleasant way to introduce themselves to aviation without any physical upset. As to safety, the Federal Aviation Agency indicates that hot air ballooning is the safest form of flying, with accidents of any significance a rarity. The major problems involve power lines and treetop or bumpy landings.

In ballooning, the view's the thing. Once aloft, the passenger can take in great gulps of countryside from a unique perspective. There is no feel of rushing air, since the balloon drifts horizontally with the wind. A wind velocity of 8 miles per hour is considered maximum for safe ballooning. Each trip is a one-way flight. A chase car does its best to find roads to follow the balloon to its landing and carries passengers and deflated vehicle back to the launch site.

How do the big bubbles work? Well, in hot air balloons—employed for almost all sport ballooning in this country today—the operator maintains flight and vertical control with propane gas burners. To get higher, the balloon's internal air temperature is increased. The balloon operates best in cold air and can reach an altitude of 30,000 feet. But you don't have to go that high. Speed on the way up or down is normally about 300 feet per minute. The best time to fly is very early in the morning and, of course, when there is little wind to interfere with take off and flight. Gas balloons, on the other hand—used abroad but seldom in the United States—obtain life from lighter-than-air gases like helium, hydrogen or cooking gas.

Almost anybody can fly. The FAA, which controls the sport, mandates only that student flyers be at least 14 years of age and that aspiring private balloonists be 16. There are numerous opportunities for trial rides at a number of balloon-dealer schools. It's not inexpensive. A typical offer of a one-hour sample flight for two may run from $65 to as high as $150 (with champagne breakfast thrown in—a balloonist's ritual). Passengers are often called upon to lend a hand with the inflation and take off procedure—all part of the fun.

Getting a license is a bit more complicated. Required are ten hours of formal instruction, successful completion of a test and a check ride. It usually takes three weeks and can cost from $650 to $1,500. Approximately 950 hot air balloon flyers are currently licensed in this country, but many more are enthusiastic about the sport as participants, spectators or even take off aides and chasers. The ballooning population in this country has doubled in each of the past five years. You can't top that kind of testimony.

Balloons come in two basic models: the AX-6 and AX-7. The former is smaller (60 feet high and 55 feet in diameter) and more popular. It carries two people. The AX-7, which is 70 feet tall and 60 feet wide, can hold three.

The people best equipped to get you off the ground are members of the Balloon Federation of America, a division of the National Aeronautic Association, formed in 1968 to promote, develop and aid the art and science of free ballooning. Or, as one member recalls, it was started by balloonists looking for other balloonists with whom to share the joy of floating free above the earth. It now has about 950 balloon pilot members and about the same number of nonpilot members. It publishes a bimonthly journal, *Ballooning,* available for $10 a year, and sponsors the annual National Hot Air Balloon Championship Race. The winner of the race is not the pilot to get there first, but the one to come down nearest to the landing spot of the leading balloon.

Some indication of the growth of ballooning is demonstrated by the fact that last year, over 600 balloonists participated in 75 events across the country. The largest was the National Championship, with 185 balloons in flight. Just ten years ago, when there were only 20 licensed pilots in this country, a total of six people took part in the national.

Numerous schools (over 200) offer balloon instruction (see below for sample). However, some of the experts in the sport suggest that an individual instructor may be better suited for teaching. Any currently commercially licensed pilot is permitted to provide instruction. More than half of the BFA members either train or sell rides or do promotions. BFA headquarters is happy to supply names of commercially licensed pilots and schools in a given area. For this information, write BFA, Suite 430, 821 15th St. N.W., Washington, DC 20005, or contact your local FAA office.

For a new blimp-type hot airship—the first "steerable" balloon to be made—contact Cameron Balloons US in Ann Arbor (see list). Another new development is the first balloon ranch. It's located in Colorado (see list) and is a complete resort facility—with ballooning as its major attraction.

Listed below are only a sample of the multitude of balloon services now in operation. These can be called upon for information on the availability of hot air balloons and instruction.

Arizona: **Cat Balloon,** 2911 E. Sherran Lane, Phoenix, AZ 85016. Att.: Jim Kitchell. (602) 956 8945.

California: **Aerial Advertising,** 16957 Hillcrest Circle, Yorbalinda, CA 92686. (714) 524-1816.

Balloon Excelsior, Inc., 1241 High St., Oakland, CA 94601. Att.: Brent Stockwell. (415) 261-4222.

Daedalus School of Free Ballooning, Menlo Oaks Balloon Fiedl, Menlo Park, CA 94025. Att.: Deke Sonnichsen. (415) 323-2757.

Scorpion Productions, Box 1147, Perris, CA 92370. Att.: Fred Krieg. (714) 657-6930.

Colorado: **The Balloon Ranch,** Star Rt. Box 41, Del Norte, CO 81132. Att.: Link Z. Baum. (303) 754-2533.

Iowa: **American Balloon Services, Inc.,** 113 Park Ave., Muscatine, IA 52761. Att.: Tom Oerman. (319) 264-1878.

Massachusetts: **"Professor" Hall's Hot Air Balloon School of Higher Learning,** 1656 Massachusetts Ave., Lexington, MA 02173. Att.: Ralph Hall. (617) 861-0101.

Michigan: **Cameron Balloons US,** 3600 Elizabeth Rd., Ann Arbor, MI 48103. Att.: Bruce Comstock. (313) 995-0111.

Captain Phogg's International School of Ballooning, PO Box 3039, Flint, MI 48502. Att.: Capt. Phogg. (313) 629-8487.

Minnesota: **Wiederkehr Balloons International, Inc.** (1323), 1604 Euclid St., St. Paul, MN 55106. Att.: Matt or Bobbie Wiederkehr. (612) BALLOON or 774-5208.

New Jersey: **Sky Promotions,** 20 Nassau St., Princeton, NJ 08540. Att.: Bob Waligunda. (609) 921-6636.

New Mexico: **World Balloon Corp.,** 4800 Eubank NE, Albuquerque, NM 87111. Att.: Sid Cutter. (505) 345-5617.

North Carolina: **Balloon Ascensions, Ltd.,** Rt. 11, Box 279, Statesville, NC 28677. Att.: William S. Meadows. (704) 873-2266.

Oregon: **Acromania,** Box 1227, Coos Bay, OR 97420. Att.: Jim Eckford. (415) 325-8787.

Texas: **Aerostats Unlimited,** Rt. 1, Box 400, Amarillo, TX 79106. Att.: Ken Kelley. (806) 353-3553.

Utah: **Daedalus Balloons Far West,** 2706 Chadwick St., Salt Lake City, UT 84106. Att.: Jo Juliand. (801) 486-1577.

Hang Gliding

It's mans age-long dream come true—stepping off a hill or mountain and flying like a bird. No instruments. No engine. Only the air. Free flight!

Skimming over hills and dunes, suspended beneath an ultralight hang glider, is indeed the oldest *and* newest way to fly, and its popularity is—well—soaring. Some 25,000 enthusiasts have taken up the sport in this country, and the numbers are ever increasing.

What attracts so many to the sport? Environmentalists like the fact that gliders are quiet and fumeless. Compared to sailplanes and small aircraft, hang gliders are relatively inexpensive.

Another appeal of the sport is that it's for all seasons and all climates. But there's another drawing power. The very possibility of flying somewhat like a bird satisfies a yearning in the human spirit and excites the imagination of those who believe they can do it—can experience the exhilaration of unencumbered flight.

Although hang gliding actually started with the visionary but unfortunate flight of Icarus, its modern-day popularity came about thanks to Francis M. Rogallo, who invented and patented the flexible wing deltoid hang glider in the 1940s. Later NASA tested it as a spacecraft recovery system—and the art of man-flight had been altered. After 1969, when Australian Bill Bennett wowed Americans with his tow-gliding feats (different from hang gliding, since the pilot usually uses water skis, rather than just his legs, to land, and is towed by a speedboat), hang gliding really started to catch on.

Today most hang gliders are Rogallos; the rest are rigid wing gliders. One main asset of the Rogallo is its lightness and compactness when folded. Unlike the rigid wing models, Rogallos can be handled by one person on the ground in a mild wind, and he can launch by himself. The pilot shifts his weight to control the Rogallo. A rigid wing pilot also shifts his weight for some control, and in some designs also uses a rudder for turns.

A standard Rogallo glider costs $500 to $700. Used ones sell for much less. Design plans for do-it-yourselfers cost under $20, and a prepared kit runs from $300 to $400. The result is a portable craft that can be carried overhead or folded and transported underarm.

Just about anyone with a goodly amount of physical endurance and mental calm and confidence can pilot a hang glider, man or woman. Muscle is helpful, as are large doses of instinct and dexterity.

The sport is not without its dangers. Glider pilots have been killed. Many others injured. FAA investigation shows that most fatalities were caused by pilot error— taking off when the wind was too strong, failure to inspect the craft before takeoff and then experiencing a malfunction in the air, or attempting a maneuver that was too advanced.

The nature of the sport does result in most pilots having a minor mishap or two while learning. It's wise to wear a specially designed hang gliding helmet for absorbing impact. Unfortunately, very few get to the advanced stage without a broken bone or two. That is because of the scarcity of schools giving instruction to intermediates and above.

The best approach to hang gliding is first to read up on the subject, then visit a site, carefully observing how pilots take off and maneuver their gliders in the air by body shifting. Then, if you feel ready to try it yourself, take lessons.

In a good course, certified instructors offer the fundamentals including ground instruction with films and lectures as well as training in the glider. You must comprehend wind conditions, aerodynamics, weather and potential hazards. After several hours of classroom work and some time on a flight simulator, you're ready for your first flight, low and slow, progressing at your own rate. The aim is to teach safe techniques. Some schools charge from about $20 for a three-hour lesson, including equipment, to $95 for a package that includes insurance as well.

Ideal beginner or intermediate slopes are long, wide, and sandy or grassy. There should be no obstructions and at least a 600-foot clearing ahead of takeoff, plus a 100-foot clearing on the launching site itself. There should be no high brush or electrical power lines or wires ahead, and the prevailing wind should blow upward.

If you're sold on the sport after completing your lessons, you may want to join a gliding club. Most are rather informal and meet on an impromptu basis. The best source for information on where they can be located is the U. S. Hang Gliding Association (USHGA), Box 66306, Los Angeles, CA 90066. Whether you're a would-be pilot or an experienced one, a $10 membership fee will bring you 12 issues of *Ground Skimmer* magazine, plus the Association's directory of hang gliding clubs, schools and flying sites.

The USHGA, in an attempt to reduce the accident rate, has started to act as a sanctioning agency for meets, promoting and administering hang gliding contests, and through its local chapters, certifying and regulating activities at these sites.

Indeed, regulated activities seem to be the key to keeping the dangers of the sport minimal. Escape Country, a 5,000-acre motorcycle park in semiwilderness outside Los Angeles, is the first successful commercial hang gliding site, with hills varying from 50 to 5,200 feet and generally good winds year-round. For $2, hang glider pilots can spend the day flying there. Open since 1973, Escape Country is proud of its safety record, and it exemplifies what a well-run, regulated site can do to keep accidents down.

Parachuting

Me jump?

Thirty years ago an invitation to throw oneself into the air with a parachute seemed as slaphappy as rolling over Niagara Falls in a barrel. Today, twenty-odd years after the first commercial parachute center was opened by French-American parachutist Jacques Istel, there are over 200 commercial jump centers, 450 parachute clubs in nearly all 50 states, and approximately 30,000 active jumpers in the United States who make 2 million jumps per year. And parachuting has developed into a popular intercollegiate sport. Annual national championships draw teams from 43 colleges and universities.

The first truly competitive parachutists were Russians. In the 1930s they conducted contests for amateur jumpers to see who could land closest to a selected ground target. The art of sky diving, however, was developed by the French, and Istel was responsible for introducing their techniques here.

In the past decade parachuting has evolved into a complicated sport of skilled movement across the sky, quickness and accurate landings on a dime—literally. Some divers consider it an art form.

What's the attraction? Istel has one view: "When you go up in an airplane you take your environment with you—the cables, metal surfaces, everything. In parachuting, you're one with the sky. It's the difference between swimming and riding in a boat."

"And you can do anything an airplane can do except go up," adds veteran parachutist Bill Meir, director of the Parachutes, Inc., complex at Orange, MA. "You can accelerate, decelerate or move horizontally across the sky, and there's absolutely no sensation of falling."

It's not necessary to be a trained athlete to parachute. Nor does age make a difference—some in the past-65 category jump regularly, though they do have to be in above-average condition. To start, a parachutist takes basic training, which gives him all the fundamentals to make his first jump. After that, it's up to the individual's perserverance as to how far he will pursue the sport.

Some never do make it into the plane. "It's all a state of mind," says Meir. "If we feel they're not mentally ready to jump out of a plane, we tell them so. But usually, by the time they've walked through our front door, they've made up their minds."

Actually, the first freefall lasts just three seconds. Then you graduate to longer ones, using a stopwatch and altimeter, making controlled turns, and eventually doing loops and maneuvers.

The next step is formation flying. Groups of divers jump one after another and meet in midair—forming stars, caterpillars, diamonds or lines abreast. That's right, you actually join hands on your way down, dropping at 120 miles per hour. It's something else.

And—if you're willing—the final step is competition, where the diver is judged on a series of set maneuvers, much as the ice skater is judged on school figures. He will turn to the left and right and perform back and front loops. Landing accuracy is another factor.

As to safety, experts say that an average of no more than two jumps in 1,000 result in injury, and these are generally minor mishaps, like twisted ankles or knees. A broken leg is very much the exception.

To learn how to jump, you may sign up at a commercial center or join a club. The latter may offer the advantage of the camaraderie of other members who can help you through your almost inevitable case of prejump jitters and macaroni knees. (Surprisingly, there often is a greater degree of "butterflies" *after* the first few jumps, but with the proper attitude, these eventually subside.)

That first jump costs from $55 to $80, including equipment, instruction and aircraft ride to the proper altitude. Succeeding jumps with instruction will average $15 or $20. Without instruction, they run $4 and up, depending on the altitude desired.

To get the name of the club or center nearest to you, contact the U. S. Parachute Association, 806 15th St. NW, Suite 444, Washington, DC 20005. There is no charge for this information. For a fee of $2 USPA will send you their complete annual directory of centers and clubs. Annual dues of $20 include a subscription to their montly magazine, *Parachutist.* USPA is comprised of professionals, business people, pilots and, in general, a cross section of people who simply love to jump.

The first jump, naturally, requires the longest preparation and the greatest expense. The novice receives about four hours of ground training. Basic equipment includes a helmet, goggles, overalls, jump boots and 40 pounds of main and reserve parachute. Prejump instruction teaches the student how to exit from the plane, maneuver the parachute and land, and what to do in the disconcerting event of a tree landing or chute malfunction. A reassuring jolt seconds after leaving the plane indicates that the parachute has opened, released automatically by a static line attached to the plane. After five static-line jumps you advance to freefall.

You learn how to steer the chute by pulling at toggles (small wooden handles) that open and close slots in the nylon canopy. A reserve chute is strapped to your chest like a spare tire. You can inflate it manually, if need be, by pulling the rip cord. Landing is equivalent to jumping off a four-foot table. As a precaution, the novice learns to land and roll. Later he may graduate to stand-up landings.

A first-timer's emotions can run the gamut from terror to sheer exhilaration, as described by one neophyte: "My turn came around, and I was frankly terrified. I jumped on cue, however, and 'whoom,' opening shock hit before I counted to three. The fright vanished, replaced by a feeling of peaceful other-worldliness. Earth sprawled below, no more real than a picture postcard, its problems reduced to the substance of the clouds on my right. I felt completely disengaged from the rules of both man and physics. The wind was soft as a cat's paw, brushing past my face and blowing me gently across the landscape. Camping, sailing, flying: They may get you away from the humdrum. But this is away from it *all.*"*

Sky diving—plunging like a bird before pulling the cord—is the ultimate goal of the dedicated parachutist. Freefall—the very word connotes excitement. For the first twelve seconds, you accelerate, and you are very much aware of that acceleration. By the time twelve seconds pass, you're moving at 120 miles per hour, but you do have control over your body. You can move across the sky at a ratio of two to one; that is, if you jump while two miles above the ground, you have time to move one

---

* Lynde McCormick, *The Christian Science Monitor.*

mile across the sky.

A few of the parachute centers affiliated with USPA are listed below.

Arizona: **Arizona Parachute Ranch**, PO Box 698, Coolidge, AZ 85228. (602) 723-5336. Sunrise–sunset, 4 days. Other times arr.

California: **Borderland Air Sports Center**, 4627 Vista St., San Diego, CA 92116. (714) 283-8915 or 426-2055. Otay Lakes Rd., 10 mi. E of Chula Vista. 9 A.M.–sunset wkends, 12 noon – sunset wkdays.

Elsinore Parachuting Center, 20701 Sereal Rd., Lake Elsinore, CA 92330. (714) 674-2141. Lake Elsinore, 3 mi. S of city. 8 A.M.–sunset wkends, 9 A.M.–sunset wkdays exc. Tues.

Perris Valley Paracenter, 2091 S. Goetz Rd., Perris, CA 92370. (714) 657-3904 or 8727. 10 mi. N of Elsinore. 8 A.M.–sunset exc. Wed. Other times arr.

Pope Valley Parachute Ranch, 1996 Pope Canyon Rd., Pope Valley, CA 94567. (707) 965-3400. 8 A.M.–sunset wkends, 10 A.M.–sunset wkdays exc. Tues.

Florida: **Deland Sport Parachuting Center**, 1260 Flightline Blvd., Deland, FL 32720. (904) 734-9803. 9 A.M.–sunset exc. Tues. Other times arr.

Zephyrhills Parachute Center, PO Box 1101, Zephyrhills, FL 33599. (813) 782-2918. Zephyrhills Airport. 9 A.M.–sunset daily. Other times arr.

Idaho: **Jump West Parachute Center**, PO Box 7304, Boise, ID 83707. (208) 286-9419. Star. 9 A.M.–sunset exc. Tues. Other times arr.

Indiana: **Parachutes and Associates**, PO Box 65, Mooresville, IN 46158. (317) 831-5023. Kelly Airport. 10 A.M.–sunset exc. Mon. Other times arr.

Kentucky: **Green County Sport Parachute Center of Kentucky**, Rt. 2, Box 140, Bardstown, KY 40004. (606) 348-9981. 9 A.M.–sunset daily.

Maryland: **Pelican Sport Aviation**, PO Box 62, Ridgely, MD 21660. (301) 634-2723. Sunrise–sunset daily. Other times arr.

Massachusetts: **Orange Parachuting Center**, PO Box 96, 24 N. Main St., Orange, MA 01364. (617) 544-6911. Orange Municipal Airport. Sunrise–sunset exc. Tues. Other times arr.

Missouri: **Ka-Mo Skydivers**, c/o Joe Voros, Box 13564, Kansas City, MO 64116. (816) 494-5333. Lexington Municipal Airport. 8 A.M.–sunset wkends & holidays.

New Jersey: **Lakewood Parachute Center**, Box 258, Lakewood, NJ 08701. (201) 363-4900. 8 A.M.–sunset, daily in summer, wkends in winter.

Ripcord Paracenter, Inc., PO Box 172, Burlington County Airpark, Lumberton, NJ 08048. (609) 267-9897. 9 A.M.–sunset wkends. Other times arr.

North Carolina: **Raeford Drop Zone**, PO Box 878, Raeford, NC 28376. (919) 875-5626 or 3261. 3 mi. NE of city. 9 A.M.–sunset exc. Mon. Other times arr.

Texas:	**Spaceland Paracenter**, PO Box 152, League City, TX 77573. (713) 337-1713. Spaceland Airpark. 10 A.M.–sunset Wed., wkends & holidays. Other times arr.
Utah:	**Seagull Parachute Club**, PO Box 391, Brigham, UT 84302. (801) 753-9919. Logan Airport. Sunrise–sunset, Apr.–Nov.
Virginia:	**Hartwood Paracenter**, Rt. 6, Box 369B, Hartwood, VA 22471. (703) 752-4784. Sunrise–sunset exc. Mon.

Soaring

An engineless plane sailing the heavens. Rising on currents of air. No means of staying up but by riding invisible air cushions. An exhilarating, silent world. . .

The earth's contours and substances reflect the sun's heat unevenly, filling the skies with ascending and descending waves of air. They are visible only when they contain moisture or "dust devils"—whirling particles of dust. Part of the skill of a sailplane pilot is locating thermals—upward air currents on which to soar in endless spirals. Some pilots try to spot hawks that ride thermals, apparently for sheer enjoyment. "We'll get on a hawk's tail and follow him right up," one pilot says. "At 1,500 feet it's too high to spot a mouse or a chipmunk. He's there for the same reason we are." As the thermal tops off, the sleek fuselage of the craft, with its long wings, moves through the atmosphere with a hiss of rushing air, gliding from one thermal to another, like stepping from cloud to cloud.

Much soaring in the United States is conducted on thermals, but lift is also obtained from waves or air produced by high velocity winds against a mountain range, or winds hitting a perpendicular surface such as cliff. These are called wave soaring and ridge soaring.

Pulled into the air by a powered tow plane (or sometimes an automobile or winch), the sailplane runs along the runway on its single wheel before lifting up. A bubble canopy fits over the one-, two- or three-seater cockpit. Not to be confused with the glider, which simply coasts to earth, the sailplane is aerodynamically designed to gain altitude on even slightly rising air, and can fly cross-country. Except for the initial tow, the sailplane requires no fuel, and for that reason may well be widely used for energy-free transportation in the future.

The world's sailplane altitude record of 46,267 feet was set by Paul Bikle in 1961. The U.S. record for continuous flight was made on May 9, 1977, by Karl Striedieck, who flew a sailplane from Lockhaven, PA, to Oak Ridge, TN, and back—a flight of 1,015 miles in 14 hours down the Allegheny Ridge—and never more than 50 to 100 feet above the treetops!

Though Orville Wright stayed up 9 minutes and 45 seconds in 1911, soaring actually developed in Germany in the 1920s. Some years ago Charles and Anne Morrow Lindbergh both became soaring pilots. Astronaut Neil Armstrong also is one.

Today there are some 3,500 sailplanes in the United States, more than 15,000 licensed pilots, 225 soaring clubs and 125 commercial schools. The Soaring Society of America (SSA) was formed in 1932 to foster and promote all phases of gliding and soaring. A division of the National Aeronautic Association, it sanctions the annual National Soaring Championship contests and numerous regional races.

SSA has produced a soaring starter kit, which will launch you on the adventure of motorless flight. The kit includes: a brochure, *How You Can Become a Glider Pilot;* a 36-page full-color booklet with a comprehensive overview of the sport called *Gliders and Pilots. . . .and How They Fly;* a 32-page *Directory of U.S. Soaring Sites,* giving schools and flight operations; a current issue of its magazine, *Soaring;* a list of soaring clubs and schools in your area; a bibliography; and an SSA membership application. The entire kit may be ordered for $2 from SSA, 3200 Airport Ave., Santa Monica, CA 90405.

Another source of information on clubs, schools and other aspects of the sport is the booklet *How to Get Started in Soaring* ($1), put out by the leading U.S. manufacturer of sailplanes, Schweizer Aircraft Corporation, Box 147, Airport Rd., Elmira, NY 14902.

Aspiring pilots need no previous flying experience and can solo as young as age 14. It is possible to start quite inexpensively. From the introductory flight (which can be under $20, including sailplane rental, towplane service and professional instructor) through solo, the investment will be under $500—and less for power pilots. It can take as little as two weeks. To receive a private license and to be able to carry additional passengers, FAA flying and written exams are required.

Once you have begun, there is apt to be no turning back, for this is a sport that can never be monotonous or repetitive. Aside from the ever-present joy of birdlike flight, no two voyages are the same. Varying weather conditions, clouds and atmosphere make each flight unique.

A few of the larger soaring centers in the country are listed below.

California:	**Calistoga Soaring Center,** 1546 Lincoln Ave., Calistoga, CA 94515. (707) 942-5592. Calistoga Airpark. All yr., daily. 7 sailplanes, instruction, 4 towplanes. Thermal, ridge & wave soaring.
	Great Western Soaring School, Box 189, Pearblossom, CA 93553. (805) 944-2920. Crystalaire Airport, 5 mi. E of Pearblossom. All yr., daily. 15 sailplanes, instruction, 4 towplanes. Thermal, ridge & wave soaring.
	Sky Sailing Airport, 44999 Christy St., Fremont, CA 94538. (405) 657-9900. Airport 1 mi. SW of Fremont. All yr., daily. 10 sailplanes, instruction, 5 towplanes. Thermal, ridge & wave soaring.
Colorado:	**Wave Flights, Inc.,** 9990 Gliderport Rd., Colorado Springs, CO 80908. (303) 495-4144. Black Forest Gliderport, 7 mi. NE of Colorado Springs. 14 sailplanes, instruction, 4 towplanes. Thermal & wave soaring.
Connecticut:	**Connecticut Soaring Center,** Waterbury Airport, Plymouth, CT 06782. (203) 283-5474. Apr.–Dec., daily. 9 sailplanes, instruction, 3 towplanes. Thermal & wave soaring.
Florida:	**Lenox Flight School,** Rt. 4, Box 863, Arcadia, FL 33821. (813) 494-3921. Arcadia Municipal Airport. All yr., Wed.–Sun. 7 sailplanes, instruction, 2 towplanes. Thermal soaring.
Hawaii:	**Honolulu Soaring Club, Inc.,** Box 626, Waialua, HI 96791. (808) 623-6711. Dillingham Airfield, 5 mi. W of Waialua. All yr., daily. 2 sailplanes, instruction, 2 towplanes. Thermal & ridge soaring.
Michigan:	**J. W. Benz Soaring,** 3148 South State Rd., Ionia, MI 48846. (616) 527-9070 or 642-9019. Ionia Co. Airport, 3

mi. S of Ionia on Hwy. 66. Apr.–Nov., daily exc. Mon., wkends only Apr.–Nov. 7 sailplanes, instruction, 3 towplanes. Thermal soaring.

Nevada: **Desert Soaring,** 4499 Nevada Hwy. 41, Boulder City, NV 89005. (702) 293-9906. Boulder City Airport. All yr., daily exc. Mon. 6 sailplanes, instruction, 2 towplanes. Thermal, ridge & wave soaring.

New Hampshire: **Northeastern Light Aircraft, Inc.,** Box 252, Lynn, MA 01903—mail address. (603) 898-7919 or (617) 581-1030. Northeastern Gliderport, Salem. All yr., daily May–Nov., wkends Dec.–Apr. 21 sailplanes, instruction, 3 towplanes. Thermal & wave soaring.

New York: **Schweizer Soaring School,** Box 147, Elmira, NY 14902. (607) 739-3821, ext. 10. Chemung Co. Airport, 10 mi. NW of Elmira. May–Oct., daily. 10 sailplanes, instruction, 3 towplanes. Thermal & ridge soaring.

Wurtsboro School of Aviation, Wurtsboro Airport, Wurtsboro, NY 12790. (914) 888-2791. All yr., daily. 12 sailplanes, instruction, 5 towplanes. Thermal, ridge & wave soaring.

Ohio: **Cardinal Aviation,** Box 2106, East Liverpool, OH 43920. (216) 386-3761. Columbiana Co. Airport. All yr., daily. 3 sailplanes, instruction, 2 towplanes. Thermal soaring.

South Carolina: **Bermuda High Soaring, Inc.,** PO Drawer 809, Chester, SC 29706. (803) 385-6061. Chester Airport. All yr., daily exc. Mon. 10 sailplanes, instruction, 2 towplanes. Thermal & wave soaring.

Texas: **Windermere Soaring School,** Rt. 2, Box 491, Spicewood, TX 78669. (512) 695-4663 or 327-3230. Windermere Gliderport. All yr., daily exc. Tues. 6 sailplanes, instruction, 3 towplanes. Thermal soaring.

Vermont: **Sugarbush Air Service, Inc.,** Box 68, Waitsfield, VT 05673. (802) 496-2290. Warren-Sugarbush Airport, 2 mi. NE of Warren. All yr., daily. 8 sailplanes, instruction, 4 towplanes. Thermal, ridge & wave soaring.

Washington: **Soaring Unlimited, Inc.,** Box 548, Kirkland, WA 98033. (206) 454-2514. Fancher Field. All yr., daily Mar.–Nov., wkends Dec.–Feb. 10 sailplanes, instruction, 3 towplanes. Thermal, ridge & wave soaring.

Wisconsin: **West Bend Flying Service,** Box 409, West Bend, WI 53095. (414) 334-5603. West Bend Municipal Airport. Apr.–Nov. daily. 6 sailplanes, insturction, 2 towplanes. Thermal soaring.

Colorado Adventuring, CO.

Baja Expeditions, CA.

VIII   ADVENTURE ROUNDUP

Wilderness Living

Though nearly every chapter in this book concerns wilderness living of one sort or another, this chapter is added to tell of special excursions where you and the wilderness may mix in a variety of ways.

Some of these treks focus on natural history, marine biology, anthropology or geology. To reach the wild places where your study and observation take place, you may travel by charter aircraft, helicopter, jeep, river raft, nonluxurious cruiser, fishing skiff, by horse, by foot or by motorcoach. Most likely it will be a combination of these modes of travel.

Expedition goals are varied. They may deal with whale watching off the coast of Baja California, or experiencing a Swiss Family Robinson survival situation on an island off Maine's rocky shore. Or the exploration of volcanoes, marine life, and tropical birds in Hawaii. . . wildlife and Eskimo anthropology in Alaska and the Pribilof Islands. . . the canyons, rivers and Indian culture of the Southwest.

Wilderness schools that give leadership training in wilderness education, nature study, caving, survival techniques and environmental courses are noted in this chapter. Also to be found here are unusual combination trips, such as one that involves cycling, horseback riding and canoeing in Vermont, with overnights at comfortable inns. Or flying to a pioneer ranch in Idaho's Primitive Area, and proceeding by horseback and raft to a river lodge. . . a hiking, backpacking, canoeing, beachcombing and exploring safari in British Columbia. . . backpacking, rock climbing, rafting and riding in the Rockies while studying orienteering and ecology.

For those seeking a more individual and relaxed wilderness experience, this chapter calls attention to already established base camps where you may hike or ride in, and spend your time fishing, observing wildlife, hiking or doing nothing at all. For more of this unprogrammed type of wilderness living, please see the chapter "Pack Trips by Horse." The mention of "drop pack trips" in that chapter indicates that the outfitter can pack a family or group into the wilderness by horse, help set up their camp, and leave them there until an agreed-upon pickup date.

ALASKA

Kachemak Bay Wilderness Lodge, China Poot Bay—via Homer, AK 99603. Att.: Michael McBride. Radio tel: (907) 235-8910. All yr. Arrival: Homer, AK.

You fly in from Homer to a lodge on the Kenai Peninsula surrounded by wilderness. It overlooks snowcapped mountains, waterfalls, fjords, volcanoes and glaciers. The "Old World crafted" cabins have wood stoves, electricity, a private bath and a sauna bathhouse. With your wilderness hosts, Mike and Diane, their 2 children and several staff, you'll visit sea bird rookeries, photograph seals, bear, moose and goats, and observe archaelogical sites and 30-foot tides. Says one guest, "Mike is a super Kit Carson, and Diane a fantastic cook. About as close to Paradise as one can get in this world." Allow time for mail: Mike travels 5 miles by skiff, weather permitting, to pick it up once a week. Rates of $125/day per guest include meals, private cabin, guides and round-trip from Homer via boat or floatplane.

CALIFORNIA

Baja Expeditions, Inc., AGI, PO Box 3725, San Diego, CA 92103. Att.: Tim Means. (714) 297-0506. (See also *Scuba Diving*.)

The focus of Baja Expeditions' trips is for naturalists, wilderness seekers, geologists, biologists. . . and anyone wanting to gain insight into the spirit of Baja's unique wilderness on nonluxury cruises to remote and wild places. Specialties of various trips center around the rich contrasts of plants, birds, fish life, land forms, marine mammals, whale watching, skin diving and living close to the sea. Trips begin in San Diego with travel by bus to a 75- or 36-foot cruiser or a 22-foot Mexican fishing skiff. Most trips include return by air from La Paz (or the same route in reverse). These are fascinating and unique wilderness expeditions. Rates range from $475 to $575 for 6- to 8-day trips; group discounts.

Nature Expeditions International, PO Box 1173, 4564 El Camino Real, Suite F, Los Altos, CA 94022. (415) 941-2910.

This nonprofit educational group, founded in 1973, offers expeditions (and short courses in the Bay Area) to provide a stimulating way for the nonspecialist to experience the natural world through discovery and instruction. Experts in anthropology, marine biology, natural history, photography or related fields accompany trips to the Hawaiian Islands, Mexico, Southwest Indian country, Grand Canyon, Utah's canyonlands, Wyoming, Hells Canyon, Alaska, the Pribilof Islands and other areas worldwide. The trips involve rafting, skin diving, hiking, sailing, air charters, comfortable motorcoaches and other modes of travel.

COLORADO

Colorado Adventuring, 219 Main St., Westcliffe, CO 81252. Att.W: Bill Crowell. (303) 783-2763.

"Although carrying a pack over a high pass or climbing a 14,000-foot mountain can be exhausting, our programs are not designed as grim exhibitions of endurance. They give people a chance to learn a variety of wilderness skills in a supportive atmosphere. "Bill and Penny Crowell and Gary Ziegler, with impressive academic, teaching and outdoor experience, provide the support for exhilarating backpacking, rock climbing, rafting and horseback adventures. They emphasize camping skills, orienteering and ecology on 3-week Rocky Mountain treks—$460, including pickup at Colorado Springs or Pueblo, June to August. They also offer a Mexican expedition by train and by foot to explore Copper Canyon, cliff dwellings and communities in the state of Chihuahua. From El Paso: 13 days, $280.

Rocky Mountain Expeditions, PO Box CC-AG, Buena Vista, CO 81211. Att.: Dick Scar. (303) 395-8466. (See also *Backpacking, Float Trips, Ski Touring*.)

For people who are venturing for the first time beyond a vehicle camper, RME offers base-camp wilderness trips in the central Colorado Rockies. On some you ride in and out on horseback; on others you hike one or both ways, with pack animals carrying the gear. At the tent camps you learn about environmentally sound procedures, observe wildlife, identify wildflowers, star-gaze, use map and compass, fish and relax. A great family trip. For 5 days, $210–$260; bring sleeping gear; group rates. July through September.

GEORGIA

Wolfcreek Wilderness, PO Box 596-W, Blairsville GA 30512. Att.: Keith W. Evans. (404) 745-6460. (See also *Youth Adventures*.)

This private nonprofit organization teaches wilderness adventure education. Its seminars and courses, given all year, center around leadership training, backpacking and caving trips. Besides a 3-week young adult summer course, there are 4-day winter courses, $110–$115; weekend medical aid seminars, $55; and a 2-week instructors' course, $275. A 5-day winter hike carries the Christmas spirit into the high country (Dec. 26–31, $135).

IDAHO

Mackay Bar Lodge & Stonebreaker Ranch, Drawer F, Room 1010, 1 Capital Center, Boise, ID 83702. Att.: Dick Perkins. (208) 344-1881. May–Oct.

In the mountainous Idaho Primitive Area, wild and remote, the only exceptions to pioneer conditions are a few airstrips and radiotelephones. At the Stonebreaker Ranch, reached by charter flight, cabins are made of hand-hewn logs, tents (for guests) are heated with wood-burning stoves, and light is provided by kerosene or Coleman lamps. It's a place to ride, fish, hike and feel like a pioneer. The Mackay Bar Lodge, reached by air charter, jet boat or raft, is a landscaped wilderness haven on the Main Salmon River where you are treated to excellent accommodations, splendid meals, riding, fishing, a float trip and jet boating. For a really unique wilderness vacation, ask Dick Perkins about his special combos. On one you fly first to a mountain ranch (Big Creek) for days, then travel 3 days by wagon and horseback to the Middle Fork of the Salmon for 2 days of rafting. Or stay 3 days at Stonebreaker then ride horseback 3 days to the Main Salmon for a few days of rafting to reach Mackay Bar Lodge. Rates, including air charters, begin at around $65/day per person.

MAINE

Island/Wilderness Expeditions, Ltd., Rockport, ME 04856. Att.: David Lyman. (207) 236-4788.

Island/Wilderness, explains Director David Lyman, offers expeditions centered around nature photography. A series of 1-week expeditions for basic nature photographers and 10-day expeditions for advanced photographers and naturalists are led by *National Geographic* photographers. One expedition for families is a Swiss Family Robinson experience—learning about camping, sailing, and how a family can live in a survival situation. About their locale, Lyman says, "The islands off the Maine coast are a rare and fragile example of a unique wilderness. Each is a microcosm of vegetation and wildlife, nature living in delicate balance." Trips are limited to 12 participants; 6 days, $175–$225; 11 days, $300.

NEW MEXICO

Southwest Safaris, PO Box 945, Dept. AG, Santa Fe, NM 87501. Att.: Bruce Adams. (505) 988-4246.

Bruce Adams has solved the problem of how to cover the vast distances of the magnificent Southwest by transporting guests by air, hopping from one spectacular scene to another. At one spot, you'll continue by jeep or by horseback, at another by foot or by river raft. In summer you camp out, but in colder months he arranges lodging. The emphasis is on geology, archaeology, ecology and history. The aircraft doubles as a portable classroom from which to study huge geological landforms or grasp the relationships among widely separated Indian ruins. "Yet one must climb into a cliff dwelling, raft down the San Juan or jeep through Monument Valley to appreciate the lifestyle of the Navajo community today,'' Bruce explains. He offers day excursions for $99 to $199, and 2- to 6-day safaris from $239 to $660, all-inclusive.

NORTH CAROLINA

Mondamin Wilderness Adventures, PO Box 8, Tuxedo, NC 28784. (704) 693-7446. (See also *Youth Adventures.*)

Mondamin sponsors a series of wilderness-oriented adult programs. On base-camp trips in the Cataloochee Valley of the Great Smokies (3–4 days, $110–$140), participants hike to valley floors, coves and ridges to study the native mountain plants. For summer camp staff and schoolteachers, there is a Nature Leadership Conference (3 days, $75) specializing in flowers, trees, shrubs, birds and other animals. Wilderness photographers may join a backpacking trip designed to improve their photographic skills, plus a day of rafting (4 days, $145).

OHIO

Wilderness Trails, 728 Prospect Ave., Cleveland, OH 44115. Att.: Gary Newman. (216) 696-5222 or 543-8639. (See also *Backpacking, Ski Touring.*)

Gary offers 5- and 10-day Wilderness School experiences in West Virginia's Monongahela National Forest. On the shorter trip, participants are trained for 3½ days so they can live the last 24 hours on their own with no food or gear provided beyond first-aid, matches, whistle and poncho. There's also an Ozarks Caving Trip in Missouri and Kentucky. It includes canoeing to out-of-the-way caving areas, entry to Kentucky's Mammoth Cave and 24 hours in the Ozark underground cave lab.

VERMONT

Hike-Skitour Vermont, RFD 1-A, Chester, VT 05143. Att.: Anne Mausolff. (802) 875-3631 or 824-3973. (See also *Ski Touring/Snowshoeing.*)

Wilderness living is easy, indeed, when it includes overnights at charming Vermont country inns! But there's lots of wilderness daytimes for these groups that hike trails around Chittenden, ride horseback in the Stowe region, canoe central Vermont rivers and bike over routes circling Woodstock—all in the course of a 1-week all-expense trip ($293) or 2 weeks ($526). There also are weekend backpacks, camping out or with the first night at an inn ($50–$74), with orientation slide shows on how to handle different types of trails and set up camp and live in it. Anne Mausolff has backpacked extensively, led Appalachian Mountain Club trips and participated in AMC leadership-training workshops.

WASHINGTON

Northwest Alpine Guide Service, Inc., 1628 Ninth Ave. #2, Seattle, WA 98101. Att.: Linda Bradley Miller. (206) 622-6074. (See also *Backpacking, Mountaineering, Canoeing, Float Trips, Ski Touring, Youth Adventures.*)

The Bradleys offer a dual opportunity for wilderness living—with their Wilderness Camp program in the Washington Cascades and at nature study camps in Washington, Canada and Alaska. Wilderness Camp, they tell us, "is the ideal way to camp out in this beautiful wild country without the work of packing in your own tents and equipment; yet you can enjoy the thrill of camping out." The 1-week nature study excursions venture to Alaska's Brooks Range (fantastic bird life); to Canada's Carcajou Mountains (everything from caribou to dall sheep to grizzlies); and to areas in Washington from beach to mountains. Each trip features a professional naturalist.

Ship Harbor Inn, 5316 Ferry Terminal Rd., Anacortes, WA 98221. Att.: Jack Hinshaw. (206) 293-3652.

A cabin in the pines on a craggy point with a private beach, clam-filled lagoon, shrimp hole, crab pot, clam shovel, small boat, berries in season and outdoor grill are the happy ingredients of a hideaway in the San Juan Islands. The unpretentious furnished cabin sleeps 6 with a tent for more. A great get get-away place for family or friends. Group rate of $285 per week includes a 10-minute flight to and from the island from Anacortes.

WYOMING

National Outdoor Leadership School, PO Box AA, Lander, WY 82520. (307) 332-4381. (See also *Mountaineering, Ski Touring, Youth Adventures*.)

The basic NOLS course is a 35-day wilderness expedition in the Wind River, Beartooth, Absaroka or Uinta ranges. You learn a multitude of skills, from cooking to compass use to edible plants to judgment and leadership. A biology expedition (35 days) places equal emphasis on "leadership, scientific education, and wilderness skills." A Baja expedition includes a "19-day mobile folbot course covering 85 miles of the most dramatic coastline the peninsula has to offer." Skills taught include kayaking, snorkeling and sea food gathering. A 35-day Cloud Peak Wilderness and speleology course includes 12 days of studying La Caverna de Tres Charros and surrounding caves.

BRITISH COLUMBIA

Pacific Northwest Sea Trails, Inc., 13062 Caminito Del Rocio, Del Mar, CA 92014. Att.: John N. Webb. (714) 481-9540.

From its homeport in Campbell River on Vancouver Island, off the British Columbia coast, PNST offers 14-day land and sea environmental journeys in the rugged Inside Passage. Trips are limited to 20 people, 16 years and older, and are co-educational. Participants learn what is required for safe enjoyment and preservation of the wilderness. Motorized inflatable boats, 6 persons in each, travel in pairs over 150 miles during the expedition, with beach camping at night. Hiking across islands, among giant evergreens and up mountains is part of the program. No drugs, alcohol or smoking—"join us for some fresh air!" Fee: $400; individual and group discounts.

Western Outdoor Adventures Ltd., 16115 32nd Ave., White Rock, B.C. V4B 4Z5. Att.: Frank Lockwood. (604) 531-3969. (See also *Jeeping, Ski Touring, Youth Adventures*.)

With an Adventure Camp on a beautiful isolated bay in Jervis Inlet, and an Ocean Camp at the northern tip of Vancouver Island, WOA uses helicopters, charter flights, buses, ferries and trains to transport its guests between Vancouver or Port Hardy, the camps and the wilderness. Some safaris are primarily hikes or backpacking treks, others are mostly canoeing. All are combined with camping, beachcombing, fishing, swimming, and exploring, with weekly departures throughout the summer. Inlet canoeing takes place "where mountains meet the sky." WOA's most remote river tour follows the Upper Stikine River from its headwaters for 10 days. Trips are for 4 to 15 people, from July to September, up to 21 days. Sample all-inclusive rates: 3 days, $160–$170; 5 days, $205–$225; 8 days, $205; 11 days, $370.

ONTARIO

Headwaters, PO Box 288, Temagami, Ont. POH 2HO. Att.: Hugh & Carin Stewart. No tel., send telegram. (See also *Ski Touring, Youth Adventures*.)

Wilderness living, the Stewarts believe, is not just traveling from one place to another, nor is it thrill-seeking nor the excitement of a superficial brush with the wild; wilderness living also demands complete participation and attention, responsibility and accountability. And the rewards? New skills, perspectives, insights—regeneration. From their remote base camp 300 miles north of Toronto, travel is by canoe in summer. And, depending on the season, you learn cross-country skiing, snowshoeing, use of toboggans, tumplines, wannigans and packs—along with all other outdoor skills. For artists (16 yrs. and up) there is a 2-week sketching program with 10 days of canoe travel. For 6 to 10 people summer rates, including sleeping gear and Temagami flight to and from base, are $365 for 2 weeks, $500 for 3 weeks. Also group and family rates.

YUKON TERRITORY

Yukon Wilderness Unlimited, PO Box 4126, Whitehorse, Y.T. Y1A 3S9. Att.: John Lammers. Tel.: 2 M 3908 via Whitehorse mobile operator. (See also *Float Trips*.)

John and Polly Lammers offer wilderness base-camp vacations at a lake near timberline. They fly you in and set up camp for the duration of your stay. "We explore the surrounding country on foot and by canoe," John explains, "—its mountain tundra and boreal forest." There's invariably good fishing. Maximum 6 guests at a time.

Outward Bound, CT.

Youth Adventures

Whether you're under or over 21 you'll find activities described in this chapter that will limber you up, teach you many skills and provide excitement and fun. Though the focus throughout the chapter is on expeditions and programs especially for people in their teens or thereabouts, adults may participate in some of them—the year-round excursions of the National Outdoor Leadership School or Outward Bound, for example.

For a complete look at youth activities, glance also through the chapters "Backpacking/Hiking," "Mountaineering/Rock Climbing" and "Biking." Also, note the youth rates in other chapters, especially in connection with family vacations.

The variety of things you can do with the services covered in this chapter is amazing. How about hiking the Chilkoot Trail, starting in Skagway, Alaska, for instance? Or leaning to read maps and find your route through the Colorado Rockies while you live for a week with only what you carry on your back? Perhaps it's rock climbing and rappeling that will draw you to the White Mountains of New Hampshire, the Grand Tetons of Wyoming, Idaho's Sawtooth Wilderness or Washington's North Cascades.

There are outdoor travel camps that combine a variety of experiences—like biking, hiking, caving and clamming through New England; or exploring national parks, hunting fossils and white-water rafting in the West; or roaming canyons and deserts and talking with Indians, prospectors and frontiersmen on a nomadic Southwest camping trek.

You may want to learn how to build your own kayak and then run a western river in it; or join a group that is kayaking in the Sea of Cortez in Mexico; or man an oar on a roller-coaster boat ride down the Colorado River. There are outfitters with whom you can float the Yukon in Alaska, explore with Cree Indian guides the waterways of northern Quebec, navigate an outrigger in Hawaii, learn to sail in Maine's Penobscot Bay, go to sea as an apprentice on a 100-foot schooner or learn all about horsemanship on a western ranch.

Or would you like to join an expedition excavating the Natural Trap in Wyoming, observing feral ponies in Assateague Island in Maryland, exploring an underwater archaeological peak off Alaska's Aleutian Islands or focus on environmental education?

There's an educational bonus in nearly all of the adventures noted in these pages, a few of which offer college credit. Along with the fun you learn river rescue techniques, survival training, first aid and emergency care, how to camp in the wilderness, how to build a snow cave, read a map, backpack, rock-climb, sail, canoe, kayak, plan an expedition, run a wild river, fight a fire, catch a fish—these and many other skills that will increase your self-reliance and enrich your life.

ALASKA

Klondike Safaris, PO Box 1898-A, Skagway, AK 99840. Att.: Skip Burns. (907) 983-2495. [Oct.–May: 823 6th St., Juneau, AK 99801. (907) 586-3924.]

Skip Burns describes his youth trips: "For 23 days, 15 young people travel 36 miles over the Chilkoot Trail—700 miles down the Yukon River past Dawson to Eagle, Alaska, then by auto to Fairbanks, where the trip ends. The program of learning experiences offers climbing, wilderness survival, campfire cooking, river navigation, ecology and photographic awareness." Adds Skip, "Our youth trips are the least expensive per-day trips in the North Country." The cost is $34/day; trips June to August.

ARIZONA

Grand Canyon Youth Expeditions, RR 4, Box 755, Flagstaff, AZ 86001. Att.: Dick & Susan McCallum. (602) 774-8176. (See also *Backpacking, Float Trips, Ski Touring.*)

The McCallums' 18-day oar-powered trip in the Grand Canyon ($575) is their specialty. "It is designed for young adults from 16 to 25," Dick explains. Participants learn white-water river navigation, camping skills, wilderness survival, river rescue techniques, physical conditioning and safety training. He also offers a program for building and learning to use your own kayak. You start with a partially completed craft and finish it to fit to your exact size—then paddle it down the San Juan.

CALIFORNIA

Squaw Valley Mountaineering Center, Box 2288-B, Olympic Valley, CA 95730. Att.: Skip Reedy. (916) 583-4316. (See also *Backpacking, Ski Touring.*)

On a 7-day wilderness program young people from 10 to 18 hike, backpack, climb, sail, raft and learn tennis, map reading, cooking, horseback riding, ice skating and survival techniques. The emphasis is on ecological awareness. An overnight backpacking trips concludes the week. The cost: $120 living out, $180 with lodging.

COLORADO

Colorado Outward Bound School, 945 Pennsylvania St., Denver, CO 80203. (303) 837-0880.

The school bells ring on the high alpine terrain of the Colorado Rocky Mountains, the rapids of the Green, Yampa and Colorado Rivers, and the deserts of southeastern Utah. You start with a backpack and work your way up to major peak ascents. The summer session, May to November, gets into basic campcraft, mountaineering, gorge crossing, rock climbing, rappeling, wilderness travel and mountain rescue. In winter, it's ski mountaineering, ice climbing, glissading and winter campcraft. (For Outward Bound's headquarters, see CT.)

Delby's Triangle 3 Ranch, Box 14, Steamboat Springs, CO 80477. Att.: Delbert Heid. (303) 879-1257. (See also *Pack Trips.*)

Del Heid's specialty is wilderness pack trips to a base camp in the Mt. Zirkel Wilderness Area. The basic idea is to acquaint boys or girls with riding and packing, woodsmanship, animal and plant life, forest-fire prevention, and survival techniques. Also hours of trout fishing. "Qualified instructors will be with the groups at all times," Del says. "This all leads to a fuller, richer life." One-day trip $50; 3 days, $125; from June to October.

Telluride Mountaineering School, Box 67, Telluride, CO 81435. Att.: Dave Farny. (303) 925-3603. [Nov.–Apr.: Box 4, Aspen, CO 81611.] 2 terms for 30 boys 3–18 yrs., 5 wks./$900; for 15 girls 14–18 yrs., 6 wks./$1000. Spring/fall custom trips, all ages, $35/day. Arrival: Montrose, CO.

Through backpacking, rock climbing, survival training, hiking, whitewater rafting, kayaking, and desert and Indian country exploration, students (6 per group) learn to appreciate nature's simple joys. "It's great fun for any kid who needs to prove something to himself," says Dave Farny, a former B-47 pilot with SAC and an experienced ski instructor and mountain guide.

Wilderness Education, PO Box 1182, Leadville, CO 80461. Att.: Jack Saunders. (303) 486-3781.

The thrust here is conservation, and Jack Saunders, a licensed guide and outfitter, starts them young with a Discovery Program for boys 12 to 14 years old and a Mountaineers coed program for 15-year-olds and up. Programs in the Sawatch Range of the San Isabel National Forest teach fly fishing, map and compass reading, cooking and nutrition, safety and the use and care of equipment. A 1-week course costs $110. Both programs are limited to 10 students.

CONNECTICUT

Outward Bound, Inc., 165 West Putnam Ave., Greenwich, CT 06830. (203) 661-0797.

This is headquarters for a nonprofit organization that began during World War II as a training school for British seamen and has spread to five continents. Today, it offers a year-round schedule in 7 "schools without ceilings" throughout the U.S. From misty seacoasts to snow-clad mountain ranges, deserts, wild rivers, deep forests and quiet lakes, Outward Bound offers wilderness experiences for everyone from 100-pound teenagers to active middle-agers. You learn the outdoor skills you need to meet the challenges of the particular course and environment. Tuition for the standard course is $525 to $650, which includes food, equipment and instruction. The schools also offer special courses of from 3 to 28 days, ranging in price from $150 to $900. (See the 7 schools listed under CO, ME, MN, NC, and OR.)

FLORIDA

Canoe Outpost Boys Camp, Rt. 1 Box 414-K, Valrico, FL 33594. Att.: Brad Scott. (813) 681-2666. (See also *Canoeing.*)

Canoe Outpost Boys Camps is a small (12 boys per session), personally supervised camping/canoeing program on the Suwannee River. It's designed for boys 10 to 15, with no canoeing experience necessary. After base-camp preparations the boys start paddling and travel 78 miles on the river. It's a 7-day camp, $139, and each boy keeps his paddle.

GEORGIA

Wilderness Southeast, Rt. 3, Box 619-L, Savannah, GA 31406. Att.: Dick Murlless. (912) 355-8008. (See also *Backpacking, Canoeing, Scuba Diving*—FL.)

Sponsored by the Georgia Conservancy, Savannah Science Museum, the Jacksonville Children's Museum and the Macon Museum of Arts and Science, Dick Murlless and his staff offer a number of trips for adventurous high school students, including river runs and backpacks, sea island base camps, a tropical ecology camp in the Florida Keys and turtle research on Georgia's Wassaw Island. "Active participation" is the focus of this environmental education program. Students become involved in a variety of projects designed to develop personal skills and environmental awareness."

Wolfcreek Wilderness, PO Box 596-W, Blairsville, GA 30512. Att.: Keith W. Evans. (404) 745-6460. (See also *Wilderness Living.*)

With an individualized approach to wilderness adventure (8 participants to 2 instructors), this private nonprofit educational organization teaches the basic skills of backpacking, white-water canoeing and rock climbing. The goal—to develop self-confidence and the freedom to appreciate a wilderness environment. Each 21-day program is entirely mobile, leaving Wolf Creek Lodge for the backwoods of Georgia, North Carolina and Alabama. "The challenge and excitement of these activities are real and involving," explains Keith Evans. "It's day-to-day living on a meaningful basis with others and yourself." The 3-week coed programs, June to August, are for 14 to 21-year-olds and cost $440.

HAWAII

Hawaii Bound School, PO Box 1500, Kailua, HI 96734. (808) 262-6988.

The beauty of Hawaii—rain forests, a 14,000-foot mountain, desert and sea coast—seldom varies through the year, making this school ideal for holiday times. Minimum age is 16 for 24-day standard courses, 12 for special 12-day summer courses, with no upper limit. You follow in the paths of the island's first inhabitants and find nourishment as they did in the fruit of the island and the fish of the sea. You backpack across a vast desert of lava, rappel down a mountainside, sleep in the lush rain forest, navigate an outrigger canoe, and learn to function alone. The cost is $25 to $35 a day, with 8 to 10 in a class under supervision of 2 instructors.

O.A.R.S., Inc., PO Box 67-G, Angels Camp, CA 95222. Att.: David Wendt. (209) 736-2924. Apr. & Dec. (See also *Float Trips*—CA.)

As the ultimate way to see Hawaii, OARS recommends 10-speed bikes. You don't have to carry gear—a truck does that—but you should be able to cover from 30 to 40 miles a day. Most nights are spent camping out. Some trips are for junior-senior high students, and others for college young adult groups. For 8 days, the price of $580 includes air fare from Los Angeles, bike shipment, food, camping and 2 nights' lodging. OARS also offers similar trips in the Caribbean.

IDAHO

Leonard Expeditions, PO Box 98, Stanley, ID 83278. Att.: Joe Leonard. (208) 774-3325. (See also *Kayaking, Ski Touring.*)

During Christmas and spring vacations, students from 9 to 12 years old, and 13 to 18, can learn a lot about how to cope in a winter environment. At his Youth Wilderness Camp in the Sawtooth National Forest, Joe Leonard gives training in building snow caves, safe winter travel, avalanche awareness, ski touring, route selection, map and compass, downhill skiing on touring skis and weather forecasting. They use his Hut System deep in the Idaho back country. In summer (minimum age, 7) the wilderness experience involves backpacking, camp setup and cleanup, fishing, cooking, climbing and kayaking. Maximum enjoyment and learning are the goals. Maximum 8 per group.

INDIANA

Canada by Canoe, Inc., Metamora, IN 47030. Att.: R. T. Ritz. (317) 647-5434.

Canada by Canoe is "a unique travel camp designed to open the sport of canoe camping to the beginning canoeist who, due to lack of equipment and knowledge, could not otherwise enjoy it." Open to boys and girls from 10 to 17, the 3-week trips begin with a bus ride to the Canadian wilderness for 300 miles of waterway. "One soon learns that compared to portaging, canoeing is really an efficient means of travel," Ritz comments. Participants also learn woodlore, view wildlife, and sometimes work their way up to becoming guides.

Grand Canyon Youth Expeditions, AZ.   Sea Education Association, MA.

MAINE

Hurricane Island Outward Bound School, PO Box 429, Rockland, ME 04841. (207) 594-5548.

Old salts and new salts mingle at this school off the rugged Maine coast, where the setting is so nautical you almost learn by osmosis. The curriculum includes ocean sailing, navigation, seamanship in 30-foot open pulling boats, emergency medical aid, rock climbing, rappeling and finally, an island solo. In winter the school hauls anchor inland for snowshoeing, cross-country skiing, map and compass reading and the warmth of snow caves. (For Outward Bound's headquarters, see CT.)

Maine Wilderness Canoe Basin, Springfield, ME 04487. Att.: Carl W. Selin. (207) 989-3636, ext. 631. (See also *Canoeing, Ski Touring, Snowmobiling.*)

With canoeing headquarters on Pleasant Lake in the Maine wilderness, and a sailing center on Deer Isle in Penobscot Bay, Captain Selin offers both fresh-water and salt-water activities to 10- to 18-year-olds. They have their choice of camping, canoeing, sailing, cycling, backpacking and kayaking in separate or combined programs. Instruction is thorough and intensive, with a camper/counselor ratio of 5 to 1. There are frequent starting dates through the summer. Most programs are for 2 weeks ($275), others up to 6 weeks ($775) or 8 weeks ($1,025).

St. Croix Voyageurs, Box A-197, China, ME 04926. Att.: George L. Dwelley. (207) 968-2434. Jul.–Sept. (See also *Canoeing.*)

Since 1938 the Dwelley family has been taking teenagers down the St. John, Allagash and Penobscot rivers. The main feature of the trips is thorough training in canoeing and camping that prepares them to be wilderness guides by the time they're in college—a skill that lands many of them summer jobs with Dwelley and other outfitters. They also learn much about the North Woods, and the multiple-use tradition in which recreation and lumbering are co-operatively developed. For 15 girls, 3 weeks $450; for 30 boys, 3 weeks, $450, or 7 weeks, $840.

MASSACHUSETTS

Earthwatch, 10 Juniper Rd., Box 127, Belmont, MA 02178. (617) 489-3030.

If you're 16 or older, you are eligible to join some really unique expeditions—a survey of Provincetown Harbor in Cape Cod, for instance, or excavations of Natural Trap in the Big Horn Mountains of Wyoming, observation of feral ponies of Assateague Island in Maryland or of racoons on St. Catherine's Island, Georgia. Earthwatch organizes research teams in the U.S. and abroad in groups of 20 for 2- or 3-week expeditions. Most fees (tax-deductible) are from $490 to $690.

Expedition Training Institute, Inc., Box 171, Prudential Center Station, Boston, MA 02199. Att.: Richard E. Enright, Jr. (617) 894-7674.

This unusual foundation was organized by members of The Explorers Club of New York to place high school and college students on 4- to 6-week field science research expeditions in the U.S. and abroad. It could be an underwater archaeological peak off the Aleutian Islands or a probe into Borneo's forests. The students share costs up to $450, plus fares to the research sites. Scholarships are available for advanced and graduate college students. The institute's newsletter gives fascinating details for expeditions involving archaeology, ecology, geology, marine biology and zoology.

Infinite Odyssey, (J), 14 Union Park St., Boston, MA 02118. Att.: Jenny Russell. (617) 542-0060. Jun.–Aug., 21–45 days.

This nonprofit organization conducts journeys in the western mountains and canyonlands of the U.S., and in Alaska, British Columbia and New England, which teach wilderness skills and build confidence. Trips vary with each area but include activities such as hiking, backpacking, camping, rock climbing, rafting, visits to Indian reservations, biking, sailing, canoeing and ski touring. They are open to a maximum of 12 participants per trip, 16 years and up, with 2 leaders for each group. Some secondary schools and colleges grant academic credit for Infinite Odyssey participation and limited financial aid is available, particularly for students who work to pay for their trip. Costs vary, from $710 for a 4-week exploratory trip in canyonlands of the Southwest (trip begins and ends in Farmington, NM), to $1,580 for 7 weeks in Alaska (from and to Seattle).

Keewaydin Wilderness Trips, Box 307G, Ashburnham, MA 01430. Att.: Abbott T. Fenn. (617) 827-5206.

This is the oldest tripping camp in America, established in 1893. In summer, Indian guides join groups of coeds or boys, 9 to a trip with 2 adult leaders, for 29 days of canoeing and 8 training and travel days in northern Quebec in the trapping grounds of the Cree Indians. Trips start with training at Lake Dunmore in Vermont before paddling the 350-mile wilderness route from the Hudson's Bay Post on Lake Mistassini. You bake your own bread, catch fish, paddle and pole on rivers and lakes, and are resupplied midway by plane. Minimum age is 15; cost. $925.

Sea Education Association, PO Box 6-AT, Church St., Woods Hole, MA 02543. Att.: Corwith Cramer. (617) 540-3954.

In sea semesters at the college level, accredited by Boston and Cornell universities and other colleges, SEA (a nonprofit organization) aims to increase the understanding of our oceanic environment. Teachers and visiting lecturers include nationally known scientists and marine policy experts. Intensive study during the shore session provides solid preparation in theory before apprenticeship at sea. For the sea study session, students sail aboard the 100-foot schooner *Westward* on a "demanding, rigorous expedition with hard work and few amenities." They help with research, data collection and processing. In the last 2 weeks each student, in rotation, assumes responsibility for all phases of ship operation and oceanographic laboratory activities. Six-week shore sessions are $950, and 6 weeks at sea in Atlantic or Caribbean waters are $2,050. SEA is open to 18-year-olds and up.

MINNESOTA

Bear Track Outfitting Co., Box 51, Grand Marais, MN 55604. Att.: David & Cathi Williams. (218) 387-1162. (See also *Backpacking, Canoeing, Ski Touring*.)

Isle Royal National Park, the Boundary Waters and the Canadian wilderness are the areas for a traveling camp that combines outdoor education with canoeing and backpacking. It's for people 11 to 17 years old. David Williams, a teacher, brings ecology together with history on these trips. You'll know a lot more about the Indians, fur traders and loggers as well as the wilderness when it's over. Contact Bear Track for dates and rates.

Minnesota Outward Bound School, 1055 E. Wayzata Blvd., Wayzata, MN 55391. (612) 473-5476.

There's water everywhere in the Quetico-Superior wilderness of Minnesota and Canada. You learn canoe rescues, portaging, night paddling, drownproofing and other techniques to navigate powerful white water. A winter course puts you on cross-country skis and teaches the teamwork for warm winter camping. (For Outward Bound's headquarters, see CT.)

NEW HAMPSHIRE

The Biking Expedition, Inc., RD 2, Box AG, Hillsboro, NH 03244. Att.: Tom Heavey. (603) 478-5783. (See also *Biking*.)

Tom and Susan Heavey have developed their favorite mode of travel into a program for teenagers with summer trips in New England, the Amish area, C&O Towpath, Wisconsin's biking trails, the Canadian Rockies, Pacific Northwest and abroad. The bicycle, they feel, provides the most satisfying opportunities for educational and adventurous travel. Outings of 24 to 41 days are led by two experienced adults. Teenagers from 13 to 17 pedal through varied scenes, attend summer theaters and festivals, ride a lobster boat or coastal ferry, explore museums and cheese factories, visit historic spots and picturesque villages, veiw spectacular mountains and wilderness wildlife, and sometimes combine biking with hiking, canoeing, cruising or train rides. Costs vary: 24 days, $490; 31 days, $625–$685; 36–41 days, $840–$852.

Dartmouth Outward Bound Center, PO Box 50, Hanover, NH 03755. (603) 646-3359.

You're back on the campus as part of Dartmouth College. But the classrooms are in the White Mountains and Connecticut Lakes regions of New Hampshire, and in Vermont, Maine and Nova Scotia. There is lots of cycling, rock climbing and rappeling, and an adult leadership course with emphasis on first aid and emergency care. Winter focuses on snowshoeing, ski expeditions, camping and snow shelters. (For Outward Bound's headquarters, see CT.)

North Country Mountaineering, Inc., Box 951, Hanover, NH 03755. Att.: Steve Schneider. (603) 643-3299 or (212) 989-4417.

NCMI is a professional guide service that sponsors climbing trips for teenagers (14 to 20) to Colorado, Washington, South Dakota, Wyoming, California and abroad. With no more than 3 participants per guide, trips last from 1 to 6 weeks, and cost from $275 to $1,395. Most trips (an ascent of Mt. Rainier, for example) require stamina and determination, "but no one will be pushed beyond his or her abilities," Steve Schneider promises. He has made many rock and ice ascents, has taught rock climbing and winter mountaineering, and is co-author (with his sister, Anne) of *The Climbers Sourcebook*. Also climbing, summer and winter mountaineering and ski touring for adults.

NEW MEXICO

Cottonwood Gulch Foundation, PO Box 969, Thoreau, NM 87323. Att.: Thomas M. Billings, Jr. (505) 862-7503. Aug.–Jun.: PO Box 40451, Indianapolis, IN 46240. (317) 896-3842.

In the fabulous Four Corners area of the West, groups of 26 boys or girls travel in "suburbans," with truck support, on 7-week explorations of mountains, canyons, deserts and Indian country. They investigate, interview, photograph and record their observations. They meet prospectors, Indians and frontier characters, from whom they learn about plants and animals, fossil-bearing rocks and minerals. Most of their nomadic camps are set up in spectacular unspoiled wilderness. The Prairie Trek Expedition is for boys and the Turquoise Trail Expedition for girls, each 7 weeks, $920. The Little Outfit is for younger boys, 6 weeks, $550. The nonprofit foundation started its programs in 1926.

Southwest Outward Bound School, PO Box 2840, Santa Fe, NM 87501. (505) 988-5573.

This school takes you into alpine meadows rising above stark deserts and rivers flowing through timeless canyons. There's desert ecology, emergency medical aid, rock climbing, rappeling, expedition planning—and then a solo. A winter course highlight is kayaking in the Sea of Cortez (Baja California, Mexico) in addition to backpacking in New Mexico and Texas. (For Outward Bound's headquarters, see CT.)

Wilderness Experiences for Young People, Inc., PO Box 12586, Albuquerque, NM 87105. Att.: Jim Stewart. (505) 831-1941.

The purpose of this nonprofit organization is "to develop an awareness of the intricacies and interrelationships of the natural world, man's dependence on it, and his role in preserving it." For many of the 9- to 17-year-olds on these treks in the Pecos, Gila and Weminuche wilderness areas, it's a revelation that you can live for a week with nothing but what you carry on your back! Jim Stewart, a certified teacher, has trekked all through the Rockies and is an experienced outdoorsman, pilot, instructor of sport parachuting, photographer and bird watcher. Students learn many skills, from map reading and route finding to rock climbing and campcraft. The courses are from 5 to 21 days, with 6 to 10 in each group. The rate is $25 per day.

NORTH CAROLINA

Mondamin Wilderness Adventures, PO Box 8, Tuxedo, NC 28784. (704) 693-7446. (See also *Wilderness Living*.)

Viewing education as "growth" and adventure as "activity on one's personal frontiers," Mondamin's brother and sister camps offer 7- to 17-year-olds a nonregimented program emphasizing lifetime activities—swimming, sailing, canoeing, rock climbing, horseback riding and tennis. The camps' philosophy is that "resourcefulness, self-discipline, give-and-take, initiative and self-direction are more important than scores, or skills themselves." Mondamin also has a series of 3- to 5-day trips and workshops for 14-year-olds and up—clinics in white-water canoeing, counselor backpacking and tripping, and riding and wilderness back-packing/rafting trips in the Great Smokies.

Mountaineer Travel Camp, The Asheville School, Asheville, NC 28806. Att.: Pop Hollandsworth. (704) 254-6345.

Teenagers can start learning the ropes in the Appalachian Mountains and work their way out West to the Grand Tetons by their fifteenth birthdays. Jim "Pop" Hollandsworth has set up the camp so that the minimum age for Appalachian campers is 12 years. They concentrate on backpacking, caving, canoeing, kayaking and rock climbing. The western trippers must be 15 and up in order to join mountain climbing expeditions from Jackson, Wyoming. The trips run anywhere from 2 to 4 weeks, $20 a day in the East, $32 in the West.

North Carolina Outward Bound School, PO Box 817, Morganton, NC 28655. (704) 437-6112.

From the southern Appalachians and Great Smoky Mountains you backpack into green forests and laurel-covered ridges. It's the teamwork of white-water canoeing, climbing, rappeling and mountain-rescue techniques. And in winter, you adapt to 60-degree weather changes while camping, climbing, caving and canoeing. (For Outward Bound's headquarters, see CT.)

OREGON

Northwest Outward Bound School, 0110 Bancroft St. S.W., Portland, OR 97201. (503) 243-1993.

This is a mobile course, ever on the move through the North Cascades of Washington and the Sawtooth Wilderness of Idaho—mountaineering, rock climbing, rappeling, backpacking, first aid, fire fighting and running wild rivers. In winter you bivouac in the snow or caves, cross-country ski, or snowshoe or—weather permitting—climb a major peak. (For Outward Bounds's headquarters, see CT.)

Northwest Whitewater Excursions, 1726 Mill St., Eugene, OR 97401. Att.: Galand Haas. (503) 343-0450. (See also *Float Trips*.)

For young anglers Galand Haas has a 5-day fishing camp originating at his wilderness camp near Florence. The program includes deep-sea fishing, bay fishing, river fishing, crabbing, clam digging, lake fishing, jetty fishing, and tying and fishing with flies. You also learn how to take care of boats and equipment—and how to clean fish.

Whitewater Youth Camps, Inc., 12120 S.W. Douglas, Portland, OR 97225. Att.: Mike Carey. (503) 646-8849. (See also *Float Trips*—Whitewater Guide Trips.)

You begin by learning the techniques of handling an inflatable kayak in calm water, and soon become an expert in boatsmanship and "reading" the water. These camps, from 1 to 6 days, are for 14- to 19-year-olds on the Clackamas, John Day, Deschutes and Grande Ronde rivers. Days with fishing, hiking and exploring end with campfire cooking and sleeping under the stars. Rates range from $9 for a day on the Clackamas to $125 for 6 days on the Grande Ronde.

VERMONT

Killington Adventure, Killington, VT 05751. Att.: Dave Langlois. (802) 422-3333 (or 422-3139 evenings). Jun.-Aug. (See also *Backpacking*.)

Trips for teens teach living and traveling in the out-of-doors, with a little rock climbing for those interested. A 3-week trek for experienced backpackers ends with a 36-hour solo. Rates: 2 weeks, $260; 3 weeks, $345. For a 1-week leadership school: $130, plus $40 for college credit, if desired. There is also a 3-week canoe camp for 16- to 18-year-olds; a tennis school (2-day weekends, $130; 5 days midweek, $325); a 1-week wilderness trail camp for families (adult, $170; child 1-17, $115); and freestyle camps for 12 years and over (5 days, $285) with aerials, stunt ballet, modern dance, trampolines and gymnastics.

Outdoor Travel Camps, Inc., Coffee House Rd., Killington, VT 05751. Att.: Victor & Jane Kelina. (802) 422-3532.

Teenagers (13 to 16) choose between East and West. The 4-week New England camp finds campers biking on Martha's Vineyard, learning about whaling, ecology and geology. Or hiking in the White Mountains, exploring caves in Vermont, or clamming on the coast of Maine. Out West, they spend 8 weeks with naturalists and rangers in national parks, attend rock-climbing school, explore mammoth caves, fossil hunt and take a raft trip down the wild Snake River. For 20 participants, the eastern camp is $680, and the western outing, $1,280. Camps offer optional credit in natural sciences.

Student Hosteling Program, Box A, Maple Hill, Rochester, VT 05767. Att.: Ted Lefkowitz. (802) 767-3297.

Student Hosteling Program expeditions "are not for everyone," as these folks repeatedly stress. "SHP trips," they tell us, "are emotionally and physically demanding and require self-discipline and a reasonable level of maturity. No alcohol, pot or drugs are allowed." For those in grades 8 through 12 who would like to meet the challenge, SHP offers 2- to 6-week nontourist biking, hiking and camping trips. They use campsites, hostels and mountain huts, buy food at local markets and cook their own meals. The coed excursions, 14 to 45 days, travel in New England, the Canadian Maritimes and Rockies, the Pacific Northwest and abroad, averaging 25 to 40 miles on travel days. "It's a close, intense group experience," says Ted Lefkowitz. "Teenagers learn about the world, the beauty of life, and about themselves through experiences of their own making." Participants must bring a good 10-speed bike. SHP provides other equipment. Trips begin in Rochester, Vermont, and end at airports.

WASHINGTON

Northwest Alpine Guide Service, Inc., 1628 Ninth Ave. #2, Seattle, WA 98101. Att.: Linda Bradley Miller. (206) 622-6074. (See also *Backpacking, Mountaineering, Canoeing, Float Trips, Ski Touring, Wilderness Living.*)

One- or 2-week treks in the Cascade Mountains—"Youth Challenge," NAGS calls them—are far more than just hikes. Each day there's a class session to teach backpacking, progressing into off-trail alpine travel. Students learn outdoors skills that provide a lifetime of recreational pleasure. The group is limited to 10, which allows close relationships with leaders who give expert guidance. Cost: 7 days, $125; 14 days, $225.

WYOMING

National Outdoor Leadership School, PO Box AA, Dept. K, Lander, WY 82520. (307) 332-4381. (See also *Mountaineering, Ski Touring, Wilderness Living.*)

"Take a long look at Lander as you drive out; you won't see civilization again for a month." That's the NOLS promise. And the first NOLS rule: "Expect the unexpected." As the course progresses, they say, two miracles will occur: You'll get stronger and your food bag will get lighter. And you can count on the environment to pose new problems each day. NOLS emphasis is on leadership, mountaineering, low-impact camping and outdoor education on most of these rugged trips, while some also feature biology, geology, speleology, ski touring and many other aspects of outdoor life. Students trek the Wind River, Absaroka, Beartooth, Uinta and Teton mountains, and travel to Alaska and to Baja for courses ranging from 15 days to 3½ months. All programs offer college credits. The minimum age for some of these rugged trips is 13 to 15, and 16 to 19 on others, with no top limit. "The best students are not the strongest ones," the people at NOLS say, "but the ones who care most about the wilderness and each other."

Siggins Triangle X Ranch, Cody, WY 82414. Att.: Stan & Lila Siggins. (307) 587-2031. (See also *Pack Trips.*)

The boys and girls who participate in this ranch and wilderness experience become known as "Shoshonees." With riding instruction, breakfast rides and all-day trips, the emphasis is on horses. There's also swimming, hiking, arts and crafts, dances and more. An 8-day pack trip over 50 miles of lush, pristine wilderness in Yellowstone Park is a highlight, and a gymkhana (games on horseback) climaxes the program. It's for 11- to 16-year-olds, with a 10-day riding clinic in June, $250; a 1-month camp program, $759; and Yellowstone Park pack trip, $425.

Skinner Brothers, Box B-G, Pinedale, WY 82941. Att.: Monte Skinner. (307) 367-2270. (See also *Pack Trips.*)

Each summer the Skinners run a wilderness school for boys and girls in 1-month sessions. One is a graduate and leadership session. It's a wide-ranging and practical course—riding and pack trips, mountaineering, modern and primitive fishing, animal habits and habitats, survival and camping techniques. Advanced subjects include organization, equipment and logistics for pack and alpine travel. In one program kids construct a log raft and float down a section of the Green River. Glacier travel, winter camping and a 24-day expedition in the Gannett Peak region are part of the mountaineering program. Each session is $980.

Yellowstone Wilderness Guides, Crossed Sabres Ranch, Box Z, Wapiti, WY 82450. Att.: Lee Hanchett. (307) 587-3750. (See also *Backpacking.*)

"If you'd like to explore Yellowstone National Park and surrounding wilderness areas, sign on with us for 1 or 2 weeks," says Lee Hanchett. "We trek through countryside that's much as it was when Jim Bridger and John Colter 'walked the mountains to the Yellowstone' over 150 years ago." Young explorers (14 through 19) learn the skills and discipline to be at home in the back country on these safe, fun and challenging explorations that "bring to light what discovery and adventure are all about."

NATIONAL—U.S.

American Youth Hostels, Inc., National Campus, Delaplane, VA 22025. (703) 592-3271. (See also *Biking.*)

AYH members 14 years or older are eligible to join cycling, backpacking, hiking, canoeing, skiing, sailing or horseback riding trips that this nonprofit organization and its 29 local councils sponsor in the U.S. each year. (See *Biking*: AYH.) For excursions to Hawaii or abroad, the minimum age is 16. These are coed groups, usually 7 to 9 people, who travel with trained leaders and spend nights at hostels. Wherever possible AYH arranges balanced coed groups of about the same age.

BRITISH COLUMBIA

Western Outdoor Adventures, Ltd., 16115 32nd Ave., White Rock, B.C. V4B 4Z5. Att.: Frank Lockwood. (604) 531-3969. (See also *Jeeping, Ski Touring, Wilderness Living.*)

For boys 14 and over there's a western adventure camp in the remote coastal wilderness of British Columbia where they explore, learn about outdoor travel and survival skills, study nature and swim, fish and hike. All-inclusive from Vancouver, 12 days, $350.

ONTARIO

Headwaters, PO Box 288, Temagami, Ont. POH 2HO. Att.: Hugh & Carin Stewart. No tel.; send telegram. (See also *Ski Touring, Wilderness Living.*)

If you've done some canoe tripping, you qualify for 3 weeks of thorough instruction in wilderness travel by canoe. You spend 2 days planning the trip, selecting menus and organizing the equipment. Then you're off for 16 to 18 days of upstream and downstream work on the upper Lady Evelyn or Makobe River, or some exploratory traveling opening up new routes. Trips are for coeds, 14 to 16 years; cost, $500.

Organizations/Reservations

There are many ways to use this book. One is to choose your trip and get in touch directly with the outfitter or service for further information and for your reservation. You can arrange a custom (or charter) trip planned especially for your family or group, or you can inquire about group departure dates for the trip you want, and then make your individual reservation to join that group of trekkers.

These same outfitters also work with various clubs, associations and booking agencies specializing in adventurous travel, and if you prefer you can make your arrangements through them instead. Many such services have come to life in recent years with the surge of interest in outdoor vacations. Others are long-established associations with decades of experience in developing and sponsoring successful treks.

Best known among the latter are three conservation-oriented nonprofit organizations which schedule trips for their members in wilderness areas throughout the United States (and in some areas abroad). They are: American Forestry Association, 1319 18th Street N.W., Washington, DC 20036, (202) 467-5810, known especially for its program of pack trips; Sierra Club, 530 Bush Street, San Francisco, CA 94108, (415) 981-8643, which offers dozens of group departures for all kinds of adventurous treks; and Wilderness Society, 4260 East Evans, Denver, CO 80222, (303) 758-2266, with emphasis on the educational aspects of wilderness excursions. The extensive programs of these organizations include a great many horsepack trips, hiking, backpacking, rafting and canoe trips; also cycling, ski touring, underwater exploration and special purpose trips, a few of which provide college course credits.

A new service backed by years of experience is our own—Adventure Guides, Inc., 36 East 57th Street, New York, NY 10022, (212) 355-6334. AGI is the compiler of four editions of this book (since 1972) and many editions of its companion publication about farm and ranch vacations. With this expertise, AGI's reservations service includes many excursions described in these pages as well as combination trips—for example, a pack trip or river run (or both) neatly blended with a dude ranch in a single vacation package.

There is so much information available today—from friends who are veteran trekkers, from the outfitters themselves from associations and a multitude of booking services—that no longer is adventurous travel just something to dream about. It's easy to arrange. Try it!

River Runs and Outfitters

Anyone who has run the full length of the Grand Canyon, is about to float Cataract, and plans next year on Hells Canyon, speaks a language known to all river rats.

The references, of course, are to the 277-mile, eight- to ten-day trip through the Grand Canyon of the Colorado River in Arizona, four or five days through Cataract Canyon of the Colorado in Utah's Canyonlands National Park, or two to three days through the 6,500-foot-deep Hells Canyon of the Snake River south of Lewiston, Idaho.

To the river runner, these and other excursions are as familiar as a cruise to Catalina Island for the Californian, to Mackinac for the Midwesterner, or to Nantucket for the New Englander. But to the uninitiated in river travel, most rivers and canyons are names only, unrelated to any geographical concept of the region through which they flow.

The following pages list more than 150 different river runs and the professional outfitters and guides who are equipped to take you on them. For more information about each of their services, please turn to the chapter "Float Trips," page 131.

Alaska (central)—Alatna, Koyukuk and Yukon rivers

Alaska Wilderness Riv. Trips—AK   ECHO—CA   Northwest Alpine Guide Service—WA

Alaska (southern)—Alagnak, Chilikadrotna, Copper, Mulchatna, Talchulitna and Togiak rivers

Alaska Raft Adventures—AK   Alaska Wilderness Exped.—AK   Alaska Wilderness Riv. Trips—AK
Mountain Guides & Outfitters—CO

Alaska (southeastern)—Alsek, Stikine and Tatshensheni rivers, Atlin, Bennett and Tagish lakes

Alaska Wilderness Exped.—AK   Klondike Safaris—AK   OARS—CA

Alaska (northern)—Kobuk, Noatak and Wild rivers

Alaska Raft Adventures—AK   Colorado Riv. & Trail Exped.—UT   Northwest Alpine Guide Service—WA
Alaska Wilderness Exped.—AK   ECHO—CA   Sourdough Outfitters—AK

Arizona—Grand Canyon of the Colorado River

American Riv. Touring Assoc.—CA   Grand Canyon Youth Exped.—AZ   OARS—CA
Canyon Country Riv. Adventures—UT   (See *Youth Adventures*.)   Outdoors Unlimited—CA
Canyoneers—AZ   Harris Boat Trips—UT   Sanderson Riv. Exped—AZ
Colorado Riv. & Trail Exped.—UT   Hatch Riv. Exped.—UT   Tour West—UT
Georgie's Royal Riv. Rats—AZ   Henry & Grace Falany's White Water   Western Riv. Exped.—UT
Grand Canyon Exped.—UT   Riv. Exped.—CA   Wilderness World—CA
Grand Canyon Dories—CA   Moki Mac Riv. Exped.—UT   Wonderland Exped.—UT

California—American, Stanislaus and Tuolumne rivers (also East Carson, Eel, Klamath, Merced and Sacramento)

AdvenTours—CA   Orange Torpedo Trips—OR   Sundance Exped.—OR
American Riv. Touring   Outdoors Unlimited—CA   Wilderness Water Ways—CA
Assoc.—CA   Riv. Adventures West—CA   Wilderness World—CA
ECHO—CA   Riv. Rat Raft Rentals—CA   William McGinnis' Whitewater
OARS—CA   Riv. Trips Unlimited—OR   Voyages/Riv. Exploration—CA
Zephyr Riv. Exped.—CA

Colorado—Dolores River

American Riv. Touring Assoc.—CA   Fastwater Exped.—UT   OARS—CA
American Wilderness Co.—CO   Four Corners Exped.—CO   Outlaw Trails—UT
Colorado Rivers—CO   Grand Canyon Youth Exped.—AZ   Rocky Mt. Riv. Exped.—CO
Colorado Riv. & Trail Exped.—UT   Holiday Riv. Exped.—UT   Sundance Riv. Exped.—AZ
ECHO—CA   Internatl. Aquatic Adventures—CO   Tag-A-Long Tours—UT
Mountain Guides & Outfitters—CO   Wilderness Aware—CO

Colorado—Animas, Arkansas, Cache La Poudre, Colorado (Upper), North Platte, Rio Grande, Roaring Fork and White rivers

Adventure Bound—CO   Internatl. Aquatic Adventures—CO   Rocky Mt. Riv. Exped.—CO
Anderson Riv. Exped.—CO   Mountain Guides & Outfitters—CO   Snowmass Whitewater—CO
American Wilderness Co.—CO   Rancho del Rio—CO   Timber Travels—CO
Canyoneers—AZ   Richard Bros.—WY   Viking Riv. Exped.—CO
Colorado Rivers—CO   Riv. Runners—CO   Wild Water West Riv. Excursions—CO
Four Corners Exped.—CO   Rocky Mt. Exped.—CO   Wilderness Aware—CO
Wilderness Sports—CO

Georgia—Chattahoochee

Southeastern Exped.—GA

Idaho—Hells Canyon of the Snake River

Don Merrell's Northwest Whitewater   Hells Canyon Navigation—OR   Snake Riv. Packers—OR
Exped.—OR   Idaho Adventures—ID   Whitewater Guide Trips—OR
ECHO—CA   Northwest Whitewater Excursion—OR   Wilderness Riv. Outfitters &
Grand Canyon Dories—CA   Primitive Area Float Trips—ID   Trail Exped.—ID
Hells Canyon Guide Service—OR   Snake Riv. Outfitters—ID   Wilderness World—CA

Idaho—Salmon River (Main and/or Middle Fork)

American Riv. Touring Assoc.—CA   Frontier Exped.—ID   Nicholson & Sons Float Trips—ID
American Wilderness Co.—CO   Grand Canyon Dories—CA   Norm & Bill Guth—ID
Bob Smith's Salmon Riv. Boat Tours—   Happy Hollow Camps—ID   Northwest Whitewater Excursions—OR
ID   Hatch Riv. Exped.—UT   OARS—CA
Canyon Country Riv. Adventures—UT   Idaho Adventures—ID   Orange Torpedo Trips—OR
Dean Helfrich Guide & Outfitter—OR   Ken Smith's Middle Fork Riv. Exped.—   Outdoors Unlimited—CA
ECHO—CA   ID   Primitive Area Float Trips—ID
Eldon Handy Riv. Exped.—ID   Nez Perce Outfitters & Guides—ID   Prince E. Helfrich & Sons—OR

Riv. Adventures West—CA
Riv. Trips Unlimited—OR
Salmon Riv. Lodge—ID
Snake Riv. Outfitters—ID

Snake Riv. Packers—OR
Sun Valley Riv. Tours—ID
Teton Exped.—ID
Tour West—UT
Western Riv. Exped.—UT

Whitewater Guide Trips—OR
Wilderness Riv. Outfitters &
   Trail Exped.—ID
Wilderness World—CA
World Wide Riv. Exped.—UT

Idaho—Selway River
American Riv. Touring Assoc.—CA

Hatch Riv. Exped.—UT

Primitive Area Float Trips—ID
Western Riv. Exped.—UT

Idaho—Blackfoot, Bruneau, Lochsa, Snake (not Hells Canyon) and Teton rivers
Dean Helfrich Guide & Outfitter—OR
OARS—CA

Prince E. Helfrich & Sons—OR
Sun Valley Riv. Tours—ID

Teton Exped.—ID
Wilderness Riv. Outfitters &
   Trail Exped.—ID

Maine—Allagash, Kennebec (upper), Penobscot (west branch) and Dead rivers
Maine Whitewater Trips—ME

Northern Whitewater Exped.—ME

Minnesota—St. Croix River
American Riv. Touring Assoc.—CA

New Jersey—Delaware River and Barnegat Bay
Big Apple Exped.—NY

Montana—Upper Missouri and Judith rivers
Halter Ranch—MT

Missouri Riv. Cruises—MT

New York—Upper and lower Hudson River, Long Island Sound
Big Apple Exped.—NY

Canyon Cruises, Antlers Inn—PA

North Carolina—Chattooga, French, Broad and Nantahala rivers
Nantahala Outdoor Center—NC

Smoky Mt. Riv. Exped.—NC

Southeastern Exped.—GA
Wildwater—SC

Oregon—Owyhee River
American Riv. Touring Assoc.—CA
Dean Helfrich Guide & Outfitter—OR
Don Merrell's Northwest Whitewater
   Exped.—OR
ECHO—CA
Grand Canyon Dories—CA
Hells Canyon Guide Service—OR

Idaho Adventures—ID
Lute Jerstad Adventures—OR
Northwest Whitewater Excursions—OR
OARS—CA
Primitive Area Float Trips—ID
Prince E. Helfrich & Sons—OR
Rivers Northwest—WA
Rogue Excursions Unlimited—OR

Sun Valley Riv. Tours—ID
Sundance Exped.—OR
Whitewater Guide Trips—OR
Wilderness Riv. Outfitters & Trail
   Exped.—ID
Wilderness World—CA
William McGinnis' Whitewater
   Voyages/Riv. Exploration—CA

Oregon—Rogue River
AdvenTours—CA
American Riv. Touring Assoc.—CA
American Wilderness Co.—CO
Dean Helfrich Guide & Outfitter—OR
ECHO—CA

Lute Jerstad Adventures—OR
OARS—CA
Orange Torpedo Trips—OR
Outdoors Unlimited—CA
Prince E. Helfrich & Sons—OR
Riv. Trips Unlimited—OR

Rogue Excursions Unlimited—OR
Rogue Riv. Raft Trips—OR
Sundance Exped.—OR
Whitewater Guide Trips—OR
Wilderness Water Ways—CA
Wilderness World—CA

Oregon—Deschutes, Grand Ronde, Illinois, John Day, McKenzie, Metrolius, Minan, Umpqua and Willamette rivers
American Riv. Touring Assoc.—CA
Dean Helfrich Guide & Outfitter—OR
Don Merrell's Northwest Whitewater
   Exped.—OR
ECHO—CA
Grand Canyon Dories—CA

Lute Jerstad Adventures—OR
Northwest Whitewater Excursions—OR
OARS—CA
Orange Torpedo Trips—OR
Prince E. Helfrich & Sons—OR
Riv. Trips Unlimited—OR

Rivers Northwest—WA
Sundance Exped.—OR
Whitewater Guide Trips—OR
Wilderness Water Ways—CA
Wilderness World—CA
William McGinnis' Whitewater
   Voyages/Riv. Exploration—CA

Pennsylvania—Youghiogheny and other PA rivers
Canyon Cruises, Antlers Inn—PA

Laurel Highlands Riv. Tours—PA
Mt. Streams & Trails Outfitters—PA

White Water Adventurers—PA
Wilderness Voyageurs—PA

Pennsylvania—Lehigh River
Pocono Whitewater—PA

Whitewater Challengers—PA

Tennessee—Hiwassee, Nolichucky and Ocoee rivers
Hiwassee Float Service—TN

Wildwater—SC

Texas—Rio Grande and Guadalupe River
AdvenTours—CA
American Riv. Touring Assoc.—CA

Outlaw Trails—UT
Texas Canoe Trails—TX

Wilderness Aware—CO
Wilderness World—CA

Colorado Rivers—CO
OARS—CA

Villa de la Miña Rio Grande
Riv. Trips—TX

William McGinnis' Whitewater
Voyages/Riv. Exploration—CA
Wonderland Exped.—UT

Utah—Cataract Canyon of the Colorado River

Adventure Bound—CO
American Riv. Touring Assoc.—CA
American Wilderness Co.—CO
Canyon Country Riv. Adventures—UT
Colorado Riv. & Trail Exped.—UT

Hatch Riv. Exped.—UT
Holiday Riv. Exped.—UT
Moki Mac Riv. Exped.—UT
OARS—CA
Outlaw Trails—UT
Red Rock Riv. Runners—UT

Rivers Northwest—WA
Tag-A-Long Tours—UT
Tour West—UT
Western Riv. Exped.—UT
Wonderland Exped.—UT
World Wide Riv. Exped.—UT

Utah—Desolation and Gray canyons (Green River Wilderness) of the Green River

Adventure Bound—CO
Adventure Riv. Exped.—UT
American Riv. Touring Assoc.—CA
American Wilderness Co.—CO
Canyon Country Riv. Adventures—UT
Canyoneers—AZ
Colorado Riv. & Trail Exped.—UT
ECHO—CA

Fastwater Exped.—UT
Grand Canyon Dories—CA
Harris Boat Trips—UT
Hatch Riv. Exped.—UT
Holiday Riv. Exped.—UT
Moki Mac Riv. Exped.—UT
Mountain Guides & Outfitters—CO
OARS—CA

Outlaw Trails—UT
Rocky Mt. Riv. Exped.—CO
Tag-A-Long Tours—UT
Wild & Scenic—AZ
Wilderness Riv. Outfitters &
Trail Exped.—ID
Wonderland Exped.—UT
World Wide Riv. Exped.—UT

Utah—Dinosaur National Monument on the Green and Yampa rivers

AdvenTours—CA
Adventure Bound—CO
Adventure Riv. Exped.—UT

American Riv. Touring Assoc.—CA
American Wilderness Co.—CO
Colorado Riv. & Trail Exped.—UT

Hatch Riv. Exped.—UT
Holiday Riv. Exped.—UT
Wonderland Exped.—UT
World Wide Riv. Exped.—UT

Utah—San Juan River

Canyon Country Riv. Adventures—UT
Canyoneers—AZ
Colorado Rivers—CO

Fastwater Exped.—UT
Grand Canyon Youth Exped.—AZ
OARS—CA

Tag-A-Long Tours—UT
Wild & Scenic—AZ
Wonderland Exped.—UT

Utah—Westwater Canyon of the Colorado River, also Labyrinth/Stillwater canyons

Adventure Bound—CO
Adventure Riv. Exped.—UT
American Riv. Touring Assoc.—CA
American Wilderness Co.—CO
Canyon Country Riv. Adventures—UT

Colorado Riv. & Trails Exped.—UT
ECHO—CA
Holiday Riv. Exped.—UT
Moki Mac Riv. Exped.—UT
Mountain Guides and Outfitters—CO

Outlaw Trails—UT
Red Rock Riv. Runners—UT
Rocky Mt. Riv. Exped.—CO
Tag-A-Long Tours—UT
Western Riv. Exped.—UT
World Wide Riv. Exped.—UT

Virginia and West Virginia—Shenandoah River

Blue Ridge Outfitters—WV

Washington—Columbia and 13 other WA rivers

Northwest Alpine Guide Service—WA   Pacific Northwest Float Trips—WA

Rivers Northwest—WA

West Virginia—Cheat River

Appalachian Wildwaters—OH

Cheat Riv. Outfitters—WV

Mt. Streams & Trails Outfitters—PA
White Water Adventurers—PA

West Virginia—Bluestone, Cacapon, Dry Fork, Gauley, Greenbriar, New and Shavers Fork rivers

Appalachian Wildwaters—OH

Mt. Riv. Tours—WV
Mt. Streams & Trails Outfitters—PA

New Riv. Adventures—WV
Wildwater Exped. Unlimited—WV

Wisconsin—Flambeau, Menomonee, Peshtigo and Wolf rivers

American Riv. Touring Assoc.—CA

Herb's Wolf Riv. Raft Rental—WI
Riv. Forest Rafts & Campgrounds—WI

Roaring Rapids Raft Co.—WI
Wolf Riv. Lodge—WI

Wyoming—Snake River above and below Jackson

See list on pages 162–163.

Wyoming—East Fork, Green, North Platte and Shoshone rivers

Intl. Aquatic Adventures—CO
Richard Bros.—WY

Rocky Mt. Riv. Exped.—CO
Shoshone Riv. Float—WY

Viking Riv. Exped.—CO
Wild Water West Riv. Excursions—CO
Wilderness Aware—CO

British Columbia—Chilcotin, Chilko, Fraser and Thompson rivers

American Riv. Touring Assoc.—CA
Canadian Riv. Exped.—BC

Cascade Riv. Holidays—BC
Kumsheen Raft Adventures—BC

Western Tours—BC
Whitewater Adventures—BC

British Columbia—Stikine, Upper Peace and other BC rivers

Canadian Riv. Exped.—BC

ECHO—CA

McCook & Furniss Kechika
Range Outfitters—BC

Manitoba—Berens, Pigeon and Poplar rivers
North Country Riv. Trips—Man.

Northwest Territories—Coppermine and Nahanni rivers
North-West Exped.—Alta.

Yukon Territory—Fortymile, Klondike, Stewart, Yukon and other YT rivers
Yukon Rafting & Wilderness Travel— YT   Yukon Wilderness Unlimited—YT

Mexico—Usumacinta, Balsas, Chac and 10 other rivers in Mexico and Central America
Mexican & Central American   Nantahala Outdoor Center—NC   Wilderness World—CA
   Rafting Exped.—Mexico   Texas Canoe Trails—TX

Bibliography

I ON FOOT

Bridge, Raymond. *America's Backpacking Book.* New York: Charles Scribner's Sons, 1976. Pap., illus. Hefty, up-to-date volume on all aspects of ecological backpacking.
Casewit, Curtis, W. and Pownall, Dick. *The Mountaineering Book: An Invitation to Climbing.* Philadelphia: J.B. Lippincott Co., 1968. The ABCs with appendixes on clubs, schools, thumbnail descriptions of areas in U.S. and Canada.
Fletcher, Colin. *New Complete Walker.* New York: Alfred A. Knopf, 1974. Illus. Chock-full of vital, current info for hikers and backpackers.
Halliday, William. *American Caves and Caving: Techniques, Pleasures and Safeguards of Modern Cave Exploring.* New York: Harper & Row, 1974. Illus. Comprehensive study of American caves, techniques and equipment by director of Western Speleological Survey.
Kelsey, Robert J. *Walking in the Wild: The Complete Guide to Hiking and Backpacking.* New York: Funk & Wagnalls, 1974. Pap., illus. Thorough guide to going solo or with others.
Kinmont, Vikki and Axcell, Claudia. *Simple Foods for the Pack.* San Francisco, CA: Sierra Club Books, 1976. Pap. 175 trail-tested recipes using natural, inexpensive ingredients.
MacInnes, Hamish. *International Mountain Rescue Handbook.* New York: Charles Scribner's Sons, 1972. Pap., illus. Highly authoritative text on hazards, survival, transporting injured.
Mountaineering: The Freedom of the Hills, 3rd ed. Mountaineers. Illus. *The* climber's text.
Rossit, Edward A. *Snow Camping and Mountaineering.* New York: Funk & Wagnalls, 1974. Pap., illus. Cold-weather camping in comfort: clothing, equipment, snow/ice travel, hunting.
Schneider, Anne and Steven. *The Climber's Sourcebook.* Garden City, NY: Doubleday & Co., 1976. Pap. Extensive, state-by-state directory of schools, guide services, clubs, camps, expeditions and manufacturers by co-founders of North Country Mountaineering, Inc.

II BY HORSE

Davis, Francis W. *Horse Packing in Pictures.* New York: Charles Scribner's Sons, 1975. Illus. A veteran horseman's captioned line drawings on everything involved in horse packing.
Dickerman, Pat. *Farm, Ranch and Country Vacations.* New York: Adventure Guides, Inc. Pap., illus. Most ranches listed include pack trips in their vacation packages.
Merrill, Bill. *Vacationing with Saddle and Packhorse.* New York: Arco Publishing Co., 1976. Illus. Indispensable advice for horse packing and trekking, from start to finish.

III ON WHEELS

Browder, Sue. *The American Biking Atlas and Touring Guide.* New York: Workman Publishing Co., 1974. Pap., illus. Unique book mapping 150 tours throughout U.S. and Canada.
DeLong, Fred. *DeLong's Guide to Bicycles and Bicycling.* Philadelphia, PA: Chilton Book Co., 1974. Illus. Comprehensive reference covering construction, repair, safety—much more.
Sloane, Eugene A. *The New Complete Book of Bicycling.* New York: Simon & Schuster. Authoritative, all-around source of info on bikes and biking; heart of the book is maintenance.
Zern, Ed, *Your Land, Your Jeep and You.* Detroit, MI: American Motors Corp. Ecology-conscious jeeping.

IV BY BOAT

Bowditch, Nathaniel. *Bowditch for Yachtsmen: Piloting.* New York: David McKay Co., 1976. Illus. Up-to-date reference for skippers of small sail and power vessels.

Chapman, Charles F. *Piloting, Seamanship and Small Boat Handling.* New York: Hearst Corp., 1976. Illus. Encyclopedia on boating, with info fitting needs of students in courses offered by U.S. Power Squadron, U.S. Coast Guard Auxiliary, American National Red Cross.

Colgate, Stephen. *Colgate's Basic Sailboat Theory.* New York: Van Nostrand Reinhold Co., 1973. Pap., illus. The text used in Colgate's Offshore Sailing School; covers basics.

Farnham, Moulton H. *Sailing for Beginners.* New York: Macmillan, 1967. Illus. Great primer, with over 200 illustrations and brief, easily memorized chapter summaries.

V ON OR IN WATER

Anderson, Robert R. and Evans, Jay. *Kayaking.* Brattleboro, VT: Stephen Greene Press, 1975. Illus. All-inclusive how-to by former U.S. Olympic coach Jay Evans.

Belknap, Buzz (with Belknap, Bill; Evans, Laura; and Huser, Verne). *Grand Canyon River Guide, Canyonlands River Guide, Desolation River Guide, and Snake River Guide.* Boulder City, NV: Westwater Books. Mile-by-mile large-scale waterproof maps resembling auto club route maps.

Davidson, James West and Rugge, John. *The Complete Wilderness Paddler.* New York: Alfred A. Knopf, 1975. Illus. Fascinating tale of authors' excursion tells readers everything they need to know to take a wilderness canoe trip; excellent illustrations, appendices.

Huser, Verne. *River Running.* Chicago: Henry Regnery Co., 1975. Pap., illus. A professional river guide's extensive manual on history, equipment, where to go—alone or guided.

McGinnis, William. *White Water Rafting.* New York: Quadrangle, 1975. Illus. Excellent, all-around manual by head boatman of Whitewater Expeditions River Exploration, CA.

Riviere, Bill. *Pole, Paddle & Portage: A Complete Guide to Canoeing.* New York: Van Nostrand Reinhold Co., 1973. Illus. From canoe selection to paddling/poling to North American areas.

Sandreuter, William O. *Whitewater Canoeing.* New York: Winchester Press, 1976. Illus. River reading in unprecedented detail, paddling strokes, navigation, weather, schools.

Strung, Norman; Curtis, Sam; and Perry, Earl. *Whitewater.* New York: Macmillan, 1976. Illus. Mechanics of river rafting, canoeing and kayaking by river guides/outdoor instructors.

Walker, Mort. *Sport Diving: The Instructional Guide to Skin and Scuba.* Chicago: Henry Regnery Co., 1977. Illus. Thorough treatment of equipment, skills, physiology, safety.

VI IN SNOW

Bauer, Erwin A. *Cross-Country Skiing and Snowshoeing.* Hackensack, NJ: Stoeger, 1975. Pap., illus. Low-down on equipment, camping, emergencies, hunting, fishing, wildlife, 200 North American areas.

Caldwell, John. *The New Cross-Country Ski Book.* Brattleboro, VT: Stephen Greene Press. Pap., illus. One of the first books on the sport, this is an expert's relaxed how-to.

Wimer, Sally. *The Snowmobiler's Companion.* New York: Charles Scribner's Sons, 1973. Illus. Editor of *Invitation to Snowmobiling* magazine on selection, maintenance, racing, ecology.

VII IN THE AIR

Fillingham, Paul. *The Balloon Book: A Complete Guide to the Exciting Sport.* New York: David McKay Co., 1976. Pap., illus. First coast-to-coast balloonist on trial flights, licensing, schools, weather, buying a balloon.

Halacy, D.S., Jr. *The Complete Book of Hang Gliding.* New York: Hawthorn Books, 1975. Pap., illus. Good overall introduction; includes how to build your own, associations.

Mrazek, James E. *Sailplanes and Soaring.* New York: Hawthorn Books, 1973. Pap., illus. The basics for novices.

Ryan, Charles W. *Sport Parachuting.* New York: Henry Regnery Co., 1975. Pap., illus. Experienced jumpmaster helps beginners take that first step-instruction, techniques, safety, equipment, competition.

VIII ADVENTURE ROUNDUP

Acerrano, Anthony J. *The Outdoorsman's Emergency Manual.* New York: Winchester Press, 1976. Illus. Prevention and Protection for every problem for snowslides to skunk attacks.

Anderson, Bob, ed. *Sportsource.* Mountain View, CA: World Publications, 1975. Illus. An encyclopedia of over 210 sports and recreational activities, written to get you involved.

Bergland, Berndt. *Wilderness Survival: A Complete Handbook and Guide for Survival in the North American Wilds.* New York: Charles Scribner's Sons, 1974. Pap., illus. Survival geography, shelters, food, clothing based on author's experience with Indian guides.

Explorers Ltd., Perrin, Alwyn T., ed. *The Explorers Ltd. Source Book.* New York: Harper & Row, 1977. Pap. illus. Source of info on organizations, books and periodicals, places for instruction, equipment and locations for 26 outdoor activities.

Kjellstrom, Bjorn. *Be Expert with Map and Compass.* New York: Charles Scribner's Sons, 1976. Illus. Everything for novice—even sample maps and compass.

Medsger, Oliver Perry. *Edible Wild Plants.* New York: Macmillan, 1939. Pap., illus. The classic guide to more than 150 North American species.

Index